Between the Ancients and the Moderns

Between the Ancients and the Moderns

Baroque Culture in Restoration England

Joseph M. Levine

Yale University Press
New Haven and London

Set in Bembo by Best-set Typesetter Ltd, Hong Kong
Printed in Great Britain by St Edmundsbury Press

Library of Congress Cataloging in Publication Data

Levine, Joseph M.
    Ancients and moderns: Baroque culture in Restoration England/Joseph M. Levine.
    Includes bibliographical references and index.
    ISBN 0–300–07914–1 (cloth: alk. paper)
    1. English literature — Early modern, 1500–1700 — History and criticism. 2. Ancients and moderns, Quarrel of. 3. Evelyn, John, 1620–1706 — Criticism and interpretation. 4. Dryden, John, 1631–1700 — Criticism and interpretation. 5. Saint-Evremond, 1613–1703 — Criticism and interpretation. 6. Wren, Christopher, Sir, 1632–1723 — Criticism and interpretation. 7. Great Britain — History — Restoration, 1660–1688. 8. Great Britain — Civilization — French influences. 9. England — Civilization — Classical influences. 10. Baroque Literature — History and criticism. I. Title.
PR438.A53L48 1999
820.9′004—dc21

99–26545
CIP

A catalogue record for this book is available from the British Library.

10 9 8 7 6 5 4 3 2 1

Contents

Plates

For permission to reproduce the illustrations, I must acknowledge with my thanks the following. Plates 1, 2, 3, 6: By Courtesy of the National Portrait Gallery, London; Plates 8, 9, 10, 15, 18: Copyright The Warden and Fellows of All Souls College, Oxford; Plate 13: Trinity College Library, Cambridge; Plate 14: the Courtauld Gallery, London; Plates 16a and b: the Guildhall Library, London; Plates 17a and b: Copyright British Museum, London; Plate 7: By permission of The British Library, London; Plate 4: Earl Spencer, Althorp; Plates 11 and 12: Photography by Thomas-Photos, Oxford, England; Plate 5: frontispiece to *Letters of Saint-Evremond*, ed. John Hayward (London, 1930).

Introduction

In the following pages I have tried to characterize the high culture of Restoration England by concentrating on the broad and sometimes boisterous argument that broke out between the ancients and the moderns and that seemed for a time to have engaged and divided nearly everyone. An advantage of this perspective is that it takes seriously the period's own estimate of itself, determined as it was to situate itself in history and to find its place in relation to antiquity. No doubt there are other ways to view the matter, but I hope this may be useful in suggesting a certain wholeness to a culture that might otherwise appear disconnected and beyond easy definition.

Undoubtedly, there is something paradoxical in suggesting that it is through an argument that one may hope to characterize a culture. But it appears to be true that at any given moment men and women are as likely to be drawn together by common problems and disagreements as they are by shared convictions. Unfortunately, the history of argument has not, I think, always had its proper place in the telling of intellectual, much less cultural, history. The ambitious efforts that have been made to describe a consistent outlook for the Renaissance, for example, or the Enlightenment or Romantic period, have usually faltered just as far as they have neglected or suppressed contemporary alternatives. What would seem to be required for a proper understanding of past ideas is a recognition that they are likely to reflect only one side of a disagreement and therefore only one part of a culture. As a result, whenever we try to retrieve the meaning of a past assertion, we should probably try, before anything else, to recover, as far as we can, the question to which it was addressed and the alternatives that were once proposed. In reconstructing this immediate context for past ideas, the historian will be bound to retrieve the quarrels and contentions that once provoked the thought that is lodged in the old documents and around which a broad range of opinion can be recovered and related. Nor should one overlook the further advantage that such arguments are often more richly documented than agreements, just because they were once so publicly and vehemently debated.

Now if it is true that a culture can be defined by its contentions as well as its agreements, then the cultural historian, like the intellectual historian, should not overlook the opportunity. In particular, for the scholar who wishes to characterize the high culture of the Restoration period, it looks as though it may be the quarrel between the ancients and the moderns that offers the best opportunity for connecting the period's broad range of apparently conflicting interests and activities on a single common ground. I have, therefore, taken this dispute as my touchstone to the intellectual and cultural concerns of the period and in that sense tried to conflate intellectual and cultural history – or at least supplied the grounds for the one in the other.[1]

The quarrel, it is true, both preceded the Restoration and continued to be argued for a long time afterward, but it took on a peculiar form and significance in the later seventeenth century. It appears that whenever anyone at the time tried to take the measure of the modern achievement or its future prospects, he or she felt compelled to compare the present with the past, to attempt a canvas of the arts and sciences and draw up a balance sheet. That provided a framework for controversy at least from the moment when Francis Bacon set the fashion with his *Advancement of Learning* down to the Battle of the Books, when Sir William Temple and William Wotton attempted to do the same thing from opposite sides of the quarrel.[2] Apparently, everyone was profoundly concerned about the authority of classical antiquity, and everyone had to fix a position with respect to it before taking the plunge into modern life; and apparently, there was no subject, from art and literature to philosophy and science, from religion to politics, that was exempt from its concerns. It does not seem too much to say that there was then an obsession with this single overriding problem, and the peculiar ambivalence of Restoration responses to it is the subject of this book.

What I have done therefore is to tell some fresh stories about some familiar people caught up in a common dilemma in an attempt to fix their collective concerns. My cast of Restoration characters includes the virtuoso diarist, John Evelyn; the playwright and literary critic, John Dryden; the French dilettante who spent his old age at the English court, the Sieur de Saint-Evremond; and the scientist and architect, Christopher Wren – each with a large supporting company. I have told these as parallel lives, since they were lived for the most part separately, but I have not tried to force the parallels, except to notice that each of them spent a lifetime attempting to work out a position with respect to the conflicting claims of the ancients and the moderns – in their theories and in their practices. In the course of their creative lives, each of these men began with a self-consciously modern position, but after much vacillation, each wound up accepting a large dose of *ancienneté*.[3] Like most of their contemporaries, they sought a position somewhere on a sliding scale between the extreme demands of both parties, and in doing so they developed a stance to culture that has sometimes been called "baroque," but may also be seen as a prelude to eighteenth-century neoclassicism.

I am not at all sure that the label "baroque," which was originally borrowed from the history of artistic style, is very helpful in characterizing a complete and complex culture, and I shall use it guardedly.[4] But a name is convenient, and it might as well be the conventional one. To the extent that I employ it here, I shall use it in a restricted sense to mean simply the tension that occurred between modernity and *ancienneté*, a tension that had consequences for style, because it both endorsed and inhibited the impulse to classical imitation that was slowly growing and ever-present throughout the period. I shall use the word, however, not so much to define the style, or even the period, but rather to describe a particular frame of mind, or set of attitudes, which underlay both and may help to explain each.[5] Although the subject of this book is literature and the arts, it remains primarily a work of intellectual history. And whatever one may think of the label, the tension between the ancients and the moderns was undoubtedly one of the chief defining characteristics of Restoration culture and colored much of its thought.

No doubt a principal difficulty in appreciating the significance of this tension and quarrel is the result of our having become accustomed to the idea of a modern triumph and our inclination to take sides against the ancients in a debate that no longer makes a lot of sense to us. Although everyone knows that there was a classical ingredient in the neoclassical age, not everyone has been willing to acknowledge its importance in the shaping of the early modern mind. But the basic condition of the quarrel – and much of the intellectual history of the period – was a broad insistence that the ancient Greeks and Romans had set the supreme models and standards for every sort of endeavor, most particularly for politics and the humanistic arts associated with it: rhetoric and oratory, history, poetry, and moral philosophy. This old notion (which was itself borrowed from the ancients) had migrated from Italy to the England of the Renaissance and established itself after much contention slowly but steadily in the schools. In the event, no Englishman was exempt from it in early modern times, and while objections were raised occasionally, an exclusively classical education became more and more securely the foundation for all discussions of culture.

Ancienneté was thus the basic inheritance of the Restoration gentleman, as it had been earlier, reinforced now by a repugnance to the profoundly disturbing revolutionary events that had so recently challenged both the social order and the classics.[6] Now, more than ever, the Latin and Greek authors were taught in the schools, freshly edited and translated, and everywhere extolled as exemplary.[7] But even at the same time, it was increasingly apparent that much that was new in contemporary culture had only recently been invented or developed – not least the English language itself – and this was reinforced by Protestant religion and patriotic pride. Meanwhile, practical technology and the natural sciences seemed to be advancing beyond anything known in antiquity. In short, it appears that both modernity *and ancienneté* were increasing together, setting the stage for a rivalry that was to become more and more self-conscious and acrimonious with every passing year. In the following pages, I have tried to describe something of its unfolding, and I have been particularly careful not to assign a premature victory to the moderns.[8] If I am right that the quarrel was finally a draw in which the field was pretty much divided – the ancients commanding the humanities, and the moderns the sciences – the Restoration, we shall find, pretty much anticipated the outcome and defined itself in the process. But the argument was never static and looked different at different times to the different participants. The advantage of telling parallel stories is to show the differences that separated (and individualized) them, as well as revealing the common ground that they shared.

That the field was divided was not new. In fact, the quarrel between the ancients and the moderns took place within another and even older argument about the relation between the humanities and the sciences, the "two cultures" that seem to have continuously and forever divided western allegiance. I have tried to show elsewhere that by 1700 both of these quarrels had developed and separated the republic of letters into different and hostile camps.[9] Thus the Battle of the Books and the *querelles des anciens et des modernes* took place within a world already split between the men of letters and the *savants* and *érudits*. Although much of this was a recapitulation of past argument, there were nevertheless a few things that were perceived as new, in particular the recent achievements of experimental science and classical philology. These developments in learning appeared to tip the balance toward modernity, but the "ancients" responded by reaffirming their own allegiance to the classical arts and literature. In this they were helped – up to a point anyway – by an increasing knowledge of antiquity, both literary and archaeological, and an increasing affinity with ancient politics. The result was a standoff in which scientific progress could exist side by side with a reverence for humanistic antiquity, and Isaac Newton could be imagined in a Roman toga, while the great Lord Chatham was plausibly portrayed as a new Demosthenes. The tensions of an uneasy baroque could thus be resolved in the neoclassical age – though only temporarily.[10]

I have begun my narrative proper with the story of John Evelyn's long preoccupation with these problems. Evelyn was *par excellence* what the seventeenth century liked to call a virtuoso. He was a man born to moderate wealth and social pretension, and he had the leisure and position to meet everyone who mattered and the good health and long life (1620–1706) to devote to every kind of intellectual concern. He did not pretend to originality but was content to follow every event in the cultural life of his time and to contribute modestly to many. Since he kept a voluminous private diary and wrote to nearly everyone, it is possible to follow his concerns carefully from year to year, and as a "mirror of true gentility," to help take the intellectual temperature of his time. Evelyn tried to bridge the gap between the two cultures by dabbling in each, and he found it already convenient to be an ancient with respect to the arts and literature and a modern with respect to science and philosophy. Eventually, he was caught up in the Battle of the Books and took sides with his "modern" friends, William Wotton and Richard Bentley, though like them he never gave up his allegiance to the classical authors and artists. Despite his apparent serenity, there was a tension between his very real neoclassical ambitions and the practical limitations of Restoration imitation, and that may account for the "baroque" style of his prose and taste. Evelyn had been to Rome and read the classics, but it was still too early and he was still too isolated in this to assimilate the ancient style very fully. Nor was the court of Charles II a very hospitable political context for the culture of Cicero or ancient Athens. As a consequence, Evelyn's own outlook was a deliberate compromise between the claims of the ancients and the moderns, a mix still unstable, but undoubtedly anticipating much that was to come in the ensuing neoclassical age.

Evelyn knew John Dryden (1631–1700), and witnessed some of his plays, but they were not close friends. Like Evelyn, Dryden received a classical education, this time at the hands of the formidable Dr Busby. At the Restoration he began a long and memorable career as a poet, playwright and critic. From the first, he was absorbed by the claims of ancients and moderns, and he never stopped thinking about them, until he too, like Evelyn, confronted the Battle of the Books in old age. Unlike Evelyn, he does not seem to have taken much interest in natural science, though he too belonged briefly to the Royal Society. Although a great deal of effort has been expended by scholars on every aspect of Dryden's career, it does not seem that anyone has ever tried to track him through all the thickets of this particular controversy – at least with the persistence and detail that are necessary for so prolific and elusive an author. I have tried to fix Dryden – and his many friends and enemies – in the history of ideas, or at least that part of it that concerns our subject. This has meant trying to recreate the changing intellectual situation in which he confronted the rival claims of ancients and moderns, and the many ways in which he reacted, sometimes inconsistently, to the challenge. The result appears to be that Dryden too nourished an increasingly neoclassical aspiration for poetry and painting that was frequently inhibited by the taste of his audience and the requirements of popular success, as well as by an uncongenial political setting.

Next, I have tried to trace the views of Dryden's much-admired contemporary, the Frenchman who lived out his days in exile at the English court, the Sieur de Saint-Evremond (c. 1616–1703). If nothing else, this distinguished émigré is a reminder of the importance of French influence on English thought throughout the period. He won many friends in high places, knew the poet, Waller, the "ancient," Sir William Temple, and the "modern," Thomas Hobbes. Dryden admired him and eventually wrote his life. Along with so many others, Saint-Evremond kept a lifelong interest in the quarrel, particularly as it developed in France, which he reported and commented upon until his ripe old age. With Dryden especially he shared a passion for poetry and the theater as well as a more ambivalent interest in that most baroque of contemporary concerns: the opera. In his preoccupation with drama of every kind, he was typical of a culture that truly believed that all the world was a stage.[11] Even more than Dryden, however, his views remained fragmentary and elusive, and it takes at least equal persistence to ferret them out of the many fugitive pieces that soon flooded the press. Again, it is well to bear in mind the changing circumstances of the *querelle* to understand Saint-Evremond's shifting response, but again it appears that this very self-conscious modern retained a healthy respect for *ancienneté*, which may even have grown toward the end of his life.

Finally, I have concluded my parallel lives with another long survey of another long career. Christopher Wren (1632–1723) was a good friend of Evelyn's and he shared many of the same interests throughout the arts and sciences. Once again, I have tried to show that Wren gave much thought to the rival claims of ancients and moderns, and once again it appears that the famous modern also concealed a great and growing admiration for antiquity. Like Dryden, he had to temper his own neoclassical impulses with the recalcitrant taste of an audience that was not yet ready to accept a full-blown *ancienneté*. The result was that his buildings, like Dryden's plays, were something of a deliberate compromise between the ancients and the moderns – late baroque if you like. In this sense, Dryden's *Aeneis* and Wren's St Paul's have something in common, and both anticipate and pave the way for the eighteenth century: for Pope's *Iliad* and Burlington's Palladian architecture.

Needless to say, there is something arbitrary about choosing just four figures to represent Restoration culture. Nevertheless, I have resisted adding examples. It may be enough to say that each of my four was deeply and directly involved in contemporary culture and thought long and hard about the common problem that they shared with their friends and their opponents and that they certainly helped raise to a new level of self-consciousness. It would have been easy to add others, though at the risk of some redundance. Perhaps a philosopher or two (a Locke or a Boyle) might have helped to round out the picture, but I have made some suggestions about them elsewhere. More regrettable may be the absence of women. Unfortunately, the high culture of Restoration England deliberately left them out, along with the bulk of the male population, and so it seems for the most part must I. (There is typically only one fleeting reference to a woman in Swift's *Battle of the Books* – to the modern Aphra Behn, who is quickly dispatched by the ancient, Pindar.)[12] It is one of the limits of classical culture that it was both created and revived with the deliberate intention of preparing an elite group of men for public life, and classical education was for the most part confined to schoolboys.[13] It was natural therefore for the few women writers in the period largely to disregard a quarrel that did not concern them directly, though they must inevitably have inclined to the modern side. Unfortunately, Aphra Behn, for a time Dryden's one female competitor (and admirer), never wrote any criticism and only rarely expressed herself on the subject.[14] If there was one great exception, it is the formidable classical scholar, Mme Dacier, who forthrightly defended the ancients, but she was French. I have found only one English woman, the anonymous author of *An Essay in Defence of the Female Sex* (1696) who took much notice of the quarrel – and that was basically to mock both sides, though she quite clearly preferred the moderns.[15]

"He that gives a Book to be publish'd," wrote John Evelyn in the wisdom of old age, "(be the Subject whatsoever) is sayd, and that truely, to lie downe and expose himselfe to Stroaks, and not seldom to deserve them."[16] One takes a deliberate risk in writing about subjects that require a specialist's knowledge. The history of ideas has by its very definition no peculiar disciplinary home, except history, and I have tried to make up for my deficiencies by doing what the ordinary historian of any subject is expected to do, recreating, as far as possible and the sources permit, the situation in which his subjects thought and worked and wrote. I naturally owe much to the expert literature that has guided my work at every turn and which I have tried to acknowledge in my notes. But I have relied even more on a close and chronological reading of the evidence, which I do not think has ever been applied systematically to my subject, and if I err, I hope this effort will be fruitful at least in stimulating others to do better. I remain convinced that whatever flaws may appear in the result, the effort was worth making and had to be made by someone sufficiently foolhardy to attempt to cross the disciplinary boundaries that make intellectual and cultural history so difficult, and at the same time so rewarding, to accomplish.

Acknowledgements

This work is the result of a long-standing interest in the history of historical thought and a more particular concern with the apparently endless quarrel between the ancients and the moderns. It has therefore been in the works for a very long time, and I am embarrassed now to try to recall all my debts. Perhaps it is enough to thank the many friends and students, and my own little family, who have heard about it so patiently over so many years. But I must not forget to give especial thanks to Mark Phillips who bailed me out at a difficult time, and to Paul Hunter who aided in the rescue and supplied me with many useful suggestions. I am also grateful to the Evelyn conference which was organized so capably by Therese O'Malley and which launched me on the Evelyn paper that was printed in the conference proceedings, *John Evelyn's Elysium Britannicum* (1998), and which I have enlarged here. (My thanks to Dunbarton Oaks Publications for letting me reprint some of that essay.) I owe much too to those other dedicated Restoration scholars, Michael Hunter, Douglas Chambers, James Jacob, and Frances Harris. Last but certainly not least, I am grateful to my students, Jeff Anderson and Robert Brown, who helped with many tasks along the way.

Part I

John Evelyn and the Two Cultures

1. John Evelyn by Godfrey Kneller

CHAPTER I

John Evelyn and the Education of Antiquity

I

John Evelyn was not on the face of it a passionate man. Prudent in life and discreet even in the privacy of his diaries, he kept his feelings for the most part to himself. Perhaps it was the influence of an admired father whom Evelyn remembered, as "exact and temperate . . . never surprised by excesse . . . of a singular Christian moderation in all his actions." Perhaps it had something to do with the temper of an age which no longer wanted to wear its heart on its sleeve. To his friends he seemed, "a gentleman of a character highly respectable in every view . . . [of the] most elegant and useful accomplishments and blessed of the most amiable virtues."[1] Indeed, he seemed a man possessed of every virtue and in all his virtue self-possessed.

That was how he liked to present himself anyway, and that is pretty much how the readers of his diaries have found him, sometimes with disappointment, in the hundreds of pages which he apparently never meant to be read by strangers. And yet it is almost too consistent, too carefully contrived to be completely true. Virginia Woolf was not the only one who complained about the diary, that "he never used its pages to reveal the secrets of the heart." No doubt something like that was what he intended. "His writing is opaque," she continued, "rather than transparent; we see no depths through it."[2] Yet surely behind all the restraint and respectability, the facile accomplishment and easy conviviality, the cool and careful façade, there was some strain and some cost. Evelyn's life, or what he liked to show of it, was too well fashioned to have been composed casually or accidentally.

In fact there was a passion in the man, not efflorescent but slow-burning. For eighty-five years, without faltering, he kept it alight. Although Evelyn had been born to wealth and culture, to an assured income and easy connections, he was restless with activity. He could have chosen a life of ease in either court or country; instead he went to work, scribbling away unceasingly until he had filled a score of printed volumes and many more of manuscript; built, planted and collected; contributed frequently to public life; and socialized endlessly with the great and good men of his time. There is nothing more revealing of the man, I suppose, than the rules he once laid down for his daughter, "for spend-ing my pretious tyme well." The enemy was that "wasteful and ignoble sloth," which he found so often corrupting a good education.[3] Surely if there is one key to this belief, an explanation for all this persistent and apparently endless activity, it lies in Evelyn's profound conviction that there was nothing in the world that could not be molded into something useful or artful by conscious and calculated deliberation and an effort of will: not nature, the Common-wealth, the family, his gardens, himself.

And so, necessarily, Evelyn believed passionately in education, not pedagogy in any narrow sense, but *paideia* in the exact meaning of the ancient Greeks and Romans. He believed with them completely in the shaping possibilities of culture and the human soul, and he seized upon the classical teachers as his models. He subjected himself, his family and his friends, to unceasing self-examination and exhortation in an insistent effort to forge out of a recalcitrant human nature something useful and good. And when it was done, when eighty-five years had passed, he was perhaps entitled to that seeming complacency that has sometimes troubled posterity, even while it has admired his achievement and pored over his diaries. He had indeed fashioned his life and the life about him into art.

Yet all was not easy, even for this very successful man, and once at least we hear a cry of pain. On January 27, 1658 Evelyn's little son Richard died, "the prettiest and dearest Child, that ever parents had, being but 5 yeares [5 months] and 3 days old . . . a prodigie for Witt and Understanding; for beauty of body a very Angel; and for endowments of mind of incredible and rare hopes." He composed the boy's epitaph in his diary and closed it simply, "Here ends the joy of my life, for which I go even mourning to the grave. The Lord Jesus Christ sanctifie this and all my other Afflictions. Amen."[4] It was not the first child that Evelyn had lost, though all the rest were infants. But this was a loss, he explained to his father-in-law, "so much the more to be deplored, as our contentments were extraordinary."[5] Although little Richard had been cut off early, already formed and full of promise, it was his education that Evelyn recalled before anything else in his hour of grief, setting it down in precise and painful detail.

For once, however, it was not enough to record his anguish in the privacy of his diary; Evelyn wished to proclaim it aloud in a public monument for all to see. And he hoped, typically, that it might be put to practical use. At hand, he remembered a little Greek book that he had purchased abroad, on "the Right Way for Parents to bring up their Children," by the ancient church father, St John Chrysostom. It was unknown in England, indeed had only just been discovered in manuscript and printed at Paris. But it seemed exactly to the point, for it preached one simple and appropriate message: the importance of shaping a child's mind. For Chrysostom, the parent's work is like that of an architect with a building, an artist with a painting, or a prince with a city to govern or — as it must have seemed to Evelyn — like a garden to be cultivated. (Eventually, Evelyn gave instructions for all of these.) Human nature is like wax, and character can be molded into virtue. There was nothing, therefore, more important than education. What could be more fitting then than to turn the little tract into English to commemorate the shaping of his own son's mind. "The golden book of St. Chrysostum," his friend, Jeremy Taylor, wrote gratefully on receiving a copy, "in which your epistle hath made a black enamel, has made a pretty monument for your dearest, strangest miracle of a boy . . . I paid a teare at the hearse of that sweet child."[6]

Evelyn's epistle, his introduction to the little book, was just like the memorial he was writing for his diary. He wished to show there, "what may be expected from a timely education, if we will with diligence pursue it." And so he offered a brief account of Richard's education, from his learning the alphabet at three, to his construing Latin and Greek at five. Beyond the rudiments of the classical languages, the little boy had learned some French, some Euclid, music and drawing, the catechism, and more – all without the least compulsion or severity. "For so insatiable were his desires of knowledge, that I well remember upon a time hearing one discourse of Terence and Plautus, and being told (upon his enquiring concerning these authors) that these books were too difficult for him, he wept for very grief, and would hardly be pacified." Just so, Evelyn remembered, had it happened to the young Thucydides. Evelyn was tempted to say more, much more, but for once his copious pen failed and the words would not come; for "my teares mingle so fast with my ink, that I must break off here and be silent . . ."[7]

2

The ink dried in time and Evelyn's life went on. Fortunately, there was soon another son, several daughters, and eventually a grandson to renew his hopes, as there were also the children of friends and patrons to sustain his interest in the classical *paideia*. Again and again he proffered advice in an endless stream of letters for his own family and for the sons and nephews of others: the Earl of Clarendon, the Duke of Northumberland, Lord and Lady Sunderland, Samuel Pepys, and so on.[8] Always he offered it with the conviction of one who enjoyed the company of the ancients, who knew them intimately and who appreciated their practical value in the world. For the young men of ambition who had any hopes or expectations of public life, Evelyn was confident that the one secure avenue to success lay in mastering the Latin and Greek languages and imitating or emulating the best of the ancients.

In his way, Evelyn was simply repeating the wisdom of Renaissance humanism which for two centuries now had been looking back upon classical example for its inspiration to contemporary life. For the most part, his advice was commonplace and could easily be found in the schoolbooks, gentleman's manuals, and the correspondence of tutors and masters, fathers and sons, throughout the early modern period.[9] It was taken for granted that the ancients had provided the skills and knowledge for most necessary things, but especially for politics and public life. Eloquence was therefore the capstone of the education of the gentleman in England, as it had been in ancient Rome, and the examples of the ancient orators and statesmen, historians and poets, were valued as the supreme models for imitation. The ancient languages were thus the two indispensable keys to success, and the grammar school curriculum was devoted almost exclusively to them. Here was the foundation of modern *anciennetė*, and Evelyn accepted it almost without question and assimilated it easily into his own life.

Evelyn was a little reticent about his own education. It is clear that he had been born to wealth and the expectation of public service. The family had made its money in gunpowder – that supreme example of modern ingenuity – and Evelyn proudly remembered his father, who had become high sheriff of both Surrey and Sussex, holding court, surrounded by 116 liveried servants.[10] Evelyn was a younger brother and only inherited the family estate in 1699; but he was well provided for, so that, despite occasional anxieties, he never really had to work. He did not receive a very good early education, he says, but learned his Latin from a tutor and at the local grammar school.[11] He always regretted missing Eton, which he avoided because of its reputation for severity. When he visited Westminster School many years later, he was enormously impressed by the facility of the schoolboys there in Latin and Greek composition, "some of them not above 12 or 13 years of age."[12] Still, he managed somehow to attain that modicum of the classics that then seemed essential to a gentleman. Evelyn always took an interest in contemporary literature as in contemporary affairs generally, but he clearly enjoyed the company of the ancients in both literature and public life. He followed grammar school with a stint at the Middle Temple to learn some law and then went on to Balliol College, Oxford. In 1640 Evelyn returned to the Middle Temple.

The death of Evelyn's father and the Civil War interrupted his work, however, and his prospects, and after briefly rallying to the King, he went off prudently to visit the continent. The idea of a grand tour was new, but may have been encouraged by the example of his famous Surrey neighbor, Thomas Howard, Earl of Arundel. It was that great man, patron of the arts and indefatigable collector, who more than any other set the fashion of visiting the principal sites of antiquity and carrying off the remains. Evelyn's travels began in the Low Countries and France, and wound up in Italy. Twice he ran across Arundel, and each time he was befriended by him and shown the sights. On the second occasion, Evelyn received some travel instructions from the dying nobleman.[13] Later, he was able to return the favor by preserving some of his friend's collections of Greek antiquities which had been woefully neglected, the so-called Arundel Marbles, setting them up at Oxford where they still may be seen.[14] For Evelyn, Arundel always remained the first and best of aristocratic models, "the father of vertu in England, the great Maecenas of all politer arts and the boundless amasser of antiquities."[15] It may have been one of Arundel's circle, Henry Peacham, who first coined the word "virtuoso" to describe these activities and prescribed them for the life of the ideal English gentleman.[16]

Life on the continent, which extended on and off for almost a decade, reinforced Arundel's example, and stretched Evelyn's *ancienneté* beyond literature and history to classical art and architecture. In Rome, he had the services of a tour guide and paid homage to the great classical buildings, especially the Pantheon and the ancient statues in the Belvedere. He agreed with Pliny that the *Laocoön* was the finest of all ancient and modern sculptures. At the Aldobrandini Palace, he saw a Roman painting, the only one then known. At the Vatican, he was deeply impressed by Raphael's paintings in the *stanze*, which he noticed were being copied by students from all over Europe, and by Michelangelo's *Last Judgment*, despite its "multitude of nakeds and variety of posture."[17] The Farnese Palace, he wrote, was "built after the ancient manner and in a time when Architecture was but recently recovered from barbarity." St Peter's, he thought, was "the most stupendious and incomparable basilicam, far surpassing anything in the World and perhapps (Solomon's Temple excepted) any that was ever built."[18] He had the painter, Carlo Maratti, later so famous, copy the bas-reliefs for him in the Arch of Titus, more exactly (and with all their faults) than in any engravings.[19] To a friend at Siena, he wrote descriptions of the Roman ruins that were so lively that they seemed more glorious than the standing palaces of other cities. "Each day you call to mind the ages past and their Heroick actions, and never putt foot to ground but in the footsteps of Caesar."[20] While traveling, he learned to draw and to engrave after Peacham's example, and several sheets survive showing his views of "famous and renowned places between Rome and Naples."[21] Back in France, he translated a couple of works by Roland Fréart, Sieur de Chambray, who had written to expound and celebrate the architecture and painting of the ancients, which Evelyn felt the English had shamefully neglected. He was entirely contemptuous of all things Gothic, even such churches as Salisbury Cathedral and York Minster, and was embarrassed by the squalor of modern London.

Already in Paris, toward the end of his stay, he was recommending travel for its educational value and offering advice.[22] "Youth is the seede-tyme in which the foundation of all things is to be layd," he wrote a few years later, urging the Duke of Northumberland to send his son abroad.[23] At the Restoration he encouraged his nephew to visit Italy and to prepare himself by reading the history of Rome so that he might appreciate "what it was before and how it came to the condition you now find it – Illustrious in its very Ruines."[24] Long afterward, he wrote to his old companion, Thomas Henshaw, "to call to mind the many bright and happy moments we have pass'd together at Rome and other places, in viewing and contemplating the entertainments of travellers, who go not abroad to count steeples, but to improve themselves." Still vivid was "the agreeable toile we tooke among the ruines and antiquitys, to admire the superb buildings, visite the cabinets and curiositys of the virtuosi, the sweete walkes by the bankes of the Tiber, the Via Flaminia, the gardens and villas of that glorious citty." He felt young again at the very recollection.[25] Meanwhile, he was ready with advice for visiting France also and he wrote elaborate instructions about what to see there for several friends, including Samuel Pepys and Christopher Wren.[26] It looks as though Evelyn deserves special credit for helping to establish the grand tour as a necessary and ordinary part of the education of the gentleman and artist. And the visit to Rome was especially bound to affect English taste. Evelyn's friend, Robert Boyle, was undoubtedly not alone when he said (several times), that since "he had seen the antiquities and architecture of ancient Rome, he esteemed none any where els."[27] As the number of travelers began to increase, new guidebooks appeared in English to reinforce the message and help them on their way.[28]

Meanwhile, Evelyn's chief occupations during the Interregnum were to continue educating himself and to preserve and manage his estate. On the eve of the Restoration he presented himself as neither a courtier or soldier, nor churchman, "but a plain Country Gentleman, engag'd on neither side," who had had the leisure to be dispassionate.[29] He was loyal to the Church of England, devout and even a little puritanical in his own religion, but absolutely scandalized by the unrestrained enthusiasm of the sects. He naturally welcomed the return of monarchy with enthusiasm, but managed to remain detached and occasionally critical. Although he had come to know the King and court in exile, he was passed over for high office, perhaps gratefully, since he did not really approve of life at the Restoration court.[30] Nevertheless he kept busy contributing to public affairs anyway. He continued to serve the King, as he had in France, with his fluent pen, and also the Anglican Church to which he was unswervingly devoted; and he held a number of short-lived appointments to assist in emergencies like the plague and the fire. Some of his services were entirely voluntary, like the various schemes he devised for improving the quality of London life. Sooner or later, he got involved in almost every kind of government activity.[31] He received little enough in return; but he seems to have believed that service was the natural responsibility of a gentleman of means, particularly now that the government of England had been taken out of the hands of the rabble. Honor and happiness, he wrote to the Countess of Sunderland, are not likely to be found at court, but belong rather to that "brave and generous soule, that having the advantage of Birth or Laudable Aquisition, can cultivate them to the Production of Things Beneficial to Mankind, the Government, and Eminent Station in which God has plac'd him."[32] Ambition and the desire of serving your country, he advised his son, need not be motivated by avarice or vanity, "nay I am of opinion that it were to be prefer'd before our owne advantage, meaning by ambition and laudable emulation."[33] When a little tract fell into his hands in 1665, advocating a life of retirement, he immediately dashed off a reply.

The little tract was called *A Moral Essay Preferring Solitude to Publick Employment* and it appeared anonymously in 1665. Evelyn soon learned that its author was a very busy Scottish advocate named George Mackenzie, who was just then rising to fame in public life. Evelyn's reply was quickly composed and appeared the following year as *Publick Employment and an Active Life Prefer'd to Solitude*. The exchange is not memorable for its originality, since the issue had been thoroughly and continuously explored ever since the Renaissance humanists recovered it from the pages of the classical authors.[34] Both writers were pretty much content to repeat the classical commonplaces that they happily borrowed from the ancients and the moderns. But neither of them was entirely serious, inasmuch as the advocate of private life (Mackenzie) was fast becoming a public figure, while the proponent of public life (Evelyn) was only too eager to cultivate his own garden.[35] Nevertheless, the issue was still alive in Restoration England.

The fact is that the best, perhaps the only, moral justification for the life and privileges of a gentleman lay then, as in ancient Athens and Rome, in direct participation in public life – in a life of service to the community. For the citizens of the ancient commonwealth, the obligation to service was clear and was laid out for all time in the works of the orator-statesman Cicero, the most articulate exponent of the active life in antiquity and the principal source for the advocates of the Italian Renaissance and afterward. According to Peacham, who accepted the conventional advice that classical eloquence was indispensable to the gentleman, the great politician, Lord Burghley, had carried a copy of the *De Officiis* "in his bosome or pocket," to his dying day, "being sufficient to make both a Scholler and an honest man."[36] Cicero, Evelyn reminded the Countess of Sunderland on the eve of the Glorious Revolution, "reproaches a Gentleman for being solicitous about his Fish-ponde, when the Commonwealth was in danger."[37] But neither England nor Scotland was a republic under Charles II; and the life of the courtier was no easy substitute for the life of the citizen. Evelyn had helped to restore the King in 1660, but played no part in the great events of 1688–89. Retirement had always been an option in antiquity, especially under tyranny and empire, and it is no accident that Mackenzie was drawn to the Roman Stoics as his principal source.[38] Curiously, both the ancients and the moderns in this argument, as so often elsewhere, drew primarily upon the classics for their inspiration.

Here Evelyn relies not only on Cicero, "one of the great book-writers of the world," but on the Greeks before him, chiefly Isocrates. It was Isocrates, after all, who had first disputed the matter with Plato and defended the political life and the arts of eloquence against the criticism of a contemplative philosophy. And it was Isocrates who had taught Cicero how to defend the ideal of the orator-statesman in the *De Officiis* and the *De Oratore*, those two handbooks of the *studia humanitatis* that were the best foundation for Evelyn's humanism. According to Isocrates and to Cicero, the Commonwealth required for its success and its prosperity above all, the active engagement of its members, and especially the arts of communication: in a word all that pertained to classical eloquence. "'Tis plain inhumanity," Cicero had said, "to flie the congress and conversation of others." It was a pity, Evelyn added many years later, that young men were so badly prepared in history and eloquence, when these skills were so badly needed for success in government.[39] Public employment and the active life, Evelyn agreed, were responsible for all the best things in war and peace.

It was a polite exchange, and years later Evelyn was glad to meet Mackenzie and trade compliments.[40] Pepys was not much impressed by his friend's performance, "though it be pretty for a bye discourse."[41] Evelyn himself apologized to another friend, the poet, Abraham Cowley, who had also been advocating retreat. "You had reason," he admitted, "to be astonish'd at the presumption . . . that I who have so highly celebrated recesse . . . should become an advocate for the enemie." Evelyn assured him that he had not changed his mind; his own "trifling essay" was not meant seriously. On the other hand, he now urged Cowley to write a poem commemorating the activities and services of the Royal Society. And at the same time he wrote one of his own, a Pindaric ode to retirement which he thought well enough to repeat many years later in a letter to Lady Clarendon.[42] Typically, Evelyn would like to have had it both ways, to combine the virtues of both service and retirement, and he fondly remembers Cicero and Hortensius, "and the purpl'd Senators in the midst of Businesse and State Affaires," retreating for refreshment to their Tusculums and Wimbledons.[43] The irony may not have been lost on Cowley, who promptly returned a note complimenting Evelyn's contribution to "one of the noblest controversies both modern and ancient."[44] In the middle years of the seventeenth century, there was obviously much to be said on both sides. Perhaps Evelyn's ambiguity is best reflected in his own intermittent service to the state, which in itself is a fair reflection of the condition of public life during the Restoration. It was not easy, whatever one's aspirations, to play Cicero under Charles II.

3

So Evelyn went on proferring well-meaning and platitudinous advice to young men, encouraging their classical skills and their political ambitions. It was another matter for his daughters and the women in his life. Since they lacked a political role, Latin and Greek were less obvious skills for them, and it was a very exceptional woman who received a classical education in the seventeenth century. Typically, Mary Evelyn, John's wife, was an able young woman who grew up in the household of the ambassador to France with a taste for modern literature and a talent for design. She had lived, she recalled afterward, "under the roofe of the learned, and in the neighborhood of science." And she wrote well in English, especially letters which the family tutor, Ralph Bohun, thought positively "Ciceronian."[45] In 1672, however, she wrote categorically,

> Women were not borne to reade authors, and censure the learned, to compare lives and judge of virtues, to give rules of morality, and sacrifice to the Muses. We are willing to acknowledge all time borrowed from family duties is misspent; the care of children's education, observing a husband's comands, assisting the

sick, relieving the poore, and being servicable to our friends, are of sufficient weight to employ the most improved capacities amongst us.[46]

Evelyn himself seems to have had something like that in mind when he looked back late in life to the good old days when "men courted and chose their wives for their modesty, frugality, keeping at home, good housewifery, and other economical virtues then in reputation."[47] There was clearly not much place here for the classical education of eloquence. And indeed, Mary Evelyn found the Duchess of Newcastle, who had a lot of miscellaneous (but little classical) learning and who dared to publish several ambitious volumes of prose and poetry, quite ridiculous in her pretensions. Dorothy Osborne, William Temple's equally accomplished wife, could not have agreed more. The women of the Restoration, it seems, were at least as hard on their female contemporaries as the men.[48]

Nevertheless, John Evelyn did not altogether neglect the formal education of his daughters, whom he believed, like his sons, could be artfully molded into shape. Once again, however, he was stricken with grief when his favorite, Mary, was lost to the smallpox in 1685 at the age of nineteen, to his "unspeakable sorrow and Affliction." It seemed to Evelyn that Mary had come to possess almost every female virtue and intellectual attainment: beauty, goodness, piety and learning. She had kept a remarkable commonplace book, a copious record of her wide and scrupulous reading, which her parents now pored over in astonishment. "Nothing," Evelyn remembered,

> was so delightfull to her, as the permission I ever gave her to go into my study, where she would willingly have spent whole dayes; for . . . she had read aboundance of History, and all the best Poets, even to Terence, Plautus, Homer, Virgil, Horace, Ovide, and all the best Romances and modern Poemes, and could compose very happily.[49]

Especially was she immersed in religion, but she could also dance, sing, and play the harpsichord, and she could converse with everyone on every level. She had, in a word, attained to all that might be useful for that one vital role that her father could reasonably anticipate, as a helpful wife and caring mother.

In the end, Evelyn had to rest satisfied with his third daughter, Susannah, the only one to survive. If she was not quite the paragon that her older sister and her departed brother had been, she had talent enough in painting, needlework and French, and she too had read "most of the Greek and Roman authors and poets, using her talents with great modesty."[50] In short, Evelyn was persuaded that some classical reading could be useful for a woman, though perhaps not too much. When he offered some unsolicited advice to his beloved young friend, Mrs Godolphin, it was to read some Plutarch, some Roman and modern stories in French and English, some pieces of Stoic philosophy and some Roman poetry. "More than this, unlesse it be a very great deal more, is apt to turn to impertinence and vanity."[51] But if this was only a shadow of the humanist education that Evelyn had prescribed for his sons, it was by no means negligible in an age when the formal education of women was almost completely disregarded.

It is not surprising then that Evelyn greeted Mary Astell's *Serious Proposals to the Ladies* (1694–97) with admiration. He certainly agreed with her and with other contemporary advocates of women's education that it was a lack of training, not of intellectual endowment, that had handicapped them throughout the ages.[52] But it was Mrs Astell who put the political problem that was not so easily resolved. She saw that men allowed poetry, plays and romances for the entertainment of women, and on occasion (when they grudgingly allowed women some sense), they sometimes recommended history. But to what avail? History – and for that matter the whole humanist *paideia* – could only serve women for amusement and conversation. "For tho' it may be of Use to the Men who govern Affairs, to know how their Forefathers Acted, yet what is this to us, who can have nothing to do with such Business?" [53] As the Duchess of Newcastle put it bluntly, "We are shut out of all Power and Authority by reason we are never Imployed either in Civil or martiall Affairs."[54] It was only the Frenchman, Poulain de la Barre, who responded to the political exclusion of women by imagining, "that it would be a pleasant thing indeed, to see a Lady in the Chair (in quality of a Professor) teaching Rhetorick, or Medicine . . . putting in Execution Laws; playing the part of Counsellor; pleading before Judges . . . heading of an Army, giving Battel; and Speaking before States, and Princes, as the Head of an Embassy." His work was not much noticed despite an English translation.[55]

But neither Mrs Astell (who despite her feminism was both a Tory and High Church), nor certainly John Evelyn (who was at least as suspicious of social change), was ready yet for a political revolution.[56] In his last published work, the *Numismata*, Evelyn deliberately appended a long enumeration of famous women who deserved commemoration in medals, a list that implicitly argued the case for women's accomplishments and that is the most elaborate of its kind in the period. In it he recognized that remarkable classical scholar, Mme Dacier, with her "masculine talent in all parts of the politer Erudition" – but as the one great exception unlikely to be matched in his own time. He agreed that this was not "for incapacity of either equalling or exceeding her, but for want of Application."[57] Although he admitted that women were not promoted to "publicke Offices, Politicall, Ecclesiasticall or Academicall," he was as ready as his great feminist predecessor, Anna Maria van Schurman, to foster at least some learning in women both for their family functions and for "more private" ends.[58] Thus Evelyn's views were undoubtedly patriarchal and condescending, but not nearly as recalcitrant as those of some of his contemporaries.[59] When the Duchess of Newcastle sent him her works, Evelyn responded with an encomium that placed her among the great women of past times; and if it is a little hard to make out his sincerity – since his praise may owe something to her aristocratic title and the polite conventions of the day – there is no doubt that Evelyn remained open to women's basic rationality (and malleability), and thus willing to make exceptions.[60]

For the while, however, Evelyn's chief hope rested with his one remaining son, John Evelyn, Jr. He wished to "give him a good education," he wrote to his friend, Christopher Wren, so that he could become, among other things, "a perfect Grecian," and thereby lay a permanent and solid foundation for life.[61] Young Jack's tutor, Ralph Bohun, agreed with Evelyn that "nothing can be as commendable in whatever station he is then to be able to write familiarly in Latine."[62] Eventually, the boy went on to Trinity College, Oxford, the Middle Temple, and a trip to France. While there, he pleaded with his grandfather (Sir Richard Browne, Mary Evelyn's father) for a longer stay, on the ground that Cicero had spent a whole year at Athens. "If my Cicero will let me stay here so long too I will endeavor to recover my time and not return empty to follow his steps to link my Greek with my Latine studyes together, and that not only in Philosophy, but also in the practice of Eloquence."[63] Evelyn made him come home.

Somehow Jack never quite measured up to his father's expectations; a natural indolence and too much drink did not help. His Greek and Latin were good enough for him to dabble in literature – but he found it very hard to make his way in the world, despite the best efforts of his father. When he died after a long illness in 1699, Evelyn's final hope for the family was left with his one grandson, now at Oxford.

Once again the old man pinned all his faith and expectations on the education of a little boy. This time John Evelyn the third was sent to Eton where he performed prodigiously, "so that there is no dealing with him in Homer, Virgil, Horace, etc." The great classical scholar, Richard Bentley, assured his friend that his grandson was ready for the university, but Evelyn kept him on at Eton for another year to improve his Greek.[64] He meant to take no chances. Hardly a week went by without Evelyn instructing his grandson in what to read or how to compose the Latin letters that might help his prospects. The main point of academical studies, he insisted, was "conquest of the two learned languages, an easy and natural style of writing of Greek into Latine and Latine into Greek."[65] And indeed, all went well. By the time young Jack got to Oxford, his grandfather could boast of his proficiency in law and history, chronology and mathematics, not to say the flute and fencing, hunting and gardening.

In truth, Jack seemed a worthy heir. When at last it was time for the old man to draw up his final testament – when Evelyn had reached the ripe old age of eighty-four in 1704 – he repeated the convictions of a lifetime in a new memoir that was addressed to his now grown-up grandson. It was, he admitted, only a collection of "hasty notes," and they remained unpublished. As before, Evelyn meant to tie close together the education and the vocation of the aspiring young governor. Thus he hoped that Jack would gain for *his* son, "by favour or purchase" some "creditable office," just as he and his father had done before him. It was important for young gentlemen "to Advance themselves. . . by dexterity of the pen, the Latine and the modern Tongues," and so enter the

Foreign Service or even the court, and become secretaries, treasurers, clerks of council, and so on, and thus, "become usefull to the publique." Although nothing belonging to "humanity" should be neglected, "your maine study should be such as we have recommended to us by the most grave and wisest ancestors."[66] Evelyn's *paideia* had not changed much in a lifetime and must have seemed at least as suitable in the new century as it had been in the old. With the classics tucked safely under his belt, the third John Evelyn proved a perfectly acceptable, if not a particularly distinguished, heir and country gentleman.

4

Among the several lessons that Evelyn learned from the Earl of Arundel and his long sojourn abroad was that English taste was terribly backward. And Evelyn's best contribution to Restoration culture may well have been his deliberate attempt to do something about it. It was at the court of Charles I and in the Arundel circle that a first attempt was made to catch up.[67] And it was one of Arundel's servants, the Earl's faithful librarian, Francis Junius, who wrote a remarkable work of erudition on ancient painting that was meant to promote the cause.[68] In it he assembled almost everything that had been said about painting by the ancient authors to argue for the dignity and usefulness of the art and its parallel to poetry. Neither was a new idea, but both needed much propagating in England, where painting, sculpture and architecture remained lodged among the mechanical arts. Although Junius was ready to proclaim the example and perfection of the best of the ancients in these things, he was no mindless adherent and insisted that the moderns could do as well, if only they worked at it sufficiently.[69] His chief guide was the ancient literary critic, Quintilian, who taught him about imitation and gave him the vocabulary of his artistic criticism, but insisted that imitation should never be servile. It was vital to imitate only the very best artists at their very best, since even they were men who could err. The painter should concentrate therefore on imitating the spirit and principles of the art, not on its exterior ornaments.[70] (Junius does not dwell on the difficulty that was presented by the great scarcity of classical examples in England.)[71] In the terms of the argument that was then developing, Junius was undoubtedly a modern, after the example of Erasmus in the *Ciceronianus*, though typically his book is entirely dependent on classical quotations and generally ignores any later painting.[72] It was heartily approved by that other great modernist, who spent so much time copying from the ancients, Peter Paul Rubens.[73]

Evelyn knew Junius's work and perhaps the man.[74] Like the rest of the Arundel circle, like Inigo Jones, for example, whom he greatly admired, Evelyn was ready on his return to England to turn his back on contemporary English culture, which he generally despised as "Gothic," and to try to renew the standards of Greece and Rome – at least in as far as they were exemplified in the classical imitations of the Renaissance. He understood the difficulty for his countrymen, who had so little to see at home to reinforce their *ancienneté*, and nothing whatever to match the splendors of Paris and Rome. But how was one to convey the ancient forms of art and architecture to them, apart from urging them to undertake the grand tour?

Evelyn saw his opportunity in composing and translating a number of works that could promote his views about the different arts and gave some practical advice for each. He began with a pair of treatises that he translated from the French of Roland Fréart, Sieur de Chambray, on architecture and painting. Fréart had been to Italy and remained long enough to imbibe the classicizing atmosphere that was already in tension with the baroque and that had begun to influence French artists there, such as Poussin and Claude. Already, France was beginning to divide into ancient and modern factions, and Fréart enthusiastically joined battle on the side of the ancients, proposing a strict adherence to the ancient models. Evelyn hesitated a little about this, as he was to do later in the Battle of the Books, but for the moment the most pressing need appeared to be to instruct his friends at home, who needed a jolt to derail them from their medieval ways. For this purpose, Fréart's works must have seemed particularly helpful.

It was the great fire of London that gave Evelyn his opportunity. All of a sudden it was possible to imagine a new city relieved of its Gothic buildings and turned into classical magnificence. Writing from the perspective of the Restoration, Evelyn was sure that, "it is from the assymetry of our Buildings, want of decorum and Proportions of our Houses, that the irregularity of our humours and affections may be shrewdly discerned." Immediately, he drew up a scheme for rebuilding and regularizing the town in the new spirit of Renaissance planning, which he presented to the King, who was interested but in the end could do nothing.[75] Old habits and older property arrangements proved intractable, and Charles II was no Urban VIII, and certainly not a Louis Napoleon – nor was Christopher Wren to be given the opportunity of either a Bernini or a Baron Haussmann, much as (we shall see) he would have loved the role.

Evelyn had to be content with haranguing his countrymen to build their houses and temples better, that is to say along the lines of the ancients, as the Renaissance imagined them. Chambray's work was meant to be a compendium of all that was best in the architectural theory of the Renaissance, and it was sumptuously engraved. Evelyn had run across it in France soon after its publication in 1652; he was persuaded to publish it by the architect, Hugh May, who secured the plates, in 1664. It appeared as *A Parallel of the Antient Architecture with the Modern*, and when it was reissued in 1680, it was called *The Whole Body of Antient and Modern Architecture: Comprehending what has been said of it by Ten Principal Authors*. These included first of all, Palladio and Scamozzi, but also Serlio, Vignola, and the sixteenth-century interpreter of Vitruvius, Francesco Barbaro. Evelyn agreed with Fréart, that "all the mischiefs and absurdities in our modern Structures proceed chiefly from our busie and Gothic triflings in the Composition of the five Orders."[76] The *Parallel*, which was splendidly illustrated, was meant to rectify this after the example of the ancients, and was undoubtedly the best and most useful work of its kind and a real inspiration for all those like Wren (to whom the translation is dedicated) who wanted to introduce the classical manner into England.[77] We shall have more to say about it later, and about Evelyn's encouragement of Wren's architecture. Meanwhile, Evelyn did not limit himself to theory; at Cornbury Park he submitted advice and designs for the Earl of Clarendon's new house, and he actually laid out the canal and gardens at Albury for his friend, Henry Howard, which included a grotto modeled on the famous one that he had seen at Naples where Virgil was supposed to have been buried. More than a century later, William Cobbett still thought it "the prettiest garden that I ever beheld."[78]

The second of Fréart's works was translated by Evelyn as *An Idea of the Perfection of Painting: Demonstrated from the Principles of Art and by Examples, conformable to the Observations which Pliny and Quintilian have made upon the celebrated Pieces of the Ancient Painters, Parallel'd with some Works of the most famous modern Painters, Leonardo da Vinci, Raphael, Julio Romano and N. Poussin* (1668).[79] It was dedicated to Arundel's grandson, then Duke of Norfolk, and made much of his famous collection of marbles, which Evelyn hoped would soon be engraved. According to Fréart, modern painting had degenerated from the masterpieces of antiquity to "mere shadows and phantasms." The barbarity of the declining Empire had reduced the art from preeminence to a vulgar trade, until it was revived in the days of Leonardo and Raphael.[80] Fréart had earlier translated Leonardo's treatise on painting, which is here supplemented and (he hopes) completed. He relies heavily on Junius for his account of the ancients and for his critical categories, but he makes his comparison with the moderns more explicit. Generally, Fréart preferred line to color, Raphael to Michelangelo, and the ancients to both.[81] The example of Giulio Romano showed how an imitation could equal, or even surpass, an original. Among the French, only Poussin could rival the ancients, "the worthiest certainly, that has appear'd since the days of those ancient renowned Painters, Apelles, Timantes, Protogenes, and the rest." In 1639–40, Fréart had been sent to Rome by the King to woo Poussin back to France. Now, carried away by his own rhetoric, he proclaims him even above Raphael, "the most perfect and accomplish'd Painter of all the Moderns."[82] No wonder Poussin wrote to him, in a letter that sets out his own artistic ideas, to indicate his warm appreciation and agreement.[83]

Evelyn does not seem to have known much about Poussin except for his reputation and a few pictures.[84] When he wanted a portrait of himself in France, he turned to the engraver Robert Nanteuil, who with Abraham Bosse remained his best friend among the foreign artists. Forty years later he was still pleased with Nanteuil's picture.[85] For the Restoration gentleman, painting one's portrait was to a real extent an act of self-representation and the artist was largely captive to the patron. Evelyn as usual led the way. As a young man he had posed romantically for his wife, and this inspired a remarkable portrait, which "I am told, by such as pretend to profound skill . . . exceedingly resembleth the Substance in that Posture, whereunto he is (dearest for your sake) too often

2. John Evelyn by Robert Walker, 1648

reduc'd." (Plate 2)[86] Back in England he sent a copy of his Fréart to Lely (whose reply, if any, is lost), and got himself painted at Pepys's earnest request by the best portraitist of the time, Godfrey Kneller, whose impulse to classicism, such as it was, was not given much scope by his endless commissions for face-painting. The "baroque" result more than satisfied Evelyn. "Nor did Kneller," he confided to his diary, "ever paint a better and more masterly work."[87]

In his own preface to Fréart's tract on painting, Evelyn chose to concentrate on one of the most important parts of beauty proposed by Fréart and Junius: the place of decorum in a painting, that is to say, the need to design circumstances appropriate to the time and place represented. Evelyn enlarges here on the many errors of the modern painters in that respect, especially the Venetians who made so little effort, but also the learned Rubens and Fréart's favorite, Raphael.[88] He is unwilling however to accept Fréart's categorical judgment against Michelangelo, whom he believed was, on the contrary, one of the greatest masters of his time; whose sculpture rivaled anything in antiquity; and whose architecture vindicated "that Antique and Magnificent manner of Building, from the trifling Goths and Barbarians."[89] And he thinks that Fréart did not fully appreciate the importance of perspective to painting, as his friend Abraham Bosse had just pointed out again in his *Treatise on the Converted Painter* – a copy of which he gave to Evelyn.[90]

Evelyn had met Bosse in Paris and struck up a friendship that was continued by letter afterward.[91] Evelyn recognized him as a great engraver, and "a plain, honest, witty, and intelligent good man."[92] But Bosse was undeniably contentious, and he was soon locked in combat with the members of the French Academy of Painting and Sculpture. The quarrel was both personal and ideological, with Bosse a little more open to the moderns than his enemies, although he too was a great admirer of the ancients and of Raphael and Poussin.[93] He welcomed Fréart's brief book as full of good things but needing some correction.[94] It is not entirely clear how far Evelyn followed the argument in France, but he seems to have sympathized with Bosse's "modernity," such as it was. For example, in his own copy of Fréart, Evelyn expressed some regret for having followed the original too literally, and he certainly thought that Fréart had overdone his criticism of Michelangelo – an argument that had also been made by Bosse.[95] But this was typical of Evelyn, who believed profoundly in the need to imitate antiquity in a free and general way and always with the possibility of success. He managed to include in his own list of deserving moderns, not only Raphael and his pupil, Giulio Romano, and Poussin, but also Rubens and Bernini. For Evelyn they all shared the same high intellectual (i.e. classical) culture, like Cicero's ideal orator or Vitruvius's architect, far beyond the mechanical craftsman who only knew how to draw and color.[96]

5

Evelyn hoped thus to advance all the arts by returning to antiquity, and he did not overlook sculpture. Peacham had already pointed out the use of ancient statues to the modern artist, calling on the example of Rubens, and remembering Charles I's astonishing collection.[97] We have seen Evelyn's enthusiasm for the Arundel marbles. In 1662 he wrote a little book called *Sculptura*, in which he considered the matter, though most of it was actually devoted to engraving. Evelyn was among the first in England to see the great value of prints in spreading the new culture, and he formed a considerable collection of his own, as well as advising friends like Pepys on how to amass one.[98] If one could not view Raphael easily or directly, one could at least look at the reproductions of Marcantonio. Evelyn thought that the best of the Arundel marbles should be engraved as models for artists and virtuosi. But drawing and engraving were also practical arts that (like photography afterward) could copy things of use, and Evelyn presented his little book to the Royal Society confident that it would be approved on that level too. From that viewpoint, the arts could be seen as bridging the gap between the two cultures by contributing to the mechanical as well as to the liberal arts, by contributing to scientific knowledge as well as to morality. When the *Perfection of Painting* was reviewed in the Society's *Philosophical Transactions* it was greeted warmly. Painting and sculpture were "the politest and noblest of ancient arts, true, ingenious, and claiming the resemblance of Life, the emulation of all beauties, and fairest Records of Appearances." Could anything be more pleasing to a philosophical traveler, architect or mechanician? Evelyn's work, wrote the reviewer, "will doubtless animate many among us to acquire a perfection in Pictures, Draughts, and Calchography [copper engraving], equal to our growth in all sorts of Optical Aydes, and the fulness of our modern Discoveries."[99]

Evelyn's attention to engraving in the *Sculptura* seems to have been the result of his discovery of the new reproductive art of mezzotint, which Evelyn attributed (mistakenly) to Prince Rupert, who had recently shown him its secrets.[100] Apparently, he saw any form of carving or molding as a kind of sculpture. In any case, he introduces his little tract with a brief history of the art from the beginning of time, long before the biblical Flood, to its height of perfection among the Greeks, to its precipitous decline under the Goths and Saracens. Unlike Junius in the case of painting, Evelyn was not forced to rely entirely on the literary testimony of the ancients, since he had seen for himself a great many ancient sculptures in the collections in Rome. Nevertheless, Pliny remained his chief guide and his judgments seem largely a result of what he was told.[101] As a result, Evelyn was unable to make critical distinctions between early and late antiquity, or between Greece and Rome, and was as likely to admire the "baroque" works of antiquity as the much scarcer classical ones. In this of course he was not alone, and it is one reason for the confusion among the imitators of classical antiquity who chose very different stylistic models: Rubens and Poussin, for example, or Bernini and Algardi, whom Evelyn found were "most in esteeme," when he got to Rome, and who were, and still are, usually placed on opposite sides of the baroque–neoclassical spectrum.[102] For Evelyn the only distinction of any importance was between ancient and modern, and the great distance that separated all these artists from the Middle Ages. The despoilers of antiquity, he wrote, had a taste, "so depraved that they demolish'd all their goodly fabricks, and excellent Works, wherever they became Masters, introducing their lame, and wretched manner, in all those Arts which they pretended to restore, even when they became a little more civiliz'd."[103]

Like Peacham, Evelyn endorsed the art of drawing in the education of children, and he frequently recommended it for his own.[104] In the *Sculptura* he briefly traces its history too from the beginning to modern times. He points out that by his day, in sophisticated circles, even the slightest drawings of the masters were thought worth preserving for their insight into the minds of the artists, and he reveals incidentally something of the grounds of his own *ancienneté*. Besides their intrinsic worth, he suggested, one had to regard

their inimitable Antiquity, than which (according to Quintilian) nothing do's so recommend things to us, from a certain Partiality which it universally carries with it; so as we seem to review what they did of old in their kind, as if (with Libanius) the Gods have imparted something of extraordinary to the Masters of the Ages past, which the nature of man is not now capable of attaining.[105]

In his travels Evelyn had been much impressed by the collections of great men, who had assembled the drawings of old masters, as well as "Rounds, Busts, Relievos and entire Figures, cast off from the best of the Antique Statues and Monuments, Greek and Roman." He was, of course, thinking of Arundel, but also of such famous virtuosi as Cassiano dal Pozzo, who had shown Evelyn in 1644, among many other things, his "rare collection of the Antique Bassirilievos about Rome, which this curious man had caus'd to be design'd in divers folios."[106] And indeed, if one could not see and study the ancients *in situ*, or carry them off like Arundel, one could always have them copied or engraved, as when Evelyn asked his draughtsman, Carlo Maratti, to make a drawing of a statue he (wrongly) thought portrayed the triumph and sacrifice of Marcus Aurelius and which he admired for the "antiquity and rarenesse of worke."[107] Here as elsewhere, Evelyn was anticipating the great collaborative enterprise of the next few generations.

Typically, Evelyn was not content simply to preach. In a modest way he also promoted the arts as a patron whenever he could, and within his means. On one occasion he even held the candle when the King got his portrait painted by the miniaturist Samuel Cooper, and discussed the art with his dilettante sovereign.[108] His proudest moment was undoubtedly his discovery of a great artist working unknown in London, the young sculptor, Grinling Gibbons. He had spotted him through a window by mere accident, "carving that large Cartoone or Crucifix of Tintorets, a Copy of which I had also my selfe brought from Venice, where the original Painting remaines." In its handling, drawing and studious exactness, Evelyn was sure he had never seen anything like it in his life or travels.[109] He immediately brought Gibbons to the notice of Charles II and launched his career. Afterward, he helped pay for the sculpted fittings at Wren's Trinity College, for which he was rewarded with a magnificent decorated table, "incomparably carv'd with 4 Angels, flowers and fruites."[110] And he never failed to appreciate Gibbons's "stupendious" works, which he believed were, without controversy, by "the greatest Master both for Invention and rareness of Worke that the world had ever had in any age."[111]

It was by then a long time since Evelyn had been in Rome, and it looks as though the memory of the ancient sculptures he had seen there had faded. Gibbons had been brought up in Holland and raised in England and had never been to Rome. Evelyn thought that he would one day prove as great a master in statuary as he had in wood carving, but it was not to be. In the next generation, it was pointed out that he was "neither well skill'd or practiced in Marble or Brass."[112] Evelyn might think of Gibbons as "our Leucippus, comparable, and for ought it appears, equal to anything in the Antients," but the comparison was inapt.[113] The critical standards of the Restoration, in the arts as in literature, might well aspire to the classics, but the requisite knowledge was still too remote and the spirit not quite right for the imitation to be any-thing more than approximate. Gibbons's tomb effigy of Sir Cloudsley Shovell in Westminster Abbey, with its clumsy figure and large peruke, began to look ridiculous even in its own time, despite, or perhaps because of, its classicizing impulse.[114] No doubt the relative freedom from classical example could often be a virtue, and the resulting taste, which we may call baroque, should certainly be appreciated in its own right, however much it may also be seen as a pro-logue or at least a preparation for the coming neoclassicism.

6

Inevitably, Evelyn also saw the great value of the ancient coins and medals for his project – those remarkable (and relatively inexpensive) miniature sculptures. Renaissance humanists and artists had always prized and collected them, and they had invented the science of numismatics among the several sub-disciplines of historical study that they placed under the heading of "antiquities." In 1689, Evelyn recommended them enthusiastically to Pepys, who was setting up his library and had asked for advice.[115]

> Men curious of books and antiquities have ever had medals in such estimation, and rendered them a most necessary furniture to their libraries, because by them we are inform'd whose real image and superscription they beare, but have discover'd to us, in their reverses, what heroical exploits they perform'd; their famous temples, bazilicae, thermae, amphitheaters, aqueducts, circuses . . . which have been greatly assistant to the recovery of the ancient and magnificent arcitecture, whose monuments had ben so barbarously defac'd by the Goths and other truculent invaders . . . besides what they contribute to the elucidation of many passages in historie, chronologie and geography . . . Who is not delighted to behold the true effigies of the famous Augustus, cruel Nero, and his master Seneca?[116]

A few years later, Evelyn published the last important book of his old age, the *Numismata: A Discourse of Medals, Antient and Modern* (1697), an elaborate and discursive handbook for the collector.[117] Here, along with the ancient coins, he illustrates the recent English medals of Charles II and his brother, when "Models and Medalions were struck, for Largeness, Design and Excellent Workmanship, equalling many that we have left of the Antient Greek and Roman." He recalls the occasion when the great English medalist of the Commonwealth, Thomas Simon, challenged John Roettiers to a contest in 1663, and reproduces the classical medal that was struck for it.[118] It seems that Roettiers's work (which Charles preferred on political grounds) may have been modeled on the miniature portrait of Charles II by Samuel Cooper for which Evelyn had once held the candle.[119] Though the printers had mangled the text and cost Evelyn much vexation, he could think proudly that with his last effort he had more or less covered the ground in trying to awaken England from its Gothic slumbers.

Indeed, put all his works together – on education, gardening, architecture and the arts – and Evelyn could well boast of having done his countrymen some little service, "for the improving and adorning their estates and dwellings, making them in love with these usefull and innocent pleasures, in exchange of a wasteful and ignoble sloth which I had observ'd had so much corrupted an ingenious education."[120] In everything his guide had been antiquity and the classical *paideia*, though to be sure it was always an antiquity deliberately, if sometimes inadvertently, adapted to modern life.

CHAPTER 2

Evelyn between the Ancients and the Moderns

I

In dwelling on Evelyn's educational ideas, I have tried to show how insistently the classical authors were assumed by Evelyn to furnish the principal instruction of the man of affairs for practical life (and also for his retirement), and how that led naturally to a preoccupation with classical art.[1] This was, I believe, the basic ground for seventeenth-century *ancienneté*. But I have so far largely left out of account John Evelyn's commitment to modernity which was at least equally strong. How did it arise, and how far was it possible to reconcile it with an admiration for the ancients?[2]

Here, it seems to me, the key lies in the teaching of Francis Bacon, who cast a long shadow over the men of Evelyn's generation. Bacon's scientific credentials have long been disputed and his originality questioned, but he was a powerful exponent of a point of view which had particular resonance for men of Evelyn's social position, for the patrons as well as for the practitioners of the new natural science. Evelyn read the *Advancement of Learning* early and carefully and he recalled it often in his many works. In the instructions to his grandson, he applauds Bacon as an example of a learned man who was yet "a person in continual employment as a Lawyer, Judge, Privy-Counseller, and in perpetual businesse."[3] But the real influence of Bacon was broader and more pervasive. He taught Evelyn's generation how to reconcile their humanist *paideia* with the new science, how to combine *ancienneté* and modernity. And it was this view that Evelyn with many of his friends enthusiastically adopted.[4]

The trick was to keep the old idea of the usefulness of the humanities to public life and to recognize the ancient achievement in rhetoric, oratory, poetry and history, while at the same time calling for a new natural philosophy liberated from all ancient authority. Bacon despised the scholastic teaching of the (still) medieval universities, accepting the humanist criticism of traditional philosophy that it was essentially useless to practical life. By Evelyn's day, Aristotle and the whole scholastic curriculum had come under siege from the young laymen who flooded into the colleges with other things in mind. It was

Bacon, Evelyn remembered, "who by standing up against Dogmatists, was [able] to emancipate, and set free the long and miserably captivated Philosophia, which has since made such Conquests in the Territories of Nature."[5] But the peripatetic teaching remained, despite the growing displeasure of those like Bacon and Evelyn who would have replaced it, and a quarrel between ancients and moderns quickly developed. Evelyn was dismayed to find in 1699 that his grandson was still being asked to read a scholastic schoolbook at Oxford.[6] What was plainly needed, he thought, was still more of the Baconian experimental philosophy, but by then Evelyn had been a member of the Royal Society for forty years and had been friends with all the new philosophers from Hooke and Boyle to Newton and Locke.

It was Bacon's contribution to see and to articulate more persuasively than anyone else how a new natural philosophy could be practical and serve the Commonwealth as fruitfully as classical eloquence.[7] As the physician William Harvey complained, Bacon advocated philosophy like a Lord Chancellor. Yet this was just his contemporary appeal. Knowledge, Bacon never tired of saying, was power, and knowledge of nature meant harnessing nature for use. But knowledge of nature could only be derived from experiment and a new logic of induction, by abandoning the imperfect relations of antiquity and the sterile old logic of the schools and starting all over again. Bacon was thus an ancient with respect to the humanities and a modern with respect to science, content on the whole with the achievement of the one, but determined to advance the other beyond anything yet known. He saw that the advancement of learning was dependent on cooperation and collaboration, and he tried in the *New Atlantis* to envision the means by which this might be accomplished. Elsewhere he showed exactly what still needed to be done by experiment and how to do it. It is not surprising then that many of the founders of the Royal Society, Evelyn among them, looked to him as their chief inspiration both in theory and in practice.[8] Or that natural science, which had hitherto belonged to the philosopher, should fall into the hands of the gentleman and man of affairs.[9]

Evelyn's interest in the new science began early and remained always practical; he was never drawn to any speculative system. His concern was for the organization of scientific activity and the accumulation of evidence. And so he read widely in the new literature of natural history and looked everywhere at the cabinets of curiosities that were then becoming fashionable. When a young man asked his advice for a trip abroad in 1657, Evelyn told him not to neglect the excellent recipes he would find, for example at Montpellier, for perfumes, powders and pomanders. Gentlemen who despised those things, "deprive themselves of many advantages to improve their tyme." "Seeke therefore after nature," he continued, "procure to see experiments, furnish your selfe with receipts, models, and things which are rare." With such a preparation, the young man might return to England to enjoy the fruits of his experience, "either by serving in some public employment (if the integrity of the Tymes invite you), or by securing your own felicity . . . in a private unenvied condition . . . of piety and knowledge."[10]

It was just before the Restoration that Evelyn concocted a scheme of his own for encouraging the new learning. Perhaps it was his friendship with Samuel Hartlib, that great Baconian promoter of all devices for the advancement of learning during the Commonwealth, that encouraged his speculation.[11] Among other things, Hartlib had promoted a follow-up to the *New Atlantis*, which was called *Macaria* (1641), and had gone on to advocate almost every kind of educational reform and technological innovation that he could discover on the Baconian assumption that knowledge could advance only by communication. By 1655, Evelyn knew that "honest and learned" person, and they corresponded busily afterward. The two men shared a particular interest in "hortulane" (i.e. gardening) matters, although they were on opposite sides of the Civil War.[12] Through Hartlib, Evelyn met another kindred spirit in John Beale, also a Baconian, gardener, and advocate of the new learning. In a letter of 1662, Beale welcomes the *Elysium Britannicum* and hopes that the poets, Denham and Waller, will write verses for it.[13]

Evelyn's scheme was proposed to Robert Boyle, a congenial friend, who was already the most distinguished and influential Baconian philosopher in England. Because the times were unpropitious – it was the last troubled year of the Interregnum and Evelyn was thinking of the fall of the Roman Empire to the barbarians – Evelyn thought that neither the Baconian notion of a Solomon's House nor a mathematical college was likely to be realized, and that a monastic retreat was more in order. The "promotion of experimental knowledge" was to be its principal end, and all its arrangements, including provision of a laboratory, library and repository, an orchard, several gardens and an aviary, were to be directed to that purpose. Evelyn worked it out in detail and with relish, though how seriously, it is hard to say.[14] He even designed a building for it in an unmistakably classical style, with a broken pediment and free-standing statues, a columned chapel with scrolled pediment and cupola – thus joining the ancients to the moderns in his usual way.[15] With the Restoration and his involvement in the Royal Society, it was, like some other of Evelyn's schemes, forgotten.

Evelyn was swiftly elected to the Royal Society.[16] For the rest of his long life he served it faithfully, attending meetings, sitting on committees, presiding once in a while over its proceedings, and contributing occasional papers. His best service may have been to praise its efforts to the King and to the country, and urge others to write in its defense.[17] Shortly after it was founded, Evelyn dedicated a little book he had translated in France to the new Lord Chancellor, with an introduction praising the Society, which he was the first to baptise as "Royal," and for which he received its thanks. It was dedicated to Clarendon as the true successor to Francis Bacon, for having helped "to set upon a Design no way beneath that of his Solomon's House."[18] The Royal Society, Evelyn declared roundly, was an assembly as accomplished as any in the history of the world.

In its very first month, the Society called upon Evelyn to bring in his "Circle of Mechanical Trades," his history of engraving and etching, and his observations on trees.[19] All fell naturally within the Baconian (and Hartlibian) program for the advancement of practical knowledge, and eventually Evelyn was able to produce something of each. In 1662 he published his *Sculptura*, which he dedicated to Boyle and in which he announced the new art of mezzotint.[20] In 1664, he brought out his most successful and ambitious book, the first to appear under the official auspices of the Royal Society and the result of much cooperation: *Sylva, or a Discourse of Forest-Trees*, to which was annexed a treatise on cider which he called *Pomona*, and a *Kalendarium Hortense: or Gard'ners Almanac*.[21] It was the last that inspired his friend Cowley to write "The Garden" and praise Evelyn. Later he read the Society a discourse on earth and vegetation and was asked to print it.[22] In the meanwhile he bombarded his friends there with pieces from his projected history of trades: "Paneficium: or the Several Manners of Making Bread in France"; "Sembrador, or a new Invention for the more Equal Sewing of Wheate and other Grains"; "An Exact Account of the Making of Marbled Paper"; "The Construction of the Rowling Press and Manner how to worke off the Plates"; and so on. His curiosity knew no bounds and he continued to complain in old age, long after he had given up fulfilling his greater ambitions, about his "unsatiable coveting to exhaust all that should or could be heard said upon every head."[23]

2

Next to education and the arts – and religion[24] – gardening was the great passion in Evelyn's life. All his days he struggled to complete what was to have been his most ambitious achievement, the still unfinished and unpublished *Elysium Britannicum*.[25] When he brought out a fourth impression of the *Sylva* in 1690, he could look back to a time, forty years before, "when Horticulture was not much advanc'd in England," and take some honest credit for its progress. The King himself had praised him for encouraging a host of planters to "repair their broken Estates and Woods, which the greedy Rebells had wasted and made havock of."[26] Through the cultivation of the soil and the cultivation of the mind, Evelyn had tried to give shape to the world, to turn life into art. But the growing quarrel between the ancients and the moderns threatened to destroy the nice harmony that Evelyn hoped to attain. Slowly, and a little reluctantly, Evelyn was forced to take sides.

The *Elysium* is a very ambitious, though unfinished and ill-digested, encyclopedia of gardening knowledge. In his first draft of the work Evelyn sketched out a long chapter on the history of gardens which he described to his new friend, Dr Thomas Browne, in 1660. Inevitably, he divided his survey into ancient and modern gardens, with the Middle Ages typically excluded. He began with the Garden of Eden and the Elysian Fields and proceeded to enumerate the most famous gardens of Greece and Rome; then he listed the most notable modern gardens in Europe, the Near East and the New World, not forgetting his older brother's grounds in Surrey, "surpassing any else in England," and his own poor plot, perpetually green and not completely unworthy.[27]

Jeremy Taylor was not just flattering Evelyn when he referred to Sayes Court as "Tusculanum" after Pliny's ancient villa.[28]

Evelyn does not seem to have been eager at this point to make a direct comparison between the ancients and the moderns, perhaps remembering Browne's skepticism on the matter. According to Browne, apart from the Garden of Eden, about which the world was well informed, "wee know not whether the ancient gardens doe equal those of later times, or those at present in Europe."[29] He may well have doubted it, but Evelyn's horticultural friend, John Beale, was prepared to side squarely with the ancients on this matter. Although he was fully convinced, "that God in later dayes very amply improvd our knowledge, and hath given us the Light of many wonderfull experiments," he assured Evelyn that God's handiwork in Eden outdid anything modern, and that his ancestors had continued the tradition of the first monarchy more magnificently and heroically – more divinely – "then can bee paralleld by our narrowe, mimicall way."[30] Jeremy Taylor suggested that Evelyn call his great work "Paradisus" rather than "Elisium Britannicum," "seeing you intend it to the purposes of piety as well as pleasure."[31] But Evelyn held to the original title and to that combination of classical and Christian that is characteristic of his humanism – to pagan Rome and to biblical Eden. When he was finally drawn into the controversy later in life, he typically divided the question; and from the testimony of the manuscript, it looks as though he preferred the ancients for design and ornament, and the moderns for horticultural science. Thus, the effigies of great men, such as Alexander and Julius Caesar, could serve as examples to virtue when placed in gardens and homes the way the ancients had done, when "Art became a piece of State."[32] It was the Baconian solution, *ancienneté* for the arts of imitation; modernity for the arts of accumulation. Gardening, it seems, required both. Evelyn had already declared his preference for the ancients in eloquence and education, art and architecture; and for the moderns in natural history and philosophy. His position in the quarrel followed naturally enough.

But this is a little ahead in the story. It was in the early days of the Royal Society that the first open quarrel between the ancients and the moderns occurred in England. It is true that there had been some occasional feuding before, but it was the claims of Evelyn and his fellows that led to a great public altercation.[33] No need to rehearse the details here. Some of the members were concerned at the indifference and occasional mockery of the new philosophy by the general public – perhaps even by the King himself – who did not always seem to appreciate its claims. For his part, Evelyn never lost an opportunity to promote the Society with Charles, as in the *Panegyric* he addressed to the King in 1661, where he assured him of immortality in founding an institution that would "improve practical and experimental knowledge, beyond all that has been hitherto attempted, for the Augmentation of Science, and universal good of Man-kind."[34]

More seriously, some of the humanists, like the classical scholar, Meric Casaubon, and the cleric, Robert South, saw the emphasis on natural science as a danger to religion and the authority of the classics.[35] Casaubon was worried particularly by what he thought was the excessively practical concern of the experimental philosophy. He tried to defend *all* the ancient learning – Aristotle *and* the literary classics – against the upstart experimentalists.[36] As a result of these criticisms, some members of the Society thought it necessary to defend themselves, first with a *History* drawn up by Thomas Sprat, then with a series of publications by Joseph Glanvill; but these were met by further attacks, and much confusion, especially from the many pamphlets of the eccentric and relentless Henry Stubbe.[37] Throughout the quarrel the moderns were often matched explicitly against the ancients, but for the most part the quarrel was confined to the claims of natural philosophy against the Aristotelians.[38] Despite the fears of Casaubon, no one seems to have thought seriously about under-mining the authority of the ancients in literature or history, and both Sprat and Glanvill preferred to use the weapons of classical rhetoric against their oppo-nents, since neither had much direct experience of natural science, which they knew only at second hand.[39] Sprat was at great pains to show that the new science posed no danger to the education of the schools or "the old talkative arts." In this, as in everything else, he remained a proper Baconian.[40] He believed that the experimental program of the Society was a practical realization of Bacon's theories, and he used Bacon's *Sylva Sylvarum* to frame the long narra-tive of its work.[41]

Evelyn had no trouble lining up on the side of the "moderns" against Casaubon and Stubbe. He was one of the members who first selected Sprat for the job of publicizing the Society, and he encouraged the enterprise from start to finish, even coaxing Cowley to write some introductory verses for the *History*, while he (perhaps with his friend Beale) designed the frontispiece.[42] He agreed with Beale on the need to protect the Society and proclaim the advancement of learning and seems to have considered publishing something on the subject himself.[43] He was flattered afterward to be singled out by Glanvill in the *Plus Ultra* among the proponents of modern learning and happy to applaud Glanvill's victory over his "snarling adversary."[44] Meanwhile he repeated the Baconian idea that the first business of the Society was to gather a natural history as the foundation for higher things. Progress in knowledge lay in the accumulation of reliable information, and that is where the advantage of the moderns lay, and where Evelyn himself could hope to make a modest contribution.[45]

When Evelyn brought out a new edition of the *Sylva* in 1679, he rewrote the preface for the occasion and turned it into a new defense of the Royal Society. His essay is a fulsome reiteration of the Baconian arguments for natural history against the skeptics.[46] It had been necessary, Evelyn agreed, for the members first to clear away the rubbish, and so free themselves from the tyranny of opinion; but this was not done through "an abolition of the old," so much as through the introduction of the new. Evelyn and his friends did not like to be thought of as rebels and never imagined undoing the classical *paideia* in which they had all been trained. Even as they adopted the possibilities of modernity for natural science, they remained more than ever convinced of the equally practical value of *ancienneté*.

It was this peculiar combination of activities – dabbling in science *and* imitating the classics, collecting natural curiosities *and* old coins and manuscripts – that marked them out and labeled them as "virtuosi." This certainly was how Evelyn saw himself and how others represented him. In 1657 he received the dedication to a translation of Gassendi's life of Peiresc, *The Mirrour of True Nobility*, where he was extolled for possessing, along with his French predecessor, a "sprightly curiosity [that] left nothing unreacht into, in the vast all-comprehending Dominions of Nature and Art." "The compleatly-knowing man," the translator continued, "must be Janus-fac'd, to take cognizance of Times past . . . as well as of the late-past, or present times wherein he lives." He must, to be sure, be both an ancient and a modern.[47] A couple of years later, Evelyn produced his own example of the ideal type in a brief life of Seigneur Giacomo Favi, which he prefixed to his *Sculptura*, "as an Encouragement to the gentlemen of our Nation."[48] "This curious person," he wrote admiringly, overlooked no field of human accomplishment, all the while behaving in a "noble, disinterested and agreeable fashion and manner of conversation." Among many other things, Favi had actually intended, so Evelyn had heard, "to compile, and publish a Compleat Cycle and History of Trades." He was, in a word, all that Evelyn had ever hoped for of himself.

3

Yet not everyone was convinced. Sir William Temple was a country gentleman like Evelyn, who had been much abroad and who had played a great role in politics until he retired to cultivate his gardens. In old age he could reflect on the frustrations of a life of action and prefer the quiet of the countryside; his essay, "Upon the Gardens of Epicurus," sounds almost like a reply to Evelyn's youthful work on the active life. Evelyn visited Temple's gardens twice at least over the years and admired them extravagantly.[49] Both men loved the classical authors; but Temple had managed, even better than Evelyn, to use them in his public career and assimilate them into his life. He developed a supple and colloquial style that was in marked contrast to the baroque periods of Evelyn and was for a long time much admired. But he deliberately denigrated natural philosophy, both new and old, insisting that the only things that were worth the attention of a gentleman were the classical humanities. He was in this respect much more an old-fashioned humanist than a newfangled virtuoso. In a short essay in 1690, he set out his thoughts on the matter and provoked the climactic episode in the quarrel between the ancients and moderns in England: the Battle of the Books.[50]

Once again some members of the Royal Society felt the slight and thought that a reply was necessary. Evelyn was now an old man and no longer so active, but he followed events closely, particularly when it turned out that two of the main participants were friends. The Society turned first to one of these, William

Wotton, a brilliant young man who had recently become a member and distinguished himself by his knowledge of the ancient and modern languages, as well as the new sciences. Evelyn had met him as a child and been astonished by his precocity.[51] In 1694 Wotton replied to Temple with his *Reflections on Ancient and Modern Learning*, and immediately won Evelyn's applause. Wotton argued that the moderns had excelled the ancients in all the fields of natural science and philosophy, although he pretty much conceded the humanities to the ancients. On receiving a copy, Evelyn was jubilant and wrote at once to Pepys, who was equally delighted.[52] Temple replied, others joined the fray, and the battle grew more acrimonious; but Evelyn stood fast with his friend and the opinions of a lifetime.

Perhaps the only new ingredient in the contest was the claim Wotton now made for modern scholarship, and this soon became the nub of the quarrel. Wotton insisted that modern philology and antiquities had given modern scholars an advantage both of method and substance unknown to previous ages.[53] With their aid, the whole past could be recovered more fully and accurately than ever before. Temple protested, but gave new fuel to the enemy by claiming as a classical author and one of the greatest of the ancient writers, the early Greek tyrant Phalaris, whose letters were still standard in the schools, although they had begun to be suspected as spurious. Wotton persuaded Evelyn's other young scholar friend, Richard Bentley, to help him out with a dissertation to prove the epistles fraudulent, and thus show by example the superiority of modern philology to anything ancient in interpreting authors and understanding the past.[54] Evelyn and his friends saw that scholarship, like natural science, was cumulative and progressive, and that the moderns, who were really ancients in point of time, as Bacon had insisted, could still stand on the shoulders of their predecessors and see farther than they.

There is no need to rehearse here the loud and long public quarrel over the epistles of Phalaris.[55] Evelyn was not a philologist, but he did not have to be told by Wotton and Bentley how the manuscripts of classical authors could be improved by the collations and elucidations of modern critics, or how classical scholarship could generally advance the knowledge of the past. As long ago as 1666, he had advised the Lord Chancellor of the need to print the classics in England in correct, fully annotated editions like the Dutch variorums that Temple had disparaged.[56] In this matter, typically, he was ready again to throw in with the moderns and side with Bentley. And so, when the critics ganged up on the young philologist after his attack on Phalaris, Evelyn was among the few who remained steadfast.[57] Evelyn lived long enough to read Bentley's triumphant riposte (1699), although he also lived to see the resilience of the ancients, led by Swift and Pope, whose wicked satires kept their cause alive into the new century. The quarrel between imitation and accumulation, *ancienneté* and modernity, could not easily be resolved.

If Evelyn was willing to stand by his modern friends, they were more than willing to reciprocate. It was just at this time, just when the battle had begun, that Bentley helped Evelyn to publish the *Numismata*, and Wotton to edit the latest edition of his *Sylva*, both of which proclaimed the superiority of modern learning. The *Numismata* had expressly justified the "Vocal Monuments of Antiquity" for their use to modern historical scholarship.[58] And in the *Sylva* we have seen Evelyn pleading the case for modern experimental science.[59] He was also called upon to contribute to that wonderful epitome of modern antiquarian learning, the reissue of William Camden's *Britannia*, and he responded with some advice and some notes for the county of Surrey. Clearly, Evelyn knew and identified with all the latest and most active proponents of modern scholarship.[60] Once, during the Phalaris controversy, Bentley tried to organize a regular meeting in his lodgings of the most famous of the moderns: Wren, Locke and Newton, "and I hope when in Town, Mr Evelyn." Unfortunately, it does not seem to have transpired.[61]

In the circumstances, it is hardly surprising to find Wotton responding in his turn with a whole new chapter on gardening for the second edition of the *Reflections on Ancient and Modern Learning*, and calling on Evelyn for help. The old man was only too glad to oblige.[62] "The antients," he was now prepared to say, "had certainly nothing approaching the elegancy of the present age." What they called gardens were only spacious plots of ground with shady trees arranged in walks and surrounded by porticos, pillars and other decorations. Of course, Evelyn admired these and advocated their imitation in the *Elysium*. But his mind was now set on helping Wotton and extolling the modern achievement. The ancients, he continued, cared little for flowers and had less variety in their fruits and vegetables. "Plinie indeede enumerates a world of vulgar plants and olitories, but they fall infinitely short of our physic gardens, books and herbals, every day augmented by our sedulous botanists and brought from all over the world." Their best writers had been very industrious, but they could not stand up against the moderns, "so exceedingly of late improv'd."[63] Here Evelyn provided the usual bibliography, not forgetting to include the Royal Society's *Transactions*. In public he was now prepared to make the same point. In the preface to a new translation of a French work, *The Compleat Gard'ner*, he again proclaimed the undoubted superiority of modern gardening in almost every respect.[64] Yet the ancients were never far from his mind, and a few years later he may be found pleading to Wotton that "some lover of the rusticities" should put the old Latin and Greek gardeners into English – Cato, Varro, Columela and the rest.[65]

Wotton was grateful for the letter, which he closely followed in his chapter of the *Reflections*, and where, much to Evelyn's embarrassment, he found himself singled out for special praise.[66] Evelyn's *Sylva*, Wotton pointed out, furnished a complete treatment of the modern woodman's skill, and so clearly demonstrated the modern superiority over the ancients, since the ancients had known almost nothing about the matter. Evelyn's work "out-does all that Theophrastus and Pliny have said on that Subject."[67] Nor did the ancients know much about cider, as Evelyn's *Pomona* also showed. As for gardens, it appears unlikely that Wotton got a look at the *Elysium*, though if he had, he might have found some further fuel for his argument about the superiority of the moderns in

the kinds and techniques of modern gardening. But like Evelyn, he would probably have been willing to concede much to the ancients also, in planning and
ornament.

The Battle of the Books continued well beyond Evelyn's lifetime. Its chief
merit was to clarify the issues in the old argument between the ancients and
the moderns, even though it did not resolve them. It left the field divided,
much as Evelyn had found it.[68] All his life, he had taken an interest in the whole
realm of learning, assuming that it could somehow be fitted together nicely in
the life of a virtuoso, and to the end he did not waver. For eighty-five years
he clung to the belief that education could shape and improve the life of the
gentleman, and he welcomed both the new sciences and the old humanities
with the same Baconian justification: that together they could bring about practical benefit for the whole community. His many writings, wrote an admiring
friend in 1699, had "eternally oblig'd the whole commonwealth of learning
. . . and there is no part of useful and polite literature in which you are not
universally vers'd."[69] The *Elysium Britannicum* was meant to be a compound of
ancient art and planning with modern science and technology, Evelyn's tribute
to the best of past and present, and his conviction that the garden, like human
nature, could be molded into a shape that was both beautiful and useful. This
placed him necessarily somewhere between the ancients and the moderns,
closer no doubt to Wotton and Bentley, but like them still infatuated with the
old Greeks and Romans and still willing to use them as the models for all
public communication. The fact that he could not quite assimilate them either
to his life or his prose style may say more about the times than it does about
Evelyn's ambitions. "It is a common observation," Sprat remarks, "that men's
studies are various, according to the different courses of life, to which they
apply themselves; or the tempers of the places, wherein they live." It was
one thing under a commonwealth, another at court.[70] In the next generation,
in the mixed monarchy of the eighteenth century, it would become much
easier to be a neoclassicist, and thus to welcome in different ways both the
ancienneté and the modernity we have been describing. It looks as though
Evelyn, always ready to embrace every kind of human learning and always eager
to admire the best of the ancients *and* the best of the moderns, would have
been pleased.

PART II

JOHN DRYDEN BETWEEN THE ANCIENTS AND THE MODERNS

3. John Dryden by Godfrey Kneller, 1693

CHAPTER 3

Dryden and the Moderns

I

It is curious that through all the sound and fury of the Battle of the Books the most celebrated writer of the age stood oddly aloof. If there was one man in England who might have been expected to pronounce upon the rival claims of the ancients and moderns and thereby settle the issue, it was surely John Dryden. Long before Temple ever thought of renewing the quarrel, the young writer had himself already raised the issue, and he never stopped wrestling with it even into old age. But while he was always passionately concerned about the matter, his judgments appeared vacillating and inconsistent both to his own contemporaries and to ours, and it is not altogether clear where he stood even in that last decade of his life when the Battle of the Books confronted him again with all the old issues, and when he remained strangely silent. Here as elsewhere, Dryden remains elusive, although a careful examination of his long preoccupation with the problem may yet be worth attempting, if only to supply a missing piece of background to the battle and place him more securely in the intellectual history of his time. If one takes the trouble to track his views in their intellectual context through the whole long trajectory of his life (and here the historian may have an advantage over the critic),[1] it will be seen, I think, that Dryden, like many of his contemporaries, was increasingly drawn to the party of the ancients; and if one takes into account the whole long course of his career, he may be seen to have anticipated the neoclassical writers who were soon to follow − as an "ancient," more in the Renaissance humanist tradition than the modern that he has sometimes been proclaimed.[2] In this respect he seems to have come closer to the next generation, to his young admirers, Joseph Addison and Alexander Pope, than to his old acquaintance, John Evelyn.

Dryden had been to school with Richard Busby at Westminster when Busby was young (about 1647), and he remained loyal to his old master throughout his life, grateful to him, as he wrote, for the "best part" of his education. Afterward, he sent two of his sons to school there. Busby was notorious for his allegiance to the crown, the classics and the (birch) rod, which he wielded with impunity throughout the troubled and inhospitable time of the Interregnum.[3] So adamant was the Westminster School about the classics, even in the darkest days of Puritan revolution, that the students were forbidden to speak anything there but Latin, and many years later Dryden was forced to intervene on behalf of his son who was (temporarily) expelled for failing to adhere to the rule.[4] In the 1690s, when Dryden turned back to the classics, he remembered having translated Persius there long ago, "for a Thursday-night's exercise," and he thought that many of his compositions might still be in his old master's hands.[5] Unfortunately, Busby did not have time to set out his educational views, except to write some textbooks, but if we want to know the theory that informed his practice and that was almost universally accepted at the Restoration, we may find it spelled out in the most popular schoolbook of the day, the work of a friend and fellow schoolmaster, Charles Hoole. Hoole's book helped to rejuvenate the classical humanist pedagogy that had been briefly challenged during the Interregnum and to establish the common ground of *ancienneté* that pervaded the culture of the Restoration, and which Dryden, along with Evelyn and most of his contemporaries – even at their most modern – pretty much accepted.

Hoole's teaching career had spanned almost exactly the period of the Civil War and the Interregnum; yet the great upheaval seemed to touch him hardly more than it did Busby. His indifference to the radical views that had resounded for a while in press and pulpit is an indication of a certain lack of appeal to many even in those heady days and may help to suggest why the reformers disappeared so abruptly at the Restoration. In any case, Hoole's career offers the perfect bridge between the humanist culture of the English Renaissance in which he himself was raised and the Anglican culture which was renewed in 1660, and which he addressed immediately. He called his tract *A New Discovery of the Old Art of Teaching School*, a perfect title for one who deeply desired to resume the old tradition. He drew deliberately on his immediate predecessors and contemporaries: on Ascham and Mulcaster, Brinsley and Farnaby, and on his friend, Busby, conflating their views and methods, and adapting them to his own practical experience in the classroom. He accepted their premises without question or equivocation in deliberate disregard of the radicals, although he did manage to find a few practical ideas among the reformers, Dury and Comenius.[6]

The chief point of Hoole's grammar school was to teach competence in Latin and Greek and to introduce the student to Hebrew. English was to be learned only incidentally, though Hoole was not entirely oblivious to its value. The early humanists might well have hoped to convert the nation to classical Latin as well as to Roman institutions, but that hope had long been abandoned. The alternative was to remodel the vernacular along classical lines, to inform English expression with all the virtues, as far as possible, of ancient eloquence. It was from this intention that all the linguistic and many of the literary quarrels of the early modern period resulted, and it is possible to divide the different factions into ancients and moderns by their attitudes toward the practical question of imitation, a problem that had exercised antiquity itself only to resurface in the famous Ciceronian fracas of the sixteenth century. Thus Tudor "ancients" such as Roger Ascham declared for Cicero and were insistent on a very close imitation, though pessimistic about how far the results in English could ever match the original; while Tudor "moderns" such as Gabriel Harvey or Samuel Daniel were more flexible in their views about imitation and more hopeful about the independent possibilities of the modern language and its prose and poetry.[7] In the seventeenth century, the battle continued to be fought out between the Ciceronians and the advocates of a more modern, though still classical (if now more elliptical) style: the style of Seneca and Tacitus.[8] This quarrel, which exercised a couple of generations until Cicero returned to preeminence at the end of the century, was thus another consequence of the prevailing pedagogical *ancienneté*, of the general practice of the schools that insisted on little else but the reading, writing and speaking of Latin and Greek through the imitation of one or another of the classical authors. These habits of mind and pen were almost ineradicable, even where they gave rise to protest or qualification.[9] As a result even the moderns tended to seek precedents in antiquity.

The real merit of Hoole's work was to show exactly how classical imitation could be accomplished. A favorite device, for example, was "double translation," which Hoole borrowed directly from Ascham and Brinsley. The student was asked to translate some of Cicero's epistles into English and then back again into Latin, "to render many of them into good English, and after a while to turn the same again into Latine, and to try how near they can come to the Authour in the right choice, and orderly placing of words in every distinct Period."[10] He was also shown how to adapt a classical model to contemporary use; how, for example, to turn a Latin letter from Cicero to his wife into an English letter from a schoolboy to a friend. (Hoole writes out the example.) "Thus you may help them to take so much as is needful and fit for their purpose out of any Epistle, and to alter and apply it fitly to their several occasions of writing to their friends."[11] In such a way the epistolary style of the Augustan gentleman undoubtedly took shape and became second nature. (It was, of course, just how the ancient Sophists had taught the schoolboys of Greece and Rome.) And later, by further devices of translation and imitation, paraphrase and metaphrase, Hoole's upper classmen were taught to compose orations and poetry and so to complete their education with Greek and Hebrew. No wonder that Evelyn was astonished when he visited Westminster School in 1661 to find the boys there capable of writing themes and verses with such "readinesse and witt" in the two classical languages.[12]

Still if Hoole was in most respects an "ancient," he had no desire to be the pedantic Ciceronian of Erasmus's dialogue. In this he was close to the great Dutch humanist himself, whose educational works he warmly recommended. Like his famous predecessor, he qualified his admiration for Cicero and the ancients just enough to open the door to modernity. "He that will be excellent in any Art, must not onely content himself with the best Presidents [precedents], which in any particular may (perhaps) exceed all other; but also now and then take notice of what others have attempted in that kinde." Thus Hoole canvasses all the classics to supplement the epistles of Cicero and even endorses some of the moderns as well – those at least who had imitated the ancients – for example Ascham, Lipsius and Politian. "And if the master," he adds later, "do but consider with himself, and inform his Scholars, that they shall all erelong reap the sweet of their present labours, by a delightful and profitable perusal of the choicest Authors both Greek and Latine, whom as they must try to imitate, so they may hope to aequalize in the most noble stile and lofty strains of Oratory and Poesy; it will encourage them to proceed."[13] Reverence for antiquity was never meant to discourage modern emulation, but Hoole at least does not seem to have believed that his modern pupils could ever surpass their ancient models. For Hoole, the best of the moderns were only the most able imitators of antiquity.

Thus Hoole was neither a reformer nor an ideologue, but like most of the schoolmasters of his time (and perhaps most other times) the accomplice of tradition, seeking only for the best ways to make it available to his pupils. Hoole boasted of his method, that "for the most part it was contrived according to what is commonly practiced in England and foreign countries," and this seems to have been so. He sought only to make them "exactly compleat in the Greek and Latine Tongues, and as perfect Oratours, and Poets as both their young years and capacities will suffer."[14] It was, undoubtedly, the universal aspiration of the age, and there is every reason to believe that Dryden accepted it without qualification. The Restoration was both tired and frightened of political and religious innovation and warmly welcomed a return to the classical *paideia* with its promise of political stability – a stability based (as in ancient Rome) on deference to an aristocratic governing class that had once been, and could now be again, especially trained for its vocation. Charles II could well be seen to be ushering in a new Augustan age, as in the coronation ceremony itself, or the many panegyrics (including one by John Evelyn) that greeted his resumption of the throne – or for that matter Dryden's own most ambitious early poem, the *Astraea Redux* (1660).[15] From that point of view and for that purpose classical rhetoric could become again the most exalted of the arts, and it is indeed present everywhere in the culture of the period, not least throughout Dryden's work.[16]

From Westminster School the young man went on to Trinity College, Cambridge, where he probably encountered the new science along with the old scholasticism (still in uneasy balance after more than a century), philosophical modernity to set beside his literary *ancienneté*. Unfortunately, almost nothing is known about his life there. And when Dryden left Cambridge in 1654 to manage a small family estate, he drifted into even deeper obscurity. It is only after the Restoration that he really begins to come into view.

2

Nevertheless, Dryden's views and personality remain frustratingly elusive. It is not just that there is so little documentation for his interior life; there is something also a little puzzling about the author's character, something peculiarly evasive that left him for a long time without a satisfactory biography.[17] Still, there is, I think, more than enough in Dryden's public career to define the intellectual issues that confronted him, as both a writer and a critic, and his generation, and these are our real quarry. And if he was not always consistent in his views, he was at least always clear and articulate about the problems that he faced and always sensitive to the winds of fashion that fluttered the Restoration sensibility, to the taste of that "mix'd audience of the populace and the Noblesse," which he served so faithfully for forty years.[18] Throughout his long career, he tried again and again to bridge the gap between practice and theory, between the concrete demands of press and theater, audience and patron, and the timeless aspirations of Renaissance criticism. Since he was invariably in the thick of combat, Dryden's views were usually occasional and tied to his immediate circumstances, and this may account for some of his inconsistency; at the same time, they generally reflected the state of the argument, if not the final position of the author, and that is their main advantage to us.[19]

Dryden's first extended work of criticism appeared in 1667 as *The Essay of Dramatick Poesie*. It was the immediate result of his direct engagement in the Restoration theater as well as a first effort to come to grips with the problem of the rival claims of ancients and moderns. In the years immediately following the Restoration the young author had successfully launched his career as poet and playwright. The time was ripe for experiment; civil war and Interregnum had virtually closed the theaters and interrupted the cultural life of the court. When Charles II returned from exile, he brought the foreign mode and encouraged French fashions. Elizabethan plays were revived, it is true, and were popular, but the long hiatus and changed audience opened the way for innovation. As John Evelyn noticed after a performance of *Hamlet* in 1661, "now the old plays begin to disgust this refined age, since his majesty's being so long abroad."[20] The theater was reorganized into two monopolistic companies largely dependent on box office receipts; new theaters were built enclosing and seating the audience before a proscenium stage and painted sets; an elaborate stage machinery was introduced to great effect; and female actresses replaced young boys.[21] Above all, the drama itself changed. Among the new forms, the comedy of manners began to appear, and "heroic drama" and "tragicomedy" were concocted from an amalgam of native and French sources. Eventually there appeared that grandest confection of all the arts, the baroque opera.[22] In each case Dryden was present.

After a brief and apparently unsuccessful fling at comedy (*The Wild Gallant*, 1663), it was the new rhymed heroic play that caught Dryden's attention and quickly made his reputation.[23] Dryden was explicitly indebted to Roger Boyle, Earl of Orrery, whose *General* had been written at the request of Charles II and circulated in manuscript for three years until it was finally performed in 1664.[24] He also knew and admired Davenant's *Siege of Rhodes* which had been written and performed even earlier, was revised and played again in 1662, and about which we shall have more to say later.[25] Now, Dryden collaborated with his brother-in-law, Sir Robert Howard, on *The Indian Queen*, which became the first of the rhymed heroic plays to be acted in London (1664).[26]

Among those who rushed to see it was John Evelyn, who thought it well written and was especially impressed by the production, "so beautified with rich Scenes as the like had never been seene here as haply (except rarely anywhere else) on a mercenarie theater."[27] As it happens, it was just about then that Evelyn himself began to write a play or two of his own: a self-styled tragicomedy called *Thersander*, set in ancient Thebes, and a comedy called *The Originals*, which he barely started. He seems to have given some serious thought to the matter – perhaps inspired by the great success of his kinsman Samuel Tuke who had just written one of the most successful "new" comedies of the day – even to scratching out some notes on ancient comedy and tragedy.[28] However, Evelyn never published his work, much less saw it performed, which is perhaps as well, although he would seem to deserve a modest place in the development of the new theater. His friend Pepys thought his plays "very good, but not as he conceits them, I think to be."[29] From then on, Evelyn gradually lost interest in the drama, put off it seems by its growing immorality.

In the meanwhile, Dryden followed his first collaboration with an effort all of his own, *The Rival Ladies*, which he dedicated to the Earl of Orrery as the principal encourager of the new mode.[30] In the dedication, Dryden defended himself against following "the new way," first by claiming some (spurious) Elizabethan precedents, and then by pointing to the general practice of England's neighbors. If rhyme was new, it had many practical advantages – especially when applied (as here) to "characters and persons great and noble."[31] He soon followed *The Rival Ladies* with a sequel which he called *The Indian Emperor* (1665). About the same time, he was elected to the Royal Society and began to hobnob with the wits at court and in town.

In a way Dryden's new plays were as much a challenge to the traditional theater as the new experimental philosophy was to the traditional curriculum, and they also looked to the King for patronage. In either case it was possible to imagine a fresh start, and the impulse to the new seemed to require a comparison with and defense against the old. In the *Essay of Dramatick Poesie* Dryden considered the problems that the new drama posed. He wrote it, he says, in retreat from the plague, with the theaters temporarily closed, sometime in 1665 or 1666.[32] When he launched it in print a couple of years later, he insisted on its "problematical" and undogmatic character. "I find many things in this discourse which I do not now approve, my judgement being not a little alter'd since the writing of it." One opinion only he maintains: he continues to believe that rhyme is entirely appropriate to drama. Even so, he will not take it upon himself to settle any other issues but merely to relate them, as Tacitus said, without passion or interest, "leaving your lordship [his young patron, Lord Buckhurst] to decide."[33]

No doubt that was the reason that Dryden decided to cast his essay in the form of a dialogue. Some years before, he had written some verses for a friend, Dr Walter Charlton, and very likely the brief "Advice to the Reader" which accompanies them and praises the ancient genre for its undogmatic virtues.[34] "For besides the opportunity of commemorating worthy Friends, and of introducing several occasional and digressive speculations," the ancient dialogues "gave themselves the advantage of freely alleaging the various and different Conceptions and Persuasions of Men, concerning the subject, which they had designed to discuss." It was, in short, a nice way to air some controversial opinions, while leaving the options open.[35] Much effort has been expended on identifying the various characters in Dryden's dialogue and in trying to pin down his own opinions.[36] But Dryden had deliberately eschewed, so he says, "the stricter Method of Positive and Apodictical Teaching," which was the obvious alternative; apparently he had another purpose in mind.

The stage is nicely set on a barge in the Thames at the time of the English sea victory over the Dutch at Lowestoft (1665). A party of four – three "peers of wit and quality" and a commoner named Neander – take a barge downstream, "shooting" the old London Bridge to Greenwich and back, talking all the way. Three topics come up for discussion, in order: whether the ancients or the moderns were generally superior; whether the French or the English write better drama; and finally, whether plays should be written in rhyme or blank verse. Each is disputed by two of the party and each is left inconclusive, although the second speaker in every case gets a longer and apparently more sympathetic hearing. The order of the discussion seems to have reversed the actual occasion of the *Essay*; Dryden was provoked to think about the quarrel between the ancients and the moderns by the immediate dispute over the question of rhyme and the precedence of the French. The rest naturally followed.

It may well have been Charles II who had started the argument. Immediately upon his return to England, he seems to have presided over a discussion about the merits of rhyme, taking sides with the new fashion and urging the Earl of Orrery to prove his case by writing a rhymed play.[37] (It was the King too, who had prompted Tuke to write his *Adventures of Five Hours*.)[38] In this he was, of course, merely reopening a debate that had been going on at least since the time of the Elizabethans. Dryden himself quotes from Samuel Daniel's *Defence of Rhyme* in his *Essay*. That he had read Thomas Campion's *Observations on the Art of English Poesie* (which had started the ruckus) is more doubtful.[39]

Campion had attacked rhyme as unknown to the ancients, a barbarous invention of the Middle Ages and "lacklearning" modern times. Daniel replied with an unequivocal plea for modernity; the authority of the ancients carried no weight for him. "All our understandings," he complained, "are not to be built by the square of Greece and Italie. We are the children of nature as well as they."[40] He was willing even to defend the Middle Ages, to find light in the midst of darkness, and achievement even among the Goths and Vandals. "The distribution of giftes is universall, and all seasons have them in some sort." True, the old Romans had excelled in language (not even Daniel would deny that), but that was not everything. "Eloquence and gay wordes are not of the substance of wit; it is but the garnish of a nice time, the Ornaments that doe but decke the house of a State."[41] The revival of antiquity had, he admitted, restored the ancient rhetoric, but it had not touched a wisdom that was always present to some men at all times, however variously garnished. Daniel's defense of rhyme thus led him to formulate some powerful arguments for modernity, even to admitting a measure of cultural relativity that seems to anticipate the Romantics.[42] If his voice was almost lost in a chorus of disapproving *ancienneté*,[43] it was not entirely forgotten when the debate resumed during the Restoration.

It was Charles II's patronage, therefore, and the practices of the new London theater that seem to have reawakened the old arguments – compounded now by the influence of the French, whose alexandrines were becoming standard in the theater. Dryden knew and admired the works of Corneille in particular and he knew something also about the quarrel abroad which had surrounded that famous man and set the new drama into conflict with the old.[44] In 1663, a Frenchman named Sorbière came to visit London and took a tour of the sights from the Royal Society to the flourishing stage. He found something to admire in each, but more to criticize, and on his return to France published his *Relation d'un voyage en Angleterre* (1664), which caused a scandal. Among other things, he attacked the English theater for (still) preferring blank verse, for ignoring the unities of time, place and action, and for lacking decorum. An answer was required and the Royal Society, whose honor had been offended by some contemptuous references to its philosophical activities, turned again to Evelyn's friend, Thomas Sprat, for defense. In 1665 appeared the *Observations on Mons. Sorbier's Voyage into England* with, among other things, a long comparison of the two stages and a direct anticipation of much of Neander's speech in Dryden's *Essay*. The use of blank verse by the English, Sprat argued, gave them many advantages over the restrictions of the French. "By the liberty of Prose, they render their Speech and Pronuntiation, more natural."[45] Their varied plots and breaches of decorum were also more natural and lively, closer representations of reality than anything in French. English plays were therefore both more diverting and more instructive. Anyway, contemporary English drama had repaired the excesses of the Elizabethans and was now as polished and regular as any.

As early as *The Rival Ladies* (1665), Dryden had defended his practice of rhymed verse, which he argued was not as new as some thought and could be quite as "natural" as blank verse.[46] Lately, thanks to Waller and Davenant, rhyme had reached a new perfection in England, and if only the English would follow the example of France and establish an academy, their gains might properly be consolidated.[47] In this, Dryden's first excursion into criticism, he does not develop his thoughts very fully, although he announces some themes he will develop later. He must have been startled when, some months later, his old collaborator and patron, Sir Robert Howard, changed his mind and pronounced in favor of blank verse over rhyme as the more natural of the two. The preface to his *Four New Plays* appeared just as Dryden was about to retreat from the plague and retire into the country; it seemed to him a direct reply to his own brief remarks in *The Rival Ladies*.[48] Howard did not accept Sorbière's main contention, however, that French drama was the best; it was the English who were pre-eminent – and above all, Ben Jonson. It has usually been held that the first speaker in Dryden's *Essay*, Crites, is in fact Sir Robert, but Crites is an ancient unqualified and Howard was something of a modern.[49] Nevertheless, Dryden was undoubtedly moved to reconsider the whole matter by his friend's argument, and the identification remains possible, as long as it is not pressed too far. After all, Cicero, Dryden remembers, had turned his colleague Atticus into an enemy of philosophy, even though he was a friend and had always served the public.

In any case, it is Crites who opens the discussion in the *Essay* with a bold declaration against the moderns:

> There are so few who write well in the Age that me-thinks any praises should be wellcome; they neither rise to the dignity of the last Age, nor to any of the Ancients; and we may out of the Writers of this time, with no more reason than Petronius of his, *Pace vestra liceat dixisse, primi omnium eloquentiam perdidistis*: you have debauched the true Poesy so far, that Nature, which is the soul of it, is not in any of your writings.[50]

He is answered at once by Eugenius, perhaps Charles Sackville, Lord Buckhurst, later Earl of Dorset, Dryden's young patron and translator in part of Corneille's *Pompey*. "There is no man," he allows, "more ready to adore those Greeks and Romans than I am," but he will not disparage his own time. "I cannot think so contemptibly of the Age in which I live, or so dishonourably of my own Country, as not to judge we equal the Ancients in most kinds of Poesie and in some surpass them." In such a way, Horace (here seen as a modern) had had to defend his own time against the claims of his own predecessors.[51] Everyone agrees to limit the discussion to one kind of poetry only, to drama; but fortunately, Crites, who takes up the cause of the ancient stage, begins with a broader argument that raises some of the larger issues.

It turns out, however, that Crites is no single-minded defender of *ancienneté*, any more than Eugenius is of modernity. He concedes that every age has its own genius and that whenever men properly combine their efforts they are likely to succeed. He then detaches science and philosophy from the *litterae humaniores* in order to treat them separately. In the past century, he admits, the virtuosi have made more useful experiments and discovered more profound secrets, "than all those credulous and doting ages from Aristotle to us."[52] This is a view, incidentally, that Dryden had already endorsed in his ode to Walter Charleton and that he was to repeat just about this time in his *Annus Mirabilis*.[53] On Charleton's recommendation, Dryden was actually elected to the Royal Society, and he was certainly sympathetic to its aims, even though he was soon dropped from its rolls.[54] Nevertheless, if the moderns were allowed to have all the advantage here, it was, for Crites, otherwise with the art of writing.

According to him, the ancients had been much more enthusiastic than the moderns about poetry and rewarded their writers much more fully. As a result, drama had had the time and the encouragement, in the period from Thespis to Aristotle, to be invented, grow to maturity and come to perfection. The moderns, on the contrary, had neglected to reward their poets and thereby turned virtuous emulation into envy and malice. This is why there were now so few good poets and so many bad judges.

With this opening, Crites enlarges on the virtues of the ancient writers, extolling their style and showing how Aristotle had (properly) extracted his rules for poetry from their practice, defining and defending the three unities of time, place and action. Were one to judge the moderns by either the examples or the precepts of the ancients, " 'tis probable that few of them would endure the trial."[55] He concludes by noticing that the best of the moderns and Eugenius's own favorite, Ben Jonson, were only too willing to defer to the ancients in all matters. "He was not only a professed imitator of Horace, but a learned plagiary of all the others . . . there are few serious thoughts which are new in him . . . you will need no other guide to our party if you follow him." Imitate, if you will, the imitator.[56]

Eugenius replies by allowing that Crites was right about the modern indebtedness to the ancients but wrong to deny that they had not surpassed their models. He sees that by arguing for modern progress in science, Crites has allowed for the possibility of progress in all the arts. "I deny not what you urge of arts and sciences, that they may have flourished in some ages more than others, but your instance in philosophy makes for me: for if natural causes be more known now than in the time of Aristotle, because more studied, it follows that poesy and some other arts may, with the same pains, arrive still nearer to perfection." (This was indeed very like the argument of Sprat and the Royal Society.) Eugenius then proceeds at length to show some of the imperfections of the ancients, for example their narrow plots and characters, and some of the improvements of the moderns, for example their invention of the five-act play structure. He will not allow that the ancients perfectly observed their own unities, though characteristically, he seems anyway to accept their timeless value.

Crites is not convinced, however, and he interrupts to say that while the moderns have indeed changed, they have not necessarily improved upon their models. "I see Eugenius and I are never like to have decided this question betwixt us; for he maintains the Moderns have acquired a new perfection in writing; I can only grant they have altered the mode of it." He admits that manners do change in time and even furnishes a few examples, but that does not touch upon his main point: the essentially constant character of human nature and (therefore) dramatic representation. Neither side notices any distinction between the kind of progress attainable in assimilating knowledge (as in the sciences) and that in imitating form and style (as in poetry). Indeed, the argument turns at this point to the rivalry between the English and the French and the merits of rhyme as opposed to blank verse, from the ancients and moderns in general, to the more particular concerns of the moment.

3

The chief aim of the *Essay*, according to Dryden, was to vindicate the English writers against the French, and at this point the company takes up that question – Lisideius (who may have been Sir Charles Sedley) against Neander (who is very likely Dryden himself). Lisideius is all for the French, the rules and the unities, and he allows only one English play, Fletcher's *Rollo*, to measure up to that standard, although he has a few kind words for Ben Jonson. Neander concedes that the French plots are more regular and their decorum more exact, but he defends the disorder of the English – just as Dryden had done in the preface to *The Rival Ladies* – and sets Fletcher and Ben Jonson above Corneille. (He insists that even on purely formal grounds, Jonson's *Silent Woman* was a more perfect play than anything in French and provides, after the example of Corneille, an *examen* to prove it.)[57] He then goes on to compare the three great Elizabethans: Shakespeare, Fletcher and Ben Jonson. The first he finds lacking in learning and sometimes in error, but always great, "the man of all Modern and perhaps Ancient Poets, with the largest and most comprehensive soul." His genius was so wonderful that he did not need books but could read nature directly. Fletcher (with his collaborator, Beaumont) had the advantage of more learning, and contrived more regular plots in a more polished language. But Ben Jonson was "the most learned and judicious Writer which any Theater ever had," and in need of no correction. "He was deeply conversant with the Ancients, both Greek and Latine, and he borrow'd from them . . . But he has done his Robberies so openly that one may say he fears not to be taxed by any Law." If he "romanized" his language too much, he remains nevertheless for Neander the most correct and admirable of the English dramatists. Next to the Elizabethans the Restoration playwrights had to pale; but even so, Neander remains confident that they have "far surpass'd all the Ancients and the Moderns of other countries."[58]

This paean to modernity is too much for Crites, who interrupts again, this time with the argument against rhyme, resuming Howard's view that it is unnatural in tragedy, and relying on the authority of Aristotle and the practice of the French. Once more, however, Neander gets the last word. He insists that rhyme is not only as natural as blank verse but even more effective. The "new" mode had been introduced into the West by the Goths and the Vandals, but in the East (he follows Daniel here) it was used all through antiquity. If the Elizabethans rarely employed it, their neglect is to our advantage, for it provides the one avenue still open to progress. "The Genius of every Age is different," Neander asserts, though he does not deny the superiority of the Elizabethans (nor affirm Daniel's cultural relativity), but they did not – could not – excel in everything.[59] Rhymed verse has the great advantage of restraining the imagination. On this note, with the barge returned to Somerset House, the dialogue ends and the company parts.

Although Neander – and before him Eugenius – had clearly gotten "the better of the argument," Dryden makes plain again that he did not wish to be dogmatic. "My whole discourse was skeptical," he wrote a little later in the defense of the *Essay*, "according to the way of reasoning which was used by Socrates, Plato, and all the Academies of old, which Tully and the best of the Ancients followed." He had offered several opinions and left everything in doubt, "to be determined by the readers in general."[60] Was Dryden then an ancient or a modern in 1665? Certainly, he had developed some powerful arguments for the freedom of the dramatist from classical convention and for the achievement of modern English poetry, and this was no doubt his chief concern. Nevertheless, everything in the *Essay* is qualified. Ben Jonson is held supreme by both parties because of his *ancienneté*; freedom is encouraged, but correctness is almost equally admired; modern rhyme is endorsed, but the Elizabethans who wrote without it are exalted, and so on. Moreover, even when Dryden inclines toward one side, he argues the case for the ancients fairly and accepts explicitly and throughout the fundamental importance of classical imitation and precedent, employing it in the arguments he supplies to all parties and using it for the very form and style of his own dialogue. From this perspective and on this issue, it is hard to see how Neander and Eugenius may be left to speak unequivocally for Dryden. No doubt he leaned in their direction late in 1665, toward a patriotic espousal of English poetry and rhymed verse. And no doubt that was why he was inclined to accept the arguments for modernity (however qualified) that open the *Essay*. But it is not hard to forecast what might happen if, after the first flush of enthusiasm, Dryden or his audience should lose their taste for rhyme or the new mixed modes of tragedy and comedy.[61]

Among those who read the *Essay*, Sir Robert Howard was most unhappy. Unlike Dryden, he was a man of very definite if somewhat changeable opinions, soon to be ridiculed by Shadwell and remembered by John Evelyn as Sir Positive-at-All.[62] He took a derisive line in the preface to the *Essay* to be directed at himself. He struck back almost immediately with a preface of his own to a new play, *The Duke of Lerma*, in which he reiterated his attack on rhyme and accused Dryden, unfairly, of being inflexible about the rules.[63] Dryden responded with a public *"Defence"*, which he prefixed to the second edition of *The Indian Emperor* (1668). In it, he still holds to his convictions about rhyme but now tries to bring classical precedent to the rescue. True, the ancients did not themselves employ it; the question is whether they would have admitted it, had they known it. Certainly, Dryden argues, they would not have found it either unnatural or unpleasing. After all, the ancients wrote their own tragedies in verse – "although they knew it most remote from conversation" – and the universal modern use of rhyme is proof enough that it is pleasing. Dryden was ready now to enlist under the banner of classical precept and modern imitation, and he confidently offers Virgil as the greatest of all poets.

(Virgil, it should be said, was also the model for the *Annus Mirabilis* which he was just then composing.) Even on the rules, Dryden seems ready now to accept the ancient injunctions. "If Nature is to be imitated . . . then there is a rule for imitating Nature rightly."[64] Rules like those that Aristotle had prescribed were exactly the means to accomplish that end, and Dryden had meant merely to set out some of the opinions of the ancients and moderns to that effect. The propositions in the *Essay*, therefore, were not to be taken as Dryden's, "but derived from the authority of Aristotle and Horace and from the rules and examples of Ben Jonson and Corneille."[65] Had not Dryden already shown how Ben Jonson's *Silent Woman* was the best of all his plays precisely because it accepted the classical utilities? In short, Dryden had not meant to oppose the old restrictions, merely the "servile" observance of them by the French.

Dryden is generally thought to have gotten the better of the argument with Howard, and he certainly reads more fluently and persuasively, but his defense of the *Essay* shows him, if I am not mistaken, in full retreat, not least from the modernity of Eugenius. Indeed, just as Dryden was completing the *Essay of Dramatick Poesie*, he was setting to work on a new play, *The Secret Love or the Maiden Queen*, in which he boasted "that it is regular, according to the strictest dramatic laws," and in his next, *The Indian Emperor*, he goes so far as to apologize for its irregularity compared to Corneille. In the preface to the *Annus Mirabilis*, he even admitted that "the learned languages have certainly a great advantage of us, in not being tied to the slavery of rhyme."[66]

Howard and Dryden soon patched up their quarrel and Dryden suppressed the "Defence" of the *Essay*. Eventually, as we shall see, Dryden gave up even more ground and altogether renounced the rhyme that had brought him fame, but he never thought to alter the sentiments of his original work, even though it was one of the very few that he ever bothered to revise.[67] That, of course, was the advantage of its deliberate ambiguity; let the audience make of it what they would. As a result, Dr Johnson thought that it would be impossible to find in English "a treatise so artfully variegated with successive representations of opposite possibilities."[68] It is not surprising that when the *Essay of Dramatick Poesie* reappeared in 1684 and again in 1693, just as the Battle of the Books began, although it set out some of the issues and offered plenty of fuel for both sides it certainly did not settle anything.

4

Dryden was famous now and wonderfully productive. Comedy and tragedy poured from his ready pen and his connections at court and in town grew ever more extensive. In 1668, he succeeded Sir William Davenant as poet laureate and a little later he became historiographer royal as well. But with fame came controversy. Dryden was left with little time for sustained reflection; barely time to adjust to the changing tastes of audience and patron; just time enough, perhaps, to defend himself against a growing public criticism. Dryden had a genuine relish for theory, if only in the form of vindication, and his occasional remarks continue to reflect the rival claims of ancients and moderns. As long as everyone shared the same classical education and agreed upon the same basic principles of imitation, it was hard to confront the issues in any other terms. But a series of challenges in the 1670s sharpened Dryden's thought and forced him to reconsider. As well as the claims of blank verse and Elizabethan pre-eminence, now both revived, circumstances forced him to a closer acquaintance with the ancients directly and with their modern exponents – with the Greek tragedies and modern French criticism. The result was a shift of position, a discernible move toward the ancients, though not before he had tried out his modern optimism a little further.[69]

The criticism came from several directions. Sir Thomas Howard had dropped out, it is true, leaving the argument and the theater for a career in politics.[70] But his brother, Sir Edward Howard, continued the onslaught against Dryden in the prefaces to several new plays of his own.[71] Meanwhile, a new and more effective voice was being raised against him. Dryden's friend and rival, Thomas Shadwell, was a great admirer of Ben Jonson. When Pepys went to a revival of *The Silent Woman* in 1668, he found the young poet seated beside him, "big with admiration of it." (Pepys himself thought it was "the best comedy that was ever writ.")[72] And when Shadwell wrote his own first play, *The Sullen Lovers* (1668), it was modeled directly after the great man. In his preface he proclaimed the method of the "humours" and the unities and argued against those who were so "insolent" as to have said that Jonson wrote his best plays without "wit." (The reference to the *Essay of Dramatick Poesie* was unmistakable.)[73] For Shadwell, Jonson was the only dramatic poet worthy of imitation, a refrain he repeated in *The Royal Shepherdess* (1669) and *The Humorists* (1671). In the last, he took exception to the arguments of a nameless friend who said that Jonson had fewer failings than any other poet but who yet denied that he should be imitated. Shadwell argues that we should always follow the best, however far beyond our reach. "Men of all Professions ought certainly to follow the best in theirs."[74] It was, of course, the familiar argument of *ancienneté*, transferred for the moment to an Elizabethan.

But there were other and more formidable voices still to be raised against the poet laureate. In 1671–72, two of the most prominent of the court wits, Buckingham and Rochester, rounded on Dryden out of what appears to have been a mixture of personal motives and poetical principles. Apparently, Buckingham had written a draft of *The Rehearsal* about 1665 to burlesque the new fashion in heroic drama, with either Howard or Davenant as the butt. When Buckingham dusted off the farce in 1671, Dryden, who was now the most prominent dramatist of the day, became the object of the satire, its hero, Bayes. The ridicule of *The Rehearsal* was very effective and probably did as much as anything else to call into question the new drama to which Dryden had pledged himself. John Evelyn, who went to see it, found it "buffooning all Plays, yet prophane enough."[75] The epilogue concludes with a contrast between the ancients and the moderns and a plea:

> Let's have, at least once in our lives, a time
> When we may hear some reason, not all rhyme;
> We have these ten years felt its influence;
> Pray let this prove a year of prose and sense.[76]

It is just possible that this caused Dryden to alter his intentions and transform his next play, *Marriage à-la-Mode*, from a rhymed heroic drama into a comedy; it certainly helped to bring about a decisive shift in the taste of the public.[77] To add to Dryden's discomfort, the Earl of Rochester, a patron whom Dryden had praised extravagantly, also began to circulate another satire in manuscript on the laureate. It was an adaptation of Horace in which Dryden is mocked again for having dared to criticize the Elizabethans.

> But do's not Dryden find even Jonson dull?
> Fletcher and Beaumont uncorrect and full
> Of lewd line, as he calls them? Shakespeares stile
> Stiff and affected . . .[78]

It was undoubtedly time for Dryden to reply.

Characteristically, he took the occasion of two new plays to formulate his answer. In the preface to the *Mock-Astrologer* (1671), Dryden directed himself to Shadwell and to the charge that he had demeaned Ben Jonson and stolen his plots. He stood by his view that Jonson was the most correct of the English poets; but the shadow of the ancients as well as the complaints of the moderns continued to hover over the discussion. "I do not admire him blindly and without looking at his imperfections. For why should he only be excepted from these frailties, from which Homer and Virgil are not free." Why should there be an *ipse dixit* in poetry any more than there is in philosophy? As for Dryden's own play, he acknowledges drawing its plot from the Spanish by way of Corneille. It was easy enough to find precedents among the ancients and those who followed their example: Virgil, for example, "who translated Theocritus, Hesiod and Homer in many places," or Terence, who took from Menander, Tasso who relied on Homer and Virgil, and of course Ben Jonson himself.[79] In each case, not least his own, the borrower had transformed the original and made it his own. There was no reason why the moderns should not continue to make their way in this time-honored tradition by imitation and transmutation.

Dryden's next play was in some ways his most ambitious. *The Conquest of Granada* (1672) was double-sized, two parts and ten acts, perhaps his most successful heroic drama. Even John Evelyn, who had a generally bad conscience about the morality of the theater, enjoyed its "very glorious scenes and perspectives," but it was Mrs Evelyn who particularly relished its pure love and nice valor. She was astonished that anyone, "borne in the decline of morality," could feign such an instructive fiction. And she was quite willing to extend to Dryden a modern freedom to break the ancient rules.

Some thinke the division of the story not so well as if it could all have ben comprehended in the dayes actions: truth of history, exactnes of times, possibilities
of adventures, are niceties the antient cricks might require; but those who have
outdone them in fine notions may be allowed the liberty to expresse them their
owne way, and the present world is so enlightened that the old dramatique must
bear no sway.[80]

Dryden's own essay, "Of Heroic Plays," was his most confident declaration
about the new enterprise. "Whether Heroic Verse ought to be admitted into
serious plays, is now not to be disputed, 'tis already in possession of the stage."[81]
He doubted that any new tragedy could make its way without it. Once again,
he rebuts the argument that rhyme was unnatural and draws upon William
Davenant's defense of *Gondibert* – an epic poem of 1650 – to justify his own
reliance on epic machinery.[82] In an epilogue, he continues to deny the
authority of Ben Jonson, who is now described as having written for a simpler
audience, and he proclaims the superiority of his own age and language. It was,
he admitted, a "bold Epilogue . . . wherein I have somewhat taxed the former
writing."[83]

Too bold, no doubt, for the epilogue soon required its own apology and
Dryden had to prepare a formal "Defence of Granada."[84] In it he tried still to
preserve the precarious balance between the claims of the past and the possibilities of the future. "I would so maintain the opinion of the present age, as
not wanting in my veneration for the past; I would subscribe to dead authors
their just praises in those things wherein they have excelled us, and in those
wherein we contend with them for the pre-eminence, I would acknowledge
our advantages to the age, and claim no victory for our wit."[85] He sees everything with the eyes of Horace, who looking back upon his predecessors, faced
the very same difficulty. According to Dryden, the Roman poet had understood "that antiquity alone is no plea for the excellency of a poem; but that
one age learning from another, the last (if one can suppose an equality of wit
in the writers) has the advantage of knowing more and better than the
former."[86] Was Dryden, then, advocating an unabashed modernity? No more
than William Wotton a few years later. Dryden was not pleased with an age
that accepted nothing of antiquity on trust; in the end, he allows himself the
modest hope "that poetry may not go backward when all other arts and sciences are advancing." In the meanwhile, his immediate concern was with the
challenge of the Elizabethans and those few things that he believed his contemporaries had improved, namely language, wit and conversation. Dryden's
modernity turns out, even here, to be qualified and relative.

Of course for Dryden, who was writing directly for the theater, the problem
was always in the first place practical. *The Conquest of Granada* proved a great but
only temporary success. For one thing the King's Company to which
he was attached had fallen on hard times and seems to have had trouble
producing his plays.[87] For another, the taste of a fickle audience was already

changing. It looks as though the appetite for the heroic had already begun to falter a bit when Dryden was set upon once again by the upstart playwright, Elkanah Settle. The new quarrel cannot have helped its fortunes. In the course of picking apart each other's plays, the two rivals only succeeded in exposing some of the faults of the genre.[88] By the time it was over, Settle could write that

> Rhiming, which had once got so much your passion,
> When it became the Lumber of the Nation,
> Like Vests, your seaven years Love, grew out of fashion.
> Great Subjects, and Grave Poets please no more;
> Their higher strains now to humble Farce must lower.

Indeed, by that time (1677), and on that point, even Dryden had begun to waver. Somehow the times were unheroic, and Dryden himself had begun to feel the discrepancy.[89] According to Dryden heroic poetry had always claimed that its principal value lay in educating and encouraging the prince. So Virgil had dedicated the *Aeneid* to Augustus. "The feign'd hero inflames the true," Dryden wrote in his dedication to the Duke of York, "and the dead virtue animates the living."[90] It is possible that the exaggeration and bombast of the plays – "an extravagance bordering on absurdity," which bothered some contemporaries and consigned them to eventual oblivion – had disclosed, even to Dryden himself, a discrepancy between romance and reality and a coincidental failure of feeling that was too great to overlook.[91] It did not help that hard times in the theater were getting harder.[92]

Still the quarrel had the good effect of forcing Dryden to consider yet again the place of ancient precedent and modern practice. His last word to Settle is probably the best expression of his opinion on that subject during the years when he was most optimistic about modernity. There are some pedants, he complains, who will cite the ancients even to justify their errors,

> Who being able to imitate nothing but the faults of the classick Authors mistake 'em for their excellencyes. I speake with all due reverence to the Antients, for no man esteemes their perfections more than my self though I confess I have not that blind implicit faith in them which some ignorant Schoolmasters would impose upon us, to believe in all their errours, and owne all their crime. To some pedants every thing in 'em is of that Authoritie that they will create a new Figure out of Rhetorick upon the fault of an old poet. I am apt to believe the same faults were found in them, when they wrote, which men of sense find now.[93]

So, for Dryden, it was reason or sense, not ancient authority, that must be the final judge. Yet by itself this was not enough to settle the difficulty, for it was not entirely clear, perhaps even to Dryden himself, how far the ancients had already exploited all the possibilities of reason and sense and thereby perfected the forms of literature; how far, if at all, they had in this surpassed the moderns;

and how far, therefore, they should be imitated. It was just at this point that Dryden began to read the French critics, particularly Père Rapin and his chief English expositor, Thomas Rymer, and to consider yet again his hesitant modernity.

CHAPTER 4

Dryden and the Ancients

I

René Rapin (1621–87) was probably the most representative voice of *ancienneté* in the age of Louis XIV, the most ubiquitous and popular critic of his time. When, ultimately, his whole works were issued in English in 1706, the editor, Basil Kennett, advertised them as "still perhaps the ablest Guide thro' the whole Circle of Fine Learning."[1] Most of his books had long been known in England in earlier translations, and he found a receptive audience on both sides of the Channel. The Jesuit had obviously struck a responsive chord; in an age of Cartesian reason and experimental science, he reminded his audience of the superior virtues of the classical humanist tradition. He at least was not a bit impressed by the "ridiculous Whims in Physicks which are now alamode."[2] He dismissed Copernicus out of hand and found everything useful in Galileo and Descartes already anticipated by Aristotle. Although he admitted some advance in minor matters through the new science, he believed that moderns like Hobbes, Descartes and Sir Kenelm Digby had merely, "rak'd together old Fragments of the Philosophy of Democritus, Epicurus, Nicetas."[3] The study of natural philosophy in general seemed to him both a snare and a delusion, and he anticipates a famous argument in Vico, that men can understand the world that they have made, but hardly the world of matter, which belongs to God.[4] Although Rapin will not accept a "servile adherence" to antiquity, or making an idol of ancient authority, he profoundly distrusts novelty and would generally prefer to be guided by tradition. " 'Tis always a Sign of an evil Test in Sciences, not to love what is commonly receiv'd."[5]

Admittedly, Rapin was not much of a philosopher, though he had more of a relish for the subject than some of the other defenders of antiquity. As a Jesuit he could hardly avoid either Aristotle or St Thomas Aquinas. Perhaps as a consequence he would not accept the story of an ancient wisdom, a wisdom anterior to the classical philosophers, preferring to attribute all knowledge to the ancient Greeks rather than to their eastern predecessors. Nevertheless, Rapin's heart lay elsewhere, in the humanities like some of the English ancients to come (e.g. Temple and Swift), and he made his fame with a series of separate treatises on poetry, history and oratory. In each case, he accepted without qualification the ancient superiority and the necessity of imitation, trying only to lay out the rules that would accord with classical experience, just as he (along with Dryden and nearly everyone else) believed that Aristotle and Horace had done in antiquity. Perhaps the foremost of his works was his explication of Aristotle's treatise on poetry; it was followed shortly by a series of parallels in which the separate arts were studied, each through a pair of classical examples: Demosthenes and Cicero, Thucydides and Livy, Plato and Aristotle, Homer and Virgil.

For Rapin, the assumption was that both the practice and the rules of antiquity reflected perfectly the dictates of reason and common sense. "For none will doubt but that the Works of the Ancients are the true Fountains where we are to draw those Riches and Treasures, where good sense is form'd and compar'd."[6] Here was the clarification that Dryden needed. As Rapin explained in his *Reflections on Aristotle* (published in 1671 and translated by Rymer in 1674), "this Treatise is no new Model of Poesie; for that of Aristotle only is to be adhered to, as the exactest Rule for governing the Wit. In effect this Treatise is nothing else but Nature put in method, and good sense reduced to principles."[7] Aristotle had merely extracted the rules from the actual practice of ancient poetry, and his principles, as Rapin and his Augustan followers never tired of repeating, were thus "onely to reduce nature into Method."[8] There was thus no way of avoiding ancient precedent. "He is but capable of very little, who governs himself, and is directed onely by modern Poems; whereas nothing noble and sublime can be made without consulting the Ancients."[9] As a consequence, imitation was the only avenue to perfection, especially the imitation of ancient epic poetry, the greatest achievement of the human mind. Rapin naturally endorsed the Renaissance commonplaces for the writer, "a long commerce with the good Authors of Antiquity, whose Works are the only true Sources, whence these rules so necessary to Poetry are drawn, and whence is deriv'd that good sense and just discernment which distinguishes the true from the false in natural beauties."[10] Rapin's genius was to take the typical schoolmaster's advice and apply it lucidly and systematically to all the genres of polite literature, to eloquence and history, as well as poetry and the drama.

Just when Dryden read these words is hard to say. Their message was certainly reinforced in 1674 when Thomas Rymer elected to translate the *Reflections on Aristotle*. As a schoolboy at Northallerton, Rymer was remembered for "his great critical skill in Human learning, especially in poetry and history."[11] His poetry, however, was not very good and his one tragedy, *Edgar*, was a failure, unperformed and rarely read.[12] It was rather in criticism, and in history, that Rymer made his reputation, and if his fame has oscillated wildly since his own time, that may tell us more about the fate of seventeenth-century *ancienneté* than about Rymer's critical abilities, which were genuine though limited.[13] For a long time indeed he was respected, even feared, until he switched careers and abandoned criticism for history in his old age, edited the great collection of documents known as the *Foedera*, and died obscurely in 1713.

Rymer's translation of Rapin appeared anonymously with a preface of his own; he claimed it three years later in *The Tragedies of the Last Age*. It was a popular work and was reprinted several times. The preface was perhaps the first to introduce the English to the virtues and vagaries of the foreign critics, especially the Aristotelian "formalists" of Italy and France.[14] Rymer reminded his countrymen how very backward they were in these matters, only Ben Jonson excepted. Like Rapin, he elevated the authority of Aristotle above all other critics. "However cryed down in the Schools, and villified by some modern Philosophers, some men have had a taste for good sense, and could discern the beauties of good writing, he is prefer'd in the politest Courts of Europe, and by the Poets held in great veneration."[15] Just as had Crites in Dryden's *Essay*, Rymer was willing to concede the modern superiority in philosophy and science, while reaffirming the ancient preeminence in literature. Yet even so, he did not want to see Aristotle followed too servilely, merely on the grounds of authority. He accepts Rapin's view that Aristotle was simply codifying what he found in the great poets of ancient Greece. "The Truth is, what Aristotle writes in this Subject, are not the dictates of his own magisterial will, or dry deductions of his metaphysics" – here Rymer bows to the critics of the old school philosophy – "but the Poets were his Masters, and what was their practice, he reduced into principles."[16] It was exactly as Rapin had said, nature reduced into a method. Rymer next proceeds to examine the English poets, Davenant and Cowley, to show how even the best of them erred, "through their ignorance or negligence of these fundamental Rules and Laws of Aristotle." Nevertheless, he stands ready to uphold the English above all the other moderns, as even the Frenchman, Rapin, had had to concede in relation to tragedy.[17] In his debut as a critic, Rymer, therefore, pronounced himself an ancient, despite an honest admiration for English poetry and the English language.

In 1677 Rymer published his *Tragedies of the Last Age* and made his reputation. He sent a copy to Dryden, who read it at once. Rymer meant to take up one of the main discussions of Dryden's *Essay*, the relative stature of the great Elizabethans, Shakespeare, Fletcher and Ben Jonson. Unlike Dryden, he deliberately chose the "stricter method of Positive Teaching," and meant to leave no ambiguity. Rymer opens his argument with a stark contrast between the ancients and moderns. For the Greeks, drama had been at the center of culture, the one true school of virtue; for the English it was far otherwise. "Surely (thought I) mens brains lye not in the same place as formerly; or else Poetry is not now the same thing as it was in those days of yore."[18] It was not only that the modern drama failed in its form – its proportions and unities, its phrase and expression – but, more crucially, it failed also in its substance, that is to say in its representation of nature, manners and morals. The purpose of poetry was to mingle pleasure with instruction, but this clearly was impossible when the plots and characters of modern plays were improbable, inconsistent and ridiculous. Rymer's standard was meant to be a universal one; ordinary reason, he insists, the common sense of everyone, even including women, is exactly what Aristotle had taught.

Before he looks at some individual plays, Rymer tries to head off one obvious objection. There were those who would say that Athens and London were very different places, that ancient precedent could hardly apply to modern conditions.[19] Rymer's reply anticipates something on both sides in the Battle of the Books. "Certain it is, that Nature is the same, and Man is the same, he loves, grieves, hates, envies, and has the same affections and passions in both places, and the same springs that give them motion."[20] Classical example must still suffice. But suppose for the sake of argument that the modern world had declined in its morality, that it had become less refined and virtuous, even though it had the double advantage of both philosophers and apostles to inspire it. (Rymer, like Temple, certainly inclined to that view.) Would not the poets then have to adapt their sentiments to their debased audience? Not at all. If the moral world had decayed, it was still the obligation of the poet to try to purge and reform it.[21] Classical example remains for Rymer universal and paramount.

What were the options then? Rymer had argued already that the English poets had both the genius and the language for their task. He reiterates this view. "Certainly, had our Authors begun with Tragedy, as Sophocles and Euripides left it, had they built upon the same foundation, or after their model, we might e're this day have seen Poetry in greater perfection, and boasted of such Monuments of wit as Greece or Rome never knew in all their glory."[22] So it *was* possible, even for this most truculent of the ancients, to imagine a future progress, though only upon the basis of classical example and imitation. Unfortunately, the English poets had so far fallen short, and it was Rymer's duty to show this, to purge and reform. If modern poetry was as rude as modern architecture, it was because the English had neglected classical precept as well as practice: Aristotle and Horace, as well as Sophocles and Euripides. Rymer meant only to rehabilitate their timeless prescriptions, to renew the ancient criticism and apply it to modern practice.

The bulk of Rymer's work is a meticulous criticism of three plays by Fletcher – Shakespeare and Ben Jonson are promised for another time – along with some reflections on Milton's *Paradise Lost* in which Rymer (like Dryden) intended to defend rhyme against blank verse. His method was to examine plot and characters in detail with reference to specific passages and to set them against the standards of ancient Greece. "I never find a fault without shewing something better," he boasted; and it remains true that despite some eccentric opinions, Rymer was able to discover some telling faults.[23] Once admit his principles, and it is hard to gainsay his conclusions. On the whole, Rymer had no time for praise and that still gives his small work a one-sided and sometimes ferocious aspect; even the Roman, Seneca, fails to live up to his Greek models. But not even Rymer would admit to the pedantry of endorsing too exact an imitation. So, for example, when he comes to consider the frequent reference in the ancients to sacrifices, oracles and meddling goddesses, he admits their purpose but cautions against their employment. He was aware that the case had lately been argued and that many thought that the old superstitions would look ridiculous on the modern stage; but not many had noticed how artfully Virgil had used the gods of Homer, "nor with what judgment Tasso and Cowley employ the heavenly powers in a Christian poem." His advice to the modern poet was simple: always distinguish the essential from the accidental, the moral function of tragedy from its trappings. The appropriate hints in Sophocles and Euripides might well be adapted by modern writers, "and something thence devis'd suitable to our Faith and Customes." Rymer did not want to see the Greek oracles or goddesses on stage any more than he wanted to hear them speak in their original language. "They are Apes and not men that imitate with so little discretion."[24]

2

In its way, *The Tragedies of the Last Age* was an impressive performance, provocative certainly, yet hard to deny in a world where everyone had had the classical poets beaten into them from childhood. As an exercise in practical criticism Rymer's work could not be matched in England, and the ideas that had flooded in from abroad and that Rymer meant to naturalize in his own country could no longer be avoided.[25] Perhaps the choice was easier in France where classical precept had no Elizabethan practice to encounter; in England the problem that Dryden had put in the *Essay of Dramatick Poesie* had now to be reconsidered. Rymer had in effect taken up the cause of Crites and the ancients; would Dryden continue to urge Neander and the Elizabethans?

Rymer's gift reached Dryden in the country in 1677 and he promptly dispatched his impressions in a letter to the Earl of Dorset. " 'Tis certainly very learned," he announced, "and the best piece of Criticism in the English tongue, perhaps in any other of the modern."[26] There may have been some who wanted to dismiss it out of hand, like the playwright, Wycherly, or the satirist, Samuel Butler, but Dryden, who had pretensions to theory himself, saw the merits of the work at once.[27] "If I am not altogether of his opinion," he continued, "I am so, in most of what he says." He was only glad that Rymer had decided not to criticize him, "for he is the only man I know capable of finding out a poet's blind side."[28] He thought that if Rymer would only hold back his *Edgar*, there was no one who could or would dare to answer him. In private he scribbled into his copy some reservations, grappling as well as he could with Rymer's arguments.

Dryden's ruminations only found their way into print sometime after his death. As the "Heads of an Answer to Rymer," they have attracted much attention, although their random and unfinished nature, and their obviously tentative character, have led to much controversy about what Dryden really meant.[29] What is clear is that Dryden had to do some hard thinking about Rymer and especially to reconsider his own position *vis-à-vis* the ancients. To cope with his arguments, it occurred to Dryden that he must first decide whether Rymer's reading of Aristotle was correct. For example, it seemed to him upon further reflection that Aristotle had in fact seen the importance of manners, thoughts and words, as well as plot and character. Might not the English be superior in those respects? And was there not more to the moral function of tragedy than simply moving an audience to pity and terror? It began to look as though Rymer had read his Aristotle too narrowly, though Dryden allowed that some of the fault may have belonged to the Greek philosopher. The more basic question was whether the ancient critic had not been confined by his own limited experience with the drama of his time, "whether he having not seen any others but those of Sophocles, Euripides, etc. had or truly could determine what all of the Excellences of Tragedy are, and wherein they consist." If Aristotle had argued that pity and terror were the only ends of tragedy, was it not because he knew only the ancient works? "If he had seen ours, he might have chang'd his Mind."[30] It could hardly be denied that the plays of Fletcher and Shakespeare continued to move and entertain the modern audience – and that was the true business of a poet. They were successful, in Dryden's view, because they had "written to the Genius of the Age and Nation in which they liv'd." Was it not the poet's responsibility to adapt himself to his own time? "For tho' Nature as he [Rymer] objects, is the same in all Places, and Reason too the same; yet the Climate, the Age the Dispositions of the People to whom a Poet writes, may be so different, that what pleas'd the Greeks, would not satisfie an English Audience."[31] Apparently, Dryden found it difficult to separate the accidental attributes of tragedy from the essential, or to dismiss them.

However, Rymer had not only suggested that modern taste was different from the ancients but that it had fallen far beneath the classical standard – that the modern poet was constrained to address a debased audience – and Dryden was to some extent willing to concede this. If the Greeks "proceeded upon a Foundation of truer Reason to please the Athenians, than Shakespeare or Fletcher to please the English, it only shows that the Athenians were a more judicious People."[32] Moreover, Rymer had insisted on a loftier purpose for the poet than merely pleasing the audience; in times of barbarism, the poet should purge and reform, lead not follow. And so once again, Dryden was forced to give some ground, though he thought that Rymer had willfully exaggerated the modern weakness in plot and character and overlooked some flaws in the Greeks. Besides, there was more to tragedy than plot. "To conclude, therefore, if the Plays of the Ancients are more correctly Plotted, ours are more beautifully written; and if we can raise Passions as high on worse Foundations, it shows our Genius in Tragedy is greater, for in all other parts of it the English have manifestly excell'd them." Shakespeare's success was more the result of the excellence of his words and thoughts "than the Justness of the Occasion."[33] Yet even on this point, Dryden had to allow that the ancient epic poets, if not the tragedians, still reigned supreme, and that no one had ever surpassed Homer and Virgil.

So, whatever Dryden's attempts at refutation, he was compelled to concede much to Rymer and his *ancienneté*. As a practicing playwright with an intimate knowledge of the stage, he felt the practical limitations of Rymer's strictures and chafed at the restraints he wished to impose. As a reflective writer with pretensions to criticism and a Westminster education, he could not fail to see something in the arguments of the French formalists and their English exponent.

> My Judgement on the Piece is this, that it is extreamly Learned; but that the Author of it is better Read in the Greek than the English Poets; that all Writers ought to Study this Critick as the best Account I have seen of the Ancients; that the Model of Tragedy he has given here, is Excellent, and extream Correct; but that it is not the only Model of Tragedy; because it is too much circumscrib'd in Plot, Characters, etc., and lastly, that we may be taught here to justly admire and imitate the Ancients, without giving the Preference, with this Author, in Prejudice to our own Country.[34]

If this is still the voice of Neander, it is more defensive now and less confident. In 1677, Dryden, who was always of two minds on the matter, seems to have found himself more equivocal than ever.

3

It was probably about this time that Dryden also read the criticism of two other notable French "ancients," the Sieur de Boileau and Père Bossu. The first of them published a pair of works in 1674 that were uncommonly influential in both countries: L'Art poétique, in imitation of Horace, and a translation and commentary on Longinus.[35] The second brought out his popular Traité d'un poème épique a year later.[36] Perhaps under the influence of these writers, certainly out of a growing appreciation of the ancient poets, Dryden seems to have begun to think about writing an epic poem himself. He had long believed, with almost everyone else, that it was the most exalted form of literature, and while he had won extraordinary success in the theater, he seems to have had some nagging doubts about the ultimate value of his plays. In 1675, he completed the latest of his heroic tragedies, Aureng-Zebe, and admitted that he was tired. The truth was, he wrote to the Earl of Mulgrave, "I am weary with drawing the deformities of and lazars of the people . . . I desire to be no longer the Sisyphus of the stage: to roll up a stone with endless labour (which to follow the proverb, gathers no moss) and which is perpetually falling down again. I never thought myself very fit for an employment where many of my predecessors have excelled me in all kinds." (Shakespeare especially filled him with shame; his Roman heroes surpassed all, though penned in an age "less polish'd, more unskil'd.")[38] He hoped now to make amends for his ill plays with a heroic poem, a poem to be drawn from English history and modeled upon Virgil. Meanwhile, as he declared in his prologue, he had even "grown weary of his long-loved mistress, Rhyme."[39] The Aureng-Zebe pledged good characters, scenes entire and not too bloody, a great action and unity of time, no forced rhymes and moderate passions: in short, nearly all the values prescribed by the French critics and thought to be ancient. If Dryden now seemed to doubt the taste of his English audience, who generally preferred a bear-garden fray (while the French stood aside and muttered, "Ha, gens barbare!"), the time would come eventually, he hoped, when the English too would become more civilized and recognize the virtues of his play.[40] For the while, uncharacteristically, he wrote little.

It is not easy to estimate the impact of French fashions upon Dryden and his contemporaries.[41] The fact is that across the Channel the quarrel between the ancients and the moderns had been going on furiously for a long time, exacerbated in science and philosophy by Descartes and his followers and in literature by a series of confrontations over the drama, beginning perhaps with the fracas over Corneille's *Cid*. If for a time the moderns had seemed to get the best of it, the ranks of the ancients quickly closed around those like Rapin who insisted upon defending the values of Renaissance humanism. Boileau was a friend of Rapin's, a member of the same circle that frequented the "academy" of the president, Lamoignan.[42] The *Art poétique* shares exactly the same literary values as the *Reflections on Aristotle*; it is indeed hardly more than a poetic version of Rapin's prose. Dryden not only read it carefully, together with the commentary on Longinus, but a few years later he helped to translate it and adapt it into English.[43] By then, the vogue for "arts of poetry" modeled on Horace and Boileau had become very much the fashion – the most notable being by friends and patrons of Dryden, the Earl of Roscommon (1680), John Oldham (1681), and the Earl of Mulgrave (1682). All three agreed upon endorsing a renewed *ancienneté*.

Dryden's immediate contribution was to revise the translation of Boileau begun by Sir William Soames. Apparently, at the behest of the publisher, Jacob Tonson, he altered the language a good deal, particularly in the fourth canto, and substituted English poetic examples for the French. Much of Boileau's original was devoted to a survey of the ancient genres with some generalized advice about how to compose in them. As with Rapin, reason and common sense were identified with classical precedent and enjoined upon the poet. For pastoral, the guides are Theocritus and Virgil; for elegy, Tibullus and Ovid; for satire, Horace, Persius and Juvenal; for tragedy, Sophocles; for comedy, Terence; for epic, Homer and Virgil. In every case, the prescriptions were laid out as the judgments of reason confirmed by the practice of the ancients, and most modern works were shown to have fallen short. In his treatment of epic, Boileau deliberately endorsed the classical (pagan) machinery over the modern (Christian) alternative, Homer above Tasso, thus renewing another old argument between ancients and moderns. In England it had just been rekindled by Davenant's preface to *Gondibert* and Hobbes's reply.[44]

For Dryden, Boileau and Rapin were at once the best and most authoritative modern critics and he remained respectful of them for the rest of his days.[45] He knew and admired other French critics also, so much so that his enemy, Martin Clifford accused him of actually stealing everything in his work from D'Aubignac, Mesnardière and Corneille.[46] When Père Bossu's work appeared in 1675, it was accepted by Dryden and his contemporaries as particularly authoritative.

(So typically, when Lady Froth in Congreve's *Double-Dealer* – which Dryden greeted enthusiastically in 1694 – undertakes to write an "Essay towards a Heroick Poem," she proudly announces her decision to follow Bossu, as well as Rapin and (more recently) André Dacier on Aristotle and Horace.)[47] If anything, Bossu was even more emphatically on the side of the ancients than the rest, although he limited himself to epic alone and disclaimed any prescriptions for the modern poet. His task, he said, was simply to explicate the old authors, but the effect was much the same: to endorse Homer and Virgil as the most nearly perfect models of heroic poetry and Aristotle and Horace as the most exact critics. For Dryden and his generation the cumulative effect of all this reading must certainly have told. Yet it was not only the French who were singing the praises of classical *ancienneté*. In England too, besides Ben Jonson, an even more magisterial voice was being raised in its favor. In 1668 and again in 1674, John Milton published his *Paradise Lost* in blank verse; in 1671 he followed it with *Samson Agonistes* and *Paradise Regained*. The effect on Dryden was profound.

4

We are apt to forget that Milton and Dryden were contemporaries, though to be sure Milton was quite a few years older. The Restoration had, of course, quite reversed their fortunes. Milton was forced into retirement and returned to poetry, while Dryden (his allegiance to Cromwell almost forgotten) was winning popular success and the title of poet laureate. Milton published *Paradise Lost* just as Dryden was replying to Howard in his *Essay of Dramatick Poesie*. Whether Milton ever read Dryden is impossible to say; he did eventually become friends with Howard.[48] That Dryden read Milton is certain, though exactly when is less so. According to a later story, Milton's poem was discovered a couple of years after its appearance in a bookshop by Lord Buckhurst who brought it to Dryden's attention. "This Man," says Dryden, in one version, "Cuts us all Out and the Ancients too!"[49] By then it probably contained the brief preface that Milton added to the later printings of the first edition and to the new version of 1674.[50] Dryden must have been startled to discover there what still sounds like a direct rebuke.

What Milton said was this: "The Measure is English Heroic Verse without rime, as that of Homer in Greek, and of Virgil in Latin; Rime being no necessary Adjunct or true Ornament of Poem or good Verse, in longer Works especially, but the Invention of a barbarous Age, to set off wretched matter and lame Meeter." Some of the moderns had employed it, but to their general disadvantage, whereas the best of the Italian and Spanish poets, and the English tragic writers, had largely forsaken it. Milton's neglect of rhyme, therefore, was no defect, however it might seem to vulgar readers, but rather an example, "the first in English, of ancient liberty recover'd to Heroic Poem from the troublesom and modern bondage of Rimeing."[51]

Just why Milton added these peremptory lines is not at all clear, but the suspicion is that he was very well aware of the contemporary controversy.[52] If so, the author of *Paradise Lost* had no hesitation in taking the part of Crites. Milton's epic may or may not be a classical poem; it was certainly launched upon the world as a classical imitation, and Dryden could only read it and its invocation as another blow in favor of *ancienneté*. When *Samson Agonistes* appeared in 1671, the blow was redoubled.[53] It too contains a few lines of introduction, and nothing that Dryden read in those years could have struck closer to home; for now Milton was no longer talking about epic, which Dryden only aspired to write, but about tragedy, which Dryden had claimed for his own. Even the title page with its Greek quotation from Aristotle's *Poetics* must have registered uneasily in the laureate's mind.[54]

This time what Milton said was this: tragedy as anciently composed, had always been held the gravest and most profitable kind of poetry, "therefore said by Aristotle to be of power by raising pity and fear, or terror, to purge the mind of those and such like passions."[55] Milton's notion of catharsis seems to have been borrowed, like so many of his critical ideas, from the Italian commentators on Aristotle, whose works he had read long before. In any case, the greatest men of antiquity had praised and even written tragedy; St Paul had actually inserted a verse of Euripides into Holy Scripture. Milton brought this up pointedly, "to vindicate Tragedy from the small esteem, or rather infamy, which in the account of many it undergoes at this day with other common Interludes; hap'ning through the Poets error of intermixing Comic stuff with Tragic sadnes and gravity, or introducing trivial and vulgar persons . . . corruptly to gratifie the people."[56] Milton insists throughout upon following ancient example for its "authority and fame"; he therefore retains the classical chorus, "introduc'd after the Greek manner," and still employed by some of the modern Italians.[57] He also insists on imitating the ancient Greek verse forms; he only omits the division of the play into act and scene, since his work was never intended to be performed. As for the plot, he concludes, its value depends on verisimilitude and decorum. "They only will best judge who are not unacquainted with Aeschulus, Sophocles and Euripides, the three Tragic Poets unequall'd yet by any, and the best rule to all who endeavour to write Tragedy." Finally, he endorses the unity of time; everything should be accomplished within twenty-four hours, "according to antient rule, and best example."[58]

In short, there seems hardly a classical precept that Milton was unwilling to endorse and claim for his own on the basis of Aristotle's theory and the actual practice of the ancient poets.[59] As in the case of *Paradise Lost*, there has been much contention about the classical character of *Samson Agonistes*. (Is it Hellenic or Hebraic or Christian or some compound of the three?)[60] But it is plain again that Milton meant to launch his play as a classical imitation and that is the way it was then read. John Toland described it as "an admirable tragedy, not a ridiculous mixture of gravity and farce according to most of the modern, but after the example of the yet unequal'd antients, as they are justly call'd, Aeschylus, Sophocles, and Euripides."[61] And Samuel Coleridge still thought that it was "the finest imitation of the ancient Greek drama that ever had been or would be written."[62]

Certainly Dryden must have seen at once the profound contrast between Milton's *ancienneté* and his own. The one true test, Milton had fairly pointed out, was a direct comparison between the ancient and the modern tragedies, and he was confident that his own would pass. But Milton was a master of the Greek language and his long acquaintance with the Greek tragedies went back to his childhood.[63] For Dryden it was otherwise. Like the wits who followed after him, he had learned some Greek at Westminster, but it is doubtful that he had ever read a classical tragedy through in the original – perhaps not even in a Latin translation. An Englishman, Thomas Stanley, it is true, had just surprised the learned world with a superb new edition of Aeschylus in Greek and Latin (1663) with the help of the fine classical scholar, John Pearson, but there is no sign that it was ever noticed by either Dryden or his critics. Dryden's knowledge of Greek practice was therefore all indirect, largely filtered through French critics whose own acquaintance with the originals was often suspect. When Milton proposed the imitation of ancient tragedy, he had both the means at hand and the independence of mind to carry it through. *Samson Agonistes* bears a genuine resemblance, perhaps even a direct indebtedness, to plays such as *Prometheus Bound* and *Oedipus at Colonus*.[64] *The Conquest of Granada* and even *Aureng-Zebe* owe as much to the world of romance and the plays of Corneille and Racine, in the latter case even to *Samson Agonistes*, as to anything directly classical.[65] But Dryden, unlike Milton, meant to have his plays performed and was, no doubt, thinking primarily of his audience.

That Dryden read Milton's views directly and borrowed from his example we may be sure,[66] but it looks as though he also heard something directly from the old man himself. John Aubrey reports that he learned from Dryden about Milton's entertaining dinner conversation, with the implication that Dryden had been there, and there is, of course, a famous account of their meeting in 1674.[67] It seems that Dryden, who was always on the lookout for new ideas for the stage, conceived the notion of adapting *Paradise Lost* for the theater. According to Aubrey, Dryden, "who very much admires Milton, went to him to have leave to putt his Paradise Lost into a Drame in rhyme. Mr. Milton received him civilly, and told him *he would give him leave to tagg his Verses*."[68] By 1713, the story had developed a little further; a gentleman told the *Monitor* that Dryden had been accompanied by Waller. "Well, Mr. Dryden, says Milton, it seems you have a mind to Tagg my Points, and you have my leave to Tagg'em, but some of 'em are so Awkward and Old Fashion'd that I think you had as good leave 'em as you find 'em."[69] Dryden told Aubrey that he found Milton's conversation "satirical" and perhaps that is the way he remembered the meeting; it is not hard to imagine what Milton would have thought of the enterprise had he lived to see it accomplished. Andrew Marvell, who early caught wind of Dryden's project, mocked it savagely in some lines before the 1674 edition of *Paradise Lost*.[70] Undeterred, Dryden took Milton's permission and swiftly turned the epic poem into a rhymed play: *The State of Innocence*, he called it, or *The Fall of Man*.

It was by any standard an astonishing enterprise. The play was meant to be accompanied by music, dance and marvelous stage effects; it was nothing less than an opera, or nearly so, intended for the opening of a new theater.[71] In fact, it was never performed and, though it was registered with the Stationers' Company in 1674, it might never have been printed, so Dryden says, except for the circulation of some unauthorized manuscript copies. When at last he brought it out in 1677, he prefaced it with some characteristic remarks which he called "The Author's Apology for Heroic Poetry and Poetic Licence." He was truly sorry, he said, if anyone should think to compare his hasty version with the original *Paradise Lost*, "being undoubtedly one of the greatest, most noble and most sublime poems which either this age or nation has produced."[72] His new friend, and sometime collaborator, Nathaniel Lee, commended Dryden's work, however, in some prefatory verses as the best poem his collaborator had yet written, a polished version of a rough original.[73]

It is hard to make out how far Dryden really believed Lee's compliment or what he thought of the whole venture. With the passage of the years, the urge to polish Milton only deepened for both the ancients and moderns (for example both for Bentley, who was to edit the epic, and for Atterbury, who urged an improved version of *Samson Agonistes* on his friend Alexander Pope).[74] Later, when Dryden was writing about verses proper for satire and heroic poetry, he remembered a conversation that he had once had with "that noble wit of Scotland," Evelyn's old foil, Sir George Mackenzie. Mackenzie asked Dryden why he didn't look to the poets, Denham and Waller, for guidance about beautiful and elegant turns of phrase. Dryden admitted that he had not paid much attention to the problem up to then, and took Mackenzie's hint, only to be disappointed with his English contemporaries, even including Cowley, who preferred turns of wit and quirks of epigram to what he thought was required of an heroic poem. From the metaphysical poets he turned with pleasure to Milton, and "found in him true sublimity, and lofty thoughts, which were clothed with admirable Grecisms," although still not the refinement that he desired. Apparently, the trouble was that Milton had faithfully followed Homer, "whose age had not yet arrived at that fineness," rather than Virgil and Ovid, who had inspired Spenser and Tasso and could better supply the moderns with the turns of phrase that they needed. If only the English would now (as in France under government patronage) create a prosodia, or at least a proper English dictionary.[75]

How far Dryden improved Milton's language may be doubted; Walter Scott was neither the first nor the last to be dubious about it, though he saw the point.[76] Long before Scott, John Dennis remembered that Dryden himself had confessed to him how little he had appreciated Milton's merits when he wrote *The State of Innocence*.[77] For the while, Dryden hoped that Lee's flattery would "rather be esteemed the effect of his love to me than of his deliberate and sober judgment."[78] And he displays a new admiration for Longinus which allows him to defend the sublime above the correct (on classical authority) – Homer and Milton, despite their blemishes, over lesser and more careful writers. He contrasts the modern "hypocrites of English poetry" with the best judges of antiquity and their recent Italian and French followers. "I could reckon up, amongst the moderns, all the Italian commentators on Aristotle's book of poetry: and amongst the French, the greatest of this age, Boileau and Rapin; the latter of which is alone sufficient, were all the other critics lost, to teach anew the rules of writing."[79]

As usual, Dryden meant first of all to defend his own practice, and once again to balance the claims of originality and tradition, the moderns and the ancients. Longinus gave him the chance to argue for all those features of a modern poem that could not find easy precedent in the examples or precepts of the ancients. "Are all the flights of heroic poetry to be concluded bombast, unnatural, and mere madness, because they are not affected with their excellencies?" Yet, like Longinus and Boileau, he would set strict limits to the boldness of the poet. What, then, was to be the ultimate standard: reason or tradition, modernity or antiquity? Dryden, drawing upon Rapin, tried to accommodate the two. Virgil and Horace, he asserts, "the severest writers of the severest age," must be allowed to settle the matter, "for in this case, the best authority is the best argument." Why? Because their authority was nothing else than the result of reason, reason demonstrated by their long-continued reputation.

> For generally to have pleased, and through all ages, must bear the force of universal tradition. And if you would appeal from thence to right reason, you will gain no more by it in effect, than, first to set up your reason against those authors; and secondly, against all those who have admired them. You must prove why that ought not to have pleased, which has pleased the most learned and the most judicious; and to be thought knowing, you must first put the fool upon all mankind.[80]

In short, you may think you can do better than the ancients, and you may try, but it is not likely that you will see more deeply into human nature than they. "Aristotle raised the fabric of his *Poetry* from observations of those things in which Euripides, Sophocles and Aeschylus pleased: he considered how they raised the passions, and thence has drawn rules for our imitation." Since nature was the original, Dryden agrees that all poets should study her, as well as Aristotle and Horace, her best interpreters. "But then this also undeniably follows, that those things which delight all ages must have been an imitation of nature; which is all I contend."[81] It may not have seemed a very original observation in 1677, but it was a powerful argument for *ancienneté* and for neoclassical imitation. It is true that Dryden concludes with some words in favor of poetic license, but they are a bit perfunctory, and he does not try to define its limits – on the grounds that Horace had not done so either. He thinks that the old Roman would not have approved the use of a Christian argument and that he would not (like Rapin condemning Tasso) have approved of employing the pagan deities. There may be a difference in the manners and customs of the ages, as Dryden had always insisted, and therefore in the forms of poetic license, but now his emphasis was all on the fundamental uniformity and constancy of human nature. Whatever his practice, he seemed to be inching further and further toward the *ancienneté* of his old character Crites.

5

Dryden continued to praise Milton, and he continued to nourish some doubts. The gulf that divided the two poets in so many ways was impossible to bridge, not least between their different apprehensions of antiquity. Both men had praised Aristotle and the rules and then broken them;[82] but Milton had read and assimilated ancient practice as well as theory, while Dryden remained largely ignorant and oddly indifferent to the Greek dramatic writers, even while insisting on them as the source of Aristotle's wisdom. There is, as a consequence, a vast difference between *Samson Agonistes* and *Aureng-Zebe*; *Paradise Lost* and *The State of Innocence*. Dryden's apologetic preface suggests that he understood something of this; but in case he missed the point, in 1675, Milton's nephew, Edward Phillips, made it clear once again.

Phillips was one of two nephews who had been tutored by Milton in Latin and Greek; he later wrote his uncle's biography.[83] The young man never lived up to his uncle's accomplishments and he turned out to be something of a hack author, though his English dictionary was very popular, and he wrote some other useful things. In 1670 he added an appendix to a standard school-text, a brief Latin history of modern poetry.[84] Already, he defends *Paradise Lost* there as the one successful epic of modern times, dismissing the neoclassical pretensions of Davenant's *Gondibert* and Cowley's *Davideis*. In 1675 he enlarged his views in a more ambitious work, *Theatrum Poetarum: Or a Compleat Collection of the Poets, Especially the Most Eminent in All Ages. The Ancients distinguish't from the Moderns*. The material is largely borrowed and hastily assembled; the arrangement is alphabetical, and the brief entries are only slightly enlarged.[85] But the dedication is to two distinguished Greek scholars, Thomas Stanley and Edward Sherburne, and it allows Phillips a chance to put his own views.

Not surprisingly he sounds just like Milton. No more than his uncle was Phillips taken in by changing fashions; what was *verum* and *bonum* once remains so always. "To the Antient Greeks and Latins, the modern Poets of all Nations and for several Ages, have acknowledged themselves beholding, for those both Precepts and Examples which have been thought conducing to the perfection of Poetry."[86] Unfortunately, the vogue for rhyme in the modern languages had come to replace the ancient measures. But the truth is that blank verse was better, more ample in scope and liberty, than anything conceivable in rhyme – "as evidently appears from an English Heroic Poem which came forth not so many years ago, and from the style of Virgil, Horace, Ovid, and other of the Latins."[87] Like Milton, Phillips advocates decorum and verisimilitude; approves reviving the chorus for tragedy and the unity of time; and decries "that Linsie-

Woolsie intermixture of Comic mirth with Tragic seriousness." And he reaffirms the precedence of epic. Characteristically, Phillips found it difficult to imagine any new form of literature. "Whosoever should desire to introduce some new kind of Poem of different fashion, from any known to the Antients, would do no more then he that should study to bring a new order into Architecture."[88] Judicious criticism, it is hardly necessary to say, depends first of all upon the knowledge of ancient authors.

About particular authors Phillips is less interesting. He is modest about his uncle, leaving it to others to decide "how far he hath reviv'd the Majesty and true Decorum of Heroic Poetry and Tragedy," though in a later place he does speak of him as "the exactest of Heroic Poets . . . either of the Ancients or Moderns, either of our own or whatever Nation else."[89] His views about the Elizabethans sound very like the *Essay of Dramatick Poesie*, and Dryden is acknowledged for his wonderful success in the theater. In 1670, Phillips had found the comedies admirable but too French. In 1675, he discovers the same fault in the tragedies, but allows Dryden an excuse. To the extent that Dryden had followed the French in over-emphasizing love and honor and continuous rhyme, Phillips thought it must be simply out of dependence on the debauched taste of the times, rather than his own "well examined judgement."

It was a shrewd hit, and by 1675 it looks rather as though Dryden had come to very much the same conclusion.

6

Dryden had deliberately matched himself with Milton and unwittingly revealed the limits of his modernity. After a long pause and some considerable reflection, during which he seems to have given up the idea of writing an epic,[90] he returned to the stage and matched himself again, this time with Shakespeare and Sophocles. The result clearly reflects his recent reading of the French critics and Milton and his deepening admiration for the ancients.

In 1677, Dryden took the story of Shakespeare's *Antony and Cleopatra* and reworked it after his own fashion as *All for Love*. It is usually thought his best play, and Dryden himself was very fond of it; it was the only one, he said, that he had written for himself. He did not so much intend to "improve" Shakespeare, as he was to do a year or so later with *Troilus and Cressida*, as to "imitate" him; to attempt a new version of a familiar story that had in fact already served more than one seventeenth-century author. Dryden, thus, invited a comparison which has continued to fascinate his readers.[91]

His preface sets out the terms of the contest. It was, he says, the many versions after Shakespeare that had given him the confidence "to try the bow of Ulysses amongst the crowd of suitors." One of them, by Sir Charles Sedley, the Lisideius of Dryden's *Essay*, had just appeared, though with only the slightest reference to Shakespeare.[92] What Dryden set out to do was to regularize the complicated plot and bring it into close harmony with the unities – perhaps even more, he remarks, than the English theater required. "Particularly, the action is so much one that it is the only of the kind without episode or under-plot; every scene in the tragedy conducing to the main design, and every act concluding with a turn of it."[93] It was thus meant to be a far cry from both Shakespeare's and Dryden's own heroic dramas. In fact, Dryden managed to reduce his predecessor's cast from thirty-four characters to ten and the time and place from about twelve years and twelve scenes to Alexandria in a few hours. He omits completely the first three acts of Shakespeare to concentrate on the denouement. As a result of these cuts and concision, the "panoramic" enterprise of Shakespeare is transformed into a close-knit classical drama. What-ever else one may think of it, "the plan of Dryden's play," said Walter Scott, "must be unequivocally preferred to that of Shakespeare in point of coherence, unity, and simplicity" – and to that extent, it must be admitted that Dryden succeeded in his efforts.[94] As Gerard Langbaine explained, "If Mr. Shakesper's Plots are more irregular than those of Mr. Dryden's (which by some will not be allow'd) 'tis because he never read Aristotle or Rapin!"[95] Dryden himself denied acceding to the over-nice punctilios of the French, and he criticized Racine's recent *Phèdre* for transforming the Hippolytus of Euripides into Mon-sieur Hippolyte.[96] Nevertheless, he had clearly taken the counsels of French criticism, if a little less the practices of the French stage, to heart. Although he imitated Shakespeare's style, he had, he insisted, "endeavored in this play to follow the practice of the ancients, who, as Mr. Rymer has judiciously observed, are, and ought to be, our masters."[97] And he "disencumbered" himself at last from rhyme.

How well Dryden accomplished all this, with what loss as well as gain, we must leave to Dryden's critics.[98] The fact is that he had deliberately and suc-cessfully imposed the precepts of classical criticism on his recalcitrant material and in so doing had shifted his point of view from Neander to Crites, from a qualified modernity to an explicit *ancienneté*. Yet even so, the imitation of classical precept, imperfectly understood, was hardly sufficient, as Dryden himself was occasionally aware, to recapitulate classical practice. For that, the ancient tragedies alone could instruct the modern playwright, as once they had the ancient critic. Racine's *Phèdre* could not therefore be allowed to stand as a model before Euripides's *Hippolytus* – not if true *ancienneté* was to be attained.

Curiously, having dispatched Milton and Shakespeare, albeit with some embarrassment, Dryden turned next to Sophocles. In the spring of 1678 he joined forces with his new young friend, Nathaniel Lee, to rewrite *Oedipus*, "the most celebrated piece of all Antiquity."[99] Dryden was in bad spirits at the time and obviously depressed about the condition of the stage. His sudden return to the theater seems to have been more the result of financial hardship than any thirst for literary immortality. Perhaps he was also concerned about the impending political crisis that threatened English stability. *Oedipus* is a col-laboration in which Dryden claimed the first and third acts and the overall design. His partner, Lee, had recently had a splendid success with a couple of plays that in some ways (their blank verse, for example) anticipated Dryden's

All for Love. If the two men were unevenly matched and temperamentally at odds, their association remained firm until Lee was carried off to Bedlam in a fit of madness.[100] Their adaptation of *Oedipus* was necessarily a failure next to the original, although it was a prodigious popular success and had some good things in it. But it is clear from the preface that the two authors were much more anxious to have their work compared to other adaptations than to Sophocles's original.

There were two of these especially: one by the Roman, Seneca, the other by Corneille. In each case, the judicious reader was asked to notice "How much the copy is inferior to the original."[101] Seneca had abandoned nature for a pompous style and a closet philosophy; Corneille had foundered especially with his hero, who to gain pity should have been shown a better man. All that Corneille could offer the new adaptation was one episode which had to be changed, and Seneca, one brief relation with an account of the appropriate rites and ceremonies which had to be corroborated. For the rest, since Sophocles alone is "admirable everywhere," he had to be followed as closely as possible.[102] In fact, the new play has been described as a motley compound of Greek and Latin, French and Elizabethan sources, closer to the Jacobeans in spirit than to the ancient Greeks. A generation later Addison deplored its rant and bombast, more by Lee perhaps, but enough by Dryden.[103] And, if it is not clear how far Dryden and his collaborator would have recognized the flaw, or seen the contrast with their ancient source, it is perfectly plain that his audience (which had no way of knowing) did not much care one way or the other.

Nevertheless, it appears that the two authors at least had now actually read the original, probably in the collection of Sophocles's plays published in Greek and Latin at Cambridge in 1665.[104] They knew that their play had been universally praised throughout antiquity, especially by Aristotle (but not by Horace, as Dryden supposed); now they discovered in it "the noblest, manliest and best design,"

> And every critic of the learned age
> By this just model has reform'd the stage.[105]

Unfortunately, as Dryden noticed, the Athenian theater was very different from its modern London counterpart; reform of the stage had therefore to be carried out within a very different set of circumstances. In Greek tragedy, the chorus was prominent and a principal figure always predominated. In the English theater, the minor characters were much more important and had to be kept in view; moreover (despite the example of *All for Love*), custom demanded a subplot which was separate but dependent on the main story. At first, Dryden put aside the question as to which of these dramatic conventions was the better, but in the end he had to admit that the Greeks were superior. "Perhaps, after all, if we could think so, the ancient method, as 'tis easiest is also the most natural and the best. For variety, as 'tis managed, is too often subject to breed distraction."[106] As always, Dryden seems to have found himself caught between two stools: the lofty literary pretensions of the past and the immediate practical expectations of the present, halfway again between the ancients and the moderns. Whether Dryden and Lee were really able to outdo Corneille and Racine in their adaptations of Greek tragedy we must leave again to the critics; it is clear that the authors at least preferred not to be judged against their ancient model.

7

Finally, as though to fix his position in these matters more precisely, Dryden returned to Shakespeare and corrected *Troilus and Cressida* for performance and publication early in 1679. Once again he pruned the plot and regularized it, corrected the language, and generally refurbished the old play, this time, however, deliberately attempting to improve the original. "I new modelled the plot; threw out many unnecessary persons; improved those characters which were begun and left unfinished, as Hector, Pandarus and Thersites, and added that of Andromache. After this I made with no small trouble, an order and connection of all the scenes, removing them from the places where they were inartificially set."[107] A new scene (among many additions) between Troilus and Hector has reminded many of Brutus and Cassius in *Julius Caesar*, though Dryden claims to have drawn his inspiration directly from Euripides's *Iphigenia*, perhaps at the suggestion of Thomas Rymer. Dryden's critic, Gerard Langbaine, usually hostile, thought the adaptation a masterpiece, "cultivated and improv'd" upon the original. (Modern critics have not always been so appreciative.)[108] Langbaine may well have been swayed by Dryden's preface, an even more ambitious apology than usual, which he called "The Grounds of Criticism in Tragedy," and which he seems to have intended to publish separately. Here at last was Dryden's full public response to Rymer, the French critics, and his recent encounters with Milton, Shakespeare and the ancient Greeks.

"The Grounds of Criticism" begins with a prologue in which Dryden excuses his alterations of *Troilus* by quoting from Longinus:

> We ought not to regard a good imitation as a theft, but as a beautiful idea of him who undertakes to imitate by forming himself on the invention and the work of another man; for he enters the lists like a new wrestler, to dispute the prize with the former champion. This sort of emulation, says Hesiod, is honorable when we combat for victory with a hero, and are not without glory even in our overthrow.[109]

This time Dryden does not fear comparison with the original; apparently even Shakespeare does not have anything like the authority of the ancient Greeks. One reason that Dryden offers is that the Greek language had reached its perfection in the fifth century, while the English of Shakespeare, even in the refined English of Dryden's time, still lacked a regular grammar. Dryden had no hesitation, therefore, in removing "that heap of rubbish under which so many excellent thoughts lay wholly buried." The only question that remains for him is the one that had dogged him ever since the *Essay of Dramatick Poesie*, that is to say, whether, or how far, to imitate the Elizabethans. He is not, he says, afraid to retract his earlier errors; this time he will rely only on the authority of the ancient critics, Aristotle (and his commentators), Horace and Longinus.[110]

He begins by asserting that the excellence of tragedy depends upon plot, reiterating (with Aristotle) the importance of unity of action; he compares his own *Mariage A-la-Mode* with its double plot unfavorably in this respect with *Oedipus*. The "innovation" (as it once was) had been invented by Terence and reproduced by the English to doubtful effect. Dryden follows Rapin in arguing that tragedy should teach by example and Rymer that it must conclude with poetic justice. (Even Euripides had faltered here.) And he quotes Bossu that all the arts, and especially poetry, had been brought to perfection by the great men of the past, "and therefore they who practice afterwards the same arts are obliged to tread in their footsteps, and to search in their writings the foundation of them; for it is not just that new rules should destroy the authority of the old."[111] How far, then, should the Elizabethans be imitated? "We ought to follow them so far only as they have copied the excellencies of those who invented and brought to perfection dramatic poetry." The Elizabethans, like all other moderns, must be measured against the ancient standard. Once again, however, he distinguishes accidental things, "superstructures," he calls them here (religion, customs and language), from essential matters, that is to say, "the foundation of the design."[112] He agrees with Rymer completely that the Elizabethans were defective in the last, though he does suggest that only one of Sophocles's tragedies perfectly realized Rymer's ideal.

For character and manners, Dryden accepts the usual neoclassical notions of decorum; resemblance, and consistency, and he finds Ben Jonson generally superior in these things to all the other modern poets. On the whole, he accepts Rymer's criticisms of Fletcher and continues to use Sophocles (the *Antigone* now as well as the *Oedipus*) as a standard of comparison. Shakespeare is praised again for his characters and defended again with the aid of Longinus for his description of the passions, but even he is found guilty of confusing "the blown puffy style" with true sublimity.[113] The author of *The Conquest of Granada* has the nerve to accuse Hamlet of rant! But of course, Dryden well knew the temptation, "for bombast is commonly the delight of the audience which loves poetry but understands it not." In any case, Shakespeare was not often guilty and was less reprehensible than those who lived in a more polite age. Dryden closes by insisting that the rules and principles he has laid down, though drawn from the ancient critics and their modern imitators, were ultimately enjoined by experience. The rules, as Rapin had said, were only nature reduced to a method. "They are founded upon good sense and sound reason, rather than on authority; for though Aristotle and Horace are produced, yet no man must argue that what they wrote is true because they wrote it."[114] Thus *ancienneté* is here defended (as it was generally), not because it was old, but because it was true. With the passage of the years Dryden had finally discovered a way to endorse the arguments of Crites and Lisideius, and he begins to sound suspiciously like Sir William Temple.

8

No doubt other circumstances contributed. By 1680, Dryden's career was ready for a new turn. For five years or so after the writing of *Aureng-Zebe*, he had been chafing under the restrictions of the stage. Now in the spring of the year, he delivered up another play, *The Spanish Friar*, and once again bade farewell to the theater. In his new preface he looks back upon his career and under the pressure of the "young gallants who pretend to criticism," he admits his mistakes. His heroic plays, he allows, were too full of bombast and exaggeration; his heroes, Maximin (in *Tyrannic Love*) and Almanzor (in *The Conquest of Granada*), "cry vengeance upon me for their extravagance."[115] In his new play he has tried to avoid those excesses while striving for the new-found virtues of proportion and decorum. Even the sublime, he repeats, must be just and proper. If *The Spanish Friar* is a tragicomedy with two plots, it is because Dryden has deliberately broken a rule for the pleasure of variety. No tragedy, he was sure, could possibly succeed for the time being without verse and a leaven of mirth.

The trouble lay, of course, with the audience.[116] When Dryden looked back afterwards upon *The Spanish Friar*, he was willing to admit its flaws and ready to assign them to the whole genre. The play "was given to the people; and I never writ anything for myself but *Antony and Cleopatra*."[117] In his dedication to *The Spanish Friar*, he wrote that he was resolved to seek no reputation, "by the applause of fools," but in his heart of hearts Dryden knew he could not avoid the difficulty. If he had erred in writing his tragedies, he had known, "they were bad enough to please, even when I writ them." Writing for performance meant writing to please an audience whose taste was invariably low; and the ordinary reader was little better. "If the Ancients had judged by the same measures which a common reader takes, they had concluded Statius to have written higher than Virgil." As a child, Dryden had himself preferred the dreary poet Du Bartas to his great contemporary Spenser.[118] Dryden found himself still in 1680 caught between the expectations of a modern audience which he contemned and an ancient idea of fame which he coveted. It looked more than ever impossible to please immediately and still be read in the future, and Dryden increasingly inclined toward the latter.

Unfortunately, the times were not propitious and financial necessity continued to press.[119] It was the midst of the Exclusion Crisis and political conviction, as well as a royal paymaster, turned Dryden to politics. He enlisted at once in the King's cause and discovered a satirical gift which inspired some of his best poetry, *Absalom and Achitophel*, for example, and *The Medall*.[120] Now also he began to take his duties as historiographer royal more seriously and composed a series of prose works, polemical and historical, on behalf of the royal cause and at the royal command.[121] At the same time, and to help him eke out a living, he began to work for the enterprising young publisher, Jacob Tonson, and to translate and edit a number of important and popular classical works. For nearly a decade, Dryden gave up the theater almost altogether for his new vocation of politics and the classics; and so the quest for literary immortality had still to be shelved.

It seems likely, however, that both of these new activities reinforced Dryden's growing *ancienneté*. To write politics was certainly not incompatible with the classical viewpoint, as was clearly the case with those classical republicans, Milton and Marvell. It was less easy for a royalist like Dryden to pretend to be Cicero, but Dryden's notions of rhetoric and history, if less vehement, were still squarely within the Renaissance humanist tradition.[122] More obviously, Dryden's immediate practical concern with the classics in translating for Tonson must now have deepened his reverence for, as it certainly extended his familiarity with the ancient writers. His very livelihood had come to rest somehow upon his ability to advertise and propagate them, to make them accessible and intelligible to the Restoration world. If his commitment to scholarship did not noticeably improve, his intimacy with the ancients did, and his conviction in their immediate relevance and application.

Dryden's first effort for Tonson was a version of Ovid's *Epistles* (1680), translated by several hands, including Thomas Rymer. The preface is notable this time for Dryden's views about translation, a subject to which he was to return often. He argues here for a mode halfway between the literal which he calls *metaphrase* and the uninhibited which he calls *imitation*.[123] Ben Jonson had practiced the first in his version of Horace and been criticized for it fairly enough by the Earl of Roscommon. Cowley and Denham had tried the second, imagining what their authors would have said had they lived in their own age and country. The danger of such modernization, Dryden saw, was that it was bound to create something new, occasionally better than the original (though never in the case of Virgil), but almost certainly unlike.[124] For Dryden the *sense* of an author should be inviolable, though the language must necessarily differ; the best recourse, therefore, was to preserve the first while altering the second, which he calls *paraphrase*. Here, in a word, was the very essence of Dryden's *ancienneté*, halfway still between pedantic imitation and unrestricted freedom.[125]

Of course, Dryden was not alone in his new occupation and he could draw sustenance equally from his old schoolmasters and his new aristocratic patrons. The first had long set about the task of editing the classical texts and supplying the commentaries; the second were now hoping to make them popularly available in English. Dryden's friend, the Earl of Roscommon, was particularly busy at it in these years. As a boy, he had studied abroad during the Interregnum, returning to England an accomplished Latinist.[126] According to tradition, on his return he set about at once founding an academy like the one he had found at Caen, "for the refining and fixing the standard of our language; in which design his great friend Mr. Dryden was a principal assistant."[127] A contemporary, Knightly Chetwood, who left a biography of Roscommon in manuscript, thought Dryden less important in the scheme, but placed him in a group around the Earl that included the Marquis of Halifax (who undertook to revise D'Ablancourt's translation of Tacitus), Lord Maitland (who began to translate Virgil), the Earl of Dorset, Lord Cavendish, Heneage Finch, and some others. "They aim'd at refining our Language, without abating the force of it . . . A great many Innocent and not useless Projects were form'd which . . . were not executed."[128] For Dryden, it was neither the first nor the only effort to reform the language in which he was implicated. We have seen John Evelyn and the Royal Society set up a short-lived committee for much the same purpose, and Jonathan Swift was to resume the cause later.[129] Roscommon himself wrote an *Essay on Translated Verse* (1684) in which he emulated the Earl of Musgrave's earlier *Essay upon Poetry* and to which Dryden attached some complimentary verses.[130] Clearly, Dryden had lots of company in thinking about the state of the language and the problems of translation – almost all of it decisively inclined toward the ancients.

Admittedly, the high station of Dryden's friends had something to do with the reputation of their little works; they seem commonplace enough to us.[131] But that, of course, was part of their contemporary appeal. For the seventeenth-century advocate of the ancients there was no point in writing something new, especially in the realm of literature. When the Earl of Roscommon adapted Horace's *Art of Poetry* in 1680, all he claimed was to write what Horace would have said if he were alive. For Mulgrave, two years later, there was nothing left to add: "Echoes at best, all we can say is vain." He admitted being unable to find much worth commending, "because of those great Ideas I have of the Antients."[132] Though a hostile critic decried his work, not entirely unfairly, as "Scraps of Bossu, Rapin, Boileau, Mr. Dryden's preface and Table Talk," that was very probably its appeal to Pope, Addison and the rest, who insisted on calling it a masterpiece.[133] Dryden recommended to Tonson that he reprint Roscommon's *Essay* of 1684 in a thousand copies, and he accompanied the original with some complimentary verses that show that he had gone a long way toward accepting his patron's view of antiquity.[134] British poetry, he wrote there, however admirable, could not yet claim to rival the classics – except, of course, for Roscommon! There is a story that one day Buckingham, Rochester, Dorset, and some others, gathered together for a literary competition with Dryden as judge. When Dryden examined them, he picked out Dorset's lines as best. "This kind of writing," he pronounced, and the whole company agreed, "exceeds any other, whether ancient or modern!"[135]

Something like this, then, provided the setting, when Tonson turned to Dryden for help with an ambitious new version of Plutarch's *Lives* and called forth Dryden's most unequivocal assertion of *ancienneté*. It is not entirely clear how the forty or so contributors were assembled or just what their qualifications were, but it looks as though it was Dryden who collected them and prepared the life of Plutarch and the introduction that preceded the work.[136] The first volume, with Dryden's contributions, was printed in 1683, the last in 1686.[137] The publisher claimed to have replaced North's Elizabethan version (from the French of Amyot) with a direct translation from the Greek. The translators, however, appear to have generally relied on the Greek–Latin version of Joannes Rualdus (1624). The result is readable but lacks both the high literary distinction of the Elizabethan and the scrupulous scholarship of the modern versions. Dryden's biography is basically a conflation of the lives in Rualdus and North (by Simon Goulart), though the last is not even mentioned.[138] His one real contribution is rhetorical – selection, compression and rewriting – but without any pretense at scholarship, unencumbered, as Dryden says, by the "usual vanity of the Dutch Prefacers."[139] He takes the occasion to expound on Plutarch's moral philosophy, which he found very congenial; on the value of history and biography, which he now emphasized enthusiastically; and on the ancients and the moderns.

It must have seemed a lifetime to the poet since he had first begun to think about the problem in the *Essay of Dramatick Poesie*. In the two decades since, no one had lived closer to the mainstream of English literary life or felt its shifting currents more sensitively. Now in 1683, Dryden resumed the subject with a description of the decay of the world that might well have come from the pen of William Temple. "It appears plainly, that not only the Bodies, but the Souls of Men, have decreas'd from the vigour of the first Ages; that we are not more short of the nature and strength of those gygantick Heroes, then we are of their understanding, and their wit."[140] Dryden passes over the patriarchs (mere striplings at seven or eight hundred years) to dwell on the age of Socrates. "How vast a difference is there betwixt the productions of those Souls, and these of ours! How much better Plato, Aristotle, and the rest of the Philosophers understood nature; Thucydides and Herodotus adorn'd History; Sophocles, Euripides and Menander advanc'd Poetry, than those Dwarfs of Wit and Learning who succeeded them in after times!" Only the Romans, it seems, had been able to revive that learning successfully, though the Greek Plutarch was one who had rivaled the best of the Antonine writers. Indeed, "Antiquity has never produc'd a man more generally knowing, or more vertuous; and no succeeding Age has equall'd him." By contrast, his own time, he says later, was an age fit only for satire.[141]

Had Dryden turned finally into an unreconstructed ancient by 1683? It is hard to know for sure. Like Plutarch, he considered himself a skeptic, though in these matters he was always ready to advance an opinion to meet the occasion, however undogmatically. The circumstances of 1683 must certainly have seemed right for an unabashed *ancienneté* and Dryden's words proclaim, if nothing else, that such a view was growing ever more plausible on the eve of the Battle of the Books. As he penned these words, he very probably understood their full force and believed them altogether. But it must not surprise us to find that they were neither his last nor his definitive expressions on the matter. New circumstances and the actual Battle of the Books compelled new thought – not for Dryden alone. In 1684, Dryden carefully revised the *Essay of Dramatick Poesie*, altering its language in precise detail. But he left all its arguments intact, even to giving to Neander still the last and fullest word. If there was some evident inconsistency in Dryden's thought, it never seemed to bother him.

CHAPTER 5

Dryden and the Battle of the Books

I

Meanwhile, in his gardens at Moor Park, Sir William Temple, the new champion of the ancients, was also reading the French critics. He was not impressed. "There has been so much paper blotted upon these subjects," he complained, "in this curious and censuring age, that 'tis all grown tedious or repetitious." He found the criticism of the moderns, like their poetry, no improvement over antiquity – even when it tried to be ancient. "The modern French wits (or pretenders) have been very severe in their censures, and exact in their rules, I think to very little purpose; for I know not why they ought not to have contented themselves with those given by Aristotle and Horace."[1] Typically, Temple would have preferred to see some fresh translations of the ancient theorists before the endless commentaries on their works which now passed for modern criticism.

Temple's remarks, "Of Poetry," were set out in 1690 in a separate little piece which accompanied the "Essay on Ancient and Modern Learning" and began the Battle of the Books. In his skepticism about the rules, Temple was characteristically English, but he had no modern sympathies. Like Dryden he did not want to fetter the poet needlessly and cost him his natural spirit and grace. The rules might discourage mistakes, but of themselves they could never make good poetry; only look at those modern French writers who had tried to abide by them! Even the ancient poets whom he most admired had written before Aristotle and Horace had laid down the law in their two languages. (The only exceptions he was willing to allow, Theocritus and Lucan, were limited and dubious.) The earliest poems in Greek and Latin were the best in antiquity and for all time, particularly the two great epics, and all the rules must derive from their example. "I think no man has been so bold . . . to question the title of Homer and Virgil, not only to the first rank, but to the supreme dominion in this state, and from whom, as the great lawgivers as well as princes, all the laws and orders of it are or may be derived."[2] Suspicion of the rules was thus combined with a stalwart *ancienneté*. For Temple, as for Rapin or Bossu – or Dryden, for that matter – Homer and Virgil "Must be allowed to have so much excelled in their kinds, as to have exceeded all comparison, to have even extinguished emulation, and in a manner confined true poetry, not only to their two languages, but to their very persons."[3]

Since there was not much point in legislating, Temple is satisfied with a few generalizations before he turns to his real subject, the history of poetry. He argues that poetry was the first kind of writing in the world and that its use to memory, and therefore to instruction, led to its priority over prose. He finds early examples in Greece, the Gothic world and the Old Testament. As always, his sweep is wide but his scholarship is shallow. He is interested in the broad changes that have taken place through the centuries, for example in the transformation of poetry to prose fiction, from Aesop to Petronius to Philip Sidney, whom he admired above all other moderns, apparently because he best displays "the true spirit or vein of ancient poetry in this kind."[4] He describes also the decay of ancient Latin writing, already evident in Lucan and Seneca, and the collapse brought about by the invasions of the Goths and the Vandals. From this cultural and poetic nadir, which continued for many ages, he turns hastily to "the dawn of a new day, and the resurrection of other sciences and the two learned languages."[5] From runes to romance to Renaissance, he charts the reawakening of poetry – but this time all in rhyme. He manages to find some sweetness in the lyrics of Petrarch, Ronsard and Spenser, but denies the success of Ariosto and Tasso in imitating ancient epic. Like Boileau and others, he doubts that Christianity can be adapted to fiction in the way that pagan religion could. (He seems not to know either Dante or Milton.) He concludes with Spenser's *Faerie Queene*, to which he also denies success, despite some fine flights of poetic fancy. Since that poem was written, the moderns have confined themselves to the little forms, "as if, not worthy to sit down at the feast, they contented themselves with the scraps . . . wanting either genius or application for nobler or more laborious productions, as painters that cannot succeed in great places take to miniature."[6]

In short, Temple finds modern poetry, like everything else, in decline. Even such specific modern inventions as epigrams, or ridicule and burlesque (Rabelais, Cervantes and the rest), or the recent efforts to polish the language in France and England, seemed to him either superficial or inept, incapable of "supplying the defects of modern poetry." It was all due, no doubt, as Crites had argued in the *Essay of Dramatick Poesie*, to the relative indifference of modern patronage. In ancient times the best and greatest men, from Solon to Caesar, either wrote or favored poetry; since then, there had hardly been a great prince who cared, or a great poet who had written. "Whether it be that the fierceness of the Gothic humours, or noise of their perpetual wars, frighted it away, or that the unequal mixture of the modern languages would not bear it; certain it is, that the great heights and excellency both of poetry and music fell with the Roman learning and Empire, and have never since recovered the admiration and applauses that before attended them."[7] Temple allows only one exception: of all the forms of literature known to history it was in the drama alone that the moderns were able to excel.

It looks as though Temple had been following that particular controversy, though just what he read is not easy to say. In his retirement, it is unlikely that he had actually seen much recent drama and he makes no explicit references to any individual plays. It is modern comedy that he approves, and it is the English since the time of Shakespeare who have excelled all others at it, both ancient and modern. (He finds even Molière a little too farcical for his taste.) It was a defect of the ancients to circumscribe their characters too much; the strength of the English was in their variety. "This may proceed from the native plenty of our soil," he explains, "the unequalness of our climate, as well as the ease of our government, and the liberty of professing opinions and factions."[8] The English have more "humour," because in England any man may follow his own and take pride in it. And variety of humor is the soul of comedy. Temple (who had traveled much abroad) thought that he could characterize the English impartially, proclaiming their virtues and their defects: their courage and beauty, their natural genius and wit, their range of fancy and depth of thought, but also their spleen and inconstancy and their obstinate divisions over government and religion. "I have had several servants far gone in divinity, others in poetry; I have known, in the families of some friends, a keeper deep in the Rosycrucian principles, and a laundress firm in those of Epicurus." However inconvenient this might prove for life or government, such a medly of humors could only have a good effect on the stage, "so that, in my opinion, there is no vein of that sort, either ancient or modern, which excels or equals the humour of our plays."[9] It begins to look as though Temple's views, here as elsewhere, had been set a long time before, probably back in the days when Howard and Shadwell and Settle had fought with Dryden, and the abbé D'Aubignac with Corneille.

2

Dryden seems not to have read Sir William Temple – or if he did, he was not much impressed. It was rather that other and still more dogmatic ancient, Thomas Rymer, who returned now to the scene to needle him, and who reminds us how relative and vacillating his commitment to antiquity really was. As we have seen, Dryden seems to have grown more conservative with the passing years, but his views continued to oscillate even in old age between the poles of ancient and modern allegiance as he was forced to face the practical problems of his craft and the changing circumstances of his life. In this he may well have been a truer mirror of his age than any of his contemporaries. Toward the end of 1692, Rymer, who had been silent as a critic for fifteen years, came trumpeting back with his long-promised follow-up to *The Tragedies of the Last Age*. His viewpoint remained much the same – French Aristotelian formalism, the rules and the unities – but this time more strident than ever. The result was a new quarrel to set beside, or within, the Battle of the Books.

Just why Rymer should have chosen this moment to come out of retirement is not at all clear, although it may well be that Dryden had something to do with it. Despite a rather formidable contemporary reputation, Rymer remained always an obscure and private person, and even the outlines of his career remain a little uncertain. His play, *Edgar*, had failed, and Rymer never again attempted drama, although he did write some occasional verses and even contributed a life to Dryden's *Plutarch* in 1683. It seems likely that the relationship between the two men must have begun to degenerate at the time of the Exclusion Crisis, when both entered the political arena on opposite sides. And it surely must have worsened with the accession of James II and Dryden's conversion to Catholicism. In 1688, Rymer chided Dryden with an anonymous broadside poem (attributed to him only in 1707) and welcomed William and Mary with two others. With the Glorious Revolution, Dryden found himself suddenly bereft, losing both his position as poet laureate and historiographer royal, first to Shadwell, then in 1692 to Nahum Tate and to Rymer himself. Thus, the views of the two men, which had already diverged over drama, came into head-on collision over politics as each was paid in turn (though not very well) to support the policies of an inimical prince.

As Rymer rose, Dryden fell. He had certainly toiled hard for crown and Church and suffered a great deal of contumely for it, but at least James paid his pension. In 1689, he suddenly lost everything and was forced to return to the theater to eke out a living. "While I continue in these bad circumstances," he complained in the preface to a new play, "(and I truly see little probability of coming out) I must be oblig'd to write." He made no bones about his loathing for the stage which he felt, like himself, was quite worn out. He would do what he could, "condemn'd to dig in these exhausted Mines."[10] *Don Sebastian* was the first play by Dryden to be performed in seven years. It was published in January 1690 and followed by a comedy, *Amphytrion*, a tragedy, *Cleomenes*, and an opera, *King Arthur* (with Henry Purcell), all of which were successful, though none brought him much money. A last play, *Love Triumphant*, failed in 1694 and closed Dryden's career in the drama once and for all.

If it was hard for Dryden to resume his theatrical career, it was no doubt partly because he was still unsure just how to reconcile ancient principles with modern circumstances, his artistic conscience and his fee-paying audience. It did not help that his political and religious position had been severely compromised by the events of 1689.[11] In 1690–92, he took up a position not unlike the one he had first set out at the beginning of his career and for much the same reasons, though he was wearier now and less confident. In *Don Sebastian*, he is at great pains to defend his borrowed plot against the perennial charge of plagiarism. It was, he pointed out, only what the best of the ancients had done, "who were never accused of being plagiaries for building their tragedies on known fables." He remembers also a modern precedent, Corneille's *Oedipus*, as well as his own. " 'Tis the contrivance, the new turn, and new characters, which alter the property and make it ours." As always, he accepts the notion of classical imitation but interprets it liberally: a good imitation was certainly not a theft.[12] As for the rules, he remains expressly deferential to Rymer, but he will not keep exactly to the "Mechanick unities." "I knew them, and had them in my eye, but followed them only at a distance: for the genius of the English cannot bear too regular a play."[13]

It was a familiar refrain. In *Amphytrion*, later the same year, he admits to borrowing from Plautus and Molière, "the two greatest names of ancient and modern comedy," but again, adding and altering to make the imitation his own and to adapt the play to English taste – so very different from that of the Romans and the French. In *Cleomenes* (1692) – with its ancient sources and modern political implications[14] – he again deplores the condition of the contemporary stage and the classical rules, though conceding (as always) their normative status. If he introduces a new scene that appears nowhere in his sources, it is simply "to gratify the barbarous part of my audience," and despite the fact that no self-respecting French poet would ever allow something "which debases a Tragedy to show upon the Stage." He sticks close to the mechanical rules, especially unity of action and place, and departs only a little from the twenty-four-hour limit. Dryden's independence thus continues to be affirmed within a framework of orthodox *ancienneté*. "It is better to trespass a rule, than leave out a beauty," he allows, but it was generally best to abide by their restrictions. Meanwhile, he concluded, "the Reward I have from the Stage is so little, that it is not worth my Labour."[15]

So even while Dryden was busy at his new plays, he continued to translate for Tonson. He seems to have begun to turn something of Juvenal and all of Persius into English just after the Revolution, although the work was not finally finished until 1692. The preface was one of Dryden's more ambitious critical and apologetic statements, "A Discourse Concerning the Original and Progress of Satire," addressed to that same Earl of Dorset to whom he had long ago dedicated the *Essay of Dramatick Poesie* – and which now reappeared in a third unrevised edition.[16] Dryden begins his encomium for his old patron, full of nostalgia for their youth and promise, and he recalls how he had written his first criticism almost without an English precedent. "Before the use of the loadstone, or knowledge of the compass, I was sailing in a vast ocean, without other help than the pole-star of the Ancients and the rules of the French stage among the Moderns, which are extremely different from ours."[17] At once, he resumes the old question of ancients and moderns and the posture of Neander in the *Essay of Dramatick Poesie*. Reason and good sense have been the same in all ages; therefore it seemed to Dryden that it was time that generally brought improvement. Yet he has no notion whatever of an unrestricted progress. "What has been, may be again, another Homer another Virgil, may possibly arise from those very causes which produced the first, though it would be imprudent to affirm that any such have yet appeared." No one age, he believed, had had a monopoly of success, although the Romans at the end of the Republic and under Augustus had come close. The Italian Renaissance had produced a great modern age when painting revived, poetry flourished, and the Greek language was restored.[18] (The triumphs of modernity were for Dryden, as for nearly everyone else, usually dependent on antiquity.) In short, it was possible to imagine new geniuses arising *equal* to any of the ancients, "abating only for the language," although Dryden remained a little uncertain about epic. He seems for a moment to be alluding to Temple's pessimism, as he was certainly responding to Rymer, though neither is named. Dryden had no doubt that, in tragedy and satire anyway, the moderns had actually surpassed the ancients. "I offer myself to maintain against some of our modern critics that this age and the last, particularly in England, have excelled the ancients in both these kinds; and I would instance in Shakespeare of the former, of your Lordship in the latter sort."[19]

It was a graceful compliment. But Dryden betrays the ambiguity of his modern sentiments by looking across the Channel to discover a "living Horace and a Juvenal" in the person of the admirable defender of the ancients, Boileau, and a new Augustus (or almost so) in Louis XIV. He then returns — or as he admits, digresses — to reconsider epic poetry, then obviously much on his mind, and the undeniable superiority of Homer and Virgil to all rivals, ancient and modern, including Statius and Lucan, Tasso and Ariosto, Spenser and Milton. When he comes to the last, he says that he has no wish to forestall Thomas Rymer, who had once promised the world a criticism of *Paradise Lost*. He allows that there are some things that could be said against Milton, but he hopes that Rymer, " 'Tho' he will not allow his poem for heroic," will nevertheless find Milton's thoughts elevated, his words "sounding," and no modern anywhere closer to the manner of Homer and Virgil.[20] If Dryden imagined that these shafts at Rymer were restrained and tactful, they certainly did not seem so to his old rival, who saw them only as a deliberate and provocative rebuff.

Before Dryden arrived at his proper subject, satire, he added a last comment about heroic poetry, for him still "the greatest work of human nature."[21] Like everyone else who thought about the subject, he worried about the pagan machinery that was so integral to the classical epic. Could a modern Christian find an appropriate substitute? He does not accept Boileau's denial — nor by implication, Rymer's — and proposes instead an innovation of his own; a scheme of Neoplatonic angels to replace the pagan gods. If this was something entirely new and unprecedented, he was willing to submit that not all innovation was bad, although the chances of success were small. In words that seem to echo the *Essay of Dramatick Poesie*, Dryden again defends the idea of progress, at least in some things. "We see the art of war is improved in sieges, and new instruments of death are invented daily. Something new in philosophy and mechanics is discovered almost every year; and the science of the former ages is improved by succeeding."[22] Yet even so, and allowing every advantage to the modern poet, Dryden can only conceive of a new epic poem more perfect "than any yet extant *since* the Ancients." Homer, he says later, wrote the "most absolute heroic poem" ever, and any modern who would attempt it must take Homer and Virgil as models, Aristotle and Horace as guides, and Vida, Bossu and the rest as commentators.[23]

Nor was it, finally, any different with satire, Dryden's belated subject, despite his praise for the moderns, Dorset and Boileau. Much of his long essay is devoted to a history of satire and an elaborate comparison of the ancient satirists, drawing deeply but independently on European scholarship for his learning: Casaubon, Scaliger, Heinsius, Dacier, and some others. Dryden accepts the notion that satire was a peculiarly Roman accomplishment and he rates the Latin writers as the best models for all time; Juvenal, Horace and Persius were above the Greeks and any of the moderns – excepting only Dorset and Boileau. How, then, should a modern write? Inevitably, Dryden recommends classical imitation and the rules. "I will not deviate in the least from the precepts and examples of the Ancients, who were always our best masters. I will only illustrate them, and discover the hidden beauties in their designs, that we thereby may form our own in imitation of them."[24] The essay concludes with this undertaking as well as a few remarks on translating that echo the ideas of the preface to the *Miscellanies* of 1685.

<h2 style="text-align:center">3</h2>

For Rymer, the success of Dryden's new plays and their apologetic prefaces was a sudden reminder of the pretensions of the moderns and their contempt for the rules. The "Discourse Concerning Satire" must have been the last straw. Not only did it take issue with him directly, its whole tone and point of view were profoundly irritating, whatever its concessions to the ancients. *The Tragedies of the Last Age* had prompted a sequel, but Rymer seems to have laid it by. At the end of 1692 he dusted it off, padded it out, and hastily rushed it off to the printer. *A Short View of Tragedy* is more than an answer to Dryden; it is an effort, as the whole title explains, to expound again, with uncompromising *ancienneté*, a complete theory of the drama, *Its Original, Excellency and Corruption with some Reflections on Shakespear and other Practitioners of the Stage*. Rymer addressed his preface to the very same patron as Dryden, the Earl of Dorset, as though he expected a sympathetic arbiter, and he invokes at once the full authority of Aristotle and Horace and their commentators, Bossu and Dacier. We are back in the familiar world of the rules and the unities. From that point of view, it seemed to Rymer that there were only a few ancient works that could claim perfection: the heroic poems of Homer and Virgil and one tragedy, the *Oedipus* of Sophocles. Since then, nothing had quite measured up, certainly not the imitations by Corneille, "and others of a Modern cut," for whom Rymer had only a sneer, *quantum mutatus!*[25]

The tract itself divides roughly into two parts: a rambling history of the theater – all decline after the Greeks – followed by a detailed analysis of three modern plays: *Othello, Julius Caesar* and Ben Jonson's *Catiline*. For the first half, Rymer's learning is elaborate and obtrusive and borrowed largely from the French; for the second, he is more original and uses what may well have been the early draft promised in *The Tragedies of the Last Age*. The work on the whole is undoubtedly "chaotic, ill-digested, unnecessarily erudite,"[26] and the disproportion of the chapters is remarkable, the discussion of *Othello* taking up nearly a third of the book. Nevertheless, Rymer had thought the matter through and his critique of *Othello* in particular was formidable and discomforting. (T. S. Eliot doubted that he had ever read a more cogent refutation!)[27] If one only accepted the premises, the conclusions followed readily enough.

From Rymer's perspective, Shakespeare had failed miserably by violating all the conventions of classical drama, and it is hard to tell whether he was more offended by the plot of *Othello*, which to him seemed improbable and amoral; the characterization which was offensive and indecorous; or the style which was vulgar and scandalous. Rymer's enthusiasm for the rules had only stiffened with time and he received much support from André Dacier's new commentary on Aristotle's *Poetics* which displayed a kindred spirit.[28] At the same time, his determination to revive even the Greek chorus was reinforced now by recent French practice, in particular by the last two plays of Jean Racine who had come out of retirement to show the way. Unlike Dryden, or even Sir William Temple, Rymer was unwilling to make the slightest concession to modern taste, or to the gap in manners and circumstances which he, like the others, perceived to have opened up, though he too was willing to make an exception for comedy. Even Ben Jonson, who ought to have known better, is shown to have failed. "When some senceless trifling tale, as that of *Othello*, or some mangl'd, abus'd, undigested, interlarded History on our Stage [as that of *Catiline*] impiously assumes the sacred name of Tragedy, it is no wonder if the Theatre grows corrupt and scandalous, and Poetry for its Ancient Reputation and Dignity, is sunk to the utmost Contempt and Derision."

For all its vehemence and exaggeration, there was something to be said for Rymer's viewpoint – as Pope remembered later.[29] Dryden, of course, had never given up his enthusiasm for the Elizabethans, whatever reservations he may have harbored about them, but this left him, as we have seen, between two stools, accepting the classical rules and models but hoping to escape their absolute authority. When Rymer picked out the famous scene in *Julius Caesar* between Brutus and Cassius in order to deride it, he was deliberately choosing a passage that Dryden had singled out for praise in his preface to *Troilus and Cressida*. Rymer only mentions Dryden once in his work to criticize him, but there was no mistaking his animus; he several times goes out of his way to praise *The Rehearsal* which had so effectively mocked the dramatist's heroic pretensions. "We want a law for Acting the *Rehearsal* once a week, to keep us in our senses, and secure us against the Noise and Nonsense, the Farce and Fustian, which, in the name of Tragedy, have so long invaded, and usurped our theater."[30] Dryden, of course, could not miss the point, although he never admitted in public to being the hero of Buckingham's work. Nor was it any easier for him that he was at least half convinced by its satire and (in much the same way) by Rymer's criticism.

4

Yet Dryden could hardly duck the issue. In 1693, he was not in a good position to strike back, suspected still because of his politics and religion, "my salary ill-paid, and no prospect of a future existence." But answer he must, and so he took the occasion of a new miscellany by Tonson to reply to Rymer with yet another, mercifully briefer, preface. "You know," he explained to Tonson, "He has spoken slightly of me in his last Critique, and that gave me occasion to snarl again." The *Examen Poeticum* had been a long time in preparation, but it was ready at last in the summer of 1693; it contains a volume of miscellaneous poetry, ancient and modern, including a hundred pages of Ovid by Dryden; some Homer by Dryden and his new young friend, William Congreve; and a variety of pieces by such as Addison, Lee, Mulgrave, Buckingham and Waller. Dryden's hasty preface is one last attempt after so many that had gone before to clarify his views about the problem of the ancients and moderns.

Clarification was necessary because it was harder than ever for Dryden to stake out a middle way between the extremes of *ancienneté* and modernity. Not only had he now to face Rymer's renewed contempt, he had also to consider the startling claims for the moderns that were suddenly being launched across the Channel by Charles Perrault. Dryden's preface is an attempt to adjudicate between these contrary views and to assess the various kinds of criticism that were abroad in the world to see whether he could distinguish the truest and most useful. He begins naturally with Rymer, who was certainly meant when Dryden observed that "the corruption of a poet is the generation of a critic."[31] Rymer, he insisted, belonged with those, like the ancient, Zoilus, or the modern, Scaliger, who tear down Homer out of envy because they only know how to find fault. These are, at best, "wits of the second order," whose only credit derives from the fame of the authors they attack.[32] If, after three thousand years, Scaliger had in fact been able to find a few faults in Homer, who would not rather be Homer than Scaliger? Among the English, Dryden detects two sorts of such critics. The one (Dryden is probably thinking of Shadwell) seems to vilify the moderns in favor of their predecessors, but this is only pretense, for they do not so much venerate the Elizabethans as use them as a device for attacking their contemporaries. The other and more contemptible (Dryden is now certainly thinking of Rymer) will allow nothing to the English of any age. They attack the moderns directly by raking up the ashes of the dead, not excepting Shakespeare and Ben Jonson. Dryden did not doubt that he could defend the Elizabethans convincingly and show that the ancient Greek writers only invented the rudiments of a stage which they never anticipated, and "that many of the tragedies in the former age amongst us were without comparison beyond those of Sophocles and Euripides." At present, he disclaims the time and means for the task but he threatens the possibility of a future answer to Rymer's *quantum mutatus*.[33]

As for the modernity of Perrault, whose third volume of *Parallèles* had just appeared, Dryden supposed that there was a vast difference between arguing for contemporary French writers against Homer and Virgil, which he thought preposterous, and upholding the English tragic writers against the claims of the Greeks, which he thought plausible. "For if we, or our greater fathers [the Elizabethans], have not yet brought the drama to an absolute perfection, yet at least we have carried it much farther than the ancient Greeks."[34] Eliminating the chorus, for one thing, seemed to him a great improvement. As for those who insisted upon a slavish adherence to the rules and the superiority of the French, Dryden again upholds the English values of variety and sublimity and the paramount need to please an audience, although he admits that "we assume too much license to ourselves, in keeping them only in view at a distance." A little later, he contemptuously dismisses the scholar-critics also, those translators who insist on the literal meaning of the text against all changes in manners and customs, and the "Dutch commentators," who obscure the originals with their erudition, those "heavy, gross-witted fellows, fit only to gloss on their own dull poets."[35] He even promises a satire on their wit in full anticipation of the Scriblerians a generation later.

Dryden's true critic was, of course, himself, although he pays a compliment to his patron, Lord Radcliffe, by proposing him as the model. (In fact, Radcliffe's real claims appear to have been very modest.) "Being yourself a critic of the genuine sort, who have read the best authors in their own languages, who perfectly distinguish of their several merits, and in general prefer them to the Moderns; yet I know you judge for the English tragedies against the Greek and the Latin, as well as against the French, Italian and Spanish of these later ages."[36] The true critic was thus an ancient, not entirely like Temple, nor dogmatically like Rymer, but in general outlook and disposition willing to make exceptions and admit possibilities, not quite to the extent of William Wotton perhaps, but enough at least to free him from absolute dependence upon the past and to encourage him to modest experiment.

No doubt, this had always been Dryden's view, although the exigencies of combat sometimes obscured it. (It was about this time, we have seen, that there appeared still another unchanged edition of the *Essay of Dramatick Poesie*.) A little later in 1693, Dryden repeated himself in some complimentary verses to William Congreve; but he couldn't help taking another swipe at his two old rivals, Shadwell and Rymer. He would not, he said, have minded resigning his position in Congreve's favor.

> Well had I been depos'd, if you had reign'd!
> The father had descended for the son;
> For only you are lineal to the throne.
> Thus when the state one Edward did depose,
> A greater Edward in his room arose.
> But now not I, but poetry is curs'd;
> For Tom the Second reigns like Tom the First.[37]

5

For all Dryden's annoyance, his replies to Rymer remained restrained; he was not, after all, in a position to do much more than complain. His last play, *Love Triumphant*, was a failure, and Dryden knew it when he was called upon to publish it. In the preface, he defends himself as well as he can against his (unnamed) adversary. If he had departed from the Aristotelian injunctions for the end of his play, then so too had Corneille in the very best of his tragedies, *Cinna*. Was not Aristotle limited by the practices of the Greek tragic writers and their "poverty of invention"? Had Aristotle been able to see *Cinna*, he must surely have changed his mind – "let Dacier, and all the rest of the modern critics, who are too much bigoted to the ancients, contend ever so much to the contrary." For the moment, apparently, Dryden thought that he had invented a new and unprecedented design for his third act. "If it were so, what wonder had it been that dramatic poetry, though a limited art, yet might be capable of receiving some innovations for the better?"[38] Dryden was always ready to leave the doorway to modernity ajar. But upon second thought, he found himself anticipated by both Menander and Terence. As for the "mechanic unities," he had managed to keep within the twenty-four-hour rule only to violate (a little) the unity of place, this despite the example of the French poets and his friend, Congreve. But wasn't there something just a little ridiculous in asking an audience to restrict its imagination to one place on the grounds of plausibility when it knew perfectly well that it was not present in the action but rather in the theater? Finally, he had abandoned the unity of action once again in favor of a double plot. Although there was some classical precedent for that (Dryden may have been thinking of the *Amphytrion* of Plautus), he remained mildly apologetic; it was a peculiar fault of the English audience to demand variety, and so he had submitted. "On occasion that they were cured of this public vice," he concludes a little wistfully, "I could be content to change my method, and gladly give them a more reasonable pleasure."[39] As usual, Dryden's endorsement of modernity turns out to be half-hearted, more self-defense against the shafts of his ancient-minded critics than any deep-seated desire for change.

Dryden was not in a position to do more. Fortunately, there had collected about him in his fallen station a group of young men who aspired to wit and literature and who looked to the old poet with reverence. Their favorite gathering place was Will's Coffee-house in London, where they showed off their work, plied Dryden with questions, gossiped about their love-lives, and talked heatedly about politics and literature. Several of them rallied now to their hero and offered to answer Rymer. One of them, William Walsh, even proposed to write a preface to *Love Triumphant*, though it was not in the end accepted. Walsh, according to Dryden, meant to enter the lists, not so much against Rymer, "yet as a champion for our cause, who defy the chorus of the Ancients."[40] Apparently, Walsh's essay grew too large for its purpose, but Dryden continued to encourage it. Poets, he wrote, would be generally grateful to him for freeing them "from the too servile imitation of the Ancients." If the audience, Dryden repeated, would only come to accept the constraints of the unities (but he doubted that the English ever would), playwrights would have no trouble submitting to them. "I will never defend that practice, for I know it distracts the Hearers," though it satisfied the taste of the audience for low comedy. Dryden offered to correct Walsh's book for the press and to see it printed well; he thought it would be best to publish it separately so that there would be no suspicion that Walsh had been too partial to Dryden as a friend.[41]

Another young man, new to London and to Dryden, did even better. Even before the year was out, John Dennis was ready to publish a long essay, which he called *The Impartial Critick: or, Some Observations upon a Late Book, Entitled, A Short View of Tragedy, Written by Mr Rymer.* Apparently, Dennis had just entered into correspondence with Dryden, who encouraged his poetry and received his effusive praise. For Dennis, who was just launching a literary career, this was invaluable. He was thirty-six years old and had only published so far a brief translation from Ovid's *Metamorphoses* (1692) and some *Miscellanies in Verse and Prose* (1693), with some Pindaric odes that Dryden praised extravagantly.[42] With such encouragement, Dennis was ready to take on Rymer. *The Impartial Critick* is a series of short dialogues preceded by an introduction that strikes out boldly against Rymer on behalf of Dryden. The tone is light, as befits an aspiring wit and gentleman (a role that Dennis was not long able to sustain). Beneath the bantering, a sober and earnest young man was attempting to come to grips with some of the chief critical problems of the age and finding himself caught, like his elders, between the subtle and conflicting claims of liberty and authority, the ancients and the moderns.[43]

According to Dennis, Rymer wished to reform the stage by recalling the methods of the ancient drama, but he did not see how that could be done in modern England. "For to set up the Grecian Method amongst us with success, it is absolutely necessary to restore not only their Religion and their Polity, but to transport us to the same Climate in which Sophocles and Euripides writ."[44] Different circumstances required different means; and the customs of one time and place appeared absurd and ridiculous to another. This was, of course, the position of Dryden and also the Frenchman now living in England, Saint-Evremond, who was in fact twice quoted by Dennis for support. The Greek chorus was a good example, sensible in terms of ancient religion, incongruous and absurd in the modern world. Love was another, inevitable upon the modern stage, but outrageous and improbable for the Greeks. It was foolish, therefore, "to think of setting up a Chorus upon the English Stage, because it succeeded at Athens; or to think of expelling Love from our Theaters, because it was rarely in Grecian Tragedies."[45] To illustrate the difference in cultural values, Dennis hits upon a passage in the *Antigone* of Sophocles where the heroine, condemned to die, can only think that she is bound to Hell with her maidenhead! It was, he felt sure, a difference that could only be explained by climate and custom. The introduction closes with a paean to the poetry of Dryden, which he prefers (against Rymer) to both Waller and the French. Unless due credit was given to the living, and some public patronage, it was not possible to imagine much progress or improvement.

The dialogues proper begin with general disapproval of Rymer's style, which seemed flippant to Dennis, as did his method and design. When it comes down to cases, however, Dennis's strictures begin to show some of the same qualifications as Dryden's, and a strong dose of *ancienneté* begins to leaven what started out so boldly. So, Dennis at first approves of Dryden's *Oedipus* (and Corneille's) against the contempt of Rymer's *quantum mutatus*; but when he comes actually to compare Dryden and Sophocles, it is all to the disadvantage of the modern for having altered the character of Oedipus and weakened the moral and cathartic effects of the story. Dryden would have done better, says Dennis, to have written the whole thing himself (instead of collaborating with Lee) and to have stuck closer to Sophocles! Would Aristotle have condemned the English *Oedipus*? Yes indeed, or be forced to give up his own principles. "But at the same time that he passed Sentence on it, he would find it so beautiful, that he could not but love the Criminal; and he would certainly crown the Poet, before he would damn the Play."[46]

Dennis distrusts Rymer, but he continues to give his allegiance to Aristotle. In the fourth dialogue (after rebuking Rymer for praising Waller unduly), Dennis returns to a consideration of the chorus. Now he tries to show that Aristotle's notions about the end and purpose of tragedy are not served by the chorus. Racine's example in his recent plays is dismissed as "convenient" rather than "necessary," a result of Mme de Maintenon's command, rather than any real desire to imitate ancient practice, from which in any case Dennis believed he had deviated. Tragedy could achieve its purpose of exciting pity and terror in the modern world only by forsaking the chorus. But didn't Aristotle and Horace and Dacier all give rules for its use? No doubt; however, the ancients were constrained by their religion, and even Dacier (whose Catholicism was as superstitious as pagan religion) conceded that there was something unnatural about its use. The chorus, Dennis insists, is implausible and unnecessary, even on ancient terms, and ought to be left to rest in the ancient works.

There was surely something paradoxical about Dennis's attempt to confute ancient practice with ancient theory, to correct Sophocles's *Electra*, for example, with Aristotle's rules, which he does in the last dialogue. But there was a simple explanation. Like almost all the other critics of his generation, including Rymer, he assumed that Aristotle's authority lay not in his dates but in his arguments. Human nature, Rymer had pointed out, was the same in Athens and London, and so was the effect of tragedy.[47] Dryden had objected, but only about the accidentals.[48] As a result, Dennis could repeat, with Rymer and Rapin, that "the Rules of Aristotle are nothing but Nature and Good Sense reduc'd to a Method."[49] It was thus possible, though not easy, to correct or modify Aristotle – to adapt the ancient principles to modern practice, not slavishly, but flexibly. So the contemporary translator of Terence (Lawrence Eachard) can typically propose Terence as "the best and most perfect Model for our Dramatick Poets to imitate, provided they exactly observe the different Customs and Manners of the Roman and English People."[50] The argument in the end was therefore not so much about the absolute authority of the ancient rules as it was about their relative value to the modern world, and a strong dose of *ancienneté* was accepted here, as it was to some degree by nearly everyone else. Dennis closes his work by accepting with Rymer (and with Temple) the superior value of

English comedies, setting Congreve's *Plain Dealer* above Plautus and Terence, but promising to return to the field to defend Shakespeare against his critic, even though in most of his particulars he allowed that Rymer's censures were "very sensible and very just"![51]

6

Dryden must have been very pleased with Dennis's work. In an undated letter written about the time of its appearance (March 1694), and published two years later, Dryden is full of praise for his friend's poetry and full of antipathy for Rymer. "Your own Poetry is a more Powerful Example, to prove that the Modern Writers may enter into comparison with the Ancients, than any which Perrault could produce in France."[52] (The praise was typically exaggerated, to judge by Dennis's few Pindaric odes.) On two points, both neglected by Dennis, Dryden reiterated his public views. He answers Boileau again with his Neoplatonic angels, but he doubts that anyone will actually accomplish a great modern epic, since no one is fit to write after Virgil, "in a barbarous Modern tongue"; and he attacks Rymer for "blaspheming" Shakespeare. Like Dennis, however, he is forced to admit that "almost all the Faults which he has discover'd are truly there." Yet who, in the end, will prefer to read Rymer than Shakespeare? "For my own part, I reverence Mr Rym-s Learning, but I detest his Ill Nature and his Arrogance. I indeed, and such as I, have reason to be afraid of him, but Shakespeare has not." It was nice for Dryden that there were others, younger and more foolhardy, who were ready to take on the irascible old critic.

Dennis must have been encouraged by Dryden's response and he soon decided to reenter the fray more directly. In 1696 he attacked Sir Richard Blackmore's attempt at a modern epic on the grounds that it had "neither unity, nor integrity, nor morality, nor universality," and that it was generally contemptible next to the great classical poems – in particular, the *Aeneid* – that it had tried so feebly to imitate.[53] Blackmore had attacked the wits in his preface, especially Dryden, and this may have provoked Dennis, as it certainly annoyed Dryden.[54] A few years later (1701), Dennis entered the fray again with a more substantial treatise in which, among other things, he took a stand directly in the Battle of the Books. Dryden had just died without declaring himself, but it is very likely that he would have approved the manifesto of his young disciple, and the work is addressed to Dryden's old friend and patron, the Earl of Mulgrave, the author of the much-admired *Essay upon Poetry*. Dennis's design, he says, was "to set the Moderns upon an equal Foot, with ever admir'd Antiquity," but he begins by setting the *Oedipus* of Sophocles above the *Julius Caesar* of Shakespeare, and reaffirming the necessity of the rules in poetry, as in painting and music.[55] He had in mind the particular example of Homer and Virgil, and his sentiments would surely have been approved by his older friend.

They wrote not with a little narrow Design, to please the tumultuous transitory Assembly, or a Handful of Men, who were call'd their Countrymen; They wrote to their Fellow-Citizens of the Universe, to all Countries, and to all Ages; and they were perfectly convinc'd, that tho' Caprice and Extravagance may please the Multitude, who are always fluctuating, and always uncertain; yet that nothing but what is great in Reason and Nature, could be able to delight and instruct Mankind.[56]

The case for modernity, if such it was, could hardly be argued more moderately or with more qualification.

In fact, Dennis deplored the extremes of both sides. The moderns had argued from reason that the ancients were men like others and had no obvious advantage in themselves or their circumstances. The ancients replied with the simple observation, universally held by critics, that the classical poets were superior, and that only the ignorant could deny it. The moderns called the lovers of the ancients slavish pedants, while the ancients responded by labeling the moderns ignorant fools. Dennis thought he could find a middle way, acknowledging ancient precedence but not placing it so high as to preclude modern possibility.[57] He pointed out how the moderns had improved many of the arts with their inventions and discoveries; but he was willing to acknowledge that favorable political conditions had fostered classical eloquence above anything modern. As for poetry, it was his view that ancient superiority (which he readily accepted) derived from the excellence of their moral and religious subjects, but that it could be matched by the moderns if they so chose. Indeed, the superiority of Christian religion offered the promise of a superior modern poetry. Milton had already shown the way, excelling Virgil in thought and spirit, though not quite in his versification or beauty of expression. But Milton had not fully understood the art of heroic poetry, since he wrote before Bossu – and John Dennis – had explained it![58] With this in mind the moderns could look forward to advancing beyond even the greatest poets of antiquity. "Whatever the Ancients justly did" – he wrote later in an essay directed against Alexander Pope's "servile deference to the Ancients" – "the Moderns may justly do." But for the while, he was forced to admit that "the actual Preheminence" of some of the ancients still had to be acknowledged.[59]

7

The next to befriend Dryden was another young man named Charles Gildon. Already in 1692, Gildon had translated a piece by André Dacier that took the side of the ancients in the French *querelle*. Dacier pretended to judge between the ancients and the moderns, owning great veneration for the one, even while supporting the claims of the other. He conceded that "there are a great many who are the Honour to our Age, and wou'd have adorn'd the Ages pass'd." But the best of the moderns were those who had best respected the ancients and followed their lead.

If you go never so little from them, you go at the same time from Nature and
Truth; and I shall not be afraid to affirm, that it wou'd not be more difficult to
see without Eyes, or Light, than 'tis impossible to acquire a solid Merit, and to
form an Understanding by other Means, than by those, that the Greeks and
Romans have trac'd for us.[60]

The moderns (Perrault and Fontenelle) were wrong to decry antiquity, when
they knew so little about it; they were barbarians worse than the ones who had
once ravaged Greece and Italy. How far Gildon subscribed to these sentiments
is not clear, but he was offended a year or two later when Rymer said much
the same thing in his attack on Dryden.

Gildon had held back, he explained to Dryden, in the expectation that
Dennis would provide the *coup de grâce* in his promised attack on Rymer's
Shakespeare. When the months passed and nothing appeared, he decided to let
fly himself. The result was a couple of pieces and some random remarks that
appeared together in 1694 in a collection of *Miscellaneous Letters and Essays on
Several Subjects*. Gildon was still very young and a little frivolous. Unlike Dennis
who went on to a long career of single-minded devotion to his muse, Gildon
became something of a hack author and party writer. Nevertheless, he sincerely
admired Dryden, despite his own inclination toward *ancienneté*, and Gildon
meant to do what he could to bring Rymer down and help the cause.

Unfortunately, Gildon probably did more to muddy the cause than to clarify
it, perhaps because he accepted the same basic framework of *ancienneté* and
meant only to qualify it. Simple patriotism seems to have been his chief
critical principle, but even so, he constantly gives the game away. He begins his
preface, for example, by lamenting "that a Man of Mr Rymer's Learning shou'd
be so biggoted to the Antients, as to become an Enemy to the Honor of his
own Country." But immediately, he allows that in things like courage, virtue
and wisdom, "Greece and Rome will never be out-Rivalled."[61] In an essay
entitled "An Apology for Poetry," he takes back something of the enthusiasm
of his preface by deploring the lack of public patronage for the arts in modern
England. "Had our Poets this Encouragement, they wou'd surpass the Romans
and the Greeks too, and England wou'd have her greater Horace and Virgil."
It is true that Gildon preferred English tragedy to the Greeks, and Dryden
above Sophocles, but he ends his essay by regretting again the "degeneracy" of
an age which, "tho' bless'd with as great Poets as ever Greece or Rome produc'd has so very little regard to them."[62] His own essay quotes Latin verse on
nearly every page to support his views.

Gildon's best arguments were reserved for the essay entitled "Some
Reflections on Mr Rymer's Short View," which was addressed to Dryden. Here
too, however, it turns out that Gildon's chief complaint against Rymer was lack
of balance rather than outright error. Dryden was far superior as a critic because
he was able as a poet himself to see the beauties as well as the weaknesses of
his predecessors. No one ever denied that Shakespeare had faults, but that
should not be allowed to obscure his merits; and only a pedant would deny

that Homer had *his* faults, though Gildon would not allow that to obscure *his* merits. In short, Gildon's modernity consisted chiefly in his attempt to redress the balance between ancients and moderns by pointing out both that the classics could err and that the moderns could succeed. Nevertheless, it was only in respect to dramatic poetry that he was prepared to assign a clear and unqualified superiority. Dryden's *Oedipus* and *All for Love* had settled that – "for all the *Quantum mutatus* of which another time."[63]

In the course of the argument, Gildon offered two other modernist views: that the Romans were superior in many respects to the Greeks, despite their own frequent reservations on the point, and that in philosophy anyway, clear progress had been made in recent times. In general, he prefers Virgil to Homer; Cicero to Demosthenes; and (on Pliny's authority) Roman art and government to the Greeks. As for philosophy (though typically, Gildon has not much use for philosophy), "Since the time of Des Cartes, when the Dictates of Greece began to be laid aside, what a Progress has been made in the discovery of Nature? and what Absurdities laid open in the School Precepts, and Terms of Aristotle?"[64] In a later essay, "For the Modern Poets against the Ancients," Gildon resumes the point. "I will be more just than my Adversary, I will yield that Greece had Great Poets, notwithstanding all those monstrous Faults and Absurdities they abound with, tho' he will not allow the English any Honour."[65] Indeed, the poetry of Greece was her greatest achievement and would last forever, even while her philosophy was now being refuted. Although Gildon has no room for a thorough parallel between the ancients and the moderns (like Perrault whose work he had heard about but not yet read, or William Wotton, who had just set about writing one), he hastily compares the ancient and modern writers for their genius, metrical skill and judgment, and finds for Virgil above Homer with respect to the first, and Dryden above Sophocles and Euripides with respect to the last. Disregard of the rules is for him no disadvantage, since liberty and variety are both useful – the proof again being demonstrated by Dryden, who always understood the necessity of satisfying an audience.

What about Shakespeare, then? Rymer, according to Gildon, had "scarce produc'd one criticism, that is not borrow'd from Rapin, Dacier or Bossu, and mis-apply'd to Shakespeare."[66] (He admits his own debt to Dryden, Saint-Evremond, and to Rapin, whom he now turns back upon his translator.) His chief method is to parallel the alleged faults of the Elizabethans with as bad or worse in the Greeks. And to shore up Shakespeare's reputation he remembers a story that Dryden had once told him. It seems that the Master of Eton College, John Hales, one day announced that he would show that Shakespeare had outdone all the poets of antiquity in all poetical matters. Naturally, there were immediate objections, and it was agreed to meet in Hales's chambers to argue the point. Many books were assembled by the enemies of Shakespeare and at length the company gathered: Lord Falkland, Sir John Suckling, and many others of wit and quality who had been aroused by the controversy. The debate was held and the judges agreed unanimously to give preference to

Shakespeare. "The Greek and Roman Poets were adjudg'd to Vail at least their Glory in that to the English Hero."[67]

It remained for Gildon to answer Rymer in relation to the rules in general and *Othello* in particular. He admits that Shakespeare had not come close to observing the Aristotelian injunctions; that he may not have even known what they were. So what? Everyone but Rymer agreed that poetry depended upon joining art *and* nature. If Shakespeare was deficient in the one, he had made up for it with the other; great genius transcends the rules and glories in a "noble irregularity." Even so, Gildon will not advise against the rules or the ancient plays. "I do not think that to be a Great Man, one must necessarily be wholly exempt from the Rules, so I must grant, that Virgil, Sophocles, and Yourself are very great, tho' generally very Regular."[68] He would simply allow a less perfect literature to have its merits also. Shakespeare, for all his faults, was able to accomplish the true ends of poetry, pleasure and profit, by moving his audience to terror and pity. The defense of *Othello* relies on comparing the play with several Greek tragedies and the *Aeneid* to show that its faults and absurdities were outdone by one or another of the ancients. Unlike Rymer, Gildon finds the plot and characterization both plausible and moral and the numbers harmonious, and the scene between Brutus and Cassius admirable. He closes by commending Dryden's good nature as too equable to have permitted him to reply to his opponents.

Gildon was not quite done, however. In still another brief essay in the collection, addressed to Dennis, he defends the theme of love in tragedies against the strictures of Rapin and Rymer. Once again, he finds the authority of ancient precedent in the way. Authority, he insists, should never outweigh reason; the same *ipse dixit* that had been shunted aside by philosophy, should also be dismissed from poetry, "since 'tis perhaps about as prejudicial to an imitation of Nature in this, as our discovery of it in the other."[69] Unfortunately, Gildon does not develop this idea further with its crucial distinction between imitation and discovery, but simply quotes Dennis (who was, of course, quoting Rapin and Rymer) that Aristotle's rules were "nothing but good Sense and Nature reduc'd to Method." If this was so, as Gildon saw, then Aristotle himself could be corrected by reason. Nor was anyone obliged "to a servile Observation" of his precepts or ancient practice without addition or improvement. Had not Sophocles and Euripides improved upon their models? Why then deny the moderns the same liberty, "to forsake the Steps of the Greeks?"[70] In this way, eliminating the chorus or adding the theme of love could easily be defended as improvements, which Dennis proceeds to do – however relying all the time on the reasoning of that staunch defender of the ancients, Père Rapin!

Indeed, Gildon was not a very powerful critic or original mind. All his points were commonplaces in a debate that had been going on now for a long time. No doubt he felt very bold in striking out against so formidable a target and on so topical a cause. And Dryden was certainly happy to have his support, however qualified. But his arguments remain useful chiefly in reminding us how hard it was to think about literature in this period, however daringly, outside the framework of *ancienneté* and apart from its assumptions. Perhaps it is not surprising that Gildon spent the rest of his career retreating from this early work, until in the end his position became almost exactly like the one he had first set out to defeat; by 1718, Gildon's views were almost indistinguishable from those of the despicable Rymer. "We are not for excluding the Moderns from their Merits, but insist, that no Modern has any Merit but what he owes to the Rules and Precedents of Art as establish'd by the Ancients." And now he expressly sides with Temple and Boileau over Wotton and Perrault. Under the circumstances, it is not surprising that the old allegiance to Dryden fails; he was a good poet, he writes now, but not much of a critic, and dramatic writing was not his talent![71]

CHAPTER 6

Dryden's Virgil and the Triumph of Antiquity

I

In 1694, the "modern," William Wotton, decided to answer the "ancient," Temple, or rather (as he preferred to think) adjudicate between the claims of Temple on the one hand and Perrault on the other. And so began the Battle of the Books. Like Temple, Wotton did not have any special acquaintance with the drama; unlike Temple or the other combatants, he had no pretensions whatever to polite letters. Nevertheless, he could hardly avoid the quarrel about literary imitation that was so central to the dispute and that raged all around him, or fail to take a position. It was, however, one of Wotton's merits to see that the issue about classical imitation was really quite different from the issue about the extent of modern knowledge and to try to distinguish between the two.[1] The difference, he thought, lay in the fact that some human activities, particularly those that were immediately practical, were interesting to everyone and quick to develop; they were therefore capable of an early perfection. They were, as Dryden admitted of the drama, "limited arts."[2] So, in morals and politics, in poetry and rhetoric, even in history and grammar (but with some qualifications) – in short, in all those subjects that were linked together in the *studia humanitatis* – the first men on the scene had had the best and fullest advantage of creativity and left to their successors little more than the possibility of imitation. Wotton believed that it was otherwise with philology and natural science, which were forced to grow more slowly to their perfection by the need for painstaking observation and experiment, by the accumulation of scholarly and scientific knowledge. In those subjects, learning was truly progressive and could easily be demonstrated by a comparison of past and present achievement.

The ancients, therefore, really were superior to the moderns in the humanities, just as Temple had said, accepting pretty much the same assumptions, although one could quibble about details.[3] Since human nature was basically the same in all ages, the human virtues and passions and the forms of eloquence and poetry must all be permanent and unchanging. As a result, Aristotle and Cicero, among others, had known just about everything in those matters already. Only the accidentals, local customs and different languages, varied over time and were the result of changing circumstances. For Temple, the causes that affected such things and had been so favorable in antiquity were largely climatic; for Wotton they lay in a superior language and politics. For Temple, the causes were often beyond the control of men and the result was dispiriting; for Wotton the accidents that had led to the classical achievement could recur, and he was generally optimistic. Yet even so, he thought that the best of the moderns were those who imitated the ancients and used their rules. For both men, the claims of Charles Perrault and the French moderns, who (from patriotic motives only) had dared to place the poets and orators of the age of Louis XIV above the Greek and Latin classics, seemed absurd.[4]

Wotton accepts that poetry was the earliest kind of writing. The Greeks had the advantage, he believed, because the language they inherited had a natural variety and smoothness beyond any yet cultivated. Certainly, the modern tongues all suffered by comparison – not least the French language with its lack of variety and strength. Perrault knew no Greek and was thus unable to appreciate the difference, as indeed were all those who had to rely only on the inferior translations of the moderns. (Here Wotton leans on Boileau and cites the egregious D'Ablancourt.) Even the Romans had had to admit Greek superiority in eloquence and poetry, though Latin possessed some natural advantages of its own. The Greeks had taken full advantage of the possibilities of their language and brought the humanities to swift perfection so that even their own later writers were reduced to imitation, which they accomplished by using examples or by extracting rules. Thus, Virgil followed the *Iliad* and Aristotle devised the rules of epic poetry from the practice of Homer. Temple was right to say that no copy could reasonably hope to excel its model. And when the language was "dead," as in the case of modern Latin, imitation was especially bound to fail. Wotton was not much more optimistic than his rival about the modern vernacular poets, though he has some kind words for the free imitations of Milton, Cowley, Butler and Dryden, and he never quite shuts the door to further possibility. The fact is that Wotton agreed basically with Temple, "that former Ages produced greater Orators, and nobler Poets, than these later ones have done."[5]

As a result, Wotton's *Reflections* was meant to reply at least as much to Perrault and the moderns as to Temple and the ancients – though Wotton complained that the world kept insisting that he was partial to the former. Wotton thought it was nonsense for Perrault to have admired Boileau over Horace, and Corneille and Molière over the ancient dramatic poets. The Frenchman had argued that they were superior because they knew the rules better and followed them more exactly. But Wotton believed that the rules derived from examples and replied that time did not always bring improvement in these matters – as the decline in classical Latin after Cicero plainly showed. (To be sure, Temple too had downplayed the rules.) Perrault had argued that politeness had increased since antiquity, especially in the matter of love. "The Writings of the best bred Gentlemen of all Antiquity, for want of modern

Gallantry, of which they had no Notion, were rude and unpolish'd, if compar'd with the Poems and Romances of the present Age."[6] But modern French politeness was, from an Englishman's perspective (as well as that of an older French generation too), degenerate and over-refined, an aberration rather than an improvement on nature. Moreover, the ancients did know much that was important about love; Wotton was ready to place Ovid and Tibullus far above the authors of *Pharimond* and *Cassandra*:

> That Simplicity therefore of the Ancients, which Monsieur Perrault undervalues, is so far from being a Mark of Rudeness, and Want of Complaissance, that their Fault lay in being too Natural, in making too lively Descriptions of Things, where men want no Foreign Assistance to help them to form their Ideas; and where Ignorance, could it be had, is more valuable than any, much more than a Critical Knowledge.[7]

It was an argument that was to be taken up again in France by that most formidable of the ancients, Mme Dacier, in the next great episode of the Battle of the Books.

Yet Wotton was right to say, as he looked around him in 1694 (and again in 1705), that "the Excellency of Ancient Eloquence and Poetry . . . is so generally held, that I do not fear any Opposition here at home. It is almost an Heresie in Wit, among our Poets, to set up any Modern Name against Homer or Virgil, Horace or Terence. So that though here and there one should in Discourse preferr the present Age, yet scarce any Man who sets a Value upon his own Reputation, will venture to assert it in Print."[8] Despite several decades of sporadic pleading, the moderns had made very little headway in claiming poetry and literature for their side; and only a few eccentric Frenchmen were prepared to disagree.

2

What Dryden made of all this must remain a little uncertain; he knew the French *querelle*, but he was content to stay clear of the English Battle of the Books. At this stage of his life, old and still in need of friends, there was not much point in entering gratuitously into a quarrel that was not his own. Moreover, it looks as though Dryden was still not ready in the 1690s to throw in unreservedly with either side. As a former student at Westminster *and* a former member of the Royal Society, his personal allegiance must surely have been divided between the two factions. We have seen that he continued to accept with Wotton the precedence of the moderns in philosophy and natural science; and it is likely that he preferred Wotton's qualified *ancienneté* in the humanities to Temple's outright pessimism. On some other matters, on the fine arts for example, and philology, Dryden seems to have preferred the other side. In the case of histories too, he took the ancients to have provided the models for all time.[9] As always, his thinking was independent, a result of practical experience as well as theoretical considerations, of a desire to please his contemporaries and make a living, as well as a hope for literary immortality.

On January 11, 1694, John Evelyn dined with a relative and heard Dryden say that he "was intent upon the Translation of Virgil" and would write no more plays. *Love Triumphant* was about to be performed, his "last Valedictory Play," and Dryden read the prologue and epilogue to the company.[10] Dryden meant what he said; for the next several years, Virgil became his chief and almost his only occupation. The poet was now sixty-three, and his career in politics and the theater was pretty much in ruins, though his lifelong aspiration for literary immortality had not entirely disappeared. When the publisher Tonson offered him a contract to translate the poems, it may well have seemed to him like a last opportunity to achieve a kind of greatness that even his successes had somehow obscured. Here was a chance to redeem his career – and to make some money too.[11] For once contemporary fortune and literary greatness – and the claims of modernity and *ancienneté* – all seemed to coincide. The old man, tired and ill, threw caution to the winds and took on the task with renewed vigor. The work was to be sold by subscription, and a large public began to look forward to the event. It seemed that the greatest of the Roman Augustan poets was to be rendered anew by the one modern who could hope to carry it off.[12] According to the *Gentleman's Journal*, "if anyone can assure himself of success in so bold a task, it is doubtless the Virgil of our Age." Dryden himself was more modest. As he wrote to the young Dennis, "the Translation will shew at least, that no man is fit to write after him in a barbarous Modern tongue."[13]

"Virgil," Dryden wrote in 1693, "has ever had, and ever will have, the reputation of the best poet."[14] Virgil was Dryden's favorite and a favorite of the age; from 1684, Dryden began to translate some bits and pieces of his work.[15] A decade later he signed a contract with the publisher Tonson in which he promised to translate Virgil's works without interruption until completed. For the next three years or so that is all that he did, except for a translation of Du Fresnoy's *De arte graphica* and a hasty life of Lucian. His translation was thus accomplished just when the Battle of the Books began; and it was published in August 1697, just when the second round resumed. Although Dryden does not mention the quarrel, the dedications, prefaces and notes which decked out his work supply many clues to his convictions.

Of course, the very choice of Virgil was a declaration of sorts. We have seen that virtually everyone, including Dryden, agreed that epic was the highest form of literature, and that the ancient poems of Homer and Virgil were the best of their kind. "A heroick Poem," he repeated now, "is undoubtedly the greatest Work which the Soul of Man is capable to perform." It easily surpassed tragedy in depth and effect.[16] To be sure, Dryden had said as much even when he was still writing tragedies, though he had typically argued the reverse in the *Essay of Dramatick Poesie*.[17] "The File of Heroick poets is very short," he wrote now, and not many modern poets could aspire to it. There was only one *Iliad* and one *Aeneid*, and not even Tasso or Milton could quite measure up, much less any of the minor authors who had tried.[18] It is true that opinion had long been divided as to which of the ancients deserved precedence, and one could, after a fashion, separate the ancients from the moderns on that question. In the *Examen poeticum* (his miscellany published in 1693) Dryden renewed the old comparison and drew a fairly even balance. Virgil, "though he yielded much to Homer in invention, more excelled him in his admirable judgment."[19] Temple was characteristically more forthright. The English champion of the ancients maintained that Homer was the best, as the original was always more deserving than any imitation. And Wotton agreed. But the champion of the moderns typically imagined the possibility of modern emulation and encouraged the hope of rivalry. Dryden was content for the moment that whoever deserved the prize, "I am satisfied they will never have a third concurrent."[20]

In short, it must have seemed in 1694 that the problem for the poet who aspired to true greatness was whether to attempt a modern epic after the example of the ancients (whether Homer or Virgil), as Milton had done and Sir Richard Blackmore was to do again shortly – and so risk a comparison with antiquity – or to concede precedence to the ancients and try something else altogether.[21] In his discourse concerning satire, Dryden sketched the requirements for an epic poet: great natural endowments and a genius for invention, a ripe judgment and strong memory, a gift for language and poetry, and a knowledge of all the arts and sciences. The modern poet would also require a proper doctrine and machinery, which Dryden thought could derive from a Platonic Christianity. And he would need a proper patriotic subject. Dryden himself had long imagined doing it and considered two possible subjects drawn from English history: the exploits of King Arthur (an epic subject that had also appealed to John Milton) and Edward the Black Prince. With the help of ancient examples, he thought he could have done it as well as some of his predecessors, "or at least chalked out the way for others to amend my errors in a like design." But the absence of patronage discouraged him, and now old age and need disabled him altogether.[22] In 1694, Dryden chose something less; he chose to put Virgil into English, and so create a modern poem out of an ancient one. In the competition between the ancients and the moderns, this meant to concede victory to the ancients, while yet insisting on their contemporary value. If Dryden would not emulate Virgil, he could do the next best thing: he could turn the old Roman into a modern Englishman, and by coupling his own name with the immortal poet come to share something of his fame.[23]

It seemed necessary therefore to defend the poet from several old charges, including want of invention – which Dryden proceeds to do in the dedication to the *Aeneis*. The fault might seem plausible, he allows, in the light of Virgil's many borrowings from Homer, Apollonius Rhodius, and other earlier writers. But such a charge, he points out, would work against all invention and all poetry, which necessarily involved imitation. (Here Dryden admits to borrowing much of his own argument from the French translator, Segrais.) Had not Homer taken his story from the history of Troy which was in everyone's mouth before he set it in order? "Is Versailles the less a New Building, because the Architect of that Palace has imitated others that were built before it?" There were common materials for poetry, "furnish'd from the Magazine of Nature." Virgil borrowed much from Homer, but the disposition of the parts – and therefore the poem – was very much his own.

> 'Tis one thing to Copy, and another thing to imitate from Nature. The Copyer is that servile Imitator, to whom Horace gives no better a Name than that of Animal: He will not so much as allow him to be a Man. Raphael imitated Nature: They who Copy one of Raphael's Pieces, imitate but him, for his Work is their Original. They translate him as I do Virgil; but fall as short of him as I of Virgil.[24]

In short, the poet who had borrowed nothing had yet to be born. But Virgil had not only borrowed, he had invented also and transformed the materials to his own purpose. The ancients certainly dwarfed the moderns, though it is possible (if only barely) to imagine how times could change for the better and the genius of the moderns come once again to rival their predecessors. For the moment, perhaps the best that one could do was acknowledge the fact and pay homage to the past – in a word, to translate Virgil.

3

It was not surprising that Dryden should call upon painting to make an argument for poetry, and to invoke the tension between ancients and moderns in each. He had long ago accepted the analogy of the "sister arts," a familiar notion that went back to Horace's famous tag, *ut pictura poesis*. "There are no two things in the World that have a nearer affinity and resemblance than Poetry and Painting," wrote a contemporary in 1685, "the Parallel between 'em runs throughout; every Body knows the old Adage, That Poetry is *Pictura loquens* and painting is *Poema silens*." Dryden accepted the old commonplaces that year in his ode to a young friend who was both a poet and painter, Lady Anne Killigrew.[25] In 1694 Tonson brought out a fourth *Miscellany* with two contributions by Dryden: the third book of Virgil's *Georgics* and a verse epistle to his friend, the painter Godfrey Kneller. The occasion for his tribute seems to have been the presentation by Kneller to Dryden of a portrait of Shakespeare.[26] This naturally led the poet to compliment the painter extravagantly and to defend Shakespeare against his detractors.

The sister arts, as Dryden tells it, have a parallel though not an identical history. Poetry is the older of the two, but both came to fruition in antiquity, decline in the Middle Ages (with the Goths and Vandals), and revival in the Renaissance. It is Raphael's line and Titian's color that Kneller has inherited.

But the arts have always depended on patronage for their prosperity (Apelles on Alexander the Great, for example, and Raphael on Leo X), so that the passing of Charles II – and by implication, the accession of William – was not very helpful to either painter or poet. Here Dryden almost takes back his compliment. Recent times had not been auspicious to either art, and the debased taste of the age had restrained both Kneller and Dryden from aspiring to greatness.[27]

> That yet thou hast not reach'd their high Degree,
> Seems only wanting to this Age, not thee.
> Thy Genius, bounded by the Times, like mine,
> Drudges on petty Draughts, nor dare design
> A more Exalted Work, and more Divine.

Dryden has been compelled to write heroic plays in rhyme; Kneller has been forced to paint flattering portraits instead of grand historical canvases. Without encouragement,

> You only paint to live, not live to paint.
> Else should we see your noble Pencil trace
> Our Unities of Action, Time and Place.[28]

How Kneller took these lines is hard to say. He certainly went on to paint Dryden in one of his finest portraits and to help him to promote his translation of Virgil. And whatever Dryden may have been thinking, Kneller's fortunes did not suffer in the new reign, but prospered more than ever. William III made him his principal painter and he was knighted in 1692.[29] Portrait commissions were more plentiful and lucrative than ever. Perhaps Kneller did have a hankering for history painting, for which he received an occasional commission;[30] more likely, he seems to have made an easy accommodation to his situation, which turned him into a comfortable gentleman of prominence. "He liv'd in splendour," according to Vertue, "gathering Riches and keeps a noble house." He built a nine-bay mansion at Whitton in Middlesex, probably designed by his friend, Christopher Wren about 1709 (who was rewarded with a portrait a year or two later) – a fine palace, we are told, and a country seat in which he entertained "all People of Honour and distinction."[31] There, he was celebrated in a flattering poem by the poet, Thomas Tickell, for his "Roman Grandeur and Athenian Grace."[32]

Kneller, it should be said, had been to Italy as a young man, where he had "studied the Antiques, and Copyed much after Raphael in the Vatican," probably with Maratti and Bernini.[33] His modern biographer discerns a "classicizing" element in his later career, and in 1711 he painted a set of classical reliefs for Alexander Pope – the Farnese *Hercules*, an Apollo and a Venus.[34] In his ambitious equestrian portrait of William III at Hampton Court he borrowed from Raphael and employed a Virgilian motto. But Dryden was probably right to think that there was no contemporary audience yet for neoclassical history painting and to feel some affinity with the painter's plight. Like the rest, he had to be content with the several hundred portraits that Kneller contrived to turn out in those busy years, including, among the best of them, Dryden and Wren, John Evelyn and Grinling Gibbons.

Meanwhile, Dryden's interest in the fine arts was further extended just at this time by a commission to translate into English a Latin poem by the Frenchman, Charles Alphonse Dufresnoy – for which he was willing to interrupt his translation of Virgil. In the poem he found the old analogy between poetry and painting plainly set out, and the sentiments of Horace and Simonides quoted in the opening verses. Dufresnoy, like his master Giovanni Pietro Bellori (whose work Dryden was also reading), meant to combine a Platonic idealism with an empirical notion of nature, to join ancient philosophy with the precepts of ancient rhetoric, and so justify and exalt the arts.[35] According to Dufresnoy, the artist must learn to imitate an idealized nature by combining direct observation with the guidance of the ancient Greeks and their modern imitators in the Italian Renaissance. Bellori remembers – and Dryden repeats – Cicero's story in the *Orator* about Zeuxis who had to draw upon five different models to create the perfect beauty of his painting of Helen, "because Nature in any individual person makes nothing that is perfect in all its parts." In that respect art was superior to nature, though always dependent on it.[36] Dryden says that he was asked to undertake the translation in the midst of his Virgil by some English artists who thought that it was the best rulebook of its kind. He relied on their assistance and gave two months to producing a prose version before returning to his great work. In his own preface, he uses the opportunity to make some further observations on the relation of the sister arts, drawing up a fresh new "Parallel betwixt Painting and Poetry."[37]

Dryden accepted the view of Dufresnoy and Bellori that the perfection of the arts consisted in the imitation of nature, "and that Picture, and that Poem, which comes nearest to the resemblance of Nature is best." It was a young friend, apparently Walter Moyle, who explained to him that the nature intended was not ordinary perceptible nature, but nature "wrought up to nobler pitch," a nature in which "all the scatter'd Beauties were united by a happy Chymistry" and transmuted into something without imperfection. (This notion was to be repeated endlessly in eighteenth-century neoclassicism.)[38] But how was it to be accomplished? With most of his contemporaries, Dryden believed that some combination of rules and examples was necessary. Dryden and his friends certainly agreed with Dufresnoy that good judgment in all the arts required close acquaintance with the "best pieces" of each.

For the fine arts that meant the sculpture of the ancient Greeks and the paintings of the high Renaissance: Raphael, Titian, Correggio and Michelangelo; while for poetry, it meant that "most perfect poem," the *Aeneid* of Virgil. Dryden knew his deficiency in the former, which he shared with all those who had yet to make the grand tour and which disqualified him from making the sure judgments of Dufresnoy. In those matters, therefore, he was pretty much reduced to accepting the authority of his sources (Bellori and De Piles as well as Dufresnoy) and retailing what they had said. It was, of course, otherwise with Virgil, whom he now sets above even Homer for imitation.[39] His chief intention was to show that in their desire to please by the imitation of nature the two arts closely resembled each other, and both required rules as well as examples to accomplish their common end. He quotes the critic, André Dacier, that "all who, having rejected the Ancient Rules, and taken the opposite ways, yet boast themselves to be Masters of this Art, do but deceive others, and are themselves deceiv'd; for that is absolutely impossible."[40]

Of course, the rules *derived* from examples.

> This is notoriously true in these two Arts; for the way to please being to imitate Nature, both the Poets and the Painters, in Ancient times, and in the best Ages, have study'd her; and from the practice of both these Arts, the Rules have been drawn, by which we are instructed how to please, and to compass that end which they obtain'd, by following their Example. For Nature is still the same in all Ages, and can never be contrary to herself.[41]

So Aristotle had drawn the rules of tragedy from the practice of the Greek tragedians; and so the modern French and Italian critics (in particular Bossu and Dacier) had drawn from the precepts of Aristotle and Horace and the example of the Greek poets. Unfortunately, Greek painting had pretty much perished, and only the testimony of the ancients remained. Still it was possible to examine the wonderful examples of Greek sculpture, preserved in Italy, and by taking into account what was common to both arts, repair the loss. Just so had Raphael and his contemporaries been able to restore the ancient achievement and bring a knowledge of painting to its "supreme perfection" – though it had since declined. Here Dryden thought that poetry might have a slight advantage, and he reminds his readers again of the critical importance of patronage to both the arts and the example of Louis XIV.[42]

For the rest, Dryden considers the rules of Dufresnoy, using the headings of classical rhetoric: invention, disposition, and coloring, to chart his way.[43] Once again, Dryden derides all servile imitation, and regrets that he has been reduced to the mere translation of Virgil. "But to copy the best Authour is a kind of praise, if I perform it as I ought; as a copy after Raphael is more to be commended, than an Original of any indifferent Painter."[44] He accepts the neoclassical strictures against Gothic barbarism,[45] not forgetting to apologize for his own transgressions in the drama – though he excepts his *All for Love*, the only play, we have seen, that he ever wrote wholly for himself. And he continues to praise Virgil above all, although he assigns Homer priority in invention and design. For the most part, it is hard to see how even Rymer could have disapproved now of Dryden's very real deference to antiquity, and it is even possible to accept the sincerity of Dryden's last surprising reference to his old enemy in 1700 as "that great critic."[46]

4

Three years passed and the subscribers to Virgil were restless. Dryden turned to his young friends for help. In his plight, "seeing me straitned in my time," they offered to write some of the accompanying matter: the life of Virgil, the prefaces to the minor poems, and all the prose arguments to the translation.[47] What this meant in fact was that the translator began his folio volume with several essays by his young friends who insisted on giving Virgil and the ancients even more authority than he himself had sometimes been ready to admit. So, for example, Knightly Chetwood followed Dryden's brief dedication to the *Pastorals* with a life of Virgil and a preface in which he set out deliber- ately to refute that very modern Frenchman, Fontenelle, who had argued that there was no need to accept all the old conventions of the genre. For Fontenelle, the modern pastoral did not have to be either as realistic as Theocritus or as fanciful as Virgil, and should certainly be updated to suit a more polite modern age. He was aware that there were pedants who would object to his criticism of the ancients (as Wotton noticed), and indeed Chetwood responded at once by defending Virgil and the ancients in general, who had invented all the useful arts. Boileau is for him the best modern critic, "because he never loses the Ancients out of his Sight," and Rapin seems to have furnished much of his defense of the classical pastoral. In any case, nothing could make up for him the advantages that the classical poets had in language. "Latin is but a corrupt dialect of Greek; and the French, Spanish and Italian, a Corruption of the Latine, and therefore a Man might as well go about to persuade one that Vinegar is as Nobler Liquor as Wine, or that the modern Composition can be as graceful and harmonious as the Latine it self." One pernicious result had been the introduction of rhyme. There were, he thought, hardly ten lines in Cicero and Demosthenes that were not more rhythmical than anything in modern literature and these must lose half their beauty in translation. It was ridiculous of Fontenelle or Perrault to prize the modern French above the ancients. It was impossible to conceive that any modern could survive and be read as long as the classical authors.

It is doubtful that Dryden was willing to go that far, although the words certainly appeared under his aegis and must have made some sense to him.[48] Of course, there was no one in England to rival the temerity of the French moderns, least of all William Wotton, who thought he was replying equally to them and to Sir William Temple. On the whole, Dryden and his young assistants preferred a more moderate course, somewhere between the ancients and the moderns, although they were eager to give the palm to classical poetry. It was young Joseph Addison who concluded his essay for Dryden on the *Georgics* by proclaiming the poem "to be the most Compleat, Elaborate, and finisht Piece of all Antiquity." The *Aeneid* might be nobler, but the *Georgics* were more perfect – with all the perfection of "the greatest Poet in the Flower of his Age."[49] In the end, the *ancienneté* of Dryden's young collaborators had begun to sound a lot like Temple's. And so it was to continue, pretty much unadulterated, into the next generation in the works of Alexander Pope, Dryden's greatest admirer, where it may be found in his own translation of the Virgilian pastorals, in the *Essay on Criticism*, and not least in his translation of the *Iliad* and its accompanying essays. It was only unfortunate, Pope wrote to Wycherley in 1704, that he had not known the great man directly, *Virgilium tantum vidi.*[50]

In any case, it is in Dryden's own preface to the *Aeneis* and in the translation itself that we get his final words on the subject. Dryden completed his long dedication in February 1697, just a few months before publication.[51] The essay is a characteristically disjointed ramble over familiar critical terrain, written in a "loose Epistolary way," with much deliberate digression.[52] Much of it follows his predecessor, the French translator, Jean Regnauld de Segrais, whose *Eneide* had been published in 1668. Dryden begins with a comparison between epic and tragedy in which he reaffirms the current view that epic was the highest form of literature and that no modern work could approach the excellence of the two great classical poems. Dryden goes on to defend the *Aeneid* against criticism, in particular the moral of the story and the manners of the hero, dismissing altogether the cavils of the grammarians who wished to object to the little slips or faults in the poem that Virgil was unable to correct before his early death. He makes the inevitable comparison with Homer, in which Homer is granted the benefit of a more noble theme, although the two poets are shown to have been equally valuable to their times.

Homer's theme was the advantage of unity over discord, but Dryden suggests that Virgil wrote in very different political circumstances to which he (necessarily) adapted his poem. He now describes the gradual subversion and downfall of the Roman Republic. According to Dryden, Virgil looked on, while "the Commonwealth was lost without ressource: the Heads of it destroy'd; the Senate new moulded, grown degenerate; and either bought off, or thrusting their own Necks into the Yoke, out of fear of being forc'd."[53] Virgil wrote his poem just as the old government was being subverted and the new imperial one established, "in effect, by force of Arms, but seemingly by the Consent of the Roman People." (The parallel with recent events was impossible to miss.)[54] In those circumstances, the Roman poet believed that the new despotic power of Augustus had to be accepted, though in his heart Virgil remained a republican – a charge that was now laid against Dryden.[55] For his part, Dryden thought that Augustus could not help remembering that the first Roman kings had been elected and were subject to the law, and he was even willing to overlook the fact that Virgil had placed the republican Cato in Elysium.[56]

Here Dryden interjects his own opinion (citing Montaigne), "that an Honest Man ought to be contented with that Form of Government, and with those Fundamental Constitutions of it, which he receiv'd from his Ancestors."[57] Virgil had weighed the political circumstances; he saw that full freedom was beyond retrieval; that prospects of change were unlikely; that he himself was indebted to the bounty of the conqueror; that the arts of peace were flourishing under him; that the Emperor was willing to share his authority with the Senate; and that everyone could be happy if only they were quiet. It looks as though Dryden was willing to make peace with his own new ruler on something like the same terms:

> These things, I say, being consider'd by the Poet, he concluded it to be in the Interest of his Country to be so Govern'd: To infuse an awful Respect into the People, towards such a Prince: By that respect to confirm their Obedience to him; and by that Obedience to make them Happy. This was the Moral of his Divine Poem: Honest in the Poet; Honourable to the Emperour, whom he derives from a Divine Extraction; and reflecting part of the Honour of the Roman People, whom he derives also from the Trojans; and not only profitable, but necessary to the present Age; and likely to be such to their Posterity.[58]

Virgil's poem was meant to teach Augustus how to govern well and win the affection of his subjects, to become, as it were, a new father of his country, on the model of his ancient predecessor, Aeneas.

It was surely impossible to read these lines without reflecting on the contemporary situation, with England experiencing a new conqueror and an altered constitution. Long ago Dryden had extolled that new Augustus, Charles II, who had rescued the nation from the chaos of republican dissolution.[59] Times had changed but the essential situation was familiar. It seems to have been the publisher, Tonson, who thought of altering the plates in the volume, hooking Aeneas's nose so that he might more closely resemble William III.[60] Montaigne said he would like to have been born in republican Venice; Dryden on the other hand still preferred to be an Englishman, though he clearly had some reservations. He had lost a lot in the recent revolution. Was there anything left to hope for?

The more he thought about it, the more Dryden seems to have identified himself with Virgil and read his poem for its contemporary relevance. He could, like his master, hope for a reconciliation with reality, though he was clearly less happy with William than Virgil had been with Augustus. Thus he was ready to accept the characterization of Aeneas by Segrais, who had answered his detractors by portraying the Roman as a perfect pattern and parallel. If there were some who favored the heroic courage of Achilles, Segrais preferred the piety of Aeneas, which, Dryden explains, comprehended "the whole Duty of Man towards the Gods; towards his Country, and towards his Relations."[61] Piety was the supreme virtue of the prince who would govern well, and in that sense it was superior even to the Homeric virtue of valor, which, however, Dryden insists was also possessed by Virgil's Aeneas.[62] If Virgil could teach Augustus some eternal lessons of good rule, Dryden could at least remind his audience (and his present sovereign) of their message, however gloomy the present situation.[63] A translator, Dryden kept insisting, "ought to possess himself entirely, and perfectly comprehend the genius and sense of his author." He should try to infuse the copy with as much life as the original.[64] He should opt for something between the extremes of paraphrase and literal translation, so as "to make Virgil speak English as he would have spoken, if he had been born in England, and in this present age."[65] The result, not surprisingly, was to introduce some anachronisms into the text that served to emphasize the affinity of the two authors and their times.[66]

Nevertheless, it is clear that William III was no Augustus, and Dryden no Virgil. In the inevitable comparison between the ancients and the moderns, Dryden in his heart of hearts, at the end of his life, had to give the palm to the ancients. Jonathan Swift, who memorialized the whole quarrel in *The Battle of the Books*, has the modern, Dryden, confront the ancient, Virgil, at a climactic moment in the struggle, each leading a body of troops. It is, to say the least, an unequal match:

> Dryden in a long Harangue soothed up the good Antient, called him Father, and by a large deduction of Genealogies, made it plainly appear, that they were nearly related. Then he humbly proposed an Exchange of Armor, as a lasting Mark of Hospitality between them. Virgil consented (for the Goddess Diffidence came unseen, and cast a Mist before his Eyes) tho' his was of Gold, and cost a hundred Beeves, the others but of rusty Iron . . . Then they agreed to exchange Horses; but when it came to the Trial, Dryden was afraid, and utterly unable to mount.[67]

Here Swift's manuscript (he says) fails, but not before it had vividly opened the great gulf that divided the exemplary ancient from his pitiful modern follower.

Swift may have held a personal grudge against Dryden, who told him as a young man that he was no poet.[68] But it is more to the point that Sir William Temple was Swift's hero – or at least his patron – and he appears correctly in *The Battle of the Books* as the champion of the ancients. Temple had no doubt played a larger and more direct role in the politics of the age than Dryden and was a good friend and supporter of the new monarch. But much less than Dryden did he nourish any illusions about his time and his contemporaries. No doubt, both men kept open some small space for future possibility, and neither set aside his pen altogether in despair. Of the two, Dryden had always been the more optimistic, the more hopeful of himself and his period, but he was old now and in defeat, and closer in spirit to the equally dispirited Temple. Perhaps it was the moment now, after a lifetime of vacillation, to concede that in literature anyway, as in politics and in the arts, it was the ancients who had set the standards which the moderns could only hope to imitate. Virgil's *Aeneid* was Dryden's best effort, though he turned now to Homer as an even more exalted poet, but he knew that a translation, however modernized and successful, could only shadow the antique achievement.[69] *Sequiturque Patrem non passibus aequis* was the Virgilian motto on Dryden's title page – "and follows his father with steps that match not his."[70] Not everyone, it is needless to say, was so pessimistic, and one could certainly welcome the accession of a new monarch and constitution. For the triumphant Whigs (for William Wotton, for example, or the republican Walter Moyle), history had certainly taken a turn for the better. For them, it appeared that England was ready now to resume the politics and culture of the Roman Augustan age. But now we are on the verge of the neoclassical triumph, something that Dryden and his baroque contemporaries had been unable quite to accomplish but to which they had always somehow aspired.

PART III

FRANCE AND ENGLAND:
THE SIEUR DE SAINT-EVREMOND

4. Saint-Evremond by Godfrey Kneller

CHAPTER 7

Saint-Evremond and the Moderns

I

Dryden's struggle to come to terms with the ancients was entirely character-istic of the age, though his determination to keep an open mind and his consequent vacillation were more obviously his own. As usual, it is the problem, rather than any one of the solutions, that seems to define the temper of the age. It does not seem an exaggeration to say that nearly everyone then seemed to be obsessed by the dilemma of how to reconcile the achievement of the ancients with the claims of modern life and literature, and the range of response was almost limitless. All over Europe the question was being debated, not least across the Channel in France where the extremes of response were greater than in England.

Of the many links between the two cultures in these years, one of the most persistent and interesting was undoubtedly furnished by the French aristocrat, Charles de Marguetel de Saint-Denis-le-Guast, Seigneur de Saint-Evremond (1616–1703), who spent the last forty years of his long life in England. During that time, almost exactly concurrent with Dryden's career, he turned out a cascade of little works (*bagatelles*, he called them) on many of the same sub-jects, at least as unsystematic and occasional as anything that the Englishman wrote. Throughout these essays, which were read widely and avidly in England for at least two generations, the theme of ancients and moderns sounded con-tinuously, and it is not surprising that some critics have discovered (mistakenly, I think) an influence on both Dryden and Temple, the first of whom wrote his "character" in 1692; the second of whom helped him to safety in England in 1670.[1]

Saint-Evremond was a nobleman who had studied with the Jesuits in Paris and served valorously at war until, in 1661, he fell into disgrace along with his master, Fouquet, and was forced into exile. His biographer, Pierre des Maizeaux, who collected his works and knew him in his last years, insists that his mili-tary career never interfered with his appetite for *belles lettres* and that he early won a reputation, "by his Politeness and by his Wit, as much as by his Bravery."[2] He was, however, no scholar. As his old friend, Silvestre, wrote, "He was not a

Man of Learning, but what he had read, he understood thoroughly. In reading he was more concern'd to study the Genius and Character of an Author, than to burden his Memory with pompous, and oftentimes useless Learning." When the young prince, the duc d'Enghien, asked for his help early in the 1640s, Saint-Evremond was only too happy to explain the meaning of the classical authors, leaving to grammarians "the scrupulous explanation of words and phrases." To Des Maizeaux, that looked exactly right for a "person of quality."[3] Like Temple and Dryden, he did not know, or could not remember, his Greek. In later years, he several times poked fun at the *érudits*.[4]

He had been to England for six months just before his disgrace, to celebrate the Restoration of Charles II. After his exile, he divided his time between England and Holland, settling finally in London in 1670.[5] It may have been Temple who as ambassador to Holland secured for Saint-Evremond a handsome pension from the king.[6] "A fond imagination that I might return to France," Saint-Evremond wrote to a friend, "made me pitch upon London as a medium between the French Courtiers and the Dutch Burgomasters."[7] London was not Paris but it was the next best thing, especially after the Duchess Mazarin (Hortense Mancini) also arrived in England (in 1675) and set up a flourishing salon.[8] Saint-Evremond had many friends at court and among the wits; he was especially close to the Duke of Buckingham and Edmund Waller and seems to have known Cowley and Hobbes and the Earl of Rochester. He continued to receive the favor of the court even after the Glorious Revolution, for he had known the future William III while in Holland. Though he seems never to have learned English, he had no wish to return to France, and in old age he politely declined all invitations, despite the promise of a pardon from Louis XIV. His income was just sufficient to maintain him in aristocratic dalliance and he enjoyed the life of an epicure, consorting with the great, conversing with the witty, paying homage to the beautiful, and never missing a musical event. "Reading and the Conversation of polite persons was all his Business; and we may affirm, that he liv'd as agreeably as a Stranger and an Exile could wish."[9] When at last he died at a great old age in 1703, the Huguenot *émigré*, Abel Boyer, reported that he had preserved a vigorous mind and a facetious humor to the end and a perfect neutrality in religion. He wished to be reconciled, he said, on his deathbed. To whom, he was asked? "To my appetite," he replied.[10] He was buried, like Temple, among the poets in Westminster Abbey.

To try to track Saint-Evremond's ideas through his long life and copious work is not easy. He did not write for profit and he did not publish, preferring (like Rochester, Buckingham and the rest) to circulate his manuscripts among a select few. Nevertheless, the booksellers eagerly got hold of copies and began to bring them out in France and Holland and in English translation. Saint-Evremond did not seek a popular reputation, but he got one anyway, and it was only toward the end of his life that he yielded to Des Maizeaux and authorized his works for the press, revising them a bit and weeding out the many false attributions that had accumulated under his name.[11] He was a dilet-

tante, but he was meticulous about his style and frequently altered his manuscripts so that there are often several versions of the same work. The dates of
composition remain exasperatingly elusive. Nor did Saint-Evremond, any
more than Dryden, bridle at inconsistency. "I own, I contradict my self
sometimes . . . I am neither of the same humour, nor the same opinion at sixty
years of Age, as I was at thirty; or at fourscore, as I was at sixty."[12] Like Dryden,
Saint-Evremond appreciated both sides of an argument; like Dryden, he was
temperamentally skeptical, with a penchant for satire and a taste for irony.
Unlike Dryden, however, he leaned consistently toward the moderns from the
very beginning to the end of his long career.

2

Saint-Evremond's first years are particularly obscure, but it seems that he preferred the moderns from the outset. As early as 1638, he joined some young
friends in a satire on the new French Academy, risking the wrath of the
"ancients," Chapelain and Boisrobert. Richelieu's grand institution had been
founded to regulate the language and the English (as we have seen), including
both Dryden and Evelyn, had been tempted to emulate it, but Saint-Evremond
saw only fun in the attempt to legislate in such matters. The comedy was not
performed, but it was printed in 1650 and revised twice by Saint-Evremond
after he had come to England, once about 1680 and once again for Des
Maizeaux.[13] Apparently, the exile whose political career had more than once
been compromised by the criticism of authority, never did become reconciled
to the importance of the rules.[14]

Nor did Saint-Evremond ever lose his taste for the theater. From the very
beginning, he was an ardent admirer of Corneille, who, of course, had had his
own memorable battle with the Academy. When the *Cid* was performed in
1637, it was an immediate popular success, and there were those who thought
that it surpassed anything either ancient or modern.[15] Naturally, it aroused the
jealousy of other writers, one of whom, Georges de Scudéry, attacked it vigorously for many faults, including a deliberate breach of the Aristotelian rules.
Even in his earliest critical essay, the preface to *Clitandre* (1632), Corneille had
proclaimed his freedom from ancient authority and mechanical application of
the rules.[16] Now Corneille was forced to defend himself against the charge of
modernity, and a barrage of pamphlets followed. At last the Academy was called
in to arbitrate and in a work drafted by Chapelain and annotated by Richelieu himself, the official organ of the ancients declared itself pretty much against
Corneille.[17] The dramatist submitted reluctantly, though he later denied its
authority and still later (1660) wrote those apologetics that Dryden knew so
well and used in the *Essay of Dramatick Poesie*. Nevertheless, it is clear that
Corneille's best rejoinder was the great series of plays that he composed
between 1640 and 1642 and that established his reputation for all time, the
tragedies, *Horace*, *Cinna* and *Polyeucte*. For a while, Corneille had made himself
the undisputed master of the French theater.[18]

The charge of modernity must have surprised Corneille a little, since he had labored hard in the *Cid* to reduce his Spanish source, Guillén de Castro, to something like the regularity demanded by the French theorists. The *Cid* after all is usually taken to be the first truly successful French classical play.[19] But Scudéry and Chapelain were not satisfied and objected (among other things) to some of the irrelevant material that Corneille had retained from the original and which they thought had spoiled the unity of the action. Corneille saw the point but bridled at the pedantry of his critics who continued to insist on a literal adherence to the rules. He had an audience to please and he saw the rules only as one means to that end. While the *Cid* was still under judgment by the Academy, he wrote a new preface to an earlier play, *La Suivante*, in which he expressly disclaimed an undue reverence for the ancients; argued that mere regularity was no guarantee of success; and proclaimed the freedom of the artist to find the means to please his audience.[20] When his next plays appeared, however, it was clear that Corneille had actually tried to meet the critics on something like their own ground and had conformed as closely as he could to the Aristotelian unities.[21] Yet still the critics were not satisfied. A new voice was heard now to echo Chapelain, François Hédelin, the abbé d'Aubignac, who set himself up to safeguard the ancient theater and to advise the poets, urging Corneille, among other things, to alter his *Horace*. The playwright resisted then and afterwards, and most of his later dramas are even less obviously classical, as unhappily they were also less popular.

Had Corneille momentarily buckled under criticism and, at least for a time, restrained his natural predilection for modernity? It is hard to be sure and not perhaps really our concern. Suffice it to say that Corneille found his dramas caught up in the controversy between the ancients and the moderns and was forced to take up a position somewhere between the Aristotelian critics, the practical demands of the stage and his own artistic conscience. It was, indeed, the very same dilemma that Dryden had to face only a few years later and for which he had so profound a sympathy. When at last Corneille determined to issue his collected works (1657–60), he felt it necessary to defend his career and wrote the discourses and *examens* which Dryden and his friends found so interesting.[22] Apparently, Corneille had been particularly provoked by D'Aubignac who finally published his attack on modernity in 1657. Corneille's answer, he explained to a friend, was founded on a new explication of Aristotle with some propositions unknown to the ancients. Corneille wished to reconcile the teaching of the ancients with the conditions of the modern stage, to pay homage to the rules and yet preserve a modest freedom for the artist to invent and experiment.[23] Moreover, like most of the moderns, he defended almost every innovation with an appeal to classical precedent![24]

Through all this, Saint-Evremond looked on sympathetically. If he could no longer see the plays that he loved after 1660, he took pains to keep informed and to read them as they appeared. His friends in France obliged him with news and copies. Later, at the salon of Mme Mazarin, there was much discussion and not a little argument. Saint-Evremond's English friends divided their interest between the French stage which they had known in exile and the English stage which now demanded attention, and they tried to acquaint their visitor with the local scene. "The Duke of Buckingham, my Lord d'Aubigny, and he, were together almost every day, and their conversation was often upon Theatrical performances. M. de Saint-Evremond, not understanding the English Tongue, those Gentlemen acquainted him with the best Dramatick Pieces compos'd in that Language; of which he retain'd so clear an idea, that forty years after he remember'd them very distinctly."[25] In this way, Saint-Evremond discovered the Elizabethans and especially Ben Jonson. Sometime between 1662 and 1665, he joined his friends in writing a comedy inspired by *Volpone* which they called *Sir Politick Would-Be*. The "comédie a la manière Angloise" was not published until Des Maizeaux brought it out with the rest of the works in 1705. Each of the contributors, he claimed, had "clubb'd part of the Characters, which M. de Saint-Evremond reduc'd into form."[26]

How much beyond this Saint-Evremond partook of English matters is hard to say, or how much he learned. He does not seem to have been much impressed with Dryden's plays, which he almost certainly knew.[27] At any rate, his education was soon interrupted by the plague of 1665, which drove him to Holland as it drove Dryden to the countryside to write the *Essay of Dramatick Poesie*. In the Hague, Saint-Evremond renewed his contacts with France and his hopes of returning. He learned there that Corneille had been attacked again by the abbé d'Aubignac over his latest tragedy, *Sophonisbe*, in an affair reminiscent of the *Cid*, and that it had provoked a new barrage of pamphlets; and he was sent a copy of a new play, *Alexander the Great*, by the young Jean Racine, a work that for the first time seemed to threaten Corneille's precedence.[28] A lady he had known in England, Mme Bourneau, wanted his opinion, and Saint-Evremond sent her two letters, one before reading Racine, the other soon afterwards, in which he pointed out the defects of the new work. Despite Saint-Evremond's directions to the contrary, Mme Bourneau showed it to everyone and it became necessary for him to set down his views more formally and even to encourage their publication.[29] The result was a characteristic bagatelle that appeared in a little volume of his works in 1668, revised and toned down from his first peremptory judgment but still entirely in favor of Corneille.

The contrast between the two dramatists was inevitable; in setting out his views, Saint-Evremond began a game that has never lost its savor.[30] The exile was a partisan, nostalgic for the drama of his youth, but he could not mistake the talent of the new young playwright. At once he paid tribute to Racine, who alone, he believed, could carry on the work of Corneille. Unfortunately, he still had much to learn, especially that "good taste of Antiquity," which the older dramatist possessed to such an extent and which allowed him to enter into the genius of dead nations and the characters of heroes long since gone.[31] Saint-Evremond was disappointed with *Alexander the Great* for two main reasons. On the one hand, Racine had mistaken his heroes and transformed them from their historical reality into something very like modern Frenchmen.

Alexander himself had been unaccountably demoted from his heroic stature and made unrecognizable, while Porus, whom Quintus Curtius had described as "an utter stranger to the Greeks and Persians," instead of reminding us of India, had been transformed into one of Racine's countrymen.[32] For Saint-Evremond, "We should not make the same Description of Persons of the same condition and the same time, when History gives us different characters of them."[33] The poet should renounce his own world to enter into that of his characters. It was a national fault for the French to make foreigners in their own image; even Corneille, "who is almost the only person that has a true Taste of Antiquity," had slipped in *Sophonisbe*, misrepresenting the character of Asdrubel's daughter. It was essential that "those great Persons of Antiquity, so famous in their age, and better known amongst us than the living themselves, the Alexanders and Scipios, and the Caesars, ought never to lose their characters in our hands."[34] Only writers of romance could indulge their fancies freely and deliberately misrepresent the characters of their fictional heroes.

Racine's other fault, according to Saint-Evremond, was that he had placed love too high in the constellation of values and motives; that he had subordinated the heroic to the sentimental.[35] It seemed ridiculous to him to have Porus preoccupied with his amours on the eve of an epochal battle and unfortunate that Racine should almost entirely ignore the war that was taking place. Corneille's heroes, even his heroines (like Sophonisbe), were never less than heroic. Saint-Evremond does not compare the poetry of the two playwrights, content to contrast only their subject matter. His admiration for Corneille's *ancienneté* had, therefore, nothing to do with either form or style, and he never mentions the unities. It is a world view that he is defending, but one built upon an idealization of the Greeks that had little apparent knowledge to back it up.

Perhaps that explains the paradox that Saint-Evremond, who is usually thought to be a "modern," can praise Corneille, who was also accused of modernity, on the grounds of his *ancienneté*. "The ancients taught Corneille to think well," Saint-Evremond wrote to a friend in 1668, "and he thinks better than they."[36] Corneille's Greek heroes spoke better than the Greeks, he argued in *The Dissertation on Alexander*, his Romans better than the original Romans. It seemed to him incontrovertible that Corneille could outdo the ancients on their own ground by representing heroic sentiment even better than they. Saint-Evremond understood correctly that a gulf was opening up between the generations and that Racine's tragedy represented a world of feeling that was no longer his own. What Saint-Evremond failed to see was that Corneille's heroic sensibility was no more antique than Racine's, though both would have it so; just like Dryden at this time, he had very little direct acquaintance with the Greek world he so much admired.[37] But Racine's *Alexander* was still an immature work and still Corneillian in many ways;[38] the contrast and rivalry between the dramatists was bound to grow, and with it the appeal to antiquity. To Saint-Evremond it continued to seem that his favorite had the better taste for the antique; to others, to the abbé d'Aubignac, for example, it looked exactly the reverse. In his growing mastery of the stage and all its effects, the young Racine seemed to them the one true reincarnation of the ancient Greek theater.[39] In short, the rivalry, once begun, turns out to have been not so much between ancients and moderns as between two conflicting if exaggerated claims of *ancienneté*.

3

François Hédelin, abbé d'Aubignac, had been a member of Richelieu's household and a critic of the *Cid*. His *Pratique du théâtre* was drafted under the patronage of the Cardinal but not published until 1657. It was known in England to Rymer and to Dryden and eventually found a translation in 1684 as *The Whole Art of the Stage*.[40] It is the fullest statement of the neoclassical orthodoxy of Scudéry and Chapelain and the French Academy and a fine example of one characteristic form of *ancienneté*.

D'Aubignac firmly believed that he was assisting in the renovation of French literature. "In our Age our Poets have recovered the Way to Parnassus; upon the Footsteps of Euripides and Terence . . . the Stage has got a new Face."[41] What was still needed was a systematic exposition of the principles of renovation which the abbé was prepared to expound. His own pretensions were modest. "I never affected to be thought the Inventor of any thing." " 'Tis impossible," he declared, "to understand Dramatick Poetry without the help of the Ancients, and a thorough meditation upon their Works."[42] The poet needed rules to guide him, rules determined by reason, but also − for it came to the same thing − rules extracted from the ancient plays. *The Whole Art of the Stage*, however mag-isterial it appeared, was merely an attempt to explain and codify the rules which had been handed down from antiquity and resumed during the Italian Renais-sance. To those who would deny classical authority, D'Aubignac replied that reason was the same in all ages and that what had worked in antiquity must work again in the age of Louis XIV. If this was not altogether evident, it was partly because the translators had often misrepresented the meaning of the classics. He allowed that occasionally the ancients had erred and deserved correction, but he insisted that the best preparation for the poet was a thorough grounding in Aristotle and Horace for theory and the whole of the ancient poets for practice.

Chief among the regularities that governed the stage were the unities of action, time and place, though Aristotle had somehow overlooked the last. Their purpose was to promote probability and decency, *vraisemblance* and *bienséance*, the goals and watchwords of the new classicism.[43] D'Aubignac was pleased to notice the improvement in the French theater since the days of Richelieu and he singles out Corneille's later tragedies, *Horace*, *Cinna* and *Polyeucte*, to show how the restriction of time had brought about in them a new concentration and excellence. While the abbé aimed at a balanced judgment of the playwright, whom he recognizes as "so clearly set above all the Poets of his time," his remarks are often critical and he finds serious faults in the *Cid* and *Horace* and

Rodrigue.[44] Yet even so, he admires the plays for the strength of their passions, and when at last he finds Corneille observing the rules, as in *Théodore*, which D'Aubignac declared his masterpiece, it was hard for him to see how anyone could do better. "When Monsieur Corneille has well meditated upon the conduct of an Incident, there is no Author, either among the Ancient or Modern Poets, that executes it better."[45] Thus, the defender of the ancients did not doubt that the moderns could equal the classical achievement, if only they would observe the same (ancient) principles and follow D'Aubignac's advice. *Théodore* was blemished only by the denouement; yet for the rest, "there is so much Art and Conduct shewed by the Poet, that if the choice of the Subject had answer'd the skill of the Author, I believe we might propose this Play as a most perfect Model."[46]

There was something too patronizing about all this; in fact, Corneille did not think that *Théodore* was his masterpiece, nor have many others (he preferred *Rodogune*),[47] and he could not help resenting the nitpicking of someone who had himself only written failures. Even the abbé's praise could be irritating, as when he applauded Corneille's discourses and the way he expressed violent passion, "so far that we see very irregular actions in them so accompanied with ingenious and pathetick Expression, that the fault could not be perceiv'd but by Learned Observers, the beauty of the Thoughts and Language dazzling the understanding of all the rest of the Audience!" D'Aubignac complained especially about the complexity of Corneille's plots. "All the Learned men in the Drammatick Art tell us, that those Plays which they call *Polymethes*, that is, loaded with many Incidents, either are bad, or at least none of the best."[48] Corneille had simplified, but not nearly enough to satisfy the new critics. "On the contrary, a Play which has but few Incidents, and a small Intrigue, but fill'd with Excellent Language and thought, can seldom fail of pleasing."[49] Could there have been more encouraging advice for the young Racine, when he read and – in his own copy – annotated these words?

For Corneille, it was another matter, and he set down his response in the discourses and *examens* of 1660, taking issue with D'Aubignac in almost everything, but without once mentioning his name. No doubt this rankled, and so D'Aubignac returned to the attack using the occasion of a new series of plays by Corneille, *Oedipe*, *Sertorius* and *Sophonisbe*, tackling them, one by one in reverse, and eventually promising to take on the whole Corneillian corpus. For his part, Corneille replied and others swiftly joined the fray, but the new skirmish was soon over, its only effect to reiterate and sharpen the issues that had already been raised, however clouded by the large dose of personal invective on both sides.

As we have seen, the issue that mattered most to Saint-Evremond was the question of *vraisemblance*, which for him meant historical probability. In the *Pratique*, D'Aubignac had argued that, "all passions that are not founded upon Opinions and Customs conformable to those of the Spectators," were bound to have no effect.[50] For example, the failure of tyrannicide was less likely to move a Frenchman living in a monarchy than an Athenian in a republic. In the

same way, "those Pathetick Discourses, which we read in the Greek and Latine
Comedyes, will never take with us, as they did upon the Stages of the Antients,
because we have but little Conformity to the Rules of their Lives, in many
things more abominally licentious than ours, and in others, [where] their
Customs were so . . . various."[51] Even Aristotle's precepts could not be applied
so mindlessly to the present. "The Dramatick Poem is so chang'd since the
time of Aristotle, that though we make an Allowance for his Translators and
Interpreters Errours, yet we think we have great reason not to be altogether of
his mind."[52] If this perception of historical distance is surprising in an "ancient,"
still more was the notion that the poet should be free to adjust his material
accordingly. When Corneille replied (with Saint-Evremond's hearty endorsement), it was to insist that the poet was bound to portray his story as he found
it in the sources, reproducing the customs and values of the original and *not*
of his audience, even if this meant breaking the rules.[53] He was certain that
the audience would not otherwise accept the action and be moved by the
play.

For D'Aubignac, *vraisemblance* meant representing an ideal reality, removed
from local circumstance and prescribed by the dogmatic rigor of the three
unities;[54] for Corneille, *vraisemblance* also meant representing an ideal reality, but
one set more realistically in the remote past, closer to history or legend and
(therefore) less circumscribed by an arbitrary set of rules.[55] For D'Aubignac, the
whole purpose of literature was at stake, for without a deliberate idealization,
the moral function of the drama, teaching by example, was endangered; for
Corneille (and for Saint-Evremond), the object was always pleasure before
pedagogy and with a corresponding flexibility.

Now it is easy to exaggerate the distance between these two positions; as
always there was much common ground. For example, both sides acccepted
Aristotle as authoritative, and they both allowed some deliberate latitude in
applying his rules. Both accepted the need for precepts that were tied somehow
to ancient practice. Both agreed that poetry was not history and that the poet
had some freedom to recount his tale in such a way as to persuade the audience of its probability. The chief difference seems to lie in the fact that where
D'Aubignac wanted to impose a rigid adherence to the *forms* of what he took
to be ancient drama, and to allow liberty to alter the *substance*, Corneille – and
even more Saint-Evremond – preferred to enjoin close adherence to the historical tale and a relative freedom from the rules. It was most desirable, in the
playwright's words, *accorder les règles anciennes avec les agrémens modernes.*[56] What
neither side did was to set much store upon imitation, though they both argued
from and for classical precedent, and it is possible to doubt how much either
of them knew directly about the Greek tragedies.

That there was some difference between the two sides, however, and that it
mattered was soon demonstrated by the new plays of Racine. We have seen
that *Alexander the Great* was close enough to D'Aubignac's prescriptions to
offend both Corneille and Saint-Evremond. As a consequence, when Corneille
read Saint-Evremond's critical piece, he was delighted and sent him effusive

thanks. He was especially happy that his friend should have assigned to him "the true taste of Antiquity." He agreed entirely that the ancient heroes were being undermined by modern fashions. "How agreeably you flatter my Sentiments," he wrote, "when you confirm what I have advanc'd about the share which Love ought to have in noble Tragedies, and with what Fidelity we ought to preserve to those illustrious Antients, those Characters of their Time, Nature and Honour."[57]

Saint-Evremond tried to reassure Corneille that his reputation was still high in England and Holland; across the Channel they even called Ben Jonson "the English Corneille," and his friend, Waller, who had translated some of *Pompey*, believed that "of all the French, you alone know how to think." In Holland, the learned Vossius put him above even Sophocles and Euripides.[58] When Racine published the play in 1666, however, he attached a preface that sounded like a direct rebuff. (There is a tradition that when he showed his play to Corneille, he was told that he had a great talent for poetry but that he should give up the stage!)[59] Racine defended himself against all those critics who pretended to be deeply versed in Aristotle and yet complained about his diminution of the hero. "They find it strange that Alexander, having won the battle, does not return at the head of an army, and that he should converse with his beloved, instead of dashing off to fight a bunch of desperadoes bent on lying."[60] Yet one of the greatest captains of the time thought that the task was not even worthy of Alexander's Ephestion. As for their principal objection that his plot was too simple, "I do not represent to those critics the taste of antiquity; I see well they have little knowledge of it." Racine did not find it worth entering into details; his trump card was his extraordinary success with the audience.

And indeed, after *Alexander*, the match grew more unequal. With each new drama, *Andromaque* (1668), *Britannicus* (1670), *Bérénice* (1671), Racine grew more successful until he became indisputably the first dramatist in France, while Corneille slipped badly. To the end, the older man proclaimed his independence and his right to experiment. The rules and precepts of Aristotle and Horace were valuable, he wrote in the preface to *Agesilaus* (1666), but their method could not be applied dogmatically to later centuries.[61] A servile attachment would not suit the modern audience and would bar all possibility of progress. This was exactly the sentiment of Saint-Evremond. On the other hand, Racine seemed to be fulfilling the rules of the new classicism more and more precisely with each new play. (No wonder that he grew intimate with Boileau and remained so without a ruffle for thirty-six years.)[62] The simplicity that D'Aubignac had demanded was increasingly evident, if only in the reduction of the main characters, from six in the *Thebaide* (Racine's first play), to five in *Alexander*, four in *Andromaque*, and only three in *Bérénice*.[63] If the scenes were deliberately indefinite and uncharacterized, the audience was not unhappy.[64] In their ignorance of ancient Greece, they were certainly not offended, and in their parochial confidence they were only too happy to see their own ideals inflated into timeless verities and reflected in the heroes of old. As a result, perhaps, no one, including the costume designers, seemed to require much archaeological exactitude.[65]

Oddly enough, Racine knew better, better surely than either Corneille or Saint-Evremond, just what the ancient manners were; he alone had read the Greek tragedies in the original, as well as much else from antiquity.[66] His notes to Sophocles and Euripides survive and he had once attempted a fresh translation of Aristotle's *Poetics*. (When he read D'Aubignac's *Pratique*, he corrected a faulty Greek reading in his copy.)[67] His choice to amend was thus deliberate, though he concealed it somewhat in the defensive remarks of his prefaces.

The duel between the rival playwrights did not take long to ripen. *Andromaque* was the first of Racine's works to bear his authentic stamp, even though it still owed something to Corneille. In the preface, Racine explained only that he had taken the whole subject from a few verses in the *Aeneid* and a hint in Euripides.[68] He is insistent (against the carping of Boileau and Saint-Evremond) that he has depicted his characters exactly as the ancients represented them, with one small liberty: softening the character of Pyrrhus. In fact, he changed much else in his sources to please his audience.[69] To those who thought this insufficient – and there were some who would like to have transformed Pyrrhus into a perfect French gentleman – Racine remarks caustically that Pyrrhus had not had the advantage of any modern novels and that anyway he was not free to change the rules of the drama. Neither Aristotle nor Horace had advocated a perfect moral character for the hero of a tragedy. In the preface to *Britannicus* he was more explicit in his attack on the drama of Corneille.[70] The subject now was the same as his rival's, a piece of Roman history like that in Corneille's *Othon* which had just appeared. Once again, he insists upon his adherence to the sources and the views of Aristotle. He defends his character, Junia, by comparing her to Corneille's invention of Emilia in *Cinna* and Sabrina in *Horace*.[71] Besides – for Racine would like to have had it both ways – there was an historical Junia mentioned by both Seneca and Tacitus. In a second preface, written in 1676 when the quarrel had subsided, Racine insisted that there was hardly a worthwhile thing in his play that was not inspired by Tacitus. Was there anything that he could do to placate his critics? The alternative to a simple plot, concentrated upon the passions of the characters, would be a story complicated by a flood of incidents, theatrical tricks and countless declamations. Perhaps his critics preferred a drunken hero (a reference to Corneille's *Attila*) or a chatterbox (like Agesilaus).[72] He even dares to call Corneille *malevoli veteris poetae* under the guise of a critic of Terence.[73]

Finally, there was *Bérénice*, played in 1671 within a week of Corneille's *Titus et Bérénice*. Just why the two rivals should choose the same subject for simultaneous plays has never been determined, but there was no doubt about the outcome. "For a long time," Racine wrote in his preface, "I have been wanting to see whether I could construct a tragedy with that simplicity of action so greatly to the taste of the Ancients."[74] The tragedies of Sophocles in particular seemed to him superior in this respect to any modern plays. *Bérénice* marks the utmost limit of Racine's concentration and is the briefest of his tragedies, strictly

observing the unities and stripped of all but essentials, "a psychological reconstruction based on merely six words of the Roman historian."[75] It seemed the
ultimate fulfillment of the abbé d'Aubignac's demand for simplicity, and there
is almost no context of any kind.[76] Racine concludes by doubting whether his
critics had ever read Sophocles or understood Aristotle. By contrast, Corneille's
Titus was typically complex and closer to history. For the public in general,
Racine had won the contest; but there were a few notable dissenters, particularly among the older generation, Mme de Sévigné for one[77] – and
Saint-Evremond.

4

From Holland, the exile looked on with consuming interest. His admiration
for Corneille continued undiminished. He thought that the dramatist's translation of a modern Latin poem about Louis XIV was unsurpassed, superior
even to Lucan. French, Saint-Evremond declared roundly, was a language
superior to Latin – an old modernist claim, though he does not notice his
sixteenth-century predecessors.[78] He asks his correspondent to send him
Corneille's *Attila* and Molière. The latter, he thought, had surpassed Plautus
in his *Amphitryon*, as well as Terence in his other plays.[79] When, a little later
(in 1668), he received *Attila*, it came together with Racine's *Andromaque*, and
though he had hardly time to read them, he attempted a comparison. "It appears
to me that *Andromache* has in it something very fine, and that 'tis but one degree
remov'd from the Great. Those who shall not go to the bottom will admire it;
but those who are looking for perfect Beauties, will miss something in it, that
shall hinder them from being fully satisfied." The fact that the actor, Montfleury,
had died recently would probably hurt the performance, but that would help
Corneille; Montfleury would have overplayed and exaggerated the ferocity of
the part. But that was the way the ancient Greeks had liked it, "when fierce
and bloody representations were more relish'd, than the soft and tender." As for
Corneille, the thoughts seemed very fine and there were some excellent verses,
but he needed more time to consider the plot. He only hoped that Corneille
would now take up the subject of Hannibal and Scipio.[80]

Actually, Saint-Evremond received three copies of *Andromaque* from three
different friends, an embarrassment of riches which he thought might offend
his frugal Dutch hosts. On further thought, the play seemed to him still beautiful but deficient, still too soft and tender. Racine must continue to take second
place to Corneille. Some of his friends agreed.[81] When, a little later, Saint-
Evremond received a copy of *Britannicus*, he found it superior to the earlier
plays but with a subject still unworthy. Perhaps one day Racine would do better
and begin to approach Corneille.[82] About this time, he decided to set
his thoughts down more formally about tragedy, comedy and opera.[83] As always,
he was compelled to think through again the relation between ancients and
moderns.

It was in 1669, then, or 1670, about the time when he returned to England to stay, that Saint-Evremond wrote the little essay that appears in his works, "Upon Tragedies."[84] It begins with a forthright declaration of his modernity. "I confess we excel in Dramatical Compositions; and without flattering Corneille, I think I may prefer many of his Tragedies before those of Antiquity." Saint-Evremond knows that the ancients have their admirers, but he is not so sure of their claim to the sublime. "To believe that Sophocles and Euripides are so admirable, as we are told they are, one must fancy greater matters of their Works, than can be conceived from their Translations." This admission of ignorance does not seem to embarrass him, though the liberty of the French translators with their theory of the *belles infidèles* was notorious. According to Saint-Evremond, the ancients lacked greatness, magnificence and, above all, dignity, whatever the praise of their admirers. "Wits they were indeed, but cramp'd by the frugality of a small Republick, where a necessitous Liberty was all they had to boast of."[85] The Athenians could hardly imagine the grandeur of a real king like Louis XIV! If at times they were able anyway to rise to the sublime, they usually obscured it by bringing on to the stage a host of gods and goddesses. "What was great was fabulous; what was natural, mean and contemptible."[86] Corneille, on the other hand, had been able to attain true grandeur, among other things through the very chasteness of his style.

With characteristic balance and detachment, Saint-Evremond admitted that the ancients, though they might fall short of grandeur, were more secure about the fundamentals of morality and human nature, about such things as fortitude, constancy, justice and wisdom. "They learnt to paint their Characters so well, that juster cannot be desir'd, considering the time they liv'd in."[87] Even so, they had been content to describe their characters by their actions alone, whereas Corneille was able to penetrate to their most secret hidden emotions; they were content to moralize through speeches and commentary, Corneille more profitably through a representation of the passions. Moreover the Frenchman had successfully banished all those barbarities that so delighted the Greeks in their time. And he had softened the unrelieved horror of their drama by introducing a modest leaven of love, without, however, diverting the audience from the more primary passions. Nor was Corneille alone in this achievement; Saint-Evremond applauds his other contemporaries too: Tristan, Mairet, Du Ryer, Routrou, Thomas Corneille, and, of course, the Racine of *Andromaque* and *Britannicus*.

In short, Saint-Evremond believed that no nation, not even the modern Italians, could rival the French in tragedy. There were, he concedes, some old English dramas which, if "retrench'd" a bit, might be turned into admirable plays. (Presumably Dryden may have been thinking something like this when he tried to improve Shakespeare.) "In all the rest, written in those Days, you see nothing but a shapeless indigested mass; a Croud of confused adventures, without regard to Time, Place or Decency; where Eyes that delight in cruel sights, are fed with Murders, and Bodies weltering in Blood."[88] The echoes of the unities and *bienséance* remind us that Saint-Evremond's modernity, while genuine, was only relative — as in the case of Corneille.[89] Perhaps Saint-

Evremond had seen some Shakespeare and Fletcher – and probably some Dryden – in London with his friends, Buckingham and D'Aubigny; he had certainly heard a lot about them.[90] Thank heaven, his new friends had condemned the excesses of the Elizabethan theater as savage and inhuman; unfortunately, "an antient Habit, or the humour of the Nation in general, prevails over the delicacy of a few private persons." In general, the English allowed too much that appealed to the senses on the stage; but Saint-Evremond had to concede that there was something to *their* reproaches of the French. "Our sentiments," he admitted (we have heard the same from Dryden and Rymer), "have not depth enough."[91]

5

Saint-Evremond's attempt to be fair-minded in the *querelle* shows again in the essay on comedies which he also wrote about this time.[92] Once more, he compares the French with both the ancients and moderns. Now the classical authors come off rather better, though still not unscathed. Modern French comedy, he complains, confines itself to "Gallantry," whereas the ancients represented the full diversity of life. Ancient comedy could have been nobler and more gallant but that was the fault of the age. "Now-a-days," he laments, "most of our Poets know as little what belongs to the Manners, as in those times they knew what belong'd to Gallantry."[93] The French surpass the Italians and Spanish in form but Saint-Evremond remains unhappy with too rigid an adherence to the rules. "I confess, that Judgment, which ought to be of all Countries, has establish'd some Rules, which are no where to be dispens'd with; but it is a hard Matter not to make some Allowances to Custom."[94] Aristotle himself was confined by Athenian practice. Laws should always be adapted to the different peoples who invent them. In comedy especially, where everything is calculated to please, reason ought always to be flexible.

The comparison with the English was brief and pointed. Saint-Evremond finds that with respect to manners, it is the English who are more like the ancients, while with respect to the rules, it is the French. French comedy is too stiff and formal, too "zealous to copy the regularity of the Ancients," and therefore too confined to a single principal action.[95] The variety that the English demanded precluded regularity, but they believed (correctly) "that the Liberties which are taken in order to please the better, ought to be preferr'd before exact Rules, which dull Authors improve to an Art of tiring their Audience."[96] The rules should generally be observed and fancy trimmed by reason, but never so as to fetter the mind. Saint-Evremond concludes by allowing two moderns, one English and one French, to represent perfectly the genius of their respective nations: Ben Jonson and Molière.[97] They were both fit rivals to the ancients, though each might have had a little more regard for character than plot.

So much for comedy. When, in a year or so, Corneille and Racine brought forth their rival works on Titus and Bérénice, Saint-Evremond thought that it was time to add a footnote to his earlier remarks on tragedy. As a consequence, he dashed off yet another little essay, "On the Characters of Tragedies," and reviewed the vexed question of love in the modern drama.[98] In it, he disposed briefly of Racine. "In the *Titus* of Racine, you find Despair, where there is scarce Occasion for bare Grief." History teaches that Titus, who was a cautious prince, sent Bérénice back to Judaea so as not to offend the people of Rome. But Racine makes a desperate lover out of him, resolved to kill himself rather than allow a separation. This time, unfortunately, Corneille did little better. He too shows us Titus ready to throw away an empire in order to make love in Judaea. "In this he trespasses directly against Truth and Probability, destroying the character both of the private Man and the Emperor, only to ascribe everything to a Passion that was extinguish'd."[99] Not that Saint-Evremond wished to banish all tenderness; he finds as much fault with Euripides who (reversing the priority of the moderns) denied all humanity to Achilles in his *Iphigenia* by making him completely indifferent to the demands of the heart. On this point, evidently, both the ancients and the moderns had failed.

Except for the tone, which is urbane and civilized, Saint-Evremond's stance is oddly reminiscent of his dogmatic opponent, the abbé d'Aubignac. To a surprising extent, both were agreed on proclaiming the sovereignty of what they thought was universal reason (but what is obvious to us as the taste of Louis's court) over all the values of life and art, however much they disagreed about its exact meaning and application. And even while Saint-Evremond consistently opposed the inflexibility of reason and the rules, he always assumed their use and permanence. Modernity in the age of Louis XIV, like *ancienneté*, was apparently always a matter of degree.

CHAPTER 8

Saint-Evremond, Dryden and the Opera

I

As for opera, Saint-Evremond did not find that newfangled genre – that "most baroque of inventions" – very satisfactory from either an ancient or a modern point of view.[1] It is true that the first Florentine operas early in the century made a serious attempt to revive Greek drama, but they were doomed to fail, if only for lack of knowledge about the originals, and so necessarily had to produce something modern. This was despite the best efforts of Renaissance scholars, like Vincenzo Galilei, who regretted novelties and wrote an invidious comparison between ancient and modern music; or the later Florentine theorist, Giovanni Battista Doni, who lamented the fact that modern polyphonic music obscured the meaning of the words and insisted that "means must be found to bring back music to classical times."[2] Typically, the dedication to one of the earliest of the Florentine operas, *Euridice* (1600), by the librettist, Ottavio Rinuccini, made the classical aspiration explicit, while the very same text set by Jacopo Peri (1601) preferred to welcome innovation. As always classical reform and modern novelty began to compete and divide the field, and the English, who for a long time lacked the thing itself, could at least consider the theory and watch the battle from afar.[3] In 1656, Thomas Blount provided a first definition of the new genre for his English audience:

> In Italy it signifies a Tragedy, Tragi-Comedy, Comedy or Pastoral, which (being the studied work of a Poet) is not acted after the vulgar manner, but performed by Voices in that way, which the Italians term Recitative, being likewise adorned with Scenes by Perspective, and extraordinary advantages by Musick.[4]

It was only just about then that it became possible to see one performed in England.

Saint-Evremond was very fond of music and attended many of the operas that were first introduced into France from Italy and fostered by Cardinal Mazarin. According to Silvestre and Des Maizeaux, he had "some skill in composition," and set many idylls, prologues and other pieces to be sung at the

5. *The Triumph of Saint-Evremond*

Duchess Mazarin's.[5] The first successful opera played in Paris seems to have been Luigi Rossi's *Orfeo* (1647) with a libretto by the abbé Francesco Buti.[6] It took a while to catch on, but the French poets were eventually engaged, and even Corneille tried his hand at something like it, though not (according to Dryden) very successfully.[7] In 1659, Robert Cambert and the abbé Pierre Perrin joined forces to create what they called the "first French comedy in music," and it proved very popular. A later collaboration, *Ariane*, on Bacchus and Ariadne, and another called *Pomone*, were both produced belatedly in London (1674) after Cambert took up residence there, with Saint-Evremond and John Evelyn very likely in attendance. The operas were, according to a visitor, "a novelty in this realm and have aroused everyone's curiosity to see them."[8] A published libretto for *Ariane* describes its sumptuous staging and supplies the only surviving illustration of an operatic production in the period.[9]

However, it was the young Italian, Giovanni Battista Lulli (or as he became, Jean-Baptiste Lully) who soon arrived to transform the genre and dominate the scene.[10] With his faithful librettist, Philippe Quinault, he produced a series of works that captivated Europe. Quinault was a good friend of the modern, Charles Perrault, who later wrote his life; and Dryden was very familiar with his plays.[11] Perrault watched Lully win the struggle for preeminence at Louis's court and the exclusive right to compose operas; and he helped him to obtain the great theater at the Palais-Royal for his productions. He remembered pointing out to Colbert how useful the Roman emperors had found it to provide games and spectacles for the people, and suggested that these might prove equally popular with the people of Paris. (The moderns, we have seen, rarely missed a classical precedent.)[12] Perrault naturally welcomed what he believed was a thoroughly modern invention that was unknown to Horace and beyond the possibility of the classical rules. He himself wrote at least one libretto for a "Lullian" opera.[13] In taking the part of modern French culture in his *Siècle de Louis le Grand* (1687) and again in his *Parallèles* (1687–97), he naturally enlisted the moderns in music and opera for his cause.[14]

It was one of his brothers, Pierre (or perhaps it was Charles himself), who had long before opened the contest by suggesting that Quinault had outdone Euripides in his opera about Alcestis – only to be rebutted by Racine who proclaimed his own faithful allegiance to Euripides in the preface to his *Iphigénie*. Racine was astonished that the moderns should attack the great poet, and he attempted to answer their petty criticisms chapter and verse, concluding with Quintilian that it was better to err on the side of deference to antiquity than to find too many faults. It was here that he reaffirmed his conviction that good sense and reason were the same in all centuries and the taste of Paris was identical with that of Athens.[15] It has been supposed that Racine chose his subject and wrote this play and the next, *Phèdre*, in deliberate reaction to the extravagant spectacle of the newly fashionable Lullian opera.[16]

Naturally, Charles Perrault defended his old friend, Quinault – and the cause of opera – against Racine, first in a letter to Chapelain and then in the *Parallèles*.[17] Meanwhile, another brother, Claude Perrault, was also addressing the subject in a little tract *De la Musique des anciens* (1680), in which he too refuted the claims of the ancients by showing that they had known nothing of modern harmony and counterpoint.[18] The proponents of antiquity had some trouble refuting that, but led by Boileau, they continued to oppose the new hybrid genre, "Parce que la musique ne saurait narrer; que les passions n'y peuvent être peintes." Such was Lully's success, however, that even Racine promised to write a libretto for him with a prologue by Boileau![19]

Once begun, the issue would not die, and it was soon absorbed in the more general French *querelle* where it continued to be argued for generations.[20] In England William Temple immediately picked up the cause of the ancients with a typically bold pronouncement: "'Tis agreed by the learned, that the science of music, so much admired of the ancients, is wholly lost in the world, and that what we have now is made up out of certain notes that fell in the fancy of observation of a poor friar, in chanting his matins." Just as modern poetry had degenerated into rhyme, so music had declined into fiddling – both equally dependent on the friars and barbarous Goths who had transmitted them. What had become of the charms of ancient music, that had so enchanted men and beasts and stirred and stilled the highest and most violent passions of men?[21] It took nearly a hundred years before the musical historians, Burney and Hawkins, could attempt to right the cause with their superior scholarship.[22]

Meanwhile Lully's career flourished. From 1673 to 1687 when he died, the composer wrote and produced a new opera (or *tragédie lyrique*, as he preferred to call it) every year to great and growing applause. Charles II, who had picked up a taste for French opera while abroad, had many scenes sung to him at court; and even in London, according to John Evelyn's good friend, Roger North, "All the compositions of the towne were strained to imitate Baptist's vein."[23] It was not long before Saint-Evremond was discussing the genre in the salon of the Duchess Mazarin, setting down his thoughts on the matter for the Duke of Buckingham.

It was natural for Saint-Evremond to compare the new operas with the old dramas that he loved, Lully and Quinault with Corneille and Racine, and Romain Rolland has reminded us how much in fact they owed to each other, particularly in the long recitatives that Lully developed to carry the action and which so resembled the declamations in contemporary tragedies.[24] As always in the period, the ultimate standard remained the theater of Greece and Rome. Above all, it was the hybrid nature of the opera that seemed to Saint-Evremond so awkward and improbable. When his friend D'Hervart wrote to tell him about the latest productions in Paris, just after Saint-Evremond had seen some of them in London, he responded by conceding that the music was beautiful in places and the dances marvelous, but that opera, "seeing how it is composed, should be perfect in every part, is an impossibility." The Duke of Buckingham had told him he would approve them only if they would sing such songs as, "Hola, Ho etc.!" and "Captain of the Guard, Summon Monsieur So-and-So!" "The best part of the action in Comedy and Tragedy," Saint-Evremond continued, "is expressed by lyrics or by recitative; and for this reason there is nothing so ridiculous as having an action sung, whether it be the deliberation of a Council, the giving of orders in battle, or any thing else you like." Feelings could well be expressed in music but not actions, which required words; opera appealed too much to the senses, too little to the mind. Poetry must always be sacrificed to the music. Put Lully's music and dance between the acts of Racine, and Saint-Evremond had no doubt that it would immediately kill the taste for opera. And he remembers a remark to that effect by Corneille, who was willing to allow music only for the chorus, as in ancient times.[25] It was in that mood that he wrote his little essay.

What, then, was an opera? It was, according to Saint-Evremond, nothing but an "odd Medley of Poetry and Musick, wherein the Poet and the Musician, equally confined one by the other, take a world of pains to compose a wretched performance." Saint-Evremond had no hesitation in giving precedence to the words and poetry of dramatic representation in the interests of *vraisemblance*. He objected to the mixture of music and dance and spectacle that could only detract from the subject, however seductive the arias and instrumental passages. As for the endless recitative, which was so tedious, it was neither singing nor reciting, but "an awkward use of Musick and Speech" unknown to the ancients, who obviously knew how to do these things better. It "is in vain to charm the Ears, or gratify the Eyes, if the Mind be not satisfied . . . An extravagance set off with Musick, Dances, Machines, and fine Scenes, is a pompous folly, but 'tis still a folly."[26] If one believed that opera should be a faithful representation, one was bound to be disappointed.[27] Neither the best of the Italians, such as Rossi, nor the best of the French, such as Cambert and Lully, could possibly succeed, although Saint-Evremond typically allowed that no one had done it better yet than Lully and Quinault.[28] As always, Saint-Evremond qualified his judgments carefully out of tact as well as conviction, but his views on opera show clearly that there were very real limits to his modern sensibilities – even to making him sound now more than a little like Boileau.[29]

It was about this time that Saint-Evremond wrote a satirical play on the subject, a pleasant parody that reinforced the judgments of his essay on Cambert and Lully. The heroine insists on conversing about the most ordinary matters in Lullian song, and when her father commands her to stop, she cries out,

> Père, Baptiste, Opéra, ma naissance,
> Me faudra-t-il decider entre vous?

Des Maizeaux thought that one scene in the piece in which Saint-Evremond specifically criticizes the chief operas of his day must have been based on Cervantes when he was poking fun at the most famous romances of his day.[30] Fifty years later, the defenders of opera were still finding it necessary to answer both his arguments and his satire.[31]

2

The English did not take much to opera in this period, and the strictures of Saint-Evremond and the ancients probably did not help. Sir William Davenant's *Siege of Rhodes* (1658) is usually taken to be the first English opera, but it had few immediate successors.[32] Its true roots, like most of what passed for opera in England, were in the court masques that had flourished before the Civil War and were revived after the Restoration.[33] The hybrid character of these entertainments, which combined words and music, theater, dance and costume, made the masque a particularly difficult form to define, and early raised questions about the relative importance of the parts. The debate between Ben Jonson and Inigo Jones over these matters and the breakdown of their collaboration

was notorious.[34] But the deliberately classicizing character of the masques –
their allegorical figures, costumes and staging – was invariably accepted. When,
typically, Jones staged Thomas Crew's *Coelum Britannicarum* (1633), he created
a scene "representing old Arches, old Palaces, decayed walls, parts of Temples,
Theaters, Basilicas and Thermae, with confused heaps of broken Columns,
Bases, Cornices, and Statues, lying on or under ground, and altogether resembling the ruins of some great city of the ancient Romans, or civiliz'd
Britons."[35]

It was not easy during the Interregnum to put on public performances of
any kind against the wishes of the radical Puritan party. Dryden explained later
how the royalist Davenant had added music to his play as a subterfuge to get
it performed, only to have it removed when the play was revived during the
Restoration.[36] And indeed Davenant had carefully prepared the way for the
Siege with a previous public entertainment, in which there were several "Declamations and Musick, after the Manner of the Ancients," in the first of which
the audience could hear Diogenes and Aristophanes debating (in Athens) the
virtues and propriety of opera.[37] The *Siege* was allowed and was successful, and
Davenant followed it almost at once with two more works on modern sub-
jects, "exprest by Instrumental and Vocall Musick, and by Art of Perspective in
Scenes": *The Cruelty of the Spaniards in Peru* and *The History of Sir Francis Drake*.
These extravagant entertainments, which even included some rope-dancing,
were popular enough to endure contemporary satire.[38] The music for the
Siege is lost, but the composers were able, and the sets were designed by John
Webb, the pupil of Inigo Jones.[39] Pepys loved it, but Evelyn (who enjoyed
tightrope-walking) was very disappointed when he went to see one of
Davenant's operas, finding it "much inferior to the Italian composure and
magnificence."[40] Dryden preferred to think of the *Siege*, not so much as an
opera than as the first of the rhymed heroic plays and an inspiration to his own,
while his old opponent, Edward Howard, took the opposite view, willing to
allow the rhyme (which he despised) as suitable for an opera, though not for
a play.[41]

Early in his own career, Dryden collaborated on a revision of Shakespeare's
Tempest, which was later reworked, perhaps by Thomas Shadwell (1674), and
revived as an "opera."[42] The stage directions survive with most of the music
and reinforce the baroque character of the event, which was performed in a
classical set stretched out of all shape by the deliberate introduction of modern
elements and an evident desire to surprise and awe.[43] Its success inspired a
second opera by Shadwell the next year, *Psyche*, an adaptation of a collaborative work by Quinault, Corneille and Molière, with music by Matthew Locke.
Once again, the work was splendidly set out, according to a contemporary, with
"new Scenes, new Machines, new Cloaths, new French Dances."

The poet's business, according to Shadwell, was only

> to show splendid scenes,
> T'interpret twixt the audience and machines.[44]

The music for the "tragedy" (as it was called in the printed libretto) was published with *The Tempest* by Matthew Locke in 1675 as *The English Opera; or the vocal Musick in Psyche, with the Instrumental therein intermix'd.* In the preface Locke explains that the work was an opera, a word and a concept that he had borrowed expressly from the Italians and that he defines by the recitative, or musical (as opposed to spoken) declamation. According to John Downes, "This Opera was Splendidly set out, especially in Scenes, the Charge of which amounted to above 800 pounds."[45] Nevertheless, Shadwell found it necessary to apologize:

> I do not doubt but that the Candid Reader will forgive the Faults, when he considers that the great Design was to entertain the Town with variety of Musick, curious Dancing, splendid Machines; and that I do not, nor ever did intend to value my self upon the writing of this Play.[46]

We can perhaps begin to understand the contempt of Saint-Evremond and the ancients for this new, mixed and frivolous genre – "Dorset Garden spectaculars," they have been aptly called – as well as their momentary fascination for the audience.[47]

All this seems to have stimulated Dryden to make his own attempt. The vogue for the rhymed heroic play was fading. In 1674, just when the new French import was stirring the court and the London audience and catching Saint-Evremond's attention, we have seen that Dryden hastily turned *Paradise Lost* into *The State of Innocence* or *The Fall of Man*. It was probably meant to compete with *The Tempest*, but the work was never produced and only published in 1677. Its stage directions call for machines and elaborate scenery that were probably beyond the financial reach of the company and that Dryden may have regretted. When the new playhouse of Christopher Wren opened in Oxford (1674), Dryden had already complained,

> 'Twere Folly now a stately Pile to raise,
> To build a Play-House while you throw down Plays.
> Whilst Scenes, Machines, and empty Opera's reign,
> And for the Pencil You the Pen disdain.
>
> 'Tis to be fear'd –
> That as a Fire the former House o'erthrew,
> Machines and Tempests will distroy the new.[48]

The music seems never to have been composed.

A decade later, in the same year that Lully's first opera, *Cadmus et Hermione*, was performed in London, Dryden tried again, writing a libretto for *Albion and Albanius* with the French exile Lewis Grabu as the composer. It began, Dryden explains, as a prologue for a play on the model of *The Tempest*, "a tragedy mixed with opera," though it was not quite either the one or the other. It grew into an entertainment of itself with the introduction of two more acts and a stage setting and decorations supplied by Betterton.[49] It was played privately several times for Charles II and given a few public performances before it was withdrawn. The failure is sometimes blamed on the music, but the Duke of Monmouth chose this unfortunate time to stage his own drama, and his rebellion shut down the theater, though it is doubtful in any case that the time was ripe for success. The English had only just begun to go abroad in substantial numbers on the grand tour, and the taste for classical antiquities and such modern contrivances as opera was just beginning to gather steam. To be sure, John Milton had long ago attended an operatic performance at the Barbarini Palace in 1639, and John Evelyn, always in the advance guard, had visited the opera several times on his trip to Rome and Venice in the 1640s, but they were exceptional. Evelyn had been particularly impressed with the opera in Venice with its music and recitative, scenes and machines, "so taken together it is doubtlesse one of the most magnificent and expensfull diversions the Wit of Man can invent."[50] Despite the flurry of activity that inspired Saint-Evremond and Dryden some thirty years later, the genre still remained for most Englishmen an exotic foreign import.

Typically, Dryden set out his own thoughts on the matter for the folio volume that appeared just after the death of Charles II, in 1685. Whether he had read Saint-Evremond by then is not clear, but he addresses some of the same questions.[51] "An Opera," he agreed, "is a poetical Tale or Fiction, represented by Vocal and Instrumental Musick, adorn'd with Scenes, Machines, and Dancing."[52] The characters were usually gods and heroes, which encouraged marvelous and surprising conduct. Dryden (like Saint-Evremond) insisted on the primacy of the words, but he was much more open to the union of sound and sense and to the introduction of stage effects than Saint-Evremond.[53] He allowed that arias in particular were addressed more to the hearing than to the understanding. It might seem preposterous that rhyme should take the place of reason, but how was one to settle such an affair? Dryden saw that it was a matter of artistic convention, and he responded, as so often, with a qualified appeal to ancient precedent:

> In order to resolve the Probleme, this fundamental proposition must first be settled. That the first Inventors of any Art or Science, provided they have brought it to perfection, are, in reason, to give Laws to it; and according to their Model, all after Undertakers are to build. Thus, in Epique Poetry, no Man ought to dispute the Authority of Homer, who gave the first being to that Masterpiece of Art, and endued it with that form of Perfection in all its Parts, that nothing was wanting to its excellency.[54]

That was why Virgil had been content to imitate the design of his model without any innovation; and that was what all true poets had always done. That was why Pindar had supplied the necessary model for all subsequent odes, from Horace to Cowley. And that was why any composer of opera, "which is a modern Invention, though built indeed on the Foundations of Ethnique

Worship," was obliged to imitate the Italians. It was the Renaissance Italians who had invented and perfected the genre, and it was up to the English to follow their lead, despite the disadvantages of their language. Dryden thought he might enlarge on the subject some day – "out of some Observations which I have made from Homer and Virgil who, amongst all the Poets, only understood the Art of Numbers, and all of that which was properly call'd *Rhythmus* by the Ancients."[55]

In short, the Renaissance Italians could help to supply all that was wanting in the ancients. When Dryden revised his essay for publication, he made only one change. In describing the invention of opera, he thought that he might have given too much credit to the Spanish as the inspiration for Italian opera. He had since learned from Saint-Evremond's Dutch friend, the erudite Isaac Vossius (now living in England), that it was in fact the ancients who had charted the way, and the modern Italians had simply "gathered up the Shipwrecks of the Athenian and Roman theaters; which we know were adorn'd with Scenes, Musick, Dances and Machines, especially the Grecian."[56] Thus Dryden was pleased to find an ancient precedent, if not a classical model, for his modern opera. Unfortunately, his own composition was not very pleasing and certainly did not succeed in accomplishing the transplantation that Dryden might have hoped for. Neither the modern Italians nor the French, nor the native English – and certainly not the ancient Greeks – were adequate to show Dryden how to create a new form all at once.[57]

Dryden did not really repeat the experiment, though he did turn now to a superior musician for further collaboration. In 1690, young Henry Purcell began to compose a series of "semi-operas," as Roger North called them, including the music for *Dioclesian*, and a little later, for Dryden's *King Arthur*. Purcell was already famous for composing one true (that is to say, through-composed) opera, *Dido and Aeneas*, but that dubious experiment had not caught on. According to Peter Motteux, English gentlemen would not tolerate "perpetual singing" and preferred to have music and dancing intermixed with the comedy or tragedy. He thought that "plays altogether sung" were unnatural in a way that ordinary plays were not.[58] On the other hand, not everyone approved the hybrid compromise. As Roger North put it, semi-operas had the fatal flaw that "they break unity, and distract the audience. Some [come] for the play and hate the musick, others come only for the musick and the drama is a pennance to them, and [there are] scarce any that are well reconciled to both."[59]

Nevertheless, the proprietors of the King's Theatre now turned to young Purcell to produce a new version by Thomas Betterton – to which Dryden contributed – of Massinger and Fletcher's old *Prophetess, or the History of Dioclesian*.[60] The result was so successful – not least the extended (though digressive) masque that appears in Act V – that Purcell decided to follow the example of Grabu with *Albion and Albanius* and publish the full score.[61] Dryden had already employed Purcell in his *Amphytrion* (1690) and praised him for several songs; now he helped him to write the interesting dedication that accompanied the new work.

In their dedication Purcell and Dryden claimed that music and poetry were like painting and poetry, sister arts. Though they excelled independently, they were most excellent when joined together, "because nothing is then wanting to either of their perfections: for thus they appeare like wit and beauty in the same person."[62] It was (as a contemporary composer pointed out) Purcell's ability to represent in music that was so wonderful, and therefore his ability to bring the sister arts into harmony – or rivalry.[63] Poetry and painting, Purcell and Dryden say, have already arrived at their full perfection in England, but music was still in its nonage, "a forward child which gives hope of what it may be hereafter." For the while, the Italians must lead the way, with a little help from the French. "Thus being farther from the Sun, we are of later growth, than our Neighbor Countreys; and must be content to shake off our barbarity by degrees."[64] Fortunately the present age seemed to be ready for refinement, "and to distinguish betwixt wild Fancy, and a just, and numerous Composition." It is unlikely, however, that Dryden really believed that *Dioclesian* had filled the bill.[65]

So Dryden tried again. It seems that in 1684 he had written a sequel to *Albion and Albanius*; now in 1691, in the midst of his last bitter effort to court the popular stage, he was induced to take it out and rewrite it as *King Arthur*, a play "Written in blank Verse, adorn'd with Scenes, Machines, Songs and Dances" – according to the title page, a "Dramatick Opera."[66] (His thoughts for an epic poem on that subject had long since passed.) It was only necessary to disguise or update the political allegory to meet the new situation. But it does not look as though Dryden really had much hope for it, however much he seemed to appreciate the genius of his young collaborator. It was the old problem again of the incompatibility of words and music. The poet had already complained in *Amphytrion*,

> How can he show his manhood, when you bind him
> To box, like boys, with his hand behind him?[67]

Now he writes, "The Numbers of Poetry and Vocal Musick are sometimes so contrary, that in many places I have been oblig'd to cramp my Verses, and make them rugged to the Reader, that they may be harmonious to the Hearer."[68] He did not regret writing the opera, he said, but he did point out apologetically that these kinds of entertainment were principally designed for the eye and ear and that the poet's art must be subservient to the composer's. Indeed, Roger North was still complaining about much the same thing to Betterton – who gave an answer that did not satisfy him. The true reason for their success, North wrote, was "that the towne had not will or palat enough to know what's good."[69]

And indeed, *King Arthur* was very successful, despite its formlessness and compromise, and it improved Purcell's reputation. "It was excellently adorn'd with Scenes and Machines . . . The Play and Musick pleas'd the Court and City, and being well perform'd, 'twas very gainful to the Company."[70] A little later, probably in the last year of his life (1695), Purcell composed a new score for *The Tempest* and turned yet another old Dryden piece, *The Indian Emperor*, into an opera, a less ambitious work, but a fitting *magnum opus* nonetheless.[71] Dryden did not forget to commemorate his collaborator with a moving funeral elegy. But the old man, with his mind now on Virgil, was ready at last to turn his back on his audience and the stage (in any form) and concentrate upon a loftier purpose – one more in tune with his growing *ancienneté*. And, though it does not look as though Saint-Evremond either saw or read any of Dryden's operas, it is perfectly clear that the old French critic would heartily have approved his intention.

3

Meanwhile the Battle of the Books had begun in earnest and the quarrel over opera was not forgotten. Rymer typically complained that opera was "a conspiracy against Nature and good Sense."[72] For the critic, John Dennis, opera could only be defended "by the Examples of the Antients," and modern opera could hardly stand the comparison. He agreed with Dryden and Saint-Evremond that music should be subordinate to drama, and the sensual to reason. "If that is truly the most Gothick, which is the most oppos'd to Antique, nothing can be more Gothick than an Opera, since nothing can be more oppos'd to the antient Tragedy, than the modern Tragedy in Musick, because the one is reasonable, the other ridiculous." Even the chorus, which had been the one musical part of ancient tragedy, was being abused by the modern Italians, since music should always be for the sake of sense, while in opera "the Sense is most apparently for the sake of the Musick."[73] If that sounds very like Saint-Evremond, though a little more dogmatic, Dennis seems to have been expressing what was the prevailing view at the beginning of the new century – the view of the *Spectator* and the *Tatler*, for example – though with the inevitable contemporary dissent.[74]

And so it is not surprising that the arguments of Saint-Evremond were repeated yet again by Charles Gildon in his life of Thomas Betterton, who insisted against the learned Joshua Barnes that only the choruses of the Greeks were sung, and even they were subordinated to the poetry. "Music," he wrote categorically, "ought still, as originally it was, to be mingled with the Drama, where it is subservient to Poetry, and comes into the relief of the Mind, when that has long been intense on some noble Scene of Passion, but ought never to be a separate Entertainment of any Length."[75] Baroque, it seems, was passing again into neoclassical. But if, as usual, the issues in the quarrel had come to depend in large part on a reliable knowledge of the Greeks, which could only be settled by an appeal to history, neither side as yet was very well prepared to settle the matter. According to Voltaire, modern operas were close to ancient tragedies in being sung, as well as in many other particulars. "They are at once the copy and destruction of the Athenian stage: a copy of it, as they admit of the *mélopée*, the choruses, machines, and deities, and at the same time the destruction of it, as they have taught our young men to be fonder of sound than sense; to prefer the tickling of their ears to the improvement of their minds."[76] Indeed, it was to be a very long time before a classical scholarship would appear that was at all competent for the question, and the modern, Charles Burney, was still contesting the ground with the ancient, Sir John Hawkins, a century later.[77]

CHAPTER 9

Saint-Evremond in England

I

It was just about the time that Saint-Evremond was thinking about opera, not long after he had returned to England, that he read the critical works of Rapin and Boileau. He was all admiration, despite their uncompromising *ancienneté*.[1] Inevitably, he was forced to do some more thinking about the matter and characteristically set out his ideas afresh in two essays, the first of which he entitled "Of Antient and Modern Tragedy."[2] As with the others, it was soon printed, translated and retranslated. In reconsidering the drama now and the ancient rules, Saint-Evremond decided to confront the abbé d'Aubignac head on in order to clarify the differences that had separated them ever since the assault on Corneille.

Never, he begins, were there so many prescriptions for tragedy, yet so few good plays! He remembers that D'Aubignac himself had written one according to the rules but without any success; yet that had not stopped the abbé from boasting that he alone understood Aristotle – "whereupon," Saint-Evremond reports, "the Prince of Condé said wittily, I am obliged to Mr d'Aubignac for having so exactly follow'd Aristotle's Rules; but I will never forgive the Rules of Aristotle, for having put Mr d'Aubignac upon writing so bad a Tragedy!"[3]

Once again, Saint-Evremond conceded that Aristotle's *Poetics* was an excellent work, "But however there's nothing so perfect in it, as to be the standing Rule of all Nations, and all Ages." Indeed, Descartes and Gassendi had both discovered truths unknown to the Greek philosopher; and errors had been found in the *Physics* and the *Poetics*, "at least with respect to Us, considering what great Changes all Things have undergone since his Time."[4] In addition, Corneille had discovered beauties in the drama of which Aristotle was entirely ignorant. Saint-Evremond's modernity was thus based on a real pride in the achievement of his contemporaries and a real belief in the possibility of progress. It was also based on a genuine appreciation of the gulf that separated the ancients from the moderns, not absolutely or in all things, reason and human nature remaining constant, but in respect to much of life and art.

One obvious measure of that gulf was religion. The ancients had filled their plays with the actions of the gods – all "downright Romance to us, at this time of day." Saint-Evremond (who is opposing Boileau here) had no doubt that the ancient drama would have been much improved without any of the para-phernalia of its religion: its gods, oracles and soothsayers. In an accompanying essay, "Of the Wonderful that is found in the Poems of the Antients," he makes his opposition even clearer, now criticizing Homer and Virgil (against Boileau again) in this respect.[5] Like Boileau, however, he does not think that substituting a modern machinery of saints and angels would be an improvement. Better to keep Christianity and tragedy apart, since their spirits were profoundly opposed. (Thus even Corneille's *Polyeucte* seemed to Saint-Evremond a relative failure.)[6] Let tragedy limit itself to human affairs and to those who were truly admirable and heroic. In addition, Saint-Evremond was very dubious about the therapeutic value of tragedy; he claims that Aristotle himself had never really understood how purgation (catharsis) was to be accomplished. Pity and fear, rather than improving the audience were more likely to undermine their virility, as the cowardice of the ancient Athenians proved. "For how was it possible for them not to learn Despair in this pitiful School of Commiseration?" Nor, finally, had the moderns improved the drama by introducing the motive of love. "To confess the Truth, our Authors have made as ill Use of this Noble Passion as the Ancients did of Fear and Pity." One day, we shall learn the true use of that passion, which is to animate courage and raise the spirits, rather than to effect tenderness. (Racine, clearly, was not far from his thoughts.) "Whenever this happens, we need not envy the Antients: and without paying too great a respect to Antiquity, or being too much prejudiced against the present Age, we shall not set up the Tragedies of Sophocles and Euripides, as the only Models for the Dramatick Compositions of our times."[7]

Saint-Evremond's stance continued thus to remain modern, though no less universal than D'Aubignac's. He believed that the moral and aesthetic standards of his own generation were founded "on good and solid Reasons." The ancients would have done better had they known and observed them, though of course they had not. Even if *Oedipus* could be translated into modern French and retain all the force and spirit of the original, it would certainly fail now, though it had obviously once pleased the Athenians. "Nothing in the World would appear to us more cruel; more opposite to the true sentiments which mankind ought to have."[8] It was a privilege to live in a more civilized age. When the ancients saw Agamemnon sacrifice his daughter, they accepted it in a spirit of pious obedience; in that superstitious age one could not do otherwise than be cruel and barbarous. Now, the modern theater, purged of superstition and immorality and free from the absolute rules of ancient drama, was ready to arrive at the perfection counseled by – Horace! *Omne tulit punctum, qui miscuit utile dulci.* As always, even the praise of modernity could find an ancient precedent.[9]

2

If Saint-Evremond's modernity was as forthright as we shall find in his generation, we have seen something of its limits. In his attack on the constraints of
classical authority, he had, of course, been anticipated. Even before the quarrel
over the *Cid*, for example, one François Ogier had already spun out something
like his position in a polemical preface to a play, *Tyr et Sidon* (1628), only to be
answered by the "ancient," Chapelain.[10] And in the generation following,
Perrault and Fontenelle were to develop much the same modern position more
boldly and completely, only to be answered again by the "ancients," Boileau
and the two Daciers. Saint-Evremond's role was to bridge the generations, as
well as the cultures of France and England, protesting against the rigors of the
new classicism in the name of freedom and independence, even while accepting much of its framework. If he was more radical in this respect than either
Corneille or Dryden, he still stopped short of proclaiming what otherwise
might have been expected: a complete freedom from the constraints of *ancienneté*. The ancients, he saw, were different and they were fallible, even though he
did not know them very well; but still, all must be measured by a common
standard, by a reason universal in its application, however flexible or adaptable
in practice.

It seemed to Saint-Evremond, therefore, and to all his contemporaries that
perfection, when it was achieved (as in some of the plays of the modern,
Corneille, or in the works of the ancient, Petronius), was for all time. The bar-
riers of time and custom, to which he was normally so sensible, vanished in
the face of literary perfection. If the practical limit to *ancienneté* in this period
was the fear of a "servile" imitation, then the practical limit to modernity was
the conviction of a timeless reason and good taste. What was lacking to both
was a truly relative historical sensibility – modernity in our sense. And since
the extremes were barred in this way, it is no wonder that there was always a
certain convergence, a substantial overlap between the two parties.

We left Saint-Evremond in the 1670s at the salon of the Duchess Mazarin,
where all these things were being discussed. It was the period of Racine's
greatest triumphs: of *Bajazet* (1672), *Mithridate* (1673), *Iphigénie* (1674) and
Phèdre (1677), the last of his plays before he retired unexpectedly to other things
and disappointed the world. In the meantime, Corneille had grown old and
begun to falter; his final play, *Surena* (1675), was not a success, although Saint-
Evremond could hardly wait to see it.[11] After that, he too wrote no more for
the theater, though he lived on until 1684. Eventually, Racine tried to make
amends when he addressed the Academy at the reception of Thomas Corneille
(1685) and eloquently sang the praises of his old rival to the warm applause of
the audience. He insisted now that it was Corneille alone who had reformed
the stage by a combination of extraordinary genius and the example of the
ancients.[12] All during the rivalry, however, the Duchess and her friends
supported the rising star and the party of the ancients, and it was left to Saint-
Evremond still to defend his old friend.

Racine, who knew Corneille's theory as well as his practice, aligned himself deliberately, as we have seen, with the ancients. From the beginning of his career, when he first had to defend himself against the moral scruples of Port-Royal, he took up the defense of the classical writers.[13] From about 1671, he grew intimate with Boileau who became a lifelong friend and ally, and he met and admired the other members of the Lamoignan circle. He even sent *Phèdre* to the two *pères*, Rapin and Bouhours, for correction and suggestions.[14] His son remembered how late in life he could recite whole scenes from Sophocles and Euripides that he had learned as a youth, though it seems, if anything, that he became more interested in the Greek tragedies with time. (It is hard to say just when he took the pains to annotate them.) In all his prefaces, he proclaims his fidelity to the ancient sources, and when he departs from Euripides's *Iphigenia*, it is only upon classical precedent. "Good sense and reason," he explains, "have been the same in all centuries. The taste of Paris is found to agree with the taste of Athens. My audience has been brought to the tears of the most sophisticated nation of Greece." It sounds almost as though he were directly rebutting Saint-Evremond.

If the moderns insisted upon finding fault with Euripides (here Racine seems to be thinking of Pierre Perrault's invidious comparison of Quinault's opera with the original *Alcestis*), Racine was sure it was because they did not understand the Greek correctly. He shows how they had stupidly misread the text and advises them not to make any more frivolous remarks about the ancients. For himself, he has nothing but "esteem and veneration" for the classics; as Quintilian had said so well, it was better to admire the ancients than to criticize them, lest we condemn what we do not understand. In *Phèdre* he reaffirms his admiration and debt to Euripides and his belief that his heroine has all the qualities that Aristotle required to arouse pity and terror. He only wishes that his play would be as instructive as its model.

Now it is frequently said that there is something a little disingenuous about these prefaces of Racine. The author protests too much. He admires Euripides but he does not hesitate to alter him; worse yet, he never acknowledges his (probably superior) debt to Seneca and the moderns. He proclaims the historical reliability of his works, though they impressed his audience with their modern French manners. (Even *Bajazet,* which was set in the contemporary world, disappointed many, including Corneille, by seeming to abandon Constantinople for Paris.)[15] The insistence on the moral instruction of *Phèdre* also rang hollow to many, a mere device by which Racine hoped to become reconciled to his pious teachers at Port-Royal. Moreover, Racine's plays no longer seem to us very close to the ancient tragedies that he so much admired, but belong rather to another world of feeling and discourse. They were, in a word, modern![16] But this is, after all, not so surprising. Racine was neither the first nor the last of the party of the ancients to distort (whether willfully or not) the antiquity that they claimed to find so useful. And the moderns, like Saint-Evremond, who suspected otherwise, were really not in a position to dispute the point. To accomplish that, they needed weapons and a viewpoint, knowledge and learning, for which they had only scorn. In France, even more than in England, philology had fallen on hard times and was universally despised, even by those who should have known better.[17]

Saint-Evremond may not have been taken in by Racine, but he was increasingly respectful. Still, he continued to defend Corneille against the strictures of the salon. It was objected by the French ambassador and by the Duchess herself that his characters were too cruel; their manners did not suit the *honnête homme*. But that was just the point! "I beseech you," countered Saint-Evremond, "to forget the lenity of our Temper, the Innocency of our Morals, the humanity of our Politicks, that you may consider the barbarous Customs, the cruel Maxims of Eastern Princes."[18] It was, of course, just this sense of historical (and geographical) distance that Saint-Evremond so admired in Corneille and its absence that he so regretted in Racine. He reminds the party of the ancients that such cruelty was the ordinary way in classical times. Why banish Rodogune and applaud Electra and Orestes? To present historical reality was not necessarily to advocate it, though Saint-Evremond took care anyway to extenuate the apparently bad manners of Corneille's heroes. "If you liv'd now-a-days in a Republick that should be oppres'd," he asked the Duchess, "if your Parents were outlaw'd, your House desolate . . . if one of your Equals was become your Master: that Dagger you have brought to plunge into your own Breast, upon the prospect of the Ruin of your Country, would you not try its Edge on the Tyrant, before you used it against your self?"[19] As so often, Saint-Evremond forgot, for the moment anyway, to notice the difference of times, while continuing to insist on the parallel.

Apparently, Saint-Evremond's final word on the subject, his last comparison of the two playwrights, was framed in a letter to the Duchess in 1692, just as the Battle of the Books was coming to a head.[20] He replies to her request for a canvas of modern French authors, and when he comes to Corneille and Racine, he gives them now an almost equal preeminence. Corneille is praised as usual for the force of his passions and for his grandeur and sublimity, while Racine is commended for sentiments that are clearer and more natural and a diction which is purer and simpler. "The former ravishes the Soul; the latter makes a Conquest of the Mind." "In the Conduct of the Work," Saint-Evremond continues, "Racine, more circumspect or distrusting himself, sticks closer to the Greeks, whom he is perfect Master of; Corneille, improving the Advantages which Time affords, finds out Beauties which Aristotle knew nothing of." So, the critic maintains his modernity, though by a narrow margin, and it is noteworthy that he has nothing but praise in the same work for the new chief of the ancients, Boileau, and a definite reluctance to side with the new chief of the moderns, Charles Perrault, who had just launched a fresh broadside against antiquity. Of that work, he allows only that the author had discovered the defects of the ancients better than he had made out the advantages of the moderns; that it was good and useful, but that it could have been done much better.

In short, although there was not much doubt about which side of the *querelle* Saint-Evremond preferred, he always continued to counsel moderation. In 1677 he wrote to the Duchess Mazarin that it was the moderns who were the true ancients in point of time, an idea that was at least as old as Francis Bacon and had become commonplace.[21] But he continued to affirm,

> That to make a sound judgment of Men, and of their Works, it is necessary to consider them by themselves, and to have a contempt, or a respect for things past, according to their intrinsic Worth, whatever it is. I am persuaded, that we ought not to oppose all things merely out of a spirit of Aversion; nor on the other hand, to hunt after them out of love of Novelty; but to reject or receive them, according to the true opinion we ought to conceive of them . . . The most essential point is to acquire a true Judgment, and a pure Understanding. Nature prepares us for it, but experience and conversation with polite persons, brings it to perfection.[22]

In 1697, his old friend, Ninon de Lenclos, wrote to him, that, "as you are a Modern also, I take care not to praise you before the Members of the Academy, who have declared for the Ancients."[23] But he was too old by then and too discreet to want to join the fray. And it is quite clear that he never really approved of either side in the *querelle*, certainly not the ancients, but not much more the radical modernity of the new generation of Perrault and Fontenelle.

3

In tracking Saint-Evremond through the thickets of theatrical controversy, we have overlooked his opinions about some related matters. It is true that drama was always a central concern for him, as it was for Dryden, and that it tended to dominate the literary controversy between the ancients and the moderns in France, at least as much as it did in England. But the debate extended to history and poetry more generally, and Saint-Evremond did not hesitate to offer his opinions about those things also. His peculiar vantage point helped him to mediate between the French *querelle*, which he followed with the greatest care, and the English Battle of the Books, from which (like Dryden) he remained aloof. In each case the prudence of old age may have restrained what must have been a real temptation to engage, though it is more than likely that Saint-Evremond also felt some insecurity and some gratitude as a guest in a foreign land.[24]

Certainly the issues were warmly discussed in the salon of the Duchess Mazarin, and because Saint-Evremond was known to side with the moderns, she asked him to set down his opinions about the French writers of his time.[25] The old man did not hesitate. He was full of praise for his contemporaries, especially for Corneille and Racine, but also for the champion of the ancients, Boileau. He had less to say in favor of the modern Perrault, though he does find fault with his criticism. At its best, his book was "curious, useful, and capable of curing us of abundance of errors." Still, he wished that the various characters in Perrault's dialogue had done better.[26] The letter is too brief and too circumspect to allow us to place him very exactly in the *querelle*, but it is clear that he (like Dryden) meant to take a position somewhere between the extremes in the controversy. He offers no opinion whatever about the English quarrel, but his English hosts (not least Dryden) read with the greatest attention and searched with the keenest interest for anything he had to say on the many questions at issue.

It must be emphasized that Saint-Evremond, like Dryden, but unlike Evelyn and many of the English combatants, was almost completely indifferent to the claims of science and the new philosophy in the *querelle*. He had read Gassendi in his youth and Descartes in middle age, but derived from them nothing but a little reinforcement for his native skepticism.[27] For this he found Montaigne a more congenial source. "I think therefore I am," was the whole benefit he had received from Descartes, so he said, though later on he found even that, "too cold and languishing for an old Man." He preferred to say, "I love therefore I am."[28] The only ancient he admired in these matters was Epicurus. As for the new science of experiment, "of all things in the world, it is the least to my taste. I leave it to M. Thevenot whose passion for insects has kept him for a month at Amsterdam." "Should I visit England," Saint-Evremond wrote in 1669, "it would rather be for the pleasure of conversing with my old friends than of seeing the Fellows of the Royal Society, and I should prefer the Duke of Buckingham's violin to his Laboratory, however curious it might be." The only sciences necessary to a gentleman were "Morals, Politicks, and the Belles Lettres" – the three overriding passions of ancient Rome – and the typical and predictable subject matter of classical sophistry and Renaissance humanism.[29]

As for history, it looks as though Saint-Evremond preferred it even to drama. He certainly believed that in that regard the ancients had far surpassed anything modern. "I can't imagine," he wrote in an essay on the modern French historians (*c.* 1669), "how a person, that has good Skill in Ancient Histories, could persuade himself to suffer the tediousness which ours afford!"[30] Here as elsewhere, only some act of creative imitation might eventually prevail, but Saint-Evremond could not for the moment conceive a likely modern candidate. Meanwhile, one had to rest content with the histories of ancient Rome and their subject, which remained exemplary after two thousand years and many changes in manners and customs. Saint-Evremond had already written about two of his favorite Roman historians, Sallust and Tacitus,[31] and more ambitiously, a long piece on Livy inspired by Machiavelli's reflections.[32] In them, he typically displays much admiration for the Romans, even while criticizing them for their barbarous manners and their patriotic credulity. He sees that their rudeness was necessary for a rising power, though regrettable from a civilized and rational point of view. He tries to separate the timelessness of some of them from the timeliness of the rest.

I know very well, that one may alledge some Actions of such rare and noble Virtue, that they will serve for patterns in all ages: but then these were the actions of particular persons, who had nothing in themselves of the genius of that time; or else they were actions of a singular nature, which (as it were) escaped men by chance, and had nothing common with the ordinary course of their lives.[33]

Indeed, Saint-Evremond was astounded by the extraordinary courage of the Romans, their severe austerity and great affection for their country; but he was equally appalled by the corruption that prevailed in later times, despite their continuing valor and patriotism. In drawing up a balance sheet, it seemed to Saint-Evremond that men of integrity, then and now, could see through their pretensions and make a distinction. No doubt there were some who would continue to complain about the present and would always look back upon antiquity without qualification, "those whose morose humour inclines 'em to find fault with every thing present, [and who always] cry'd up, thro' caprice, what was past." But there were others, more discerning, who could see that there were imperfections and virtues in all ages, even if they were often obliged, sometimes with reason, to admire the greatness of the past. "In so general an admiration, the Historians have not been wanting to pay the same respect to the Antients; and making a Hero of every Consul, have bestow'd all virtues on every one that had well served the Republick." On the other hand, Saint-Evremond at least was too shrewd – too modern – to be altogether taken in by that.[34]

The situation was better for contemporary poetry. In an essay of the 1680s on the ancients, Saint-Evremond writes of its present condition and prospects. Once again he emphasizes the differences between past and present cultures:

No Man pays a greater Veneration to the Works on the Antients than my self. I admire the Design, the Oeconomy, the Elevation of Spirit, the Extent of Knowledge, which are visible in their Compositions; but the difference of Religion, Government, Customs and Manners, have introduced so great a change in the World, that we must go, as it were upon a new System, to suit with the Inclination and Genius of the present Age.[35]

As in the case of drama, it was religion that made the biggest difference: subtract the gods and there was nothing much left to ancient poetry. Still there were other changes that time had wrought, including the modern morality that Saint-Evremond approved, softened and civilized from that "unbecoming freedom" of former times. One had only to consider the "vile and brutal" argument between Achilles and Agamemnon at the beginning of the *Iliad*; or their dreadful crimes in killing – with their own hands – the weak and innocent; or Achilles tying the body of Hector to his chariot and dragging him inhumanly to the Greek camp. If Homer could be excused for painting nature as he saw it, his heroes certainly could not. They lived in a world still rude and unpolished, when the good could hardly be distinguished from the bad, and the behavior of men was still childish. Neither their morals nor their customs could bear comparison with the moderns. "Politicks had not yet united men, by the bonds of a rational Society; nor polished them enough for others: Morality had not yet accomplished them for themselves."[36]

Indeed, Saint-Evremond was as exercised by the manners as he was by the morals of the ancient world. Imagine two leaders amusing themselves before battle by reciting their genealogies! Or haranguing before the contest, "just as they make Speeches in England, before they are hanged!" Nor did he care any more for the extravagant similes of the ancient poets. "Truth was not the inclination of the first Ages; an useful Lye, and a lucky Falsehood gave reputation to Impostors, and Pleasure to the credulous." As a result, all was fiction, allegory and similitude. With the moderns, things were very much better; the genius of Saint-Evremond's age was all opposed to fables and false mysteries. "We love plain Truth; good sense has gain'd Ground upon the Illusions of Fancy; and nothing satisfies us now-a-days but solid Reason."[37] Meanwhile the entire seventeenth-century view of the world had altered when the earth was put into motion around the sun. "In short, every thing is changed, Gods, Nature, Politicks, Manners, Humours, and Customs."[38] Why then should poets be expected to write like their forebears?

It followed that Saint-Evremond was opposed to all "servile and too much affected Imitation." If Homer were now alive, he would still be an admirable poet, but he would write poems suited to the modern temper. "Our Poets make bad ones because they model them by those of the Antients, and order them according to Rules which are changed with the things that time hath altered."[39] Yet here once again, at the very brink of what seems a thoroughgoing historicism, Saint-Evremond stops short and concedes that there were some rules which were eternal because they were built upon a firm and solid reason, and "they have a right to prevail at all Times." Unfortunately (but typically) Saint-Evremond has no room to develop the point. But his concession to permanence helps to explain his last paragraph with its fine sense of balance between the claims of the ancients and the moderns. "The Poems of Homer will always be a Master-piece, but they are not a Model always to be followed. They will form our Judgment; and our Judgment will regulate the present Disposition of Things."[40] It was necessary to try to combine a decent respect for antiquity with a due recognition of the claims of modernity, the good sense of the one with the novelty of the other.[41]

Even so, it looks as though Saint-Evremond's preoccupation with the Greeks had been forced upon him by the quarrel, though his affection for the Romans was more spontaneous. It is clear that he knew the Latin writers better and felt more comfortable with them. When he wrote his autobiography for his friend, the Marshal Créqui, and described his reading, he allowed that "the Latin Authors afford me the most, and I read whatever I think fine, a thousand times over without being cloy'd."[42] He preferred the republican authors of the age just before Augustus: Cicero and Sallust especially, and he had little use for

Seneca and anyone later, except for Petronius and Tacitus. Like Dryden, he appreciated translations, though he did none himself, and disapproved the pedantry of those who insisted that they be read only in Latin. He thought that the efforts of D'Ablancourt, Vaugelas, and the rest were admirable, even if they were "not critically faithful to the Originals," but he did not think that translations could ever deserve the praise of original composition. D'Ablancourt performed brilliantly in all his works – except when he was on his own![43]

Typically, Saint-Evremond expounded on the subject in still another short tract, "Reflections on the French Translators," in which he reviewed Brebeuf's translation of Lucan and Segrais's Virgil.[44] Like many of his contemporaries, Saint-Evremond had a special affection for Virgil, and he did not hesitate to place the *Aeneid* above any modern epic. How pleased was Dryden when he stumbled upon these sentiments! Yet it was necessary that Segrais fall short of an original whose beauty of expression "it must be impossible to equal in our Language, since it could not be done in his own." The translator had to be content to render the spirit of the author, which Saint-Evremond was willing to say he had done so well as to surpass any modern French poem. Once again, the words come oddly, but not unexpectedly, from a proponent of the moderns. Saint-Evremond only objects to that part of the preface where he believed Segrais had misjudged Virgil's characters.

Of course, Virgil was not without fault. Segrais, the proponent of the ancients, had typically overlooked the fact that Virgil could have done more for his hero. In making Aeneas pious, "he ought to have bestow'd upon him a Devotion full of confidence, which may agree with the spirit and temper of Heroes; and not a scrupulous Notion of Religion, which never consists of true Valour."[45] Since Virgil could have molded Aeneas any way he liked, why then did he make him subject to fears and lamentations on every occasion? When Dryden read this passage in Saint-Evremond, he was at pains to object, and it is a measure of their different commitments to *ancienneté* that the Englishman should try to find a path halfway between Segrais and his critic. For Saint-Evremond, Segrais was right to praise the *Aeneid* lavishly, especially the fourth and sixth books, but wrong to defend the characters, which were clearly beneath those of Homer. "Judged by this," he concludes, "how much ought we to admire the Poetry of Virgil, since in spite of the superlative virtues of the Heroes of Homer, and the little merit of his own, the best Criticks will not allow the Latin, to be inferior to the Greek Poet."[46]

It was, as always, a balanced judgment in a dispute which was just then beginning to heat up. As usual, Saint-Evremond had staked out a ground somewhere between the growing extremes. On the one hand, he was willing to criticize both Virgil and Homer; on the other hand, he could find no modern writer to approach them. Dryden, who dissented a little and defended the epic writers more vigorously, nevertheless would probably have accepted Saint-Evremond's general conclusion, written later to the Duchess Mazarin. By then the aging exile had seen a great many fashions come and go, along with the reputations of many popular authors, including his own favorite, Corneille. Now he was ready to condemn two vices equally: an excessive *ancienneté* and an excessive modernity. It was equally wrong to adopt either a love of novelty for its own sake or a despair of the present on behalf of the good old days. "It is necessary to consider them by themselves," he wrote wisely, "and to have a contempt or a respect for things past, according to their intrinsick Worth, whatever it is. I am persuaded, that we ought not to oppose all new things merely out of a spirit of Aversion; nor on the other hand, to hunt after them out of a love of Novelty; but to reject, or receive them, according to the true opinion we ought to conceive of them."[47]

Saint-Evremond was willing therefore to allow that the good sense that could be found in many modern works was more generally borrowed from antiquity than invented anew. "I would have the Moderns inspired by the Wit of the Ancients," he wrote to the Duchess in 1676, "but would not have them steal it, and pass it for their own. I allow 'em to teach us how to think well, but to make use of their thoughts." And he repeated the refrain that had run through almost all his reflections on life and literature. "All ages have a peculiar character proper to themselves; they have their Politicks, their Interests, their Affairs; and, in some measure, their Morals, having their particular Virtues and Vices. I own 'tis all Humanity still: but Nature is various in men; and Art, which is nothing but an imitation of Nature, ought to vary as she does."[48] Behind the balanced antitheses that marked Saint-Evremond's style and infuriated some of his readers, there was an independent mind that had weighed the claims of both the ancients and the moderns over a lifetime and found that there was, after all, something to be said for both sides.[49]

4

Despite the long years of exile, Saint-Evremond's concerns and interests remained largely French, spun out of his youthful escapades in Paris. It is true that he had come to know the older English generation and never tired of praising Waller and Buckingham. But he seems barely to have noticed Dryden at all, nor Milton, Rymer and the rest – not even William Temple who had befriended him in Holland. On the other hand, it is a tribute to the English fascination with things French that they were always eager to read his essays, and the London booksellers never tired of bringing them out in fresh translations. He was read because he wrote well and amusingly and about a French scene that interested the English even when they pretended to despise it. The plays of Corneille and Racine were widely known and often performed. The *Cid*, which had caused so much commotion in Paris, was twice translated into English, and Pepys, who saw it performed, read it "with great delight."[50]

About the same time, just as the heroic English drama was taking shape and Dryden beginning to frame the *Essay of Dramatick Poesie*, two different translations of Corneille's *Pompée* were acted on the London stage. One was by Katherine Phillips, the "matchless Orinda," the other by a consortium of

aristocrats, including Waller and Dorset. Mrs Phillips was one of the few women
writers of the period to win a solid contemporary reputation and tempt a comparison with the ancients, though her brief life and genuine modesty restricted
the match. The critic, Gerard Langbaine, was not alone when he proclaimed
her equal to the Greek Sappho and the Roman Sulpicia, who had both been
praised throughout antiquity just as Orinda was now by her distinguished
Restoration audience – including Evelyn and Dryden.[51] Her view of translation was very like Dryden's: "to write Corneille's Sense, as it is suppos'd
Corneille would have done, if he had been an Englishman not confin'd to the
Lines, nor his Numbers, but always to his Meaning." Mrs Phillips went on to
translate *Horace*, a version that was finished after her early death by Sir John
Denham and frequently performed in London. On February 4, 1668, John
Evelyn saw it acted before the King and Queen, "betwixt each act a masque
and antique dance." He saw it again the following February. Eventually,
four different versions were produced, including an excellent one by Charles
Cotton.[52]

Besides translations from the French, there were adaptations like Otway's
Titus and Berenice (1677), based on Racine, and Abel Boyer's more literal ren-
dering of *Iphegénie* (1700), which was said to have "pass'd the Correction and
Approbation of the late famous Mr Dryden."[53] The English versions certainly
varied in competence and fidelity to the originals, but even at their worst they
gave some flavor of the French, or at least the formal conventions that governed the French drama and that were the basis of contention between the
ancients and the moderns. In them echoes of the *querelle* can sometimes be
heard. As early as 1675, John Crowne complained, in his prose version of *Andromaque*, that the audience had begun to desert the heroic drama of Corneille.[54]
And when he was accused of stealing from Racine's *Bérénice*, he replied in the
preface to his play, *The Destruction of Jerusalem* (1677), with a familiar complaint:
"Since Love has got the sole possession of the stage, reason has little to do there;
that effeminate piece has softened and emasculated the vassals of the stage."
The "lusty ancients," he pointed out, had never failed in that respect, and as a
result, they would – unlike the moderns – continue to be read forever.[55] When,
a generation later, Ambrose Phillips retranslated Racine's *Andromaque*, as *The
Distrest Mother* (1712), he deliberately revised it to accord more exactly with
neoclassical principles, and produced a great popular success.[56]

We have seen that Dryden kept a close eye on affairs across the Channel and
that his own theories and practice were indebted to French tragedy and in
particular to Corneille. And he showed more than a passing interest in the
bagatelles of Saint-Evremond. In general he found "the nicety of French
manners" to be the main flaw in French tragedy. "All their Wit is in their
Ceremony," he complained in the preface to *All for Love*; "they want the Genius
that animates our Stage." Hippolytus in Racine's *Phèdre* was so punctilious about
his manners that he would rather choose death than accuse his stepmother
to his father; to an Englishman, such "excess of generosity" looked more
appropriate to a fool or madman. "In the meantime," he continued, echoing

the views of Corneille and Saint-Evremond, "we may take notice that when the poet ought to have preserved the character as it was delivered to us by antiquity . . . he has chosen to give him the turn of gallantry, and send him from Athens to Paris, taught him to make love, and transformed the Hippolytus of Euripides into Monsieur Hippolyte."[57]

It was part of Saint-Evremond's appeal to Dryden and his friends that he could write so engagingly about all these matters. And when he addressed any of the points of contention between ancients and moderns, he was likely to find an audience in both camps. So it would seem, for example, with the two collections of essays that appeared in English in 1685–86. The first, entitled *Mixt Essays*, was prefaced by an anonymous translator whose sympathies were decidedly ancient. He begins with a brief account of the revival of classical theater in Renaissance Italy and the France of Cardinal Richelieu. "If the Cardinal had liv'd some years longer, he would have carried it much higher, and even contended with Athens and Rome themselves."[58] He gives the abbé d'Aubignac special credit for writing the most perfect treatise on the subject. Besides the French critics, he singles out for praise Ben Jonson, Dryden and especially Thomas Rymer, "who hath given sufficient proofs that he hath studied and understands Aristotle and Horace, Homer and Virgil . . . so that we may justly number him in the first rank of Criticks." Saint-Evremond is praised, but in this company with some inevitable reservations. His essays on the drama were thoughtful and judicious, but just a trifle too French. His strictures on the machinery and decoration of Athenian tragedy were too "rough and peevish." In short, he had erred too much on the side of modernity.

The other version of Saint-Evremond to appear at this time was by one of the busiest translators of the period, Fernand Spence, an obscure man of modern sympathies, but sharing with Saint-Evremond a genuine respect for antiquity. He introduced his collection of the Frenchman's works with a long essay of his own that echoes many of Saint-Evremond's ideas, with only an occasional exception. "It is the happiness of this Age," Spence writes, "to equal if not to exceed all others in true Philosophy, that is to say in knowledge of men and things."[59] The chief reason for this was the accumulation of learning from other times. Spence typically had no desire to disparage the achievements of ancient Greece and Rome, "the first Museums of Art and Wit," but simply to question their absolute authority. He reverses Saint-Evremond's view, however, granting that in matters of wit their drama had "a richer Vein than we have, for the Description of Nature, and of humane Passions, and in brief, whatever bears a respect to wording and expression." It was otherwise in formal matters. The organization and contrivance of a work and its decorum required many rules and precepts, which could only be found out by "a long train of experience and reflection," in sum by the accumulated wisdom of time. "It must follow that the last Ages will have the advantage in these concerns, for as much as they have engag'd all the labour and thinking and mistakes of the former."[60] Like Saint-Evremond, however, Spence also believed in a good sense that was true for all time; and so was able to condemn equally "a contemptuous behavior towards our Forefathers," and a "neglect and disestimation of the moderns" – about which Horace had long ago complained.

Inevitably, there was one point on which Spence, like almost all his English compeers, entirely disagreed with Saint-Evremond. He was sure that English drama completely surpassed the French, and he remembered that even Rapin had conceded as much a long time ago. He makes the now familiar comparison between the two stages, discusses the rules of Aristotle and Horace, inclining toward freedom and concluding with a defense of opera against the strictures of Saint-Evremond, who we have seen had damned the hybrid form for its sensuousness and lack of *vraisemblance*. Spence admits that opera violates all the unities, but he found much to praise in Dryden's recent collaboration, *Albion and Albanus*. It was, he saw, impossible to write an opera to the prescriptions of Aristotle and Horace, who certainly could not have known a genre that was invented by the Renaissance Florentines![61] Unfortunately, Dryden's *Albion* was not a popular success, and Dryden himself had some doubts about it. He may not have welcomed Spence's praise very much either. He certainly did not approve of Spence's principal activity, the free translation of the classics. Some years later he recalled that it was Lord Dorset who said about Spence, "that he was so cunning a translator that a man must consult the original to understand the version." Spence was an admirer of D'Ablancourt and the *belles infidèles*, and this was not an unjust comment.[62] And indeed it is a reminder that Dryden was inclining toward *ancienneté* just in the same years that Saint-Evremond continued to lean the other way.

And so we discover again how easy it is to exaggerate the distance between the ancients and the moderns at the end of the seventeenth century. There were of course plenty of things to argue about, as the Battle of the Books was shortly to prove, but in 1700 classical antiquity more than ever continued to cast its spell, and in England even the honored guest from abroad, who had always been tempted by the modernist claims of his homeland and who sometimes tried to spread them abroad, was still careful to show his respect for the ancients.

5

It was in 1690 that Sir William Temple published his brief essay on the ancients and moderns and began the Battle of the Books. Whether Temple read Saint-Evremond – or Dryden for that matter – is not at all certain, although it is hard to believe that he could have remained entirely ignorant of either of their works and indifferent to their ideas.[63] It was part of Temple's effortless and colloquial style not to reveal his sources, so that it is always difficult to know just what it was that he was reading or quoting. Since he had common friends and court connections with his two contemporaries, however, it could well be that he met or conversed with them both, although again there is hardly a shred of evidence to connect them, except that once many years before Temple had helped Saint-Evremond to get from Holland to England. In a way it hardly matters, since all three men were preoccupied with the same problem, drawing each in his own way upon a common stock of ideas. In 1691, that very popular new journal, the *Athenian Mercury*, put the question this way: "Whether the Common Notion of the World be true, that those later Ages for some Centuries past, have less a share of Learning, Judgment and Invention than those which preceded?" Who were the greatest artists: ancients or moderns? Who built the better ships, or invented the compass? "Do the Modern English Dramatique Writers excell most of those of the last Age?"[64]

Temple had renewed the question by arguing vigorously and one-sidedly for the ancients in all these matters. Even before William Wotton took up the challenge a few years later and began the Battle of the Books, Temple was answered by Sir Thomas Pope Blount in a set of essays that asked, "Whether the Men of the present Age are any way inferior to those of former Ages, either in respect of Virtue, Learning or long Life."[65] Blount does not reply directly to Temple, but certainly inclines to the moderns, from a viewpoint that sounds a little like Saint-Evremond:

> We should not be so fondly conceited of our selves, and the extraordinary Abilities of the Present Age, as to think every thing that is Ancient is obsolete . . . so neither should we be so Superstitiously devoted to Antiquity, as to take every thing for Canonical, which drops from the Pen of a Father, or was approved by the Consent of the Ancients. Antiquity is ever venerable, and justly challenges Honour and Reverence; but yet there is a difference between Reverence and Superstition; we may assent unto them as Ancients, but not as Oracles.[66]

Though time could not *make* truth, truth was in some sense the daughter of time, and it was the moderns (as Bacon had said) who had all the advantage.[67] In fact, Blount's conclusion would probably have satisfied both Dryden and Saint-Evremond. "The greatest respect we can shew the Ancients, is by following their Example; which was not Supinely and Superstitiously to sit down in fond admiration of the Learning of those who went before; but to examine their Writings, to avoid their Mistakes, and to use their Discoveries in order to the Improvement of Knowledge."[68]

Nevertheless, when Wotton brought out his answer to Temple, Blount added a note to his own essay, reinforcing his modernity. Wotton had argued with others that the advantage of modern knowledge was the result of building upon the classical achievement. Blount doubted it; if anything, deference to the past had continued to inhibit modern advancement: "to walk always upon Crutches is we know the same way to lose our Limbs." He thought that translating and editing was no substitute for original writing, "for fear of our shooting our Fore Fathers Mark, we do but copy one after another."[69] He even decried the silly business of endlessly quoting the classical authors – a brush that would have tarred both the translator, Dryden, and the critic, Saint-Evremond, and most of his modern contemporaries.

As the quarrel heated up, it would be nice to know whether Saint-Evremond read Temple, or Blount, or Dryden. That Dryden, at any rate, read Saint-Evremond on these matters is beyond a doubt. (It does not appear that they ever met.) In 1683, he tells us that he had "cast his eye" over a collection of the Frenchman's works, and in 1692, he was asked to complete Saint-Evremond's "character" for a new English translation of his essays.[70] Dryden was respectful of his contemporary but held to his own ideas; and on the problem of the ancients and the moderns he was prepared to disagree.[71] Already in 1683 he was ready to dissent from Saint-Evremond's appraisal of Plutarch. In one of his bagatelles the Frenchman had resumed the comparison that had earlier been made by Montaigne between Plutarch and Seneca, which was not very flattering to Dryden's hero.[72] For much of the seventeenth century, as we have seen, a taste for Seneca was often coupled with a predilection for modernity; his concise pointed style and his sententious Stoic wisdom were frequently preferred to the more rotund periods and civic values of Cicero and the Augustans. If Seneca was an ancient, he nevertheless thought of himself as a modern, and he offered (with Tacitus and the other Silver Age authors) a convenient alternative to the more characteristic Renaissance Ciceronianism that had for a long time prevailed and that was perhaps more suited to the taste for absolutism that for a while obtained in France and England. Again and again, the moderns were ready to employ classical precedent in their favor; modernity, like *ancienneté*, was always relative. Neither Saint-Evremond, however, nor Dryden, endorsed this view – the days of Senecan ascendancy (and the taste for absolute government) were apparently fading. The old rebel, Saint-Evremond, emphatically rejected Seneca's style and, only a little less emphatically, his philosophical teaching. "His Latin comes far short of that of the Augustan Age, nothing easy or natural; but all made up of points, and strain'd witticisms, and has more of the heat of Africk or Spain, than the light of Greece or Italy."[73] As for Seneca's morality, Saint-Evremond found it hypocritical at best, and a far remove from his hedonism.

Saint-Evremond's precarious position and growing prudence made him discreet about his politics. He seems to have started out with something of that same "spirit of aristocratic rebellion" that had inspired Corneille and his generation and that led them to compare themselves (no doubt much too simply) with the Roman aristocracy.[74] Saint-Evremond remained forever nostalgic, but when he took up residence in Holland in 1665, he wrote to his friend Créqui, "After having lived in the constraint of Courts, I take up with the comfort of ending my days in the freedom of a Commonwealth, where if nothing is to be hoped for, there's at least nothing to be fear'd." And he went on to praise the Dutch for their magistrates, taxes and religious moderation.[75] When at length he returned to England, he wrote to the French minister, Lionne, "I am return'd to a Court, after having liv'd in a Republick." He found London "a medium between the French Courtiers and the Dutch burgomasters."[76] And indeed it looks as though it was this medium that was his best choice in politics – as it was in nearly everything else – a congenial milieu for his peculiar baroque sensibility. "To exercise dominion without violence," he wrote to the Duchess, "is all that the best of Princes can do; to obey without murmuring, is all that can be required of the best of subjects."[77]

For the most part Dryden agreed. (He had, after all, started out his career under Oliver Cromwell, then worked for and been betrayed by a monarchy with absolutist pretensions.)[78] Seneca's style was for him also mere "shatter'd Eloquence," broken, pompous, confused and inharmonious. The old Roman may have been a great wit, but he was not much of a philosopher, "not fit to be compar'd with Cicero, of whose reputation he was envious."[79] One might as well compare Lucan to Virgil; Montaigne had greatly exaggerated his merit. All the more reason then for Dryden to be offended, when Saint-Evremond, like his model, tried to couple Seneca with the admirable Plutarch. If a Roman comparison was required, how much more appropriate would have been the historian and philosopher, Varro. Plutarch and Seneca, Dryden insisted, had almost nothing in common, except the coincidence of their times. They were unlike in personality, moral integrity and style. It is true that the Greek language, like the Latin, had long decayed by Plutarch's day – "For the fall of Empires always draws after it the Language and Eloquence of the people" – but Plutarch's style was flowing and even; Seneca's precipitous, harsh and broken. (Saint-Evremond had prudently avoided that comparison on the grounds that he knew no Greek.) Moreover, where Saint-Evremond had found fault with Plutarch's insight into human motives, which he thought too shallow, Dryden defended him again. Saint-Evremond's judgment, he conceded, was that of "a man who has a nice taste in Authors," but he was in this case at least clearly mistaken.[80]

The defense of Plutarch and the rejection of Seneca in 1683 are indications of Dryden's growing *ancienneté*, and here as elsewhere in his preference for the earlier Roman authors, he seems to have anticipated the English Augustans.[81] To be sure, Saint-Evremond shared something of this perspective. "Never had Rome such a set of noble Genius's," he wrote elsewhere, "as at the latter end of the Republick: the reason is, because there was then Liberty enough remaining amongst the Romans, to give a due force to their minds; and Luxury enough to give them Politeness and Agreeableness."[82] For Saint-Evremond, as for Dryden and Temple, language and culture had reached a kind of perfection then, until this was corrupted under the emperors by such as Lucan and Seneca. It was a measure of the agreement beneath the argument that the two men were not really very far apart on such matters. Indeed, all that would seem to have been required for a revival of true Ciceronian eloquence was an appropriate political scene; and here England must have begun to seem more congenial than the France of Louis XIV. For the moment, it remained only to ask whether or how far the present culture in either country might attain to the high standards of Augustan Rome.

It was in 1692 that Dryden was asked to complete a character sketch of Saint-Evremond for a new collection of his *Miscellaneous Essays*.[83] The appreciation seems to have been begun by Knightly Chetwood, whose name however does not appear, and who gave it up for unknown reasons. In any case, it was an opportunity for Dryden to praise his contemporary again, while registering another mild dissent.[84] We have seen that the two critics disagreed about Virgil, a typical example of the different shades of commitment to the antique that were then appearing even among the moderns, just as the Battle of the Books began. In Saint-Evremond's essay on the French translators, which was reprinted in this collection, he had described the recent version of the *Aeneid* by Segrais, and considered the praise that the French translator had lavished upon the original. Saint-Evremond largely agreed with Segrais, but dissented on two points: he found the character of Aeneas beneath heroic dignity; and he preferred (though by a slender margin) the *Iliad* of Homer.[85] Like Rapin, Bossu, and the rest of the "ancients," he accepted the classical epics as the loftiest achievement in all poetry, surpassing anything in modern times; but unlike the more dogmatic of the ancient party, he was typically ready to find fault even with the best of the old poems.

For Dryden now, who was just about to undertake the *Aeneid*, there was a great deal to praise in Saint-Evremond. He seems to have agreed with Chetwood and Saint-Evremond that even the best writers of his own time could not measure up to those who had written under the Roman Emperor, Augustus, "when the Empire and Language were in some Sence Universal."[86] They had written to the world, while the moderns were largely confined to their own countries – except when they were translated. Saint-Evremond deserved to be better known, if only because he wrote like an ancient Roman. "The same Spirit, the same Noble Freedom, the same unaffected Greatness appear in both." There is, Dryden agreed, "not only a justness in his Conceptions, which is the Foundation of good Writing, but also a Purity of Language, and a beautiful turn of Words, so little understood by Modern Writers, and which indeed was found at Rome, but at the latter end of the Common-wealth and ended with Petronius, under the Monarchy."[87] Thus at a stroke, the modern, Saint-Evremond, was turned into an ancient Augustan! Unfortunately, the Frenchman had pressed his criticism of Virgil too far, and Dryden, who presents himself as a "religious admirer of Virgil," found it necessary to correct his judgment. He briefly describes the extenuating literary and political circumstances that confined the ancient poet. In particular, he follows Bossu here, "that the Roman Commonwealth being now chang'd into a Monarchy, Virgil was helping to that Design: by insinuating into the People the Piety of their New Conqueror, to make them the better brook this Innovation."[88]

It would be easy to exaggerate the distance between these two modern judgments. Dryden does not. He ends his character with "respect and deference" to Saint-Evremond, especially for his penetration. "He generally dives into the very bottom of his Authors; searches into the inmost recesses of their Souls, and brings up with him, those hidden Treasures which had escap'd the Diligence of others." Dryden particularly admired Saint-Evremond's criticism of Racine's *Alexander the Great* and thought that had the Frenchman only seen the English theater with his own eyes, rather than those of others, his opinions would have been as definitive there as upon his home ground. "But conversing in a manner wholly with the Court, which is not always the truest Judge, he has been unavoidably led into Mistakes."[89] To the extent that Dryden tries to put some distance between himself and his fellow critic, it was upon two points only: their practical experience in the world of poetry and drama and their adherence to the standards of classical Rome. As might have been expected, it is Dryden who turns out to be the more devoted exponent of antiquity, though not perhaps by much of a margin; and it is not accidental that he it was also who should have been more actively engaged in the life and art of his time.

Part IV

Christopher Wren and the Quarrel between the Ancients and the Moderns

6. Christopher Wren by Godfrey Kneller, 1711

CHAPTER 10

Restoration Architecture and the Young Christopher Wren

I

For Dryden and his generation, it was inevitable that the fine arts should become, along with history and literature, a battleground for ancients and moderns. Certainly architecture had an old claim to be numbered among the liberal arts, and it was natural that the same issues should arise for it as for the rest: about the uses of imitation, the authority of the ancients, and the immutability of the rules.[1] When Dryden wanted to praise his young friend Congreve, he turned spontaneously to architecture to make his compliment. It was under Charles II, he recalled, that the stage had revived, but what it had gained in skill, it lost in strength.

> Our Builders were, with want of Genius, curst;
> The second Temple was not like the first:
> Till you, the best Vitruvius, come at length;
> Our Beauties equal; but excel our strength.[2]

In architecture, as in everything else, the golden age was past, though not quite beyond retrieval.

It was just a year or two earlier that William Temple had characteristically proclaimed the superiority of the oldest buildings against anything modern, insisting in a forceful passage on the "stupendous" monuments of antiquity that had certainly dwarfed everything since: the Pyramids and the Hanging Gardens of Babylon, the Colossus of Rhodes, and the wonderful works of ancient Rome – palaces, theaters, aqueducts and bridges.[3] It seemed to the party of the ancients exactly as in the case of literature, that the old monuments, like the ancient poems, orations and histories, continued to cast their long shadows over the modern world. Typically, Joseph Addison was persuaded that for architectural greatness, "the ancients, especially among the Eastern nations of the world, [were] infinitely superior to the moderns."[4] And a few years later the Austrian architect, J. B. Fischer von Erlach, published a sumptuous volume – soon turned into English – where the Seven Wonders of the World and the rest of Temple's ancient buildings was each illustrated and shown to surpass anything modern.[5]

Inescapably, William Wotton was forced to examine the question in his survey of ancient and modern learning, and he devoted a whole chapter to the subject, although he admitted to little personal knowledge of the matter. He began by conceding that nearly everyone in his time accepted the preeminence of the ancients in painting, sculpture and architecture, not least those modern Italians who were the "genuine successors of the old Romans," and the best of their kind today.[6] Here, it seemed, even more than in literature, *ancienneté* appeared securely ensconced. Wotton allowed that even Michelangelo and Bernini had admitted that their finest works were inferior to some of the old statues standing in Rome. And it looks as though he might have left it at that, except for the sudden appearance, he says, of Charles Perrault's *Parallèles*, where he found the controversy renewed and the arguments for modernity boldly set out. Wotton was impressed, though not quite convinced. Perrault's credentials as "Chief Surveyor of the King's Buildings" lent authority to his arguments there – much more than about eloquence and poetry – and Wotton thought it worth translating them, but without offering any judgment of his own.

Perrault, as Wotton relays his argument, had admitted that the rules of the ancients for architecture were timeless, like the rules of rhetoric, and he granted that they were the foundations of the modern achievement. Nevertheless, he insisted that the modern architect, like the modern orator, had been able to improve upon the ancients by employing their rules for use and beauty more successfully than the originals. Here, Perrault distinguished some rules that were eternally true, such as those that prescribed how to choose and cut and fix the stones together, from those that were only customary, like the different orders of the columns, which, he insisted, were mere accidental beauties.[7] He accepted that the Pantheon in Rome was the "most regular and exact Building now extant," but he pointed out several instances of negligence in the stonework that he thought unpardonable. (Wotton adds that the ancients lacked the necessary modern machinery for the job.)[8] Perrault concluded by choosing two modern buildings that he thought excelled anything in antiquity; Versailles and the colonnade of the Louvre.

Wotton passed quickly over Perrault's account of sculpture and painting, noticing only that in those matters too, the Frenchman had generally argued for the moderns. In particular, Perrault had applauded their discovery of perspective, and he had proposed two neoclassical painters for the highest honors: Raphael and Le Brun. Wotton adds nothing himself, but closes with a brief mention of Poussin, Bernini and Le Brun. It is clear that he felt uneasy about these things and anxious to get on to the stronger ground of scientific modernity. Still, the fact is that he must have known much more about the cause of artistic *ancienneté* than he let on, since one of his close friends and supporters was John Evelyn whom we have discovered defending the ancients in those matters – whatever he thought about the moderns elsewhere. It was just about the time that Wotton was working up his thoughts in the *Reflections upon Ancient and Modern Learning* that Evelyn asked him to help him republish his old treatise on architecture. And while it is doubtful that Wotton ever gave him any actual assistance, he could not have remained ignorant of Evelyn's arguments, so that his silence in the later versions of his own work is suggestive.[9] Wotton meant to be fair in the quarrel between the ancients and the moderns, but in these matters, and at this time, it must have seemed that it was the moderns who needed all the help that they could get.

2

In his travels abroad, Evelyn had been embarrassed to discover the backwardness of his countrymen, and on his return, had decided to do something to contribute to the "renascency" of the arts that he believed Charles II had begun to encourage.[10] In Italy, Evelyn had looked at the old Roman buildings directly, as well as such modern counterparts as the Palazzo Farnese, which had been designed soon after architecture was recovered (as he puts it) from Gothic barbarism, or the buildings of Palladio, which had been recommended to him by the Earl of Arundel. He even did some sketching, as we have seen, perhaps under the tutelage of Carlo Maratti.[11] He particularly admired St Peter's as the greatest church that had been built since Solomon's Temple – especially its "frontispiece" with the famous colonnade, the great dome, and Bernini's *Baldacchino*. He was entranced by Bramante's Tempietto.[12] In Paris too, he was impressed by such neoclassical structures as had recently appeared and the fine collections of paintings and antiques. On the other hand, Notre Dame appeared to him "a clumsy Gothic pile."[13] On his return to England, he looked about him with new eyes and was satisfied with only two buildings in all of London: the Banqueting House at Whitehall Palace and the new portico of St Paul's, both by Inigo Jones, the first English architect to learn abroad and the first to work directly from classical models. (It is interesting that Evelyn neglects to mention the most austerely classical of Jones's London buildings: St Paul's Church, Covent Garden.)[14] Evelyn believed that it was essential now to cast off the barbarous Gothic style and resume the mantle of antiquity, and he saw that the French could help teach the English here, exactly as in literature. Roger Pratt, his friend and fellow in exile, came to just the same conclusions. "No man," he wrote in 1660,

> deserves the name of Architect, who has not been very well versed both in the old ones of Rome, as likewise the more modern of Italy and France, etc., because that with us, having nothing but the banquetting house at Whitehall and the portico at St. Paul's, it is no ways probable that any one should be sufficiently furnished with the variety of invention, and of excellent ideas, which it will be necessary for him to have, who has but a great scarcity wherein to employ his judgment.[15]

As a result, Evelyn chose to translate what he thought was the latest and most useful manual on the subject by Fréart de Chambray. His hope was to revive the Augustan age, with Charles playing the role of Emperor, and Evelyn (by means of Fréart) taking on the role of the theorist, Vitruvius, and showing the way.

The *Parallel of the Antient Architecture with the Modern* was meant, therefore, to offer a practical compendium of traditional knowledge about the classical orders.[16] Fréart had been sent to Italy by Cardinal Richelieu and knew the works of the Renaissance and antiquity directly. In his book, he examined the most famous classical buildings in detail, comparing the accounts of ten modern interpreters, and treating each order in turn. He accepts only the three classsical orders (Doric, Ionic and Corinthian), dismissing the Tuscan and composite as later, inferior, Roman copies. He pretends to no novelty; his only aim, he insists, is to return the art of architecture to its original Greek splendor. His work was meant to answer anyone who dared to claim "that the mind is free, not bound, and that we have as good a right to invent, and follow our own Genius, as the Antients, without rendring our selves their Slaves." For Fréart, it seemed "vain and frivolous" to imagine that "Art is an infinite thing, growing every day to more perfection, and suiting it self to the humor of several Ages and Nations, who judge it differently, and define what is agreeable, everyone according to his own mode."[17] (It would be nice to know just who, if anyone, was prepared to make such an extravagantly modern claim.) On the contrary, the Greeks had long ago brought architecture, and a great deal else, to perfection. Fréart's claims were almost as broad as Temple's and extended to all the arts and sciences. "Let us not then forsake the paths which those excellent guides have trac'd before us; but pursue their footsteps, and generously avow, that the few gallant things which have yet reached down to us, are due onely as deriv'd from them." The alternative was that miserable "libertinism" which disdained both the rules and examples of classical art.[18] Fréart's work was meant to clarify just what those rules were, by generalizing from the authority of individual examples, and to resolve the difficulties and obscurities in the tradition, even to "correcting" Vitruvius, just as the humanists were doing with their classical texts, so that they might be properly employed in the present.

To most of this Evelyn agreed, although he registered what sounds like one reservation in his own "Account of Architects and Architecture," which he appended to the translation. Evelyn saw that Fréart had limited himself simply to the orders and that there remained a need for a more comprehensive work that would treat the whole art. He hoped that someone would come along soon and take the job in hand, and (as he put it), "advance upon the Principles already establish'd, and not so acquiesce in them as if there were a *Non Ultra* Engraven upon our Columns like those of Hercules, after which there remained no more to be discovered."[19] It must have been hard for this very loyal member of the Royal Society, and perhaps unnecessary, to give up all hope of the advancement of learning and concede to the *ne plus ultra* which was for his colleagues the barrier to all progress.[20] Evelyn's *ancienneté*, which was genuine in these matters, was thus tempered by a small and ambiguous dose of modernity, and his position sounds a little like that of the many moderates, who were just then trying to steer a path between the poles of authority and freedom. Even so, we should probably not make too much of this remark, since it is not entirely clear whether Evelyn was willing to accept Fréart's effort to clarify the ancient orders as a (somewhat paradoxical) example of progress, or whether he believed that architecture itself could be perfected in the future.

The *Parallel* won an audience, including the Royal Family, and after a time, Evelyn determined to bring out a new edition. In the meantime, however, architectural theory was stirred up in France by a new outbreak between the ancients and the moderns and a spasm of further publications, which Evelyn examined closely. In particular, he looked on with interest at the contest that developed over the work of Charles Perrault's older brother, Claude. The ambivalence of "classical modernism" could hardly be expressed better than in the career of this man who was responsible at the same time for an excellent translation of Vitruvius and the great colonnade of the Louvre and also for several books in which he challenged the classical precepts of Fréart and his followers. Claude Perrault loved a paradox and his colleagues found him inscrutable. Charles Perrault felt it necessary to defend his memory and popularize his theories. Here, then, was some of the background to the *querelle* that Wotton seems to have missed, but which Evelyn could easily have supplied.

3

Claude Perrault is another example of the seventeenth-century virtuoso who set no boundaries to his competence. He began life as a physician and for a time taught medicine at the University of Paris. He was an active member of the new Academy of Sciences where he offered many papers on various subjects, all the time reaffirming the modern battle-cry against that "blind veneration" for antiquity that seemed the ever-present obstacle to progress. In the 1680s, he published four volumes of *Essaies de physique* in which he recorded many new discoveries in natural science and several novel theories. It was here that he set out his views on the superiority of modern music which helped to fuel the battle over opera. He was also a fertile inventor with a keen interest in machinery of every kind. In 1688, according to his brother, Charles, he attempted to dissect a camel and died of blood poisoning, a martyr (rather like Francis Bacon) to the new science. About 1667, he turned abruptly to architecture and won immediate fame for his contributions to both theory and practice.

It seems to have been Charles who inveigled him into his new role. The Perraults were a formidable family with a long record of government service, and Charles eventually became secretary to the great minister, Colbert.[21] If

Louis XIV, even more than Charles II (who always kept his sense of humor), aspired to the role of the new Augustus, it was Colbert who tried to play the role of Maecenas. In 1664, he was awarded the title of Superintendent of the King's Buildings and was put in charge of cultural affairs. Colbert hoped to galvanize the arts in the service of His Royal Majesty, to subsidize and to supervise their activities. For that purpose, he organized a small council, a *petite académie*, with Perrault as secretary. He then set about restoring the older academies of literature and painting and sculpture, and initiated new ones for science (1666), architecture (1671) and music (1672). In 1667, Charles Perrault became *Contrôleur des Bâtiments de sa Majesté*, the title which so impressed Wotton, but his chief qualifications seem to have been legal and literary. He held the job until the death of Colbert in 1683.[22]

It was Charles who got Claude on to the committee to supervise the building of the Louvre. What transpired on that occasion will probably always be a matter of controversy, but the result was the famous colonnade which Charles claimed for his brother, although Boileau and others later denied him the credit.[23] Whatever his precise contribution, he was intimately involved in the work and several others in the years from 1667 to 1670 that were indisputably his own, like the new observatory of the Academy of Sciences. After that, he withdrew from practice almost as suddenly as he had entered on it in order to concentrate upon theory and his beloved sciences. There was some doubt as to whether he had ever really put his heart into his career as a builder.

Already in his translation of Vitruvius (1673), he had offered some unorthodox notions as commentary.[24] The work was read and discussed in the Academy and there were some objections, particularly from the director, François Blondel. The result was a new work by Perrault, the *Ordonnance des cinq-espèces de colonnes selon la méthode des anciens* (1683), as well as a second edition of Vitruvius (1683). Perrault, it seems, was prepared to express his own *nouveauté* both in the façade to the Louvre and in his views about Vitruvius and the ancients.

The *Ordonnance*, like Fréart's treatise, was meant as a practical manual on the orders and was soon translated into English.[25] It is the polemical preface which focused the quarrel and furnished Charles Perrault and William Wotton with their modern arguments.[26] There Claude Perrault reiterates the views he had first set out in his *Essaies*, and specifically argues the analogy between the beauties of proportion in music and architecture, both of which were rooted in nature but needed (in different ways) to be discovered and improved.[27] Even the dedication to Colbert points out the inadequacy and obscurity of Vitruvius and the need to clarify the resulting confusion about the orders – the need, in short, for refinement and novelty. " 'Tis hardly to be imagin'd what a superstitious Reverence Architects have for the Works which we call Antique." Yet after all, Perrault continues, this "excessive respect for the Antique" was common to all the arts and sciences and was only reinforced by the "natural Docility of Men of Letters." Since the arts were almost always treated by literary men, it was no wonder that this "spirit of submission" was extended to architecture, and authority preferred above reason.[28] Yet it was obvious that no two buildings in antiquity and no two modern writers, in fact, agreed, even about so fundamental a matter as the proportion of the orders. Here, certainly, was room for clarification and progress, but only if liberty, which was necessary to the progress of all the sciences, would be allowed.

Yet Perrault's liberty was not *from* the rules but rather *within* them; like most Frenchmen in the age of Louis XIV, he accepted their value and their inevitability. Moreover, it is a very narrow liberty indeed for which he pleads. Perrault declared his own genuine respect for the works of ancient architecture; he wanted leave only "to change some Proportions which differ from the Antique in things only inconsiderable and of small Importance."[29] Perhaps more to the point, he disclaimed any desire to alter the past, but wanted only to discover and restore it to its pristine perfection by correcting the ancient and modern works, none of which – when one thought about it – were the originals, but were themselves only copies. (This, incidentally, explained the differences among them.) It was, therefore, in architecture as it was in literature: "to restore the true Sense of the Text, if I may so speak, it is necessary to search these different Copies." "My Aim is only to extend this Change a little further than has been hitherto done . . . [to give] the Rules of Architecture, that Preciseness, Perfection, and Easiness to remember, that they wanted."[30] Perrault intended, thus, to provide a kind of philological restoration of an imagined original, using the evidence of Vitruvius, but interpreting and amending it when necessary. (This "itch" to amend the originals was, of course, one of the most serious charges laid against the philologists; Richard Bentley typically raised a storm when he "corrected" the standard text of Horace in nearly a thousand places!)[31] As usual, it is not so easy in these matters to separate the modern, Perrault, from the ancient, Blondel, who also approved the rules but rejected servile imitation, found occasional faults in the ancient works, and accepted the basic grammar of classical architecture with its emphasis on the proportions of the orders.[32] To the extent that there was a difference, it was more a matter of degree than kind; but it was Perrault's cheerful recognition of the need to correct and emend the ancient texts that gave him (like Bentley) his reputation for modernity. When Perrault offered himself as a new (improved) Vitruvius to the Augustus of Louis XIV – as the little vignette in his text and a sonnet prefixed makes clear – that was audacious enough in this context to cause a brawl.[33]

It is his view of history, however, that separates Perrault most obviously from many of his contemporaries. One day, a Hebrew scholar named Louis Compiègne de Veil, approached Perrault with a problem he had encountered in his translation of Maimonides.[34] In the eighth book of the *Mishna Torah*, Veil found a discussion of the ancient Jewish Temple; in looking further into the matter, he found a great disagreement among modern scholars about its form. Every biblical commentator, it appeared, had his own notion of what it looked like. Among the many attempts to visualize the Temple, the most famous was

7. The Temple of Solomon by Villalpando

that of the Spaniard, Villalpando, who had imagined it, in his commentary on the prophet, Ezechiel, to be a perfect work of classical architecture, replete with columns, pilasters, entablatures, and the rest.[35] Models were more than once constructed according to his specifications and displayed in the seventeenth century, and Fréart published Villalpando's Solomonic order in the *Parallèle* (Plate 7).[36] John Locke was among the many who took an interest.[37] But others, moderns if you will, had criticized the reconstruction as anachronistic, believing that the evidence, properly examined, indicated a temple that was smaller and more primitive. In brief, the question was whether the first architecture (like the first philosophy) was best because it was divinely inspired, and the Greeks and Romans merely inheritors or plagiarists of the classical tradition, or whether the Greeks had developed the art to perfection from a simple and primitive beginning. As late as 1741, the "ancient" idea, so congenial to William Temple, was still being defended vigorously in England by the architect of Bath, John Wood the elder, in his work on *The Origin of Building: Or the Plagiarism of the Heathens Detected*.

Inevitably, Perrault took the "modern" side in the argument. He found it ridiculous "that God had taught the architects of the Temple of Solomon all these proportions by special inspiration and that the Greeks, who are generally believed to have invented them, had in fact studied with these architects."[38] His own reconstruction, which appeared in 1678 with three plates, shows a building almost entirely devoid of classical features. Anyone who expected either size or splendor in that ancient monument must surely have been disappointed.

In fact, no one seems to have paid much attention, though Isaac Newton, who had his own classicizing view of architectural history, apparently knew Perrault's design. In 1725 William Stukeley reported a conversation he had recently had with Newton about the Temple.

> I found Sir Isaac had made some drawings of it, and had consider'd the thing. Indeed he had study'd every thing. We did not enter into any particular detail, but we both agreed in this, that the architecture was not like any of the designs or descriptions yet publick. No authors have an adequate notion of antient and original architecture. Sir Isaac rightly judg'd it was older than any other of the great temples mention'd in history; and was indeed the original model which they followed . . . But he thought the Greeks according to their usual ingenuity improv'd architecture into a higher delicacy, as they did sculpture and other arts. I confirmed his sentiments by adding that I could demonstrate (as I apprehended) that the architecture of Solomon's temple was what we now call Doric. Then, says he, the Greeks advanced it into the Ionic and the Corinthian, as the Latins into the Composite.[39]

Perrault's reconstruction was more radical, for it has been pointed out that even those who objected to Villalpando and eliminated his Corinthian columns (including Christopher Wren, as we shall see) generally continued to attribute at least some classical features to the Temple.

Charles Perrault was content to pass over his brother's view of the Temple in order to concentrate on his chief work. In the *Parallèle*, he repeats Perrault's main contention that there were two kinds of beauty, one eternal and the other customary. But it is clear that neither of the brothers was prepared to endorse a relativist view, even for the beauty created by convention. Perrault's actual buildings, including the problematical colonnade of the Louvre, were, after all, classical imitations, even if Perrault was prepared to innovate modestly within the ancient tradition.[40] And although François Blondel disapproved of the coupled columns there, which he insisted had no classical precedent, the Academy itself pronounced in 1674 that the ancients had indeed used them so upon occasion. Christopher Wren (who owned a copy of Perrault's Vitruvius) was not the only one to employ them.[41] In due time, the building was hailed as orthodox and one of the greatest in all architecture.[42]

4

When, therefore, Evelyn determined about 1695 to revise his translation of Fréart and bring it up to date, much had happened in France and England, including the first discharge in the Battle of the Books. Nevertheless, he continued to think that the *Parallel* was still "the most useful and perfect work of its kind."[43] It is worth noticing that even as he worked over it, he remained in close contact with his two young friends, Wotton and Bentley, both of whom agreed to assist him on other modernist projects. However, with respect to architecture and the arts, Evelyn wavered; to Bentley, he wrote early in 1697 that he intended to make some large additions to his own "Account of Architecture" and to dedicate it to his old friend, Sir Christopher Wren.[44]

Among the additions is a long note at the beginning of his commentary where Evelyn recounts the history of architecture from its primitive beginnings to its pinnacle in ancient Greece and Rome, through its decline and fall in the Middle Ages, to its restoration in modern times.[45] Of course, this was no more than the ordinary view of Renaissance humanism, the view that had been adapted long ago from literature to the arts and that Dryden had typically endorsed for poetry and painting. Here in the usual way, Evelyn is concerned to contrast classical architecture, which he finds "most entirely answering all those perfections requir'd in a faultless and accomplish'd building," with that "fantastical and licencious manner of building, which we have since call'd Modern (or Gothic rather), of heavy, dark, melancholy, and monkish piles, without any just proportion, use or beauty, compar'd with the truly Ancient."[46] He is willing to except only the classical moderns from his censure: those who had restored the ancient manner, like Bramante, Raphael, Michelangelo, Palladio and Bernini, "the heroes and masters of our *Parallel*."[47] It was the good work of recent times to have brought culture back to its "pristine splendor and magnificence" – not just architecture, but sculpture, painting and letters. Closer at hand, Evelyn was willing to consign all the English cathedrals of the Middle Ages – Winchester, Salisbury, Westminster Abbey, and the rest – to that same dark night of ignorance and superstition, and contrast them with those few worthy modern buildings of Inigo Jones and Chrisopher Wren, designed "after the ancient manner."[48] It is left unclear whether the moderns, in their pursuit of antiquity, had actually equaled or might yet excel their predecessors.

Another addition to the commentary takes especial notice of the French quarrel. In it, Evelyn examines Fréart's reluctant description of the fifth, or composite order, the youngest of the classical orders and a late invention of the Romans. The French, he finds (including Claude Perrault), "of all the Nations under Heaven, being the fondest of their own Inventions," have embellished it and turned it into a new "Gallic" order. They were thus willing to alter what for two thousand years no one had been so bold to attempt. One would think, Evelyn exclaims, "we might be content with what the Romans have already set for a pattern," as indeed Fréart had taught, "who, contrary to the genius of his country-men, had the greatest aversion to the least innovation in his profession."[49] As for the Louvre, in another note, Evelyn weighs the arguments of Perrault and Blondel, for and against. He was obviously taken by Perrault's plea for a modest freedom from classical constraint, "that one is not so precisely oblig'd to rules and examples, but that in some cases they may be departed from for the better, since it were to put a stop to the improvements of all arts and inventions whatsoever, none of which were consummately perfect at the first." (Here speaks the loyal member of the Royal Society.)[50] But if changes of proportion were sometimes to be allowed, he was sure, as Perrault had been

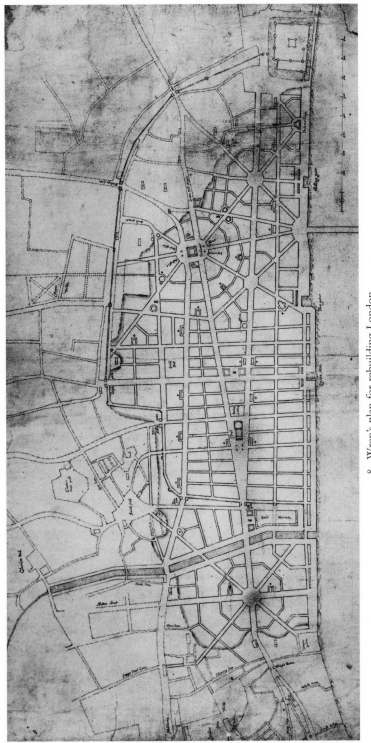

8. Wren's plan for rebuilding London

also, that they should be employed only, "very sparingly and with great consideration." In any case, Evelyn agreed with the judgment of the Academy that the ancients had used double columns upon occasion, thus lending the authority of classical example to the Louvre colonnade.

In short, Evelyn's view in 1697 was not very different from his view forty years earlier, when first ravished by classical architecture, he had returned to England to try to win back culture from the barbarians and restore, by imitation, the achievement of ancient Greece and Rome. If anything, his classicism, like that of the rest of his generation, may have hardened. Already across the Channel, his contemporary, La Bruyère, was writing with satisfaction,

> We should do by Stile as we have done by Architecture, banish entirely the Gothic order, which the Barbarians introduc'd in their Palaces and temples, and recall the Dorick, Ionick and Corinthian. What was only seen in the Ruines of ancient Rome and old Greece shines in our Portico's and Peristils, and is become Modern.[51]

5

Among the many tracts on architecture that caught Evelyn's eye in these busy years was a truly remarkable work by a young man named Antoine Desgodets. We have seen that Fréart's treatise and Perrault's books were all meant, like so much of the theory in this period, to clarify the teaching of Vitruvius, by recovering his meaning as far as possible. The problem was that while there was a general agreement to restore and use classical doctrine, the notorious vagueness and obscurity of Vitruvius's text caused great differences and uncertainties among the commentators. Since the problem had analogies in all classical literature, it was bound to occur to someone that there was a possible way to resolve the difficulties.

It was the Renaissance philologists and antiquaries who had first thought of collecting information by direct observation of the monuments, so that they could gain a better understanding of the life of the ancient world and a clearer notion of the meaning of the ancient texts. Were there not still standing in Rome the ruins of many of the ancient buildings themselves, the best possible evidence for the theories of Vitruvius? Ever since the Renaissance, scholars had been drawn to the monumental remains, identifying and describing them, locating the places and mapping the city, and reconstructing the sites of famous events and the haunts of famous men. And ever since the Renaissance, artists had followed, studying and imitating what could be seen. An early instance is Palladio's *Antichità di Roma* (1553), a work that remained popular enough to be translated into Latin and published at Oxford in 1709 under the auspices of the Dean of Christ Church, Henry Aldrich. Christopher Wren remembered that "those who first labored in the Restoration of Architecture about three centuries ago, studied principally what they found in Rome, above-ground," and he recalled himself looking at a sketchbook of Pirro Ligorio in the collection of Inigo Jones.[52] In time, the need for precision grew more insistent, encouraged no doubt both by a new interest in measurement (and new tools with which to measure) and by a more pedantic concern for exact imitation. When the English mathematician and antiquary, John Greaves, went off to Rome and Egypt, it was to bring back the first careful measurements of obelisks and pyramids that had ever been made. When Inigo Jones visited Rome in 1614, he took his copy of Palladio right to the buildings themselves to compare the proportions.[53] In 1674, Colbert sent Desgodets to Rome to try to settle matters. After some preliminary misadventures, the young man quickly established himself and set to work.

In just sixteen months' time, Desgodets was able to make a meticulous canvas of all the Roman monuments, in Evelyn's words, "a more exact and nice Research among the Antiquities of that City, Remeasuring and Recalling to a new Calculation what had been done before so often." His achievement was to establish a new standard of accuracy, "a Precision so Delicate (and even to a Hairs-breadth as they say, so scrupulously Nice) as reaches not only to single Feet, Inches and Lines alone, but even to the minutest Part of a Line."[54] He brought his drawings back to Paris and had some of them engraved with specifications as *Les Édifices antiques de Rome* (1682). Eventually, this work too found an English translation.[55]

In short, what Desgodets had done was to improve vastly on his predecessors by applying something of the spirit and technique of the new science and the new philology to the ancient monuments. Once again, he was employing the familiar *explication du texte* of the humanists and with the same hope of determining the exact rules for imitation. But as so often in these matters, the result was unexpected. Desgodets's measurements showed beyond doubt that the ancients themselves, and all their modern commentators, had varied seriously in their accounts of the proportions. It is no wonder then that when the Academy received these results, it immediately shelved the report and refused to discuss it for many years![56]

In fact, the response was very like William Temple and Jonathan Swift in the Battle of the Books refusing to read the philologists, and for much the same reason. The director of the Academy, Blondel, who was especially embarrassed, defended himself by ridiculing the pedantic attention to detail that marked the whole enterprise and that even poor Desgodets had feared might put off some of his readers. What did such piddling accuracy matter when it was the spirit that counted, not the letter? Blondel's "Platonic" perspective allowed him to sidestep the inconvenient facts by claiming that it was the apparent proportions that meant everything in a work of art rather than the actual ones. This gave the architect some freedom to manipulate the visible proportions accordingly. Blondel was dismayed "to see so many persons interested in architecture take such pains to check with over-scrupulous accuracy the measurements of antique buildings, down to recording the imperceptible parts of a module."[57] For the practical man who wanted to erect buildings, Desgodets appeared a useless pedant, just as to Temple and Swift (those practical men of the world who wanted to write their way into public life) Dr Bentley looked no more than a clown. Evelyn, as always, was caught somewhere between the ancients and the moderns, and wavered. The "minutiae and animadversions" of Desgodets, "So nicely insisted on (tho' I do not say there are none more material) but whether worth his travelling so far and Suffering so much to bring Home . . . I leave to others." In any case the cost of reproducing them made it impossible to add to his revised version of Fréart, "nor was it thought of so great Importance considering . . . the Modest Liberty, which 'tis known has now and then been taken, even by the Antients themselves."[58]

For Claude Perrault, the appearance of Desgodets's work must have seemed providential, and he leaned on it heavily for his *Ordonnance* and in his battle with Blondel.[59] He had started off on the premise that Vitruvius needed explication and that none of the commentators was sufficient, and here was all the proof that was needed. As usual, it was the moderns who benefited most from the exercise of scholarship. Desgodets had gone to Rome to restore the authority of Vitruvius and returned "paradoxically" to undermine it by showing the disparity between Vitruvian doctrine and the reality of the ancient buildings. Inevitably, it was Perrault who understood that better than Blondel and was willing to accept the implications; but it is worth repeating that he was still far from ready to draw any relativist conclusions or even to advocate anything more than that "modest liberty" that Evelyn also prescribed. For the time being, the injunctions to follow the rules of Vitruvius and the models of classical Rome remained almost completely intact, with only a modest latitude of invention to separate the moderns from the ancients.

6

John Evelyn first met Christopher Wren on July 10, 1654, at Wadham College, Oxford, and duly noted the occasion in his diary.[60] It was during the Interregnum, but Wadham was full of excitement under its Master, John Wilkins, and there Evelyn met many of the future members of the Royal Society. Wilkins showed him some of his collections, mathematical and magical curiosities, shadows, dials and perspectives, "most of them his owne and that prodigious young Scholar, Mr Chr. Wren." Young Wren promptly presented Evelyn with a red-dyed piece of marble, "as beautiful as it had been naturall."[61] It was the beginning of a lifelong friendship, cemented in later years by frequent collaboration and sealed by intellectual and familial ties.

Despite immense energy and ninety-one busy years, Wren is not easy to get at. Unlike Evelyn, he kept no diary, wrote very little, and published nothing at all. Still his career in natural science and in architecture is well enough documented to fix him in our story, thanks to his son who drew up the family accounts in the *Parentalia*, and the Wren Society which has since printed most of the existing documents and drawings.[62] It is clear from this that Wren was a modern, like Evelyn, with respect to the new mathematical and experimental philosophy, although equivocal again with regard to literature and the arts. Like

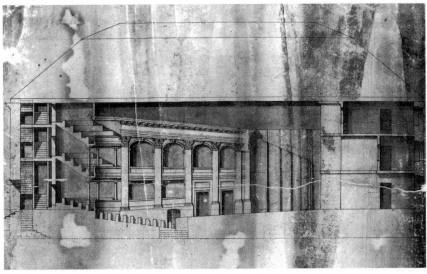

9. Wren's design for Drury Lane, 1674

Dryden he was a clergyman's son; a Westminster boy who had learned the classics under Busby; a Fellow of the Royal Society; and he was almost exactly the
same age, but they seem to have had no contact.[63] It is true that, when
Killigrew's theater at Drury Lane burned down in 1672, Wren was employed
to design the new one, a "plain built house," that was meant to compete with
Dorset Garden (which has also been attributed to Wren), and Dryden prepared
his reworked *Paradise Lost* for it as *The State of Innocence*.[64] (His plan for the
theater at Drury Lane with its amphitheatrical seating (Plate 9) has been
described as "an attempt to combine in a Restoration playhouse some of the
essential features of an antique theatre.")[65] But the opera remained unperformed
and there is no evidence that the two men ever met, though they probably
knew a good deal about each other. In any case, Wren the architect, like the
playwright Dryden, found himself caught uneasily between a sophisticated
ancienneté borrowed from France and an unsophisticated audience whose sensibilities were still not very classical. And, like the poet, we shall see, he was
continuously forced into compromise.

Wren's activity in science is too rich and various to chronicle here.[66] He
seems to have been a genuinely modest man who liked to collaborate with
others and rarely took credit for his ideas and inventions. Robert Willis used
his drawings for a remarkable atlas of the brain; Newton acknowledged his
contributions to the laws of motion; Robert Hooke called him the Archimedes
of his time.[67] Thomas Sprat set aside a whole section of his *History of the
Royal Society* to record his many under-appreciated contributions.[68] Among
some early lists of "new theories, inventions, experiments and mechanick
improvements," that the youthful Wren drew up, there is one alone that has

some fifty-three entries, including some "New Designs tending to Strength, Convenience, and Beauty in Building," which suggests that architecture was already on his mind.[69] Still another list of remarkable contrivances (drawn up in 1661 for the entertainment of the King) also offers some "Designs in Architecture."[70] His son says that he taught himself how to draw, and also how to engrave, etch, and turn.[71] Among his many inventions was "a very curious and exceeding speedy way of Etching," a peculiar instrument to draft perspectives, and a way of drawing pictures by microscopical glasses.[72]

When, still very young, Wren was appointed Professor of Astronomy at Gresham College (1657), he gave an inaugural lecture in praise of modernity. He used the opportunity to applaud the new astronomy of Copernicus and Kepler as "that first happy Appearance of Liberty, oppress'd by the Tyranny of the Greek and Roman Monarchies."[73] He was pleased to celebrate the telescope and the microscope and the particular English contributions to the new science: the discovery of logarithms, the circulation of the blood, and above all, magnetism. Nor did he forget the usefulness of the new astronomy to history and chronology; we shall not be surprised to find him later in the company of Newton and Bentley. In all these things, he was sure, "the Mathematical Wits of this Age have excell'd the Ancients." In a letter to the Royal Society, a few years later, he adopted the characteristic Baconian idea of progress through experimental science. For the moment, he thought it was only necessary to be patient and "to plant crab-stocks for Posterity to graft on."[74] For Wren, as for Hooke and Boyle and Evelyn, advancement in these matters was only a question of time.

Wren was especially close to Robert Hooke, whose diary records many conversations about science and a few about architecture.[75] In these years, Hooke was secretary of the Royal Society and its quasi-official experimenter; Wren eventually hired him to assist him with his architecture. At the Rainbow, Wren "shewed his projection of mapps supposing the eye at the distance of the Radius which reduced the Parallels to equal distances." At the Crown, they spoke about Kepler and medicine. "Sir Christopher told of killing the wormes with burnt oyl and of curing his lady of a thrush by hanging a bag of bog lice about her neck." At Wren's, until five, they "Talked of Scotoscopes, Cylinders, Chariotts, Shipps."[76] Once, they imagined Porsenna's tomb, which Wren had tried to construct, and discussed Persepolis.[77] Apparently, it was preparation for a mausoleum to commemorate Charles I. The mausoleum was never built, although the plans survive. "The Form of the Structure," according to the young Wren, "is a Rotunda, with a beautiful Dome and Lantern; a circular Colonnade, without, of the Corinthean Order, resembling the Temple of Vesta."[78]

That Wren should have intended a classical imitation at that time was no longer surprising. It was another matter, when many years earlier, he had first unveiled his plans for St Paul's. As Evelyn and Pratt had noticed, England had then almost no classical architecture to offer, apart from a few buildings by Inigo Jones. Domes and colonnades were an exotic import in a thoroughly Gothic landscape. The very language of classical architecture was

late in arriving.[79] Apart from Jones's pupils and those, besides Evelyn, who had
lived or traveled abroad, there were few who were prepared to accept the innovation, particularly for an English church. And yet the ground had been well
laid in the classical education which then prepared every young man for life
and which inevitably whetted the appetite for classical things along with classical words. Wren, like the Christ Church defenders of antiquity in the Battle
of the Books, had received the best education of his time.

His enthusiasm for the classics was genuine. At home, under his father and
a famous uncle, and at school, Wren had learned how to read, admire and
imitate the ancient authors.[80] Once, he translated a poem by Horace and sent
it to his good friend, the able classicist (and defender of both the English stage
and the Royal Society), Thomas Sprat. This sparked an exchange in which both
agreed that the Roman poet was "one of the most accomplish'd Men of that
incomparable Age."[81] When Sprat came to write the history of the Society,
he paid Wren a special compliment as the ornament of his country and
the hope of the future. Among other things, he recalled how they had "sometimes debated together, what place and time of all the past, we would have
chosen to live in, if our fates had bin at our disposal." Not surprisingly, both
agreed "that Rome in the Reign of Augustus, was to be preferr'd before all
others."[82]

Of course, everyone knew that Augustus had found Rome made of brick
and left it marble. As Wren and Evelyn, and the King himself, looked out on
the timbered London of their day, they undoubtedly made invidious comparisons and nourished something of the same hope. Wren believed with most
of his contemporaries that architecture, like literature, had a general political
use. (In time he became a member of Parliament and a commissioner for several
prominent institutions.)[83] "Publick Buildings," he wrote in old age, "being the
Ornament of a Country, it establishes a Nation, draws People and Commerce,
makes the People love their native Country, which Passion is the Original of
all great Actions in a Common-Wealth." The Romans, above all, had understood as much, and the modern Italians.[84] For Wren and Evelyn, London looked
like a congestion of misshapen and extravagant houses, though they knew only
too well that there were others who seemed to prefer it that way.[85]

Just what Augustan Rome had looked like, however, was not so easily
apparent to an insular Englishman who had only the classical authors to go
by. There was, it is true, a growing literature on the subject supplied by antiquaries and architects, but the best remedy for ignorance and the surest impulse
to classical imitation was (as Evelyn never tired of counseling) continental travel
and direct inspection.[86] So far, it had been difficult for Englishmen to journey
abroad safely except in exile; now, at the Restoration there began that characteristic English enterprise that was meant to complete the education of a
gentlemen. It was the beginning of the grand tour.

Meanwhile, the sketches of Evelyn and Wren both imagine London transformed into a centrally planned Renaissance city with wide streets and open
piazzas and a privileged place for St Paul's Cathedral. "The City would then

have been built in such a Manner," Nicholas Hawksmoor recalled later, "as to
have stood foremost at this Day amongst the Wonders of the World, for Extent,
Symmetry, Commodiousness, and Duration, at much less Expence than the
Citizens have been at, in the Rebuilding it in the confused, irregular, and per-
ishable Manner 'tis now left in."[87] The failure to implement Wren's scheme was
still being regretted long afterwards.[88]

7

When Charles II made Wren his deputy surveyor, it was probably out of admiration for his practical and scientific abilities; there was as yet only the barest
recognition of architecture as a profession.[89] Of course, Charles had spent a lot
of time in France and was thoroughly up to date in aesthetic matters. (Once
Evelyn called upon the King, who immediately asked for a crayon and paper,
"and then laying it on the window stoole, he with his owne hands, designed
to me the plot for the future building of White-hall.")[90] Though Wren had not
yet been abroad, he began to build anyway in the classical manner at Pembroke
College, Cambridge, and the more ambitious Sheldonian Theatre, Oxford (Plate
10). His equipment consisted of the best books that he could find on the subject
and his own mechanical and mathematical ingenuity. For the Sheldonian,
he seems to have taken Sebastian Serlio's plan for the ancient Theater of
Marcellus as his model.[91] But the Romans had no need to roof their theaters,
so Wren set himself the awkward mechanical problem of constructing an
exceedingly large ceiling supported only by side walls. For this, he developed
an idea that had been suggested by his friend, John Wallis, a "geometrical flat-
floor," which, when it was erected, astonished his contemporaries.[92] The whole
exercise had no English precedent and the building was described by
one witness as the contrivance of "an English Vitruvius."[93] For Sir John
Summerson recently, it is "like a Latin poem on a modern theme composed
by a careful but not absolutely fluent scholar."[94] When it was finally completed
and opened in 1669, it had cost the Archbishop of Canterbury a great sum.

Wren had attempted a classical theater in a modern setting, an adaptation of
an ancient model to contemporary circumstances. And the interior decoration
was contrived to further the effect. This was just the time when all over Italy
great illusionist ceilings, with classical mythological and historical stories, were
being designed for public buildings and private palaces, but the idea was relatively new in England; perhaps only Rubens's paintings for the Banqueting
House could serve as a model. Robert Streater had recently been appointed
serjeant-painter to the King and may have visited Italy during the Commonwealth period.[95] By 1658 he had already won a reputation for painting, etching,
architecture and perspective, "not a line but is true to the Rules of Art and
Symmetry," though it is hard to know how well it was deserved, since most of
his work has perished.[96] In any case, Streater was engaged to paint an elaborate mural for the Sheldonian ceiling, which was deliberately intended to evoke
the ancient Temple (Plate 11). It was a complex allegory set against an open

10. The Sheldonian Theatre engraved by Loggan

sky, and curtained around with a satin cloth held open by putti. Here is how it was explained by a contemporary:

> In imitation of the Theaters of the ancient Greeks and Romans, which were too large to be covered with lead or tile, so this by the Painting of the flat roof within, is represented open: and as they stretched a cordage from Pilaster to Pilaster, upon which they strained a covering of cloth, to protect the people from the injuries of the weather, so here is a cord-molding guilded that reaches cross and cross the house both in length and bredth, which supporteth a great reddish Drapery, suppos'd to have covered the roof but now furl'd up by the Genii round about the House toward the walls, which discovereth the open Air.[97]

The subject of the allegory was "Truth Descending upon the Arts and Sciences," each of which is portrayed by an appropriate figure, while the enemies of truth, Envy, Rapine and Ignorance, are shown tumbling down, "thrown head-long from the Clouds." Pepys went to see the canvases before they were installed and found Wren and a number of virtuosi admiring them and comparing them favorably with Rubens. He was not so certain, though he thought they were very noble. Later James II had reservations also, but a contemporary, Robert Whitehead, went so far as to place them above Michelangelo.[98] And when Streater finally got a biography at the end of the

11. Ceiling of the Sheldonian by Streater, 1669

century, he was praised above all other English painters in his time, for possessing "the highest Italian Gusto, both for Pencilling, Judgment and Composition" – which the author attributed to his wide reading in history and his fine collection of books and prints.[99] Perhaps we should rest content with the modern judgment; whatever its faults, the Sheldonian ceiling was surely "the most ambitious baroque composition that had yet been attempted by an Englishman."[100]

Evelyn (who had early been shown the model by Wren and offered some advice) was there to applaud the opening. It was, he was glad to say, "a fabrique comparable to any of this kind in former ages, and doubtlesse exceeding any of the present."[101] Evelyn too remained a great admirer of Streater, who went on (among other things) to paint the scenery for Dryden's *Conquest of Granada*.[102] The only thing perhaps to mar the Sheldonian ceremony and spoil the occasion was a speech by the university orator, Dr South, an unreconstructed "ancient" and another Busby scholar, who liked the building but went out of his way to disparage the new natural philosophy and its proponents in the Royal Society. Evelyn was not alone in finding this deeply regrettable.[103] It is true that for the modern critic, the building shows a little uncertainty in its classical intentions – not altogether surprising in the work of a beginner.[104] Nevertheless, there was one point at least on which everyone then was prepared to agree: England had discovered a new architect of genius and a new building style that was striking in its medieval Oxford setting and full of possibilities for the future.

CHAPTER 11

Restoration Architecture between the Ancients and the Moderns

I

Even before the Sheldonian was completed, Wren had seen the need to improve his "Latin scholarship" with a trip abroad. Evelyn showered advice on him and gave him a fresh copy of Fréart.[1] In the meanwhile he prepared himself also with letters of introduction to many savants and architects. Wren hoped especially to meet the two greatest living architects, Mansart and Bernini. He was soon able to report his progress.[2] "I have busied myself in surveying the most esteem'd Fabricks of Paris and the Country round." He was spellbound by the Louvre where no fewer than a thousand workmen were employed in the building, "a School of Architecture, the best probably, at this Day in Europe." He swiftly sought out Bernini, fresh from Italy, to see his designs for the Louvre. Unfortunately, "the reserv'd Italian gave me but a few Minutes View." Wren admits that he would have given his skin for the designs but that he had time only to copy them in his fancy and memory. Nevertheless, he thought he could, "by Discourse, and a Crayon, give you a tolerable Account of it." (In fact, Bernini's designs for the Louvre were not used, no doubt in part because of the opposition of the Perraults.)[3] Meanwhile, there was much else to see: the College of the Four Nations by Le Vau, the royal palaces at Fontainebleau and Versailles, the country houses, learned societies, collections of paintings, coins and medals, and so on. Wren did not forget to call on the scientists, but it was the arts that captivated him. "Painting and Sculpture," he adds in a postscript, quoting Fréart, "are the politest and noblest of the Arts . . . And what can be more helpful, or more pleasing to a Philosophical Traveller, an Architect and every ingenious Mechanician? All of which must be lame without it." Wren sent along a list of the best architects and artists in Paris; he hoped on his return to write some "Observations on the present State of Architecture, Arts and Manufactures in France." Apparently, he never did.

The visit lasted about six months. It would be nice to know whether Wren ever met Claude Perrault, or what he thought of some of the other new domes that he could now see for the first time, at the Sorbonne, for example, and the Val de Grâce. Once you have seen the latter, Evelyn wrote to Pepys, "your Eyes

12. Christopher Wren by Verrio, Kneller and Thornhill, 1669

will never desire to behold a more accomplished Piece. There it is you will see the utmost effects of good Architecture and Painting, and heartily wish such another stood where St Pauls was, the boast of our Metropolis."[4] When, however, one of Wren's companions asked him what the greatest building in Paris was, he replied, the Quay, "which he demonstrated to me, to be built with such expense and such a great quantity of materials, that it exceeded all manner of ways the buildings of the greatest pyramids of Egypt."[5] The moderns in France seem to have had as much to offer as the ancients to the inquisitive Englishman. Apparently, Wren saw no need to go on to Rome. The journey was expensive; he had seen enough for his purposes.[6]

2

Wren had crossed the Channel with a commitment to classical architecture; he returned with a redoubled sense of *ancienneté*. Two kinds of evidence make this commitment unmistakable: there are the buildings on which he worked, and there are the occasional comments and half-completed theories that appear in the *Parentalia*.[7] It would be impossible here to recount the long and complicated story of how Wren designed and built St Paul's, though a hasty recapitulation of that familiar tale may be helpful. Wren was called in as early as 1663 to survey the old church which was suffering from disrepair, and he offered some comments even before the great fire made the work more urgent. For the rest of his life, the design and construction of the cathedral remained a central preoccupation, as scheme after scheme was abandoned or modified to meet the changing circumstances.[8] What is clear is that from the first, Wren cleaved closely to an essentially classical line, to a building that was intended to depart radically from the original Gothic church and that would employ the whole new vocabulary of the ancients, from columns to dome. Already in his plan for rebuilding London after the fire, he had proposed a domed building, something like the Pantheon, which had no precedent in England and hardly any in all of Europe.[9] Wren understood the difficulty of promoting so radical an enterprise. As he wrote to the Dean, Sancroft, just before the fire in 1666, "*Carmina proverbia* soundes better to most Eares than Horace, and wee have fewer Judges of a Latine style in building than in writing, but I hope you will goe to the charges of trew latine."[10]

Wren's first scheme was intended to preserve a good part of the old fabric, but to introduce a large dome – "A spacious Dome or rotunda with a Cupola or Hemispherical Roof" – between the Gothic choir and the Norman nave, and to replace the old tower. This he proposed as a "middle way" between a too audacious and too expensive new building and merely patching up the old. Even so, he thought it best not to tear down the tower at once, but to build a scaffolding around it, so as not to disappoint conservative viewers until the replacement was actually visible.[11] The new dome, like Inigo Jones's portico, was meant to be an "absolute piece of itself," and could be completed quickly and inexpensively. It would make an appropriate monument for a city that deserved renown. Wren reminded the commissioners that he had been abroad and understood how the work could be done. The cathedral roof also needed mending, but that too could easily be accomplished in the "good Roman manner," rather than in the "Gothic rudeness of the old Design." "This may be safely affirmed not only by an Architect, taking his measures from the Precepts and Examples of the Antients, but by a Geometrician."[12] It was typical of the new age that reason and *ancienneté* should be brought into convenient harmony.

Still, the commissioners had to be persuaded; even the more progressive were staggered by the size of the project. "If all incongruities must be reformed,"

Roger Pratt exclaimed, "what pillars, and arches, to be pulled down! what new ones to be erected! what Scaffolds and Engines!"[13] On August 27, 1666, Evelyn went to visit the cathedral with Wren and the commissioners, and joined in the argument about the roof and dome. With his help, Wren carried the day and it was agreed that the steeple must go, not only out of necessity, but because "the shape of what stood was very meane." "We had in mind," Evelyn wrote, "to build it with a noble Cupola, a form of church-building, not as yet known in England, but of a wonderfull Grace."[14] A month later the fire toppled what was left of the steeple, and much else, including Jones's portico. Repair was no longer a plausible option.

Wren was free now to plan with less constraint, and he turned more forthrightly than before to classical inspiration. All his other work in these years reflects a similar conviction: his scheme for rebuilding the city (with its Patheon-like St Paul's); his designs for new churches; and the great column known as the Monument which he built with Hooke between 1671 and 1675.[15] St Maryle-Bow in Cheapside, for example (designed in 1670), was expressly modeled after the Roman building known then as the Templum Pacis, now as the Basilica of Maxentius, and known to Wren through Palladio's reconstruction. Wren proposed an ingenious classical substitute for the traditional Gothic spire, an elaborate construction in which he was able to display from top to bottom, "all the five orders, regularly executed." St Stephen's Walbrook (1676) was thought to be his masterpiece. "Perhaps Italy itself," it was suggested, "can produce no Modern Building that can vie with this in Taste or Proportion."[16] The same critic placed the Monument alongside the Columns of Trajan and Constantine; but Wren's son pointed out the characteristic freedom of the architect in exceeding "the received Proportion of the Order, one Module, or Semi-diameter."

It was Wren's way. His admiration for classical architecture was profound but he was never a slavish imitator. In part this was due to circumstances; the site of the building, its function, the audience and patron, all forced on him adaptations not necessarily to his taste. (Was this not the case for Dryden also?) When he had least interference, he produced what was probably his most thoroughly classical work, the library for Trinity College, Cambridge (1676–95) (Plate 13). In a letter to Isaac Barrow, Wren made clear his intention of using the ground floor there to recreate the ancient stoa, "according to the manner of the ancients who made double walkes (with the rowes of pillars, or two rows and a wall) about the forum."[17] Even so, Wren took the usual liberties, so that Nikolaus Pevsner, for example, finds a disjunction between some of the inside and some of the outside features which he thinks is "typically baroque." Nevertheless, the library presented Gothic Oxford with a startling Roman simplicity that must have made everything else look suddenly "fussy and finicky."[18] For Sir John Summerson it is without a doubt, "the essential Wren in epitome."[19]

It is not surprising, then, that Wren's next design for St Paul's was for a church that was also to be classical in form, a single rectangular choir, with a domed

13. Trinity College Library engraved by Loggan, 1690

vestibule at one end – though under the pressure of finances, very modest in size, indeed too modest, as it turned out, for his patrons. The real objection, however, according to Wren's son, was that "being contriv'd in the Roman Stile, it was not so well understood and relish'd by others, who thought it deviated too much from the old Gothick Form of cathedral Churches, which they had been used to see and admire."[20] Wren tried again immediately with his so-called Great Model design, his own favorite (Plate 14).[21] Here was a truly magnificent church meant to rival the best of ancient Rome or modern France and Italy. "He endeavour'd to gratify the Taste of the Connoisseurs and Criticks, with something coloss and beautiful, with a Design antique and well studied, conformable to the best Stile of the Greek and Roman Architecture."[22] But still the chapter and the clergy were dissatisfied; they clung to the tradition of the Gothic nave.[23] It was only the next design (1675), a deliberate compromise, that won the King's assent and allowed Wren to build. If the Great Model had been a truly classical attempt, the "warrant design" (Plate 15) was meant "to reconcile, as near as possible, the Gothick to a better Manner of Architecture; with a Cupola, and above that, instead of a Lantern, a lofty Spire, and large Porticoes."[24] It has since been characterized by Summerson as "a Gothic building in classical dress," with a traditional cathedral plan, even including buttresses, though hidden behind "sham" walls.[25] Still, Wren now had his warrant and some real latitude to amend the plan as he went, so that he could implement his scheme for a great dome based on the St Peter's of Bramante and Michelangelo.[26]

    In fact, Wren published no more plans and used his liberty to restore some of his original intentions. The new cathedral held its first service in 1697, though

14. The Great Model of St Paul's

still lacking its dome. Evelyn had gone to see it earlier and taken exception to one or two details, but endorsed it, on the whole, as "a piece of Architecture without reproach."[27] "If the whole Art of Building were lost," he wrote in his new version of Fréart, "it might be recovered and found again in St Paul's, the historicall Pillar, and those other Monuments of his happy Talent and extraordinary Genius."[28] St Paul's seemed to him the very culmination of the change in taste that had first been introduced into England by the Earl of Arundel and Inigo Jones and that he had tried so hard to foster.[29] Largely as a result of these works, it appeared to him that England "was now beginning to be somewhat polish'd in the manner of their building," as "indeede in the accomplishment of the English language also."[30] And when the dome finally appeared (about 1708), it certainly won great praise, though even so, Wren was forced to accept a balustrade on the outside and some decoration on the inside that he did not want. "Persons of little skill in architecture did expect, I believe, to see something they had been used to in Gothick Structures; and ladies think nothing well without an edging." He would have been willing to comply with the vulgar taste, but he was unwilling to "break the harmony" of the whole work and create a disagreeable mixture against the principles of architecture. Unfortunately, his old friend, Isaac Newton, seems to have joined in the majority against him. As usual, the result was not quite what the architect had intended.[31]

Whether the result is truly classical or baroque is perhaps beside the point, though a matter of much discussion among modern critics. Certainly, there are

15. The Warrant Design of St Paul's

many features of the finished cathedral that owe little directly to classical precedent and much to Wren's engineering strategies (like the supporting dome
within the dome), or that seem to owe something to Italian baroque examples
(like the late west towers, which were not anticipated in the warrant design).[32]
If one accepts with Geoffrey Webb that the opposition between the authority
of antiquity and modern freedom is the first condition of the baroque, then
Wren was *par excellence* a baroque architect.[33] He certainly valued classical
imitation, but needed freedom to accommodate his own buildings to the practical exigencies of time and place. Wren owned a copy of Desgodets, and his
son defended Wren's departures from the Templum Pacis by remarking on
the disagreement of the ancients in their measurements.[34] He thought that
the double columns in Wren's work, like Perrault's at the Louvre, could be
defended by ancient precedent; but that they could also be sanctioned by
the freedom of the architect–imitator to alter his classical models – as indeed
the ancients themselves had done, who "generally took such Liberties, well
knowing that the Orders were to be adapted to their proper Use, and not
the Design too servilely to the Orders."[35] "We now esteem the Learning of
the Augustan Age," he continues, "yet, no question there were then many
different Styles in Oratory, and perhaps some as good as Cicero's." But liberty
did not mean license. "This is not said as any Inducement . . . to fall into crude
Gothick Inventions, far from the good Examples of the Ancients, no more than

to encourage a barbarous Style in Latin, and yet surely we cannot but with Erasmus, laugh at him who durst use one Word that he could not find in Tully."[36] The plea for modernity was, as always in this period, severely circumscribed.

From this vantage point, then, Wren's baroque is but another variety of classicism, freer and less dogmatic, but still deferential to antiquity. In the words of a nineteenth-century admirer, "Wren in this most splendid of modern buildings, has powerfully exemplified that just and effective imitation, which is essential to the elevation of pure style in architecture, and at the same time, leaves room for all the exercise of linguistic invention. St Paul's is [just] such a free imitation of St Peter's as the *Aeneid* is of the *Iliad*."[37] When, at the end of Wren's long career, he was ousted from his position, he protested against the balustrade and decorations proposed for the cathedral. He had wanted four statues only, one for each pediment, "which will be a most proper noble and sufficient ornament to the whole fabric, and was never omitted in the best ancient Greek and Roman architecture, the principles of which, throughout all my schemes of this colossal structure, I have religiously endeavoured to follow." If Wren deserved any glory, he added, "it is in the singular mercy of God, who has enabled me to begin and finish my great work so conformable to the ancient model."[38] This was not a new conviction, but one he had shared throughout his long friendship with John Evelyn, and it seems to have had a growing appeal to both the ancients and the moderns in the period – perhaps especially to those who found themselves somewhere in between: contemporaries such as John Dryden and William Wotton, who, in so far as they trusted their own critical judgment, must have found much comfort in the great modern architect's liberal neoclassical sentiments.

3

Wren also had strong and deliberate ideas about the interior decoration of his buildings, but here too he was forced into compromise. At Trinity College, he looked after the moldings with characteristic attention. "Wee are scrupulous in small matters," he explained to the Master, "and you must pardon us: Architects are as great pedants as Criticks or Heralds." He had parts of the design copied out to guide the workmen.[39] In the next years Wren worked closely with Grinling Gibbons and seems to have continued to restrain something of the great carver's natural exuberance at Hampton Court and at St Paul's.[40] For the architect, all decoration was naturally subordinate to the overall effect.

Things seen near at hand may have small and many Members, be well feuled with Ornaments, and may lie flatter; on the contrary, all this care is ridiculous at great Distances; there bulky Members, and full Projectures casting quick Shadows, are commendable; small Ornaments at too great Distance serve only to confound the Symmetry, and to take away the Lustre of the Object, by darkening it with little Shadows.[41]

Nevertheless, we have seen that Wren was forced to stand by while railings and sculptures were added to the cathedral, and in much the same way he was now compelled to accept a decoration for the interior of the dome that he never intended. It appears that he first imagined a plain coffered ceiling, like that at the Pantheon, which appears in the Great Model. Later he seems to have thought of a mosaic, perhaps in imitation of the early Christian churches in which he took a great interest.[42] Now he still preferred something simple, a painting with "Ornaments of architecture in Basso Relievo, and the mouldings heightened with gold," which he pointed out could be done at a third of the price of the mosaic.[43] For some years the jockeying continued and the decision was several times deferred as the rise and fall of Whigs and Tories affected Wren's fortunes. Long before, he had complained about the uncertainties that political life enjoined on him, "bound to our good behavior, uncertain which way the next wind may tosse us."[44] In the end, he had to stand aside while it was decided to paint the ceiling with an illusionist picture. A competition was held and the winner was a brash young Englishman named James Thornhill.

Decorative painting had come into its own in the years since Streater had completed the Sheldonian ceiling. Once again it was foreigners who led the way, imported by the court and aristocracy. In particular, the Italian-born, French-trained Antonio Verrio had painted one ceiling and staircase after another for the last two Stuart kings and their courtiers, covering them with illusionist figures set in perspectival scenes.[45] At Windsor he collaborated with Grinling Gibbons under Evelyn's architect friend, Hugh May, to redecorate the hall and chapel in the most resplendent baroque fashion.[46] When Evelyn visited Windsor in 1683, he particularly admired the staircase with Gibbons's carvings and Verrio's figures, "full and flowing, antique and heroical." The hall seemed to him equal to the most famous Roman masters. On his return a year or two later, he was overwhelmed by the "stupendious" paintings there of Edward II receiving the Black Prince – "coming towards him in a Roman triumph" – and the roof with the history of St George, "incomparable" he supposed, "and I think equal to any and in many Circumstances exceeding any I have seen Abroad."[47] About the same time, he looked at Verrio's work at Montagu House, with its depictions of Dido's funeral pyre and the Labors of Hercules, and found it "both for design, Colouring, and exuberance of Invention, comparable to the greatest of old Masters, and what they so celebrate in Rome."[48] Even the Catholic chapel at Whitehall, which was decorated by Verrio and Gibbons, impressed him, though he found it hard to believe that he could have witnessed such a thing in Protestant England.[49]

Verrio fell from royal favor after the fall of his Catholic masters, though he did not lack employment by others who were hungry to emulate the court as well as their own foreign counterparts. And in a few years he was back in favor, contributing to the Protestant cause with a frescoed staircase and some colorful ceilings at William III's Hampton Court.[50] But now there were other artists from abroad to supply the demand and furnish the new taste, foremost among them the indefatigable Louis Laguerre, a Frenchman who had been trained at Versailles, and who did much painting at Blenheim and Petworth, as well as helping to decorate Kneller's new country house.[51] Led by these visitors, history painting came suddenly into fashion and with it a reinvigorated taste for the antique.[52] It was in this company that the young Thornhill appeared to challenge the field and won the commission at St Paul's.

The young painter was still hardly known. He had learned his craft as an apprentice to Thomas Highmore and been admitted to the Painter-Stainers Company in 1703. His first work was in country houses where he picked up the new style of Verrio and Laguerre. In 1705 he contrived the sets for the opera *Arsinoe, Queen of Cyprus*, "the design of this entertainment being to introduce the Italian manner of Musick to the English Stage, which has never been before attempted."[53] It was a foretaste of things to come. Like Streater earlier, Thornhill graduated from the theater to history painting and gained his first large commission in 1707 to decorate the hall of the new hospital that Wren had built at Greenwich. It was just after he started work there that the competition for St Paul's was held. According to Vertue, Laguerre won the original contract, but the commissioners suddenly reversed their decision and held an open competition.[54] It was ordered, according to the minutes, "that the inside of the Dome be painted with figures, but confined to the Scripturall history taken from the Acts of the Apostles, and that such Painters as are willing to undertake the same, do bring their Designs and proposalls (both as to summe and time) to the Commissioners."[55] Half a dozen artists submitted designs, all but Thornhill foreigners. Eventually the field was winnowed down to two, the Venetian, Antonio Pellegrini and the young Englishman whose chiaroscuro design was surprisingly chosen. It may have been the Archbishop of Canterbury who swung the balance. "I am no judge of painting," he is reported to have said, "but I think I may fairly insist: first that the Painter employed be a Protestant, and secondly, that he be an Englishman." It was a victory, as Vertue reported later, "by political contrivance."[56] Pellegrini was disappointed and left England, as did his talented countryman, Sebastiano Ricci, who also seems to have sought the commission. According to Vertue, it was the intercession of Lord Halifax that won the job for Thornhill. "His reason was this, that Mr Thornhill our Country man has strove against all oppositions and difficulties and now got near the very Top of the Mountain and his grace [the High Chamberlain, the Duke of Shrewsbury] would throw him down and crash all his endeavors which would discourage all our country men ever after to attempt the like again."[57] In any case, the decision had been wrested from the architect, and Wren told the commissioners pointedly that he would take no responsibility for it whatever.[58]

The years passed as Thornhill labored on his two great projects, while his reputation began to grow. It was about this time that he fell out with Godfrey Kneller in the Academy of Painting that the latter had founded, and for a time took control.[59] In 1716, a young student named Dudley Ryder decided to visit St Paul's and have a look. Unfortunately, he was told that Thornhill would let no one see his work in progress. He persisted, however, and was reluctantly admitted to the great man's presence. Ryder told him that he had a great curiosity to see "so extraordinary fine a piece of painting," and begged to have the liberty of viewing it. Thornhill made an exception for the eager young man, who replied that "we should now be able to vie at least with Paris for history painting which we have been so deficient in before." Thornhill said he expected to finish the work in a year or so. All the architecture was complete but the history painting was not yet begun (Plates 16a and b). Ryder reported that "there are three models hung up with different designs, one of which is chosen, and all the models are divided into eight columns or pieces of architecture, in each one of which some one story of St Paul is described . . . The models have a pretty good spirit in them, but there does not seem to me that air of grandeur and majesty in describing the postures and faces which appears in the most masterly pictures."[60] It does not look as though Ryder knew the Raphael cartoons which were Thornhill's immediate inspiration.

Perhaps Ryder was disappointed that the color had been banished, though he does not say so. The decision to paint in grisaille was evidently meant to bring out the purely sculptural and architectural character of the scene, and the result is more deliberately classical (and dull) than the more boisterous designs that Thornhill was painting simultaneously at Greenwich. Whether Wren had any influence on this is hard now to say. Thornhill supposed Ryder must be a virtuoso, and Ryder replied by saying modestly only that he took pleasure in seeing a fine painting. He confessed he was not himself a painter, but was afraid to say more, "lest I should discover my ignorance." Thornhill was pleased, "glad that anybody that was a judge should come to take notice of his performance." Ryder climbed to the top of the scaffolding to admire the roses painted at the very top of the dome, and to watch the workmen peforming under Thornhill's direction. Afterward he couldn't help boasting of his exploit to his cousin Billio.

4

It seems likely that Ryder would have enjoyed Greenwich better. A hospital for seamen had been Evelyn's idea ever since he was appointed by Charles II in 1665 as a commissioner to look after the sick and wounded; and now after so many years Queen Mary was enthusiastic.[61] In 1694 a commission was set up to attend to it, and Evelyn was asked to be the treasurer, while Wren was appointed the architect. They had already worked together at the new hospital for soldiers in Chelsea, which had just opened its doors. Now Wren was to work at Greenwich without any remuneration for more than a decade.[62] At first he proposed a great single domed building, but he was as usual forced to adjust his plan to the site and the wishes of the Queen, who insisted on protecting the house and view that Inigo Jones had created there, as well as the block that Webb had begun under Charles II.[63] By 1698 he completed his scheme for a pair of domed buildings with an avenue between, connected by

a

16a and b. Designs for the dome
of St Paul's by Thornhill, c.1720

b

two long colonnades leading to the Queen's House, and this was pretty much the way the project was finally completed, although some further alterations were made. Already, in 1696, Evelyn had helped Wren to lay the foundation stone, and in the next years he visited the site often to support his old friend and watch his progress, while he looked after the accounts. In 1700 they went together to show the King a model and some drawings, and were received warmly.[64]

The hospital turned out to be a characteristic compound of classical and baroque elements – with double columns borrowed again from Perrault's Louvre. Evelyn, who had made a large donation, was more than satisfied.[65] However, in 1702 the commission was suddenly dissolved for a new board of directors, after which Evelyn resigned and Wren gradually withdrew. It was his younger associates now, Vanbrugh and Hawksmoor, who saw the work through to its final execution, though it remains hard to assign their exact responsibilities. Who was it, for example, who decided to raise the low cupolas to their present dramatic height? If it was Vanbrugh, as is sometimes said, why did Wren give his approval?[66] Still, it is not likely that Wren had much influence over Thornhill when he was chosen to decorate the hospital in 1707 and there is a tradition that he actively opposed it.[67] For the next eighteen years the artist worked there intermittently, decorating first the lower hall, then the upper hall and vestibule. The result has been called "perhaps the most effective piece of Baroque painting by any English artist," and "the richest baroque painted room in England."[68]

In 1715 Richard Steele was invited to see the new ceiling in the Great Hall and he deciphered the allegory in an issue of the *Lover*. Later Thornhill incorporated Steele's words in his own printed "Explanation" that appeared in English and French.[69] The colorful painting that he admired shows William and Mary surrounded by the cardinal virtues, with many figures representing such things as Truth and Peace, Wisdom and Strength, triumphing over Tyranny, while Architecture holds up a design for the Hospital, and the four seasons and the four elements appear supported by much naval equipment. According to Steele, Thornhill had accomplished his great and noble design with uncommon genius. "The Regularity, Symmetry, Boldness and Prominence of the Figures are not to be described, nor is it in the Power of Words to raise too great an Idea of the Work."[70]

In the Upper Hall (Plate 17), Queen Anne and George I preside, while on the walls grisaille paintings show the arrivals in England of William III and George I. As Edgar Wind pointed out long ago, it is possible to make out something of what Thornhill had in mind for these two paintings from his scribbles on some of the preparatory sketches that survive.[71] The interest of Thornhill's notes is that they put the question that then beset every history painter – and every poet and dramatist – in the period: how, in brief, to picture the exploits of heroic contemporary figures against the exemplary models of antiquity. Should they be portrayed realistically in present-day costume or idealized in classical dress?[72] Thornhill lists the objections to showing the King

17a and b. Sketches by Thornhill for the Upper Hall at Greenwich

arriving at Greenwich on September 18, 1716, dressed in the modern way, and suggests an answer to each. First he remembers that it was night, which is hard and ungraceful to paint. Perhaps he could "take the Liberty" of showing an evening sky and adding some torches. Then the boats were small, so perhaps it would be best to paint the royal yacht brightly with guns firing. As to the nobles who accompanied the King, some were now in disgrace, and it would be too partisan to represent them as they were. Perhaps this could be avoided by selecting a few and leaving the rest in the background. Thornhill thought it would be good to find out just what they were wearing, but the King's dress was not in fact graceful enough, "nor example worthy to be transmitted to Posterity." Best to garb him "as it should have been than as it was." And finally, since it would be ugly to represent the vast original crowd, he considered taking the liberty again of reducing the numbers, "as they ought to have been then."[73]

Thornhill had a genuine interest in realistic representation, and in this he seems to have influenced his son-in-law, Hogarth.[74] But here he chose to idealize his historical subject, as it was increasingly thought proper to do. Though the notion of decorum was generally invoked to prescribe an historically accurate dress, the need to moralize encouraged the artist and writer to improve his subject, and that usually meant to classicize it. So, for example, the author of *The Art of Painting* insisted on the need to study history and disapproved of the idea of using the costume of one nation for another. But still, "we may neglect the Nicety of the Story for the Advantage of the Picture as putting any famous Hero in better grace and posture (if a great Action) than perhaps History hath transmitted to us."[75] Joseph Addison drew the consequences for the *Spectator*:

> Great Masters in Painting never care for drawing People in the Fashion; as very well knowing that the Head dress or Periwig that now prevails and gives a Grace to their Portraitures at present, will make a very odd Figure and perhaps look monstrous, in the Eyes of Posterity. For this reason they very often represent an illustrious Person in a Roman habit, or in some other dress that never varies.[76]

Not everyone was happy with this. Martin Lister denied that Roman dress was appropriate for a contemporary, "as though the present day need be ashamed of their Modes." When Charles II chose imperial dress for Grinling Gibbons to execute at Windsor and in the old Exchange, it seemed ridiculous to him. "I appeal to all Mankind, whether in representing a living Prince now a days these naked Arms and Legs are decent, and whether there is not a barbarity very displeasing in it."[77] But the movement was growing against the moderns and inclining toward neoclassicism, and Thornhill had no wish to interfere.[78] The historical paintings at Greenwich (Plates 18a and b), like the building which housed them, were something of a compromise, but an undoubted success, whatever Christopher Wren may have thought of them.

18. Sketch by Wren for the Royal Hospital for Seamen, Greenwich

Thornhill had taken the job on speculation, asking only that his fee be determined by experts at the work's completion, and the group of painters who were called on for their opinion then agreed unanimously that Thornhill's work was "equal to any in England, of the like kind, and superior in number of figures and ornaments."[79] In 1685, William Aglionby had lamented the fact that no Englishman had yet produced a history painting worthy of the name; by 1720 Thornhill more than filled the bill, though one could still cavil a bit about the authenticity of either his classical or his classicizing representations. "Here," according to *Vitruvius Britannicus*, "Foreigners may view with Amaze, the Beauty, the Force, the Majesty of a British pencil."[80]

5

How nice it would be if we could eavesdrop somehow on that conversation in Richard Bentley's rooms in St James's Palace, 1697, when Wren was invited to join his friend, along with John Evelyn and Isaac Newton for what was intended to be a regular gathering![81] Wotton's *Reflections* and Bentley's *Dissertations* had just appeared and it is hard to believe that they had no word for that second round in the Battle of the Books. For Wren, as for Locke, it was out of character to join directly in the fray, but there is not much difficulty establishing just what his position was. Like the rest of the company, we have seen that he was a "modern," unabashedly in favor of the new science, more guardedly in favor of artistic liberty, yet with a conviction of universal standards and the need for classical imitation. If this is clear enough of his scientific and architectural works, it is confirmed by his fragmentary and occasional forays into theory, particularly the several essays that have come down to us unfinished in the *Parentalia*.

There are five tracts in all, intended apparently "to reform the Generality to a truer Taste in Architecture."[82] Wren seems to have felt himself continually at odds with an audience whose sympathies were still "Gothick" and that still had only a hazy notion of what was truly classical. In these overlapping and incomplete essays, Wren seems to have intended a systematic treatise on architecture that meant to distinguish (rather like Claude Perrault) the eternal factors in building from the ephemeral, and that would have recounted the whole history of construction from the beginning of time. Wren believed that reason and history, mathematics and classical authority, could be joined in a harmonious fashion to underpin his architectural practice. In this sense he may have hoped (rather like Wotton) to remove the rigid antithesis between ancients and moderns that had been proposed by Temple and Charles Perrault.

Wren begins with the familiar distinction between the essential and the accidental, the eternal and the ephemeral. Already in Paris, he had written to complain how the French, under the influence of female fashions, sometimes confused the two. "Building certainly ought to have the Attribute of the eternal," he wrote then, "and is therefore the only thing uncapable of new Fashions."[83] (At the end of his life, he was still complaining about this confusion in the ornament that was imposed on St Paul's.) "Architecture," he repeats now, "aims at Eternity; and is therefore the only thing uncapable of Modes and Fashions in its Principals."[84] Apparently, Wren meant to distinguish between two kinds of principles: the proportions of the different orders, on the one hand; and such things as beauty, firmness and convenience (the Vitruvian virtues), on the other. In either case, he opposes frivolous change. The classical orders, Wren explains, are the result of the experience of the ages, of Phoenicians, Hebrews and Assyrians, as well as Greeks and Romans, of great wealth expended and the skills of artists and geometers throughout the centuries, each emulating the one before. Since experiments in architecture are costly and hard to correct, it is essential now to study antiquity, rather than to consult the imagination. As a result, Wren concludes, "an Architect ought to be jealous of Novelties, in which Fancy blinds the Judgment: and to think his judges, as well those that are to live five Centuries after him, as those of his own Time. That which is commendable now for Novelty, will not be a new Invention to Posterity, when his Works are often imitated, and when it is unknown which was the Original; but the Glory of that which is good of itself is eternal."[85]

As for beauty, Wren believed with Claude Perrault that it had two causes:

natural, that is to say based upon geometrical proportions; and customary, that is to say based upon the senses and not intrinsic to the object.[86] (Here, Wren appears to borrow from the new philosophy the distinction between primary and secondary qualities, but he modifies Perrault in applying the distinction.) Natural beauty is universally acknowledged and eternally true; customary beauty is variable and uncertain and requires the architect's experience and judgment. For Wren, the superior authority must always be natural or geometrical beauty. Regularity is a law of nature and is always preferable to irregularity; oblique positions are always discordant unless they come in pairs like an equilateral triangle. "Therefore Gothick Buttresses are all ill-favored, and were avoided by the Ancients." Symmetrical, well-proportioned columns are essential to good architecture, although the details might vary according to the judgment of the architect and the perception of the viewer.

Apparently, Wren used to hold forth on these matters on Saturdays when he made his weekly inspections of St Paul's. Roger North was a lawyer with the usual interests of the virtuoso, including the arts, music and architecture. He seems to have read most of the modern works on these subjects, from Palladio to Fréart, and had done a little building himself. One day, North took his brother to visit Wren, "who, like a true philosopher, was always obliging and communicative, and in every matter we enquired about, gave short but satisfactory answers."[87] Why, North asked him, did he use entablatures over pilasters, contrary to classical precedent? Wren explained that it was a result of practical necessity; Inigo Jones had done the same! On another occasion, they talked about beauty. Wren held "that there was a distinction in nature of graceful and ugly, and that it must be so to all creatures that had vision." North objected that the distinction was not in nature but in us, "from the judgment and use of things." Wren gave as an example, triangles, arguing that an equilateral was more agreeable than a scalene, with some other instances, such "as the stated dimensions of Columns." Typically, North's belief in custom was at least as dogmatic as Wren's in geometry and not much different in consequence. If anything, it compelled him to a more literal ancienneté, as his reservations about some of Wren's buildings and his preference for Inigo Jones seem to imply.[88]

Nevertheless, Wren's commitment to antiquity was genuine enough, for he assumed that what was true and beautiful in architecture and what was best in antiquity were much the same – exactly as in literature. But he was not pedantic. Some modern writers, he noticed (perhaps thinking of Fréart), had labored hard to discover the exact proportions of the orders in the works of antiquity and reduced them to rules. They had misunderstood their task. Geometrical principles did not require exact imitation. In fact, the ancients themselves had varied the details, and the moderns who had tried to reduce them to uniformity were being arbitrary and pedantic. The Pantheon was a case in point where no two columns measured alike; Wren's own great column was another, "the Height exceeding the due Proportion of the Order." What did it matter, since in neither case was the disproportion visible?[89] It was understandable, though unfortunate, that the moderns should confuse what was eternally true, i.e. that the columns should be employed in a geometrical way, with the ornament that was only temporary and fashionable. "Because they were found in the great Structures (the Ruins of which we now admire) we think ourselves obliged still to follow the Fashion, though we can never attain to the Grandeur of those Works."[90]

Wren's terseness here, and the collective pronoun, make his meaning a little ambiguous, but it looks as though he was willing to acknowledge the preeminence of the greatest of the classical buildings. In another of the tracts, he singled out again the Temple of Peace as a building unique in strength and size, longer than Westminster Abbey and higher than any cathedral in the modern world.[91] Wren knew that he had not attained to that grandeur in his own St Paul's. (He was not likely to forget that the greatest of modern cities had rejected his classical Great Model as heedlessly as his plan for rebuilding and rationalizing itself.) "Antiquity always carries veneration with it," Wren agreed, but he would not accept Temple's view that what was oldest was necessarily best.[92] Here, Wren turns to history, which occupies much of the rest of his work, to show how the column and portico had to develop from a simple beginning to their culmination in Augustan Rome. For Wren, as for Perrault, it was foolishly anachronistic to imagine with Villalpando that Solomon's Temple had been decked out with Corinthian columns, when it was clear that the column had first to be invented and then develop in deliberate stages from Doric to Ionic to its final Corinthian phase.[93]

Thus Wren turned to history to confirm his views and so combine rational inference with the testimony of the ancients.[94] Using some hints in Vitruvius, he imagines how primitive men must have begun to build by adopting treetrunks as their first columns. Using the Bible, he finds Cain to be the first architect, with Noah's Ark, the Tower of Babel and the Temple of Solomon among the chief pre-Doric landmarks. His intention was to show a steady development to and through Greek and Roman architecture. When he reaches classical times, he begins to draw heavily on the works of modern philologists and antiquaries. To reconstruct the appearance of an ancient building was a task that had long been shared between the humanists, who wanted to understand the literary and historical references, and the architects, who wanted to imitate the works themselves. The evidence was both literary, as in the descriptions of Vitruvius and Pliny, and monumental, that is to say in the ruins themselves. Wren took a particular interest in the archaeological discoveries that were being made in excavating St Paul's, and speculated about the earliest buildings on the site, as well as about the extent and boundaries of Roman London.[95] He possessed many antiquarian treatises as well as modern travelers' reports describing the ancient remains. We have seen him discussing with Hooke the tomb of the Etruscan King, Porsenna. In one of his tracts, he reconstructs that "Stupendious Fabrick . . . of Tyrian Architecture," using the description in Pliny. And here too he offers precise reconstructions of some of his favorite classical buildings: the Temples of Peace and Diana at Ephesus, and the

Sepulchre of Mausolus, one of the Seven Wonders of the World, and "the exactest form of Doric."[96]

In short, Wren believed that reconstructing the ancient monuments was the best possible training for the modern architect. He was even prepared to offer a philological reconstruction to help out, criticizing the work of the famous scholar, Père Hardouin, whom he believed had mistaken the meaning of a technical Greek term in his commentary on Pliny. In another place he was ready to offer an original emendation. Apparently Wren did not have to be persuaded about either the value or the achievement of modern scholarship; and there can be little doubt that he approved, as he certainly must have understood, the efforts of his new friend, Dr Bentley, in the Battle of the Books.

6

It is clear then that Wren accepted the familiar view of history that had come down from the Renaissance, and with it the belief in the authority and perfection of the classics in architecture as well as literature. The only thing that continued to divide the two parties was whether perfection had been reached at the beginning of time (as in Temple) or in ancient Greece and Rome (as in Wotton and Wren), and whether that perfection might be attained again. Either way, everyone, both ancients and moderns, agreed that the decline and fall of ancient Rome had meant the collapse of civilized culture and that the cycle of decay had only been arrested during the Italian Renaissance and afterward, when the classical models were deliberately recovered and imitated.

So too Wren believed that architecture had been restored first in Italy, when the ancient Roman remains began to be studied and appreciated. "About two hundred Years ago," his son explained, "when ingenious Men began to reform the Roman Language to the Purity, which they assigned and fixed to the Time of Augustus and that Century; the Architects also, ashamed of the modern Barbarity of Building, began to examine carefully the Ruins of old Rome, and Italy; to search into the Orders and Proportions, and to establish them by inviolable Rules."[97] In 1713, Francis Atterbury, now Bishop of Rochester and head of the commission to repair Westminster Abbey, asked Wren for advice, and he replied with a long disquisition on Gothic architecture that fleshes out the history in his tracts.[98] Wren supposed that Gothic style had been invented by the Saracens and introduced into Europe at the time of the Crusades. While he sometimes found something to admire in medieval architecture, he generally shared Evelyn's view, which his son quotes here, that it was all pretty contemptible compared to antiquity. The Renaissance had come late to England and only begun to reach fulfillment in the Banqueting House of Inigo Jones where for the first time one could make a true comparison between the ancient and the modern styles.[99] (This would have seemed sensible enough to Atterbury who believed that classical propriety in literature had only arrived about the same time.)[100] In particular, Wren criticized the building methods and structural faults that he discovered now in the Abbey, as he had once in old St Paul's. His recommendation was characteristically pragmatic. Patching a Gothic building with classical ornaments could only lead to a hodgepodge of irreconcilable styles, "a despicable Mixture, which no person of a good Taste could relish."[101] As he had many years before at Christ Church, Wren suggested a restoration in tune with the original Gothic fabric.[102] Atterbury, though still the great proponent of classical *ancienneté*, agreed.

Yet not everyone found Wren's relationship to history or antiquity satisfactory. By 1713, Wren was growing old and a younger generation began to turn away from the man who had dominated architecture since the Restoration. The battle for the dome and the portico had been won, but his own students, Hawksmoor and Vanbrugh – the "school of Wren" – were chafing a bit under his classical restraint and pressing their "baroque" freedom to new limits. To be sure, they never really disavowed their old master, nor he them, and they continued to pay homage to antiquity even in their most extravagant works.[103] No doubt it is true, as Anthony Blunt insisted, that "all the great baroque architects expressed the greatest admiration for the architecture of Classical Antiquity and it can be shown that they studied and invented their works with care and enthusiasm."[104] Of course, it complicates matters that there was also an "ancient baroque," that is to say a baroque style in late antiquity, that interested the seventeenth century, though, as we have seen, the distinction in ancient styles was hardly apparent then. As always a certain measure of ignorance, as well as knowledge, was helpful to the idea of classical imitation.[105]

Thus when Hawksmoor was asked to engrave the illustrations for the third edition of James Maundrell's popular *Journey from Aleppo to Jerusalem* (1714), he relied on his predecessor, Jean Marot, and compared the (Hellenistic) Temple of Jupiter at Baalbec (which Marot had placed in Greece) to Inigo Jones's St Paul's, Covent Garden! And indeed the portico that he designed for the London church, Christchurch Spitalfields, seems actually to have been inspired by Baalbec.[106] Hawksmoor's own ambiguous loyalty to classicism is perhaps best expressed in a letter he wrote to Lord Carlisle, for whom he worked at Castle Howard. He thought his partner, Vanbrugh, had done well to found the work "upon the Rules of the Ancients," that is to say "upon Strong Reason and good Fancy, joyn'd with Experience and Tryalls, so that we are assured of the good effect of it." That, he explained, was what was meant by "following the Ancients." If, he continued, "we contrive or invent otherways, we doe but dress things in Masquerade, which only pleases that Idle part of mankind, for a short time" – to which he added this brief postscript:

> I wou'd never mention Authors or Antiquity, but that we have so many conceited Gentlemen full of this Science, ready to knock you down, unless you have some old father to stand by you. I dont mean that we need to Coppy them, but to be upon the same Principalls.[107]

His own view of the history of architecture seems to have been borrowed largely from Evelyn and Wren, but he was annoyed at those who willfully designated everything "Gothic" because they did not like it. Not much point, he thought, in confusing the historical Gothic with moderns like Borromini, who were simply "taking too much Liberty."[108] Typically, Hawksmoor found himself defending his own work for the mausoleum at Castle Howard against the pedantic criticism of Lord Burlington and his ally Sir Thomas Robinson who wanted to correct his intercolumniations there, which they insisted (rightly) went against classical precedent, though Hawksmoor believed that the ancients, liberally interpreted, were on his side.[109]

Vanbrugh seems to have shared these sentiments, though his theoretical pronouncements are scarcer. Unlike Hawsmoor, Vanbrugh took up architecture unexpectedly, late in life after a successful career as a playwright and initiator of Italian opera. (It was Vanbrugh who designed the sumptuous new Haymarket Theatre, as well as launching it in 1705 with Italian singers and operas.)[110] Here as elsewhere, his amateur status may have helped to liberate him from too slavish a commitment to the rules. But though both men believed (with Wren) that there was a need at times to preserve and conform to Gothic style, they drew more usually on Renaissance classical theory – from Alberti to Palladio to Perrault's Vitruvius – to inspire and justify their works. The result was a baroque style that was typically "ambiguous" – and impermanent. It has been said that Vanbrugh's grand buildings, which included Castle Howard and Blenheim Palace, "stand in the same relation to orthodox classical architecture as the Heroic drama stands to Classical tragedy. Indeed, Heroic architecture is as good a description of his style as could be found."[111] Nor should it be forgotten that Vanbrugh could build on the very same grounds as the baroque Castle Howard a charming neoclassical "Temple of the Four Winds" that was modeled directly on Palladio's Villa Rotunda.

7

According to Kerry Downes, Wren "was never as whole-heartedly Baroque as Vanbrugh and Hawksmoor were." He was specifically wary of the "fancy" that "blinds the Judgment" – unlike Hawksmoor who expressly welcomed it.[112] Nevertheless, Wren was attacked more vigorously from the opposite side. Neither his theory nor his practice seemed classical enough to satisfy the dogmatism of the more adamant upholders of antiquity, the "ancients" who were daily gathering strength. For these men, Wren had departed too far from classical models and from their best modern disciples, Palladio and Inigo Jones.[113] Already in 1712, the Earl of Shaftesbury was impatient with the aging architect who had for so long monopolized English public architecture.[114] When in 1719, the young Earl of Burlington returned to England from Italy (a second time) and looked upon the new St Paul's, he could only shake his head sadly and remark, "When the Jews saw the second temple, they [remembered the beauty of the first and] wept."[115]

No matter that Burlington was only twenty-five years old when he is supposed to have uttered these words; he was already patron and inspiration for a whole new movement known to history as neo–Palladianism. That it should coincide almost exactly with the triumph of the ancients in the Battle of the Books is no accident. Burlington had met Alexander Pope as a young man and their friendship remained close until Pope's death.[116] For Pope and his allies in the new generation, Burlington became the supreme arbiter of taste, the "Apollo of the Arts." From the first, the Earl and his friends vigorously took up the ancient cause, arguing forthrightly that the best architecture lay in the classical past and that only close imitation was permissible, and for this they won the full support of the poets.[117] In general, they tried to realize their ideal in ways that had only been known imperfectly to Wren and his students: by direct inspection of the ancient buildings themselves, and by an exact study of the best of the classical imitators, Palladio and Inigo Jones.[118] As Pope put it later in his famous "Epistle to Burlington" (1731):

> You too proceed! Make falling Arts your care,
> Erect new wonders, and the old repair,
> Jones and Palladio to themselves restore,
> And be what'er Vitruvius was before.[119]

Burlington had not only been twice to Italy and studied Palladio's buildings in and about Vicenza, but he was able to purchase many of his drawings while there and after his return to England. The new architectural *ancienneté* was thus in large measure the direct result of the grand tour, now thoroughly established as the culmination of a classical education, and an improved knowledge and renewed taste for antiquity. It had finally become possible to appreciate the austere classicism of St Paul's Church, Covent Garden, which Burlington repaired out of his own pocket, and for which he won Pope's praise, and to try to replicate its simple dignity.[120]

Of course, the way for Burlington had been well prepared, not only by the deepening of classical interest that we have observed generally, but by a growing admiration for the literary and architectural works of Jones and Palladio who seemed the best interpreters of antique architecture.[121] Many years before, Evelyn had been instructed by the Earl of Arundel in the classical authenticity of Palladio's buildings, and Fréart had given him precedence in theory.[122] Jones's interest and his own studies had been kept tenuously alive by his pupils, especially by John Webb, whose work on the theater we have noticed, and which was often confused with his own, and we have seen that Wren himself consulted some of the unpublished drawings and used the printed works. In one series of surviving drawings, Webb can be seen trying to reconstruct the ancient house described by Vitruvius, using several Renaissance manuals.[123] One of Burlington's important contributions to the new classicism was to publish many drawings by Jones as well as Palladio, so that they could be made conveniently available to the student and the practicing architect.[124] That the study and imitation he advocated were chiefly of imitations (Italians copying Romans copying Greeks) passed for the moment unnoticed.

8

Among the several links between the generations, between the classicism of Wren and that of Burlington, was the work of one of the original combatants in the Battle of the Books, the Dean of Christ Church, Henry Aldrich. He had been a leader, with Atterbury, in the group that attacked Bentley over the *Epistles* of Phalaris, though his exact complicity in the affair has never been established. (He does appear to have designed the frontispiece to the second version of Swift's *Tale of a Tub*.)[125] Aldrich was a typical virtuoso, like his good friend, John Evelyn, with a particular interest in art objects and music, both of which he collected avidly.[126] He began to practice architecture about 1675 and won something of a reputation, so that when Sir Edward Hannes left a bequest to Westminster School for a new dormitory, he gave directions that Aldrich and Wren be consulted about the building. (Aldrich died in 1710 before he could do anything.) His own best effort was the Palladian Peckwater Quadrangle which he designed for his own college, built between 1707 and 1714. It is a triumph of the new *ancienneté*, a "correct" classical imitation built in a most appropriate place – the very headquarters of the neoclassical opposition.[127] Meanwhile, as we have seen, he persuaded a friend to publish Palladio's antiquarian tract, the *Antichità di Roma* (1709), and began to write up his own architectural views. Although he left his manuscript unfinished and unpublished, it amply displays his profound commitment to Vitruvius and Palladio, to the rules of the one and the examples of the other, from which he allowed only the slightest deviation.[128]

It was only in 1715–16, however, that one can speak of a concerted movement, with the appearance of a sumptuous new edition of Palladio's major treatise, the *Quattro libri*, by Giacomo Leoni, and the first volume of Colen Campbell's *Vitruvius Britannicus*.[129] In what sounds almost like a direct rebuttal of Evelyn and the Royal Society, Campbell announced flatly that Palladio had capped the Renaissance revival and arrived at the "*ne plus ultra* of his art."[130] Only Inigo Jones, he believed, had been able to match the Italian in the purity of his *ancienneté*.[131]

It was probably Campbell's influence that converted the young Earl to the Palladian cause, though the liberties that he was willing to take in his own designs may have caused a later estrangement from his patron.[132] For a time Burlington House became the center of a concerted movement that was meant to reform all the arts in a building that was refurbished to echo Inigo Jones whose Banqueting House was now declared "without Dispute, the first Structure in the World."[133] According to Richard Graham, who brought out a new edition of Dryden's version of *Dufresnoy* in 1716, a trip to Burlington House could in its perfection save an Englishman all the trouble and expense of a journey to Rome for the study of the arts.[134] The Palladians won a decisive victory over Wren when at last they managed to wrest the commission for the new dormitory at Westminster School from him and lay the foundation stone in 1724, thus sealing the triumph of their party on the very spot where many of the ancient defenders had once sallied forth into battle.[135] By 1726 a contemporary could declare, "The reigning taste is Palladio's and a Man is a Heretick that should talk of Michelangelo or any other modern architect."[136] The reputations of Vanbrugh and Hawksmoor, and Wren himself, began swiftly to fade.

Nor is it surprising that it was just in these years that James Thornhill suddenly found himself losing out to Burlington's protégé, William Kent, who had the great advantage of having gone (like his master) to Italy to study. There Kent met Burlington and came home to complete the decoration at Burlington House; in 1723 he beat Thornhill for the commission to paint Kensington Palace.[137] Thornhill's career as a history painter was pretty much over, and it became commonplace to say later that "if he had been to Italy, his work would have been more finished and more correct."[138] Be that as it may, Thornhill's own response was to turn, or return, to that most classical of all modern painters, Raphael, and he spent his last years copying out the newly recovered cartoons for which Christopher Wren had prepared a new gallery at Hampton Court. Not for the first time did an exponent of the baroque serve the classical revival.[139]

That the new Palladianism was the self-conscious assertion of ancients over moderns appears most obviously in the work that is its best theoretical expression: Robert Morris's *Essay in Defence of Ancient Architecture, or a Parallel of the Ancient Building with the Modern: Shewing the Beauty and Harmony of the Former and the Irregularity of the Latter* (1728).[140] Morris chose to use two of Pope's lines from the *Essay on Criticism* for his motto:

> Learn hence the Ancient Rules a just Esteem,
> To copy Nature is to copy them;[141]

and he saw in Palladio, "the living image of Antiquity rising from Heaps of Ruins." He advocates following the ancient guides only, and he returns to the strict notion of only three classical orders. Of these, he believed that the Corinthian came closest to perfection, where "like Hercules upon his Pillar, we see engraven *Ne plus ultra*." Morris praised Wren, along with Inigo Jones, as one of the principal restorers of ancient architecture, though a little later he added a characteristic Burlingtonian qualification about St Paul's.[142] As for Burlington, he did not write, or say, very much himself, but the brief Italian preface to his edition of Palladio in 1731 expresses the very same sentiments, and it seems to have furnished the exact theme for Pope's "Epistle to Burlington": the distinction between true and false, that is to say, chastely classical and ignorantly ostentatious architecture.[143] Pope read Palladio and took Palladian advice about his own building; in his library he placed plaster busts of Palladio and Inigo Jones; and he told his friend Spence that he had once begun writing a Latin treatise on the old buildings of Rome using the best antiquarian authorities. He even sketched a Palladian design or two of his own.[144]

The parallel between poetry and the visual arts that Dryden had proclaimed was thus repeated throughout the period. Pope had been advised as a boy by his gentry neighbor, William Trumbull, that "there may be some happy genius's, who may judge of some of the natural beauties of a Poem, as a man may judge of the proportions of a building, without having read Vitruvius, or knowing anything of the rules of architecture," but Trumbull thought it more likely to lead to mistakes and superficiality. Knowledge of the rules *and* of the examples was necessary for both literature and the arts.[145] And indeed, Burlington and his allies made just such a deliberate effort to employ classical scholarship so that the ancient sources could be better understood and harnessed directly for the purposes of imitation; antiquarian study was reunited with present practice.[146] Burlington's publication of *The Roman Baths of Palladio* (which was to be followed by another volume on arches, theaters, temples and other buildings) was obviously meant for this purpose. On occasion, he was even willing to correct or improve his secondary authorities by a more direct appeal to Rome.[147] In 1728, Robert Castell dedicated a book to him, called *The Villas of the Ancients Illustrated*, where the literary testimony of Pliny the Younger was combined with other classical writings and remains – philology with antiquities – to try to recreate the precise plans of Pliny's villas and gardens at Laurentum, Tusculum, and elsewhere. Castell's work had an immediate influence in its turn on several actual garden plans, including Burlington's at Chiswick and Pope's at Twickenham.[148] Even in Scotland, the new classicism found fresh exponents in still another effort to banish the last remnants of a lingering Gothic barbarism.[149]

9

Nevertheless, the alliance between taste and learning was uneasy, as Pope was discovering just then with his Homer. Exact scholarship never did sit well with the wits and men of the world. It was the Earl of Chesterfield, typically, who advised his son, "You may soon be acquainted with a considerable part of Civil Architecture, and for the minute and mechanical parts of it, leave them to masons, bricklayers, and Lord Burlington, who has, to a certain extent, lessened himself by knowing them too well."[150] The Palladian movement could hardly escape the same perils that faced its literary counterpart. Close imitation, we have seen, depended upon close knowledge, but the more one learned about antiquity, the harder it was to adapt the ancient models to modern conditions. Pope had praised Burlington's architecture as useful rather than ostentatious,[151] but Burlington's Chiswick House seemed at least to one contemporary, "rather curious than convenient," and the strictures on his even more pedantic York Assembly Rooms ("the most severely classical building" of its time in Europe) were even worse.[152] Inevitably, the satirists had their say. The "Man of Taste," in the poem of that name, reflects on the many houses he had seen, from Hyde Park Corner to Bethnal Green.

> Sure wretched Wren was taught by bungling Jones,
> To murder mortar, and disfigure stones
> Who in Whitehall can symmetry discern?

> I reckon Covent-garden Church a Barn.
> Nor hate I less thy vile Cathedral, Paul!
> The choir's too big, the cupola's too small:
> Substantial walls and heavy roofs I like,
> 'Tis Vanbrug's structures that my fancy strikes:
> Such noble ruins ev'ry pile wou'd make,
> I wish they'd tumble for the prospect's sake.[153]

In the *Universal Spectator*, the editor, Henry Stonecastle, writes about such oddities as Mr Inigo Pilaster, Sir Christopher Cupolo and Alderman Pantile. The latter "talks all day long of frieze, cornice and architecture," and "there is not a gate-post near the house nor a broomstick in it which he has not had some purpose of turning or carving according to one of the five orders." The pedant even rejects his daughter, whose shape, unfortunately, reminds him of the despised Tuscan order.[154] A "modern" like Hogarth could only find amusement in the collaboration between Pope and Burlington.[155]

Moreover, it was becoming clear that if one wished to imitate the best of antiquity, much remained still to be done; for Robert Adam, not even Desgodets was accurate enough, and he made a strenuous effort to revise his work. At last, it began to dawn on some that a genuine *ancienneté* could only be served by returning to the true originals of both the Romans and the neoclassical moderns. Already, at the very beginning of the new century, the third Earl of Shaftesbury was looking beyond Rome to ancient Greece for the supreme models in all the arts, anticipating Winckelmann and the triumph of the neoclassicism that was soon to come.[156] When that notion grew more obvious and opportunity offered, the neo-Palladians were doomed and the last and most powerful of the ancient movements of the eighteenth century took place: the Greek revival.[157]

In other words, from the perspective of the quarrel between the ancients and the moderns, the whole long history of English architecture, from Inigo Jones through Wren and Burlington to Stuart and Revett, shows one clear direction: here, as in literature, there was a steadily increasing desire to go back to the ancients for practical guidance and inspiration, and a more and more capable realization of it. In that long story, it is the generation of Evelyn and Wren and Dryden, and the young men who fought the Battle of the Books, who mark the decisive moment of self-consciousness about these issues. And it is at that moment too that the claims of the ancients seemed to fasten themselves more securely than ever on the arts and literature, despite the chafing of the moderns and their undeniable successes elsewhere. For the while, it seemed that only one issue remained to be resolved, and that was how far classical imitation could withstand the insidious assault of classical scholarship. On that issue, honest men could, and certainly did, continue to disagree and with an intensity that is still surprising.

Indeed, it was a long time before that issue was concluded, or rather transformed, and only then by the unexpected rise of a whole new movement of thought that turned the principles of art into timebound constructions of period and place, a viewpoint that has usually been called "historicism." Now it is true there were some intimations already of such a view in Restoration England; and far off in Naples, the eccentric Italian, Giambattista Vico, was beginning to argue forthrightly for just such a position, though to a generally uncomprehending audience.[158] But before historicism could challenge the generally held conviction that classical thought and values were universal and timeless, and Vico could become comprehensible to the world, the intellectual ground had to be well prepared. In England this meant that classicism had first to reach fruition and then to fail – had first to reveal its full value and then its ultimate inability to satisfy the demands of modern life. No doubt, the baroque writers of our study were among the first to pose the problem, but they were still too absorbed in the preliminaries – too concerned to attempt both an imitation and *at the same time* a liberation from the classics – to foresee how the classical authors and architects might eventually become inconsequential or altogether irrelevant. They were, in a word, caught still halfway between the ancients and the moderns.

Notes

Introduction

1. While not insisting on a rigid distinction, I take the intellectual historian to be confined largely to describing past ideas, whereas the cultural historian seeks to describe relationships between different fields of thought through common forms and styles – as here between ideas and practices in literature and the arts – and may include within his purview objects (like works of art) as well as words. See Francis Haskell, *History and its Images: Art and the Interpretation of the Past* (New Haven, 1993), and my review in the *Art Bulletin*, 76 (1994), pp. 539–40.

2. See Joseph M. Levine, *The Battle of the Books: History and Literature in the Augustan Age* (Ithaca, N.Y., 1991). I argued there for the importance to intellectual history of the English battle and the French *querelle des anciens et des modernes*, and I tried to show how serious were the arguments that created so much noise and amusement at the time, and that continued to generate controversy for so long afterward. In particular, I tried to show how important the issues were for employing and imagining the past and writing its history.

3. I shall use the French term for want of an English one; it is perhaps significant that there is nothing in English to match the term "modernity."

4. For the history of the expression and its gradual extension from a term of denigration in the eighteenth century to an analytical category in the history of art and literature a century later, and thence to a description of the general culture of the whole period, see especially René Wellek, "The Concept of Baroque in Literary Scholarship," in *Concepts of Criticism* (New Haven, 1963), pp. 69–127; C. T. Carr, "Two Words in Art History: I Baroque," Forum for

Modern Language Studies, I (1965), pp. 175–90; and Guiliano Briganti, in the *Encyclopedia of World Art* (New York, 1960), II, pp. 258–67 all three with excellent bibliographies. For the belated use of the term in music, see Friedrich Blume, *Renaissance and Baroque Music*, trans. M. D. Herter Norton (London, 1969), pp. 83–102.

5. For an alternative view that emphasizes both style and period, see Judith Hook, *The Baroque Age in England* (London, 1976).

6. John Evelyn, speaking of the education of children, was not the only one to attribute "the late Rebellion and uncertainties to the defect of that alone." Evelyn to Samuel Hartlib, Feb. 4, 1660, Evelyn Correspondence (formerly at Christ Church, now in the British Library). On the other hand, Hobbes thought that teaching the classics had actually helped to inspire the rebellion; see his *Behemoth* (1682).

7. The Interregnum had seen many schemes for educational reform proposed, some of them deliberately anti-classical, though all were quickly dropped at the Restoration. Dryden's teacher, the royalist, Richard Busby, managed to proclaim the classics unchallenged throughout the period, and it seems that the old curriculum remained pretty much intact in most schoolrooms. Charles Hoole's popular *New Discovery of the Old Art of Teaching School* (London, 1660) is, we shall find, a convenient bridge to the Restoration with its ambition to make the schoolboy "exactly compliant in the Greek and Latine Tongues, and as perfect Orators, and Poets as both their young years and capacities will suffer" (p. 168).

8. It was the error of R. F. Jones in his pioneering work, *Ancients and Moderns* (2nd edn, 1961) to think that scientific modernity, which was real, had to proceed at the expense of a literary *ancienneté*, which

however was equally dynamic and (for the time being) just as practical. See my "Ancients and Moderns Reconsidered," *Eighteenth-Century Studies*, 15 (1981), pp. 72–89.

9. See my essay, "Strife in the Republic of Letters," in *Commercium Litterarium: Forms of Communication in the Republic of Letters 1600–1750*, ed. Hans Bots and Françoise Waquet (Amsterdam, 1994), pp. 301–19.

10. I hope soon to complete a separate study entitled *Why Neoclassicism? Culture and Politics in Eighteenth-Century England*. Together with the present volume and *The Battle of the Books*, this will complete a trilogy of sorts, composed of a long sequence of case studies, each with an intrinsic interest, but so threaded together as to provide a fairly full narrative of the rise and fall of the classics in England from about 1660 to 1820.

11. See for example Peter N. Skrine, *The Baroque: Literature and Culture in Seventeenth-Century Europe* (London, 1978). It should be emphasized too that the Restoration theater, more than most, deliberately tried to blend all the arts with literature.

12. *A Tale of a Tub*, ed. A. C. Guthkelch and D. Nichol Smith, 2nd edn (Oxford, 1958), p. 248. So too both Temple and Wotton almost completely disregarded women in their comparisons of ancients and moderns, though Wotton noticed, probably correctly, that there were more examples of classically educated women between 1500 and 1600 than either before or since: *Reflections upon Ancient and Modern Learning* (London, 1694), pp. 349–50. Later Mary Astell turned Wotton's observation to polemical account in her *Serious Proposal to the Ladies* (1694), ed. Patricia Springborn (London, 1997), p. 22.

13. The nearest exception in Restoration England appears to be the school for girls opened by Bathsua Pell, Mrs Makin, which taught Latin and French, in addition to music and dance, and offered Greek, Hebrew, Italian and Spanish as optional subjects; see the prospectus in her *Essay to Revive the Antient Education of Gentlewomen* (1673), ed. Paula L. Barbour (Augustan Reprint Soc., 202, 1980), pp. 42–43. Still useful is Dorothy Gardiner, *English Girlhood at School* (London, 1929). I have considered women's education a little further in the chapter on Evelyn below.

14. I rely on Maureen Duffy, *The Passionate Shepherdess: Aphra Behn 1640–89* (London, 1977), Angeline Coreau, *Reconstructing Aphra* (Oxford, 1980), and Janet Todd, *The Secret Life of Aphra Behn* (London, 1996). Typically,

Aphra's plea for the equality of women is based on classical examples, as in the epilogue to *Sir Patient Fancy* (1677). However, in the play itself, Lady Knowell is ridiculed for her learned pretensions, and when Aphra translated some Ovid for Dryden in 1680, she asked him to explain to his readers that she "understood not Latin." Thus even while she protested about the exclusion of women from modern culture, she admitted her "want of languages," and professed to write only for entertainment. See for example her brief prologues to *The Dutch Lovers* (1673) and *The Lady Chance* (1687).

15. The anonymous author seems to have been Judith Drake. After drawing the characters of the pedant and the country gentleman, she finds both the "learned and the unlearned [male] blockheads" to be pretty much equal. Nevertheless, she flatly denied the superiority of the ancient authors and thought that women might actually have an advantage in not having to waste so much time on Latin and Greek when the ancients could be read in English translation. Two other candidates who might have been included are Margaret Cavendish, Duchess of Newcastle, and Katherine Phillips, "the matchless Orinda," about whom I will say a little below. Unfortunately, neither seems to have given much sustained reflection to the main themes of this book. For Mme Dacier, who did, see Levine, *Battle of the Books*, pp. 133–40.

16. Unaddressed letter, Oct. 8, 1699, Evelyn Corr., no. 648.

Chapter 1 John Evelyn and the Education of Antiquity

1. See the autobiography prefixed to *The Diary of John Evelyn*, ed. E. S. de Beer, 6 vols (Oxford, 1955: hereafter cited as Evelyn, *Diary*), I, p. 1, and the anonymous obituary quoted by Clara Marburg, *Mr Pepys and Mr Evelyn* (Philadelphia, 1935), p. 73.

2. Virginia Woolf, "Rambling Round Evelyn," *The Common Reader* (New York, 1925), pp. 113–23.

3. Evelyn to Lady Sunderland, Aug. 4, 1690, in Evelyn, *Diary and Correspondence*, ed. Henry B. Wheatley, 4 vols (London, 1906), III, pp. 463–65 (hereafter cited as Evelyn Corr.). Evelyn had rarely gotten to bed before midnight in twenty years, he wrote in 1668, and he was proud that he could "read the least print, even in a jolting coach, without other assistance." Evelyn to Beale, Aug. 27, 1668, in Arthur Posonby, *John Evelyn* (London, 1933), pp. 54–55.

4. Evelyn, *Diary*, Jan. 27, 1658, III, pp. 206–10.
5. Evelyn to Sir Richard Browne, Feb. 14, 1658, Evelyn *Corr.*, III, pp. 244–45.
6. Taylor to Evelyn, June 4, 1659, ibid., pp. 256–60. Evelyn's work is entitled *The Golden Book of St. John Chrysostum concerning the Education of Children* (London, 1659); it is reproduced in the *Miscellaneous Writings of John Evelyn*, ed. William Upcott (London, 1825); see esp. pp. 107–11, 115. M. L. W. Laistner, who furnishes a modern translation and some useful background, praises Evelyn's work for its "dignity and literary skill," but he sees evidence that it was translated from Latin rather than the original Greek: *Christianity and Pagan Culture in the Later Roman Empire* (Ithaca, N.Y., 1951), app., pp. 75–84.
7. Evelyn, Epistle Dedicatory, *Golden Book*.
8. Besides the diary and published correspondence, I have made use of the Evelyn papers, formerly at Christ Church, Oxford and now in the British Library. They include more than 2,500 letters, which will eventually be edited by Douglas Chambers. The manuscripts are being catalogued at present by Dr Frances Harris of the British Library, who has kindly helped me to navigate through them. For the time being, I have chosen to identify them simply by date under the general rubric, Christ Church MS Corr. The best descriptions of the collection are Michael Hunter, "John Evelyn's Archive at the British Library," *The Book Collector*, 44 (1995), pp. 147–209; and *John Evelyn in the British Library*, by Theodore Hofmann et al. (London, 1995).
9. See W. Lee Ustick, "Advice to a Son," *Studies in Philology*, 29 (1932), pp. 409–41.
10. Evelyn, *Diary*, I, pp. 7–8.
11. Evelyn to Lady Sunderland, Dec. 22, 1688, Posonby, *John Evelyn*, pp. 151–52.
12. Evelyn, *Diary*, May 13, 1661, III, pp. 287–88.
13. Thomas Howard, *Remembrances of Things Worth Seeing in Italy Given to John Evelyn, 25 April 1646*, ed. John M. Robinson (Roxburghe Club, 1987); Evelyn, *Diary*, II, pp. 466–67, 479. Evelyn visited Arundel at Albury, Nov. 7, 1641, *Diary*, II, p. 77; and in Italy, July 30, 1645, and again, in the spring of 1646: ibid., pp. 466–67, 479. For Arundel, see Mary F. S. Hervey, *The Life, Correspondence and Collections of Thomas Howard, Earl of Arundel* (Cambridge, 1921), pp. 449–55; Francis C. Springell, *Connoisseur and Diplomat* (London, 1963); David Howarth, *Lord Arundel and His Circle* (New Haven, 1985), pp. 214–16. And for Arundel's political career, Kevin Sharpe, *Politics and Ideas in Early Stuart England* (London, 1989), pp. 182–206.

14. Evelyn touchingly describes Arundel's deathbed scene (April 1646) in the *Diary*, II, p. 479. He persuaded Henry Howard to give the marbles to Oxford, "those celebrated and famous Inscriptions Greeke and Latine, with so much cost and Industrie gathered from Greece." See under Sept. 19, 1667, *Diary*, III, pp. 495–96 and note. He recalls the occasion in a note to his great manuscript work, the *Elysium Britannicum*, where he especially commends the use of ancient sculpture as garden decoration and also for "learned Men and Antiquaries": *Elysium Britannicum* (transcribed from the manuscript now in the British Library by John Ingram), p. 357. A facsimile edition by Ingram is promised by the University of Pennsylvania Press. See the essays collected by Therese O'Malley and Joachim Wolschke-Bulman, *John Evelyn's Elysium Britannicum and English Gardening* (Dunbarton Oaks Colloquium in the History of Landscape Architecture, 17, Washington, 1998).
15. Hervey, *Life . . . of Thomas Howard*, pp. 447–55. According to his contemporary biographer, Edward Walker, "He was the greatest Favourer of Arts, especially Painting, Sculpture, Designs, Carving, Building and the like, that this Age hath produced; his Collection of Designs being more than of any Person living, and his statues equal in Number, Value and Antiquity, to those in the Houses of great Princes . . . He had the Honour to be the first Person of Quality that set a value on these in our Nation": "A Short View of the Life of Sir Thomas Howard earl of Arundel and Surrey" (dated June 7, 1651), *Historical Discourses upon Several Occasions* (London, 1705), p. 222.
16. Henry Peacham, tutor in Arundel's family and fellow traveler, published *The Compleat Gentleman* first in 1622, then enlarged in 1634, with an important new chapter "Of Antiquities." See the edition by G. S. Gordon (Oxford, 1906). It was dedicated to Arundel's son, William Howard, and asserts its own place in a tradition that extends from Plutarch to Erasmus, Thomas Elyot and Roger Ascham. For the idea of the virtuoso, see Walter E. Houghton, Jr, "The English Virtuoso in the Seventeenth Century," *Journal of the History of Ideas*, 3 (1942), pp. 51–73, 190–219.
17. June 18, 1645, Evelyn, *Diary*, II, pp. 294–99.
18. Ibid., pp. 117, 159, 255, 285, 304, 371–72; *Elysium Britannicum*, p. 362.
19. Evelyn, *Numismata* (London, 1697), p. 72.
20. Jacob Thicknesse to Evelyn, Nov. 16, Evelyn MS Corr., no. 1230.

21. From a published set dedicated to Thomas Henshaw and drawn in the winter of 1645; see Antony Griffiths, "The Etchings of John Evelyn," *Art and Patronage in the Caroline Courts*, ed. David Howarth (Cambridge, 1993), pp. 51–67. Some of Evelyn's Italian sketches are reproduced in the Royal Institute of British Architects (RIBA) *Catalogue of the Drawings*, III (1972), pp. 114–15. Peacham had written a popular work on *graphice*, and endorsed the art, which he elevated to "liberal" in *The Compleat Gentleman*, ch. 13.

22. See Evelyn, *The State of France* (Paris, 1552), reprinted in the *Miscellaneous Writings*, ed. Upcott, pp. 39–95. In general, see George B. Parks, "John Evelyn and the Art of Travel," *Huntington Library Quarterly*, 10 (1946–47), pp. 251–76.

23. Evelyn to Edward Thurland, Nov. 8, 1658, Evelyn *Corr.*, pp. 249–52.

24. Evelyn to George Evelyn, March 30, 1664, Christ Church MS Corr. Letterbook, no. ccxii; cf. clxxxii.

25. Evelyn to Henshaw, March 1, 1698, Eveln *Corr.*, IV, pp. 21–22; *Seven Letters of John Evelyn* (Oxford, 1914), pp. 17–19; Marburg, *Pepys and Evelyn*, pp. 40–41. See also the nostalgic letter of Evelyn to his nephew's tutor, Walter Pope, March 30, 1664, Evelyn *Corr.*, IV, pp. 21–22.

26. Evelyn to Pepys, Aug. 21, 1668, Marburg, *Pepys and Evelyn*, pp. 101–8. For Wren, see below, ch. 10. See also Evelyn to Maddox, Jan. 10, 1657, Evelyn *Corr.*, III, pp. 224–27; Maddox to Evelyn, Dec. 21, 1656, Evelyn MS Corr., no. 990.

27. John Aubrey, *Brief Lives*, ed. Andrew Clark, 2 vols (Oxford, 1898), I, p. 120. Aubrey reports that Boyle spoke Latin as well as anyone he had ever met.

28. For example, Henry Cogan's *Directions for such as shall Travel in Rome* (1654), Edmund Warcupp, *Italy, in its original Glory, Ruine and Revival* (1660), and William Lodge's *Painter's Voyage of Italy* (1679), all translated from Italian works. In general, see John Walter Stoye, *English Travellers Abroad, 1604–1667* (London, 1952); Edward Chaney, *The Grand Tour and the Great Rebellion: Richard Lassells and the Voyage of Italy in the Seventeenth Century* (Geneva, 1985). By 1677, it was the subject of debate at Oxford, "whether travelling be good for an English gentleman": Thomas Isham, *The Diary 1671–73*, trans. Norman Marlow (Farnborough, 1971), p. 38.

29. John Evelyn, *An Apologie for the Royal Party* (1659), reprinted with *A Panegyric to Charles the Second* (1661) by Geoffrey Keynes (Augustan Reprint Soc., 28, 1951), p. 12.

30. "Mr Evelyn and I," Pepys wrote in his diary, "rode together with excellent discourse till we came to Clapham, talking of the vanity and vices of the Court, which makes it a most contemptible thing." A few months later, Evelyn was still talking of the "badness of the Government, where nothing but wickedness, and wicked men and women command the King": Samuel Pepys, *Diary*, ed. Robert Latham and William Matthews, 11 vols (Berkeley, 1970–83), VII, pp. 29, 183. Nevertheless, Evelyn remembered the King very fondly at his death, as always "very kind to me." See the obituary he composed on Feb. 4, 1685, Evelyn, *Diary*, IV, pp. 409–11.

31. Posonby, *John Evelyn*, p. 75. Evelyn's services on various commissions are listed by E. S. de Beer, "John Evelyn (1620–1706)," *Notes and Records of the Royal Society*, 15 (1960), p. 233.

32. Evelyn to the Countess of Sunderland, Dec. 23, 1688, Evelyn *Corr.*, III, pp. 431–34.

33. Evelyn to his son, Evelyn MS Corr., n.d., no. 1387.

34. See Paul O. Kristeller, "The Active and the Contemplative Life in Renaissance Humanism," *Arbeit Musse Meditation: Betrachtungen zur Vita Activa und Vita Contemplativa*, ed. Brian Vickers (Zurich, 1985), pp. 133–52.

35. As Evelyn noticed, " 'twere pretty, if at last it should appear, that a Publick Person has all this while contended for Solitude, as it is certain, a Private has done for Action": "To the Reader," *Publick Employment*, in the facsimile version of the debate edited by Brian Vickers (Delmar, New York, 1986), p. 135. For editions and circumstances, see Geoffrey Keynes, *Evelyn: A Study in Bibliophily and a Bibliography of his Writings* (Oxford, 1968), pp. 184–90. In a letter to Robert Plot, Evelyn described himself as "most of all affecting a private and studious life." He was pleased to say that he had "studiously declin'd knighthood, and other honorable employment at Court": Sept. 14, 1667, Christ Church Letterbook, no. ccccliv, ff. 37–38. Typically, some twenty years later, he seems to have had some second thoughts; see Evelyn to Anthony Wood, May 21, 1691, Evelyn *Corr.*, III, pp. 465–67.

36. Peacham endorses the idea and sets out a select reading list, *Compleat Gentleman*, p. 45.

37. Evelyn to the Countess of Sunderland, Oct. 12, 1688, Christ Church Letterbook, no. dcii.

38. In 1663, Mackenzie wrote an essay entitled

"The Roman Stoic." See F. S. Ferguson, "A Bibliography of the Works of Sir George Mackenzie," *Edinburgh Bibliographical Society Transactions*, I (Edinburgh, 1938), pp. 1–60; Andrew Lang, *Sir George Mackenzie* (London, 1909). One of Evelyn's opponents later pointed out that when Epicurus and his followers decided to decline all public employment, they slighted all that "paideia," or "course of studies consisting of grammar (which in its extent included all Critical Learning, History and Chronology) and Rhetorick, and Logick, even Mathematics": Henry Stubbe, *Legends no Histories or a Specimen of some Animadversions upon the History of the Royal Society* (London, 1670), n.p. For a time in the mid-century, there was a special vogue for the Roman imperial writers, Seneca and Tacitus; the classic statement remains George Williamson, *The Senecan Amble: A Study in Prose from Bacon to Collier* (London, 1951).

39. "The improvement of a more ornate and gracefull manner of speaking" would supply the nation with people, "fit for any honorable imployment, to serve and speake in Parliament, and in Councils; give us good Magistrates and Justices . . . able ambassadors and orators abroad; in a word qualified patriots and pillars of State, in which this age does not, I feare, abound": Evelyn to William Nicolson, Nov. 10, 1699, Evelyn *Corr.*, IV, p. 24; *Letters to and from William Nicolson*, ed. John Nichols, 2 vols (London, 1809), I, p. 141.

40. The two had already exchanged polite letters in 1667; see *Miscellaneous Writings*, ed. Upcott, pp. 503–4; they met in 1690, see Evelyn, *Diary*, V, p. 12.

41. Pepys *Diary*, May 26, 1667, VIII, p. 236.

42. Evelyn to Cowley, Aug. 24, 1666, and to Lady Clarendon, June 16, 1690; Douglas Chambers prints three stanzas in "'Elysium Britannicum' not printed neere ready, etc': The 'Elysium Britannicum' in the Correspondence of John Evelyn," *Evelyn's Elysium Britannicum*, ed. Therese O'Malley and J. Wolschke-Bulmahn (Washington, D. C., 1998), pp. 107–30.

43. Evelyn to Lord Danby, Dec. 3, 1686, quoted ibid., p. 112.

44. See the exchange between Evelyn and Cowley, March 12, May 13, 1667, Evelyn *Corr.*, III, pp. 349–52; and Cowley's essays, "Of Solitude," "Of Obscurity," and "Of Agriculture," in *The Writings of Abraham Cowley*, ed. A. R. Waller, 2 vols (Cambridge, 1905–6), II, pp. 316–18, 318–19, 319–20. Evelyn often proclaimed the advantages of a retired life, for example in the *State of*

France (1652), *Miscellaneous Writings*, ed. Upcott, p. 48; in a letter to Jeremy Taylor (1655), Posonby, *John Evelyn*, pp. 134–35; and in 1667 (following a spate of political activity), in a letter to Robert Plot, Sept. 14, Christ Church Letterbook (1699), pp. 37–38. No doubt much depended on Evelyn's personal political circumstances.

45. See Bohun's "Character of Mary Evelyn" (1695), printed with some of her letters in Helen Evelyn, *The History of the Evelyn Family* (London, 1915), p. 98; and in Evelyn *Corr.*, IV, pp. 49–54. The best portrait of Mary may still be in *The Home-Life of English Ladies in the XVII Century* (London, 1860), pp. 1–134.

46. Mary Evelyn to Ralph Bohun, Jan. 4, 1672, Evelyn *Corr.*, IV, pp. 57–58.

47. "The virgins and young ladies of that golden age put their hands to the spindle, nor disdained they the needle; were helpful to their parents, instructed in the management of a family, and gave promise of making excellent wives."

48. Mrs Evelyn to Edmund Bohun (1667), Evelyn, *Corr.* (Bohn's), IV, pp. 8–9. *The Letters of Dorothy Osborne to Sir William Temple*, ed. Edward A. Parry (Everyman edn), pp. 81–82. It is interesting in this regard to read the regret expressed by an admiring George Ballard about this most forthright and prolific woman writer of the age, "that 'tis to be lamented she had not the advantage of an acquaintance with the learned languages which would have extended her knowledge, refined her genius, and have been of infinite service to her in the many compositions and productions of her pen": *Memoirs of Learned Ladies of Great Britain* (Oxford, 1752), pp. 299–300.

49. Evelyn, *Diary*, IV, p. 431.

50. Ibid., April 27, 1693, V, p. 138.

51. "Oeconomica to a Newly Married Friend," quoted in W. G. Hiscock, *John Evelyn and Mrs Godolphin* (London, 1951), p. 167; see Evelyn's *Life of Mrs Godolphin*, ed. Harriet Sampson (London, 1939), app. B. Much the same advice was offered by George Hickes in his translation of Fénelon's *Instructions for the Education of a Daughter* (1688); see Myra Reynolds, *The Learned Lady in England 1650–1760* (Gloucester, Mass., 1964), pp. 294–96.

52. Mary Astell, *Serious Proposals to the Ladies*, ed. Patricia Springborg with a useful introduction (London, 1997), pp. 10–14. See Ruth Perry, *The Celebrated Mary Astell* (Chicago, 1986).

53. Mary Astell, *The Christian Religion* (London, 1705), p. 292, quoted in Perry, *Celebrated*,

p. 9. See also *Reflections upon Marriage* (3rd edn 1705), in *The First English Feminist*, ed. Bridget Hill (New York, 1986), p. 73; and Sara Heller Mandelson, *The Mental World of Stuart Women* (Brighton, 1987), ch. 3. Mrs Astell's educational aims remained limited. "It is not intended," she wrote of her prospective pupil, that "she shou'd spend her hours in learning words but things, and therefore no more Languages than are necessary to acquaint her with useful Authors. Nor need she trouble herself in turning over a great number of Books, but take care to understand and digest a few well chosen ones": *Serious Proposal*, p. 10. "She was very genteely educated," recalled George Ballard, "and altho' she proceeded no farther in the languages at that time, than the learning of the French tongue; yet she afterwards gain'd some knowledge in the Latin." He thought the *Reflections* (2nd edn 1705), the strongest defense of the female sex to that time: *Memoirs*, pp. 447, 450.

54. Duchess of Newcastle, *Philosophical and Physical Opinions* (1655, 2nd edn 1663), in Douglas Grant, *Margaret the First* (London, 1957), pp. 213–15. "Man is made to govern Common-Wealths, and Women their privat Families": Duchess of Newcastle, *The World's Olio* (London, 1655), sig. S4v. See Jean Gagen, "Honor and Fame in the Works of the Duchess of Newcastle," *Studies in Philology*, 56 (1959), pp. 519–38.

55. Poulain de la Barre, *The Woman as Good as Man* (London, 1677), trans. from the French original (1673), pp. 6–8. La Barre followed this work with another on the excellence of men which (according to Pierre Bayle) was only meant ironically to reinforce his feminism; see Michael A. Seidel, "Poulain de la Barre's *The Woman as Good as the Man*," *Journal of the History of Ideas*, 35 (1974), pp. 499–508.

56. See Joan K. Kinnaird, "Mary Astell and the Conservative Contribution to English Feminism," *Journal of British Studies*, 19 (1979), pp. 53–75.

57. Evelyn, "Some Instances of the Learned, Vertuous and Fair Sex," *Numismata* (London, 1697), pp. 264–65, 285–86. For Mme Dacier's extraordinary classical education and her career in the *querelle* as a champion of the ancients, see Joseph M. Levine, *The Battle of the Books: History and Literature in the Augustan Age* (Ithaca, N.Y., 1991) pp. 133–40. Evelyn had anticipated much of this in a letter to Pepys, Aug. 12, 1689, *Corr.*, IV, pp. 437–39.

58. Anna Maria van Schurman, *The Learned Maid, or Whether a Maid may be a Scholar?*, trans. from the Latin (London, 1659), p. 29. Van Schurman was a genuinely learned Dutch woman who recommended the whole of the liberal arts to her sex, but inevitably found law, oratory and the military discipline, "less proper and necessary" (p. 5). See the essay by Joyce Irwin in *Female Scholars* (Montreal, 1980), pp. 68–85. Evelyn singles her out for praise in the *Numismata* and his letter to Pepys; she was a chief inspiration for later feminists like Mrs Makin.

59. He might be compared with Sir Ralph Verney who advised his daughter categorically "not to threaten Lattin, Greeke, and Hebrew," but to make do with French and "bookes fit for you as Romances, Plays, Poetry, Stories of Illustrious (not learned) Woemen . . . and all manner of good housewifery." See his letter to her, July 27, 1652, *Memoirs of the Verney Family*, ed. Margaret Verney, 4 vols (London, 1892), III, pp. 73–74. Or with Lord Halifax, who wrote an immensely popular *Advice to a Daughter* (twenty-five editions from 1688) and left all learning out. Or with the misogynist tract by Robert Gould, *Love Given O'er* (1682), which provoked a lively controversy that lingered till the end of the century. See the text with a useful introduction by Felicity Nussbaum (Augustan Reprint Soc., 180, 1976).

60. Evelyn to the Duchess of Newcastle, June 15, 1674, *Corr.*, III, pp. 395–98. The Duchess was accustomed to receiving the homage of lots of men; as in *A Collection of Letters and Poems, written by several important Persons of Honour and Learning to the late Duke and Duchess of Newcastle* (London, 1678). For the contemporary argument about women's rationality, see Hilda Smith, *Reason's Disciples: Seventeenth-Century English Feminists* (Urbana, 1982).

61. Evelyn to Wren, April 4, 1665, *Evelyn Corr.*, III, pp. 304–6. Evelyn recalls his "owne defects in the Greeke tongue and knowledge of its usefulnesse."

62. See the series of undated letters from Bohun to Evelyn at Christ Church, nos 303–11. Bohun lived with the Evelyn family for five years, according to Evelyn, "well and faithfully performing his Charge": *Diary*, Dec. 10, 1670, III, p. 566. He was rewarded much later by being given the rectory at Wotton.

63. John Evelyn, Jr to Sir Richard Browne, Paris, 1676; BL Add. MS 15,948, f. 149.

64. Evelyn to Mrs Evelyn, Jan. 18, 1697, *Seven Letters of John Evelyn*, pp. 11–14. See also Evelyn, *Diary*, Apr. 23, 1696, V, p. 236.

65. Jan. 1699, Evelyn Christ Church MS Corr. Some of the correspondence is summarized

in Hiscock, *John Evelyn*, pp. 207–11. In a long letter to the young Lord Spencer, Evelyn expounded on the importance of letter-writing and the use of classical models. "What should we have done without Ciceroes [letters] and the younger Plinies? to name no more because they were incomparably the best": Evelyn to Lord Spencer, Jan. 15, 1692, Christ Church Letterbook (1699), pp. 158–59. To Pepys, he writes that young Jack "not onely keeps but greatly improves his Greek, by directly reading their historys, and now and then, among his other exercises, he turns some passages into Latine; translates select Epistles out of Cicero and Pliny, and letting them lie-by for some time . . . turnes them into Latine again, the better to judge of his improvement": Evelyn to Pepys, Jan. 20, 1703, Samuel Pepys, *Private Correspondence and Miscellaneous Papers*, ed. J. R. Tanner (London, 1926), pp. 298–302. In 1665, Evelyn had been appointed to a committee for refining the English language; his suggestion was to imitate the best of the ancients; see Evelyn to Peter Wyche, June 20, 1665, Evelyn *Corr.*, III, pp. 309–12; Evelyn to Pepys, Oct. 4, 1689, in Samuel Pepys, *Letters and the Second Diary*, ed. R. G. Howarth (London, 1933), pp. 205–10.

66. Evelyn, *Memoires for my Grand-son*, ed. Geoffrey Keynes (Oxford, 1926), pp. 15, 42–43.

67. Charles I was of course a great patron and collector; see most recently Ronald Lightbown, "Charles I and the Tradition of European Princely Collecting," *The Late King's Goods: Collectors: Possessions and Paintings of Charles I in the Light of the Commonwealth Sale Inventories*, ed. Arthur MacGregor (London, 1989), pp. 53–72; Arthur MacGregor, "King Charles I: A Renaissance Collector?" *Sixteenth Century*, 11 (1996), pp. 141–60. It looks as though the Duke of Buckingham set out deliberately to rival Arundel; in 1627 he bought Rubens's collections, including many ancient sculptures. See L. R. Betcherman, "The York House Collection and its Keeper," *Apollo*, 92 (Oct. 1970); Graham Parry, *The Golden Age Restor'd: The Culture of the Stuart Court* (Manchester, 1981), pp. 136–45. The rivalry for the spoils of the eastern Mediterranean, conducted through Arundel's agent, William Petty, may be followed in Thomas Roe's *Negotiations*, ed. S. Richardson (London, 1740); A. T. F. Michaelis, *Ancient Marbles in Great Britain* (Cambridge, 1882), pp. 185–205.

68. It was published first in Latin in 1637, and in an English translation by Junius the following year at the request of the Countess of Arundel, *The Painting of the Ancients in Three Bookes* (London, 1638). The argument was to "set forth the Art of Painting as in old times it hath begun, as it was promoted, and as it came to that wonderful perfection mentioned in ancient Authors." See the edition and introduction to *De Pictura Veterum I*, by Colette Nativel (Geneva, 1996).

69. The best artists have always hoped to do better than their predecessors, and even though "it were not in their power to overtake and to out-run the best Antients, yet did they always strive to come so neere upon their heeles": *Painting of the Ancients*, trans. Junius, p. 15. Perfection should always be the aim, even if it should exceed our grasp, and it is open to the moderns, as well as it was to the ancients: ibid., pp. 14, 40. In any case, Junius is opposed to anyone who believes that "whatsoever is not done after the example of Antiquity, goeth against their stomackes": ibid., p. 32. At the same time, he is equally against an unrestricted fancy or imagination. In this as elsewhere, Junius counsels a mean between extremes, as did many of his classical sources. Thus he quotes Quintilian that "whatsoever is excessive is faulty," a counsel that would seem to preclude at least the wilder extremes of the baroque: ibid., p. 323.

70. Quintilian, "doth not without great reason forwarne us to take good heed that wee should not too much accustome our selves to a strict course of Imitation, least we might . . . loose . . . the ready suggestions of our own naturall wit": *Painting of the Ancients*, trans. Junius, pp. 31–38. See R. G. Austin, "Quintilian on Painting and Statuary," *Classical Quarterly*, 38 (1944), pp. 17–26.

71. In Italy, Poussin was more pessimistic. Theoretical principles, he pointed out, are no use to the painter, "unless they are confirmed by evidence that is the result of practical experience . . . unless the firm guidance of good examples points the way." Poussin was in Rome; what hope could there be in England? See Bellori's account of Poussin's teaching in Anthony Blunt, *Nicholas Poussin*, 3 vols (New York, 1967), I, app. I, p. 361.

72. Just at this moment, Henry Peacham was recalling the Ciceronian debate, and how Longolius was "laughed at for apish and superstitious imitation of Tully," in *The Compleat Gentleman*, p. 43.

73. Rubens praised the *De Pictura* as "a rich storehouse of examples, opinions and precepts, which relating to the dignity and

honor of the art of painting, scattered everywhere in the ancient writings . . . shed the greatest light for us." He only wished that Junius would complete it with a treatise on the modern Italian masters, "since the examples of the ancient painters can now be followed only in the imagination": Rubens to Junius, Aug. 1, 1637, *The Letters of Peter Paul Rubens*, ed. Ruth S. Magrun (Cambridge, Mass., 1955), pp. 406–8. For Rubens's devotion to antiquity, see Wolfgang Stechow, *Rubens and the Classical Tradition* (Cambridge, Mass., 1968).

74. See Evelyn to Pepys, Aug. 12, 1689, Evelyn *Corr.*, III, p. 450.

75. Dedication to Denham, in the translation of Fréart, below. Evelyn's plan is reproduced in the *Journal of the Royal Institute of British Architects*, 3rd ser., 27 (1919–20), pp. 467–70.

76. Evelyn, *A Parallel of the Antient Architecture with the Modern* (London, 1664), "To Sir John Denham."

77. "Soon after this happen'd the dredfull Conflagration of the Citty, when taking notice of our want of Books of Architecture in the English Tongue, I publish'd those most usefull Directions of ten of the best Authors in that subject, which were very scarce to be had . . . What the fruit of that Labour and cost has been (for the sculptures which are very elegant, were very chargable) the great Improvement of our Workmen, and several Impressions of the Copy since, will best testifie": Evelyn to the Countess of Sunderland, Aug. 4, 1690, Christ Church MS Corr., no. 1560.

78. William Cobbett, *Rural Rides* (1822), quoted in Michael Charlesworth, "A Plan of John Evelyn for Henry Howard's Garden at Albury Park," *Evelyn's Elysium Britannicum*, app. pp. 289–93. Evelyn, *Diary*, III, pp. 381–82, 496. See John Newman, "Hugh May, Clarendon and Cornbury," *English Architecture Public and Private: Essays for Kerry Downes*, ed. Edward Chaney (London, 1993), pp. 82–83; Douglas Chambers, "The Truth in the Landscape: John Evelyn's Garden at Albury," *Journal of Garden History*, 1 (1981), pp. 37–54; John Dixon Hunt, *Garden and Grove: The Renaissance Garden in the English Imagination 1600–1750* (London, 1986).

79. The original was published in Paris in 1662 as *Idée de la perfection de la peinture*.

80. Roland Fréart, Sieur de Chambray, *An Idea of the Perfection of Painting* (London, 1668), pp. 1–2.

81. "Whatever my esteem for Raphael may be, my resolution is to render all just deference to these illustrious Ancients . . . and do

cheerfully acknowledg, that the Painters of the latter Age are inferior to them": ibid., p. 85. Raphael was the closest of the moderns to them; Michelangelo, on the contrary, had in the *Last Judgment* completely betrayed the ancients: ibid., p. 66.

82. Ibid., p. 123.

83. Poussin to Chambray, March 1, 1665, applauding him as the first in France to have opened the eyes of those who would not see, in Blunt, *Nicholas Poussin*, app. 1, pp. 371–72.

84. See Evelyn, *Diary*, II, pp. 113, 399; III, p. 11; IV, p. 403.

85. Oct. 31, 1698, Evelyn MS Corr. "He is the greatest Man that ever handl'd the Graver," Evelyn wrote to Pepys, "and besides, he is a scholar and a well-bred Person": Aug. 21, 1669, in Marburg, *Pepys and Evelyn*, pp. 101–8. See also William Glanvill to Evelyn, April 10 and June 14, 1669, in Evelyn MS Corr., vol. 17 and three letters of Nanteuil to Evelyn in the MS Corr., nos 1016–18. There is a reproduction of the original picture with some useful information in François Courboin, *Catalogue de L'Ouvre de Robert Nanteuil* (Paris, 1925), pp. 187–90. Nanteuil also drew Mrs Evelyn and her parents for the family.

86. Evelyn to his wife, Sept. 16, 1648, Evelyn MS Corr., no. 1405. The artist was Robert Walker and the painting may now be seen in the National Portrait Gallery, London.

87. July 9, 1689, Evelyn, *Diary*, IV, p. 644. For the copy to Lely, see Keynes, *Evelyn*, p. 192. On Kneller's "baroque classicism," see J. Douglas Stewart, *Sir Godfrey Kneller and the English Baroque Portrait* (Oxford, 1983), pp. 84–85; and below, pp. 101–3.

88. Fréart's complaint was repeated by Rubens's admirer, De Piles, in his *Abregé* (1699); see Stechow, *Rubens*, p. 27.

89. Fréart, *Idea*, preface. For the quarrel in France, see Jacques Thuillier, "Polémiques autour de Michel-Ange au xviie siècle," *Dix-huitième Siècle*, 36–37 (1957), pp. 353–91.

90. The copy is now in the British Library with Evelyn's inscription, "ex dono authoris: meliora retinete." (Evelyn's full motto was *Omnia explorate, meliora retinete*, "Examine all things, retain the better of them.") See too the marginal note on p. 44. Bosse's work, *Le Peintre converty aux précises et universelle règles de son art* (Paris, 1667), capped his theorizing and was intended to offer "belles et bonnes instruction sur l'élection du bon goust ou choix des beaux objets sur l'histoire, et aussi sur le coloris." His theory of perspective was based on the work of

Gérard Desargues, and was set out early in his *Manière universelle pour pratiquer de perspective* (1648), a copy of which he also gave to Evelyn. It was Bosse's concentration on scientific perspective, which he tried to make the official academy position, that caused the breach with Le Brun, who preferred a less rigorous "aerial" perspective.

91. On Dec. 28, 1649, Evelyn went to see Bosse for instructions on perspective, *Diary*, II, p. 568. In 1669, Evelyn's brother-in-law, William Glanvill reported from Paris that Bosse had asked after Evelyn and promised to write: Glanvill to Evelyn, June 14, 1699, Evelyn MS Corr., vol. 17. Bosse helped design Evelyn's bookplate. For Bosse's career and quarrels, see André Blum, *Abraham Bosse et la Société Française au dix-septième siècle* (Paris, 1924).

92. Evelyn to Pepys, Aug. 21, 1669, in Marburg, *Pepys and Evelyn*, pp. 101–8. In 1662, William Faithorne forestalled Evelyn by translating Bosse's *Traité des manières de graver* (1645) as *The Art of Engraving and Etching* (1662).

93. When Fréart presented his translation of Leonardo's treatise on painting to the Academy in 1651, as a rule and guide, Le Brun praised it and Bosse protested; this seems to have begun the quarrel. By 1661, he had lost and was excluded from the Academy, but the quarrel went merrily on.

94. Bosse, *Le Peintre converty*, p. 54.

95. "I have too literally followed this preface which is in the original it selfe scarce sense in some places": marginal note at the end of the preface in Evelyn's copy, now in the British Library. Ibid. Bosse told his side of the story of the quarrel with the Academy in a little work, *Au Lecteur*, that is appended to Evelyn's copy of Le *Peintre converty*.

96. "It must be consider'd that they are our Learned Men, good Historians, and generally skill'd in the best Antiquities": ibid.

97. "If a Painter will meddle with History, there are old Statues to him the only life it selfe. I call Reubens to witnesse whether his knowledge in this kind hath not been his onely making": Peacham, *Compleat Gentleman*, p. 110. For the "Royall liking of ancient statues," see ibid., pp. 123–24. Rubens left a manuscript, *De imitatione statuarum*, that was published later by De Piles (1708). See Stechow, *Rubens*, p. 27; and Jeffrey M. Muller, *Rubens: The Artist as Collector* (Princeton, 1989). Junius had also pointed out the use to artists of the Arundel collection, "on publike view in the Academie at Arundell-House": *Painting of the Ancients*, p. 271.

98. Evelyn's friend, Beale, pointed out that he had been anticipated in this by Henry Wotton: Beale to Evelyn, Aug. 30, 1662, in Hiscock, *Evelyn*, p. 49. Charles I kept "a very greate Booke in folio of Prints beeing Severall Antiquities of Statues and Roman buildings," in his cabinet at Whitehall: Lightbown, "Charles I," p. 64.

99. *Philosophical Transactions*, 39 (Sept. 21, 1668) p. 784.

100. It was only long afterward in the *Numismata* (1697) that Evelyn confessed to his mistake and correctly assigned the invention to Ludwig von Seigen; see Keynes, *Evelyn*, pp. 116–19.

101. Evelyn, *Diary*, II, pp. 216, 225, 235, 300.

102. Ibid., p. 399. On both the distinction and the common classical ground for these artists, see the very helpful essay by Rudolf Wittkower, "The Role of Classical Models in Bernini's and Poussin's Preparatory Work," *Studies in the Italian Baroque* (London, 1975), pp. 103–14. Anthony Blunt points out that while Rubens prized the "baroque" works of the ancient world, Poussin preferred more "classical" models, even to anticipating the late eighteenth-century desire to imitate fifth-century Athens: *Poussin*, I, pp. 232–35. The defining moment in separating the two parties in Rome is usually said to be the debate in the Accademia di San Luca between Pietro da Cortona and Andrea Sacchi in 1636, both advocates of classical imitation, but the one freer and the other more restrained. The immediate issue was the number of figures that could plausibly be represented in a single picture. The "classicists" invoked the Aristotelian unity of action, analogous to that in ancient tragedy; the "moderns" preferred the analogy with ancient epic. It seems to have been the later critic, Bellori, in his *La Vita de'pittori, scultori et architetti* (1672), who set up the now familiar baroque–neoclassical opposition, by defining a classical line from Raphael to Agostino Carracci, through Domenichino and Sacchi, to Poussin and Maratti, disregarding (and implicitly condemning) Pietro da Cortona and Bernini. For better or worse this determined the neoclassical canon for the next two centuries. The debate in the Academy was first described by Melchiore Missirimi in 1823, and is pretty much followed by Rudolf Wittkower (*Art and Architecture in Italy 1600–1750*, Harmondsworth, 1958, pp. 169–80), who created the label "high baroque classicism," that has been widely accepted. See, for example, Jennifer Montagu, *Alessandro Algardi* (New Haven, 1985), p. viii. However, Denis Mahon and

Anne Sutherland Harris (in *Andrea Sacchi*, Oxford, 1977, pp. 33–37) have been among recent writers who have preferred more open and fluid categories to take account of the confusion.

103. Evelyn, *Sculptura*, ed. C. F. Bell (Oxford, 1906), p. 30.

104. See the series of letters by Evelyn to his grandson, 1699–1701, several in Hiscock, *Evelyn*, pp. 207, 220–22; and especially, Jan. 14, 1701, Evelyn MS Corr., no. 1476, where he takes the young man step by step through his lessons.

105. Hiscock, *Evelyn*, p. 105.

106. Evelyn, *Diary*, II, p. 277. Another Englishman who was shown Cassiano's collections was Philip Skippon in 1663. See his "Account of a Journey," in *A Collection of Voyages and Travels* (London, 1732), VI; and in Anthony Blunt, "Poussin and his Roman Patrons," in *Walter Friedlander zum 90 Geburtstag* (Berlin, 1965), app. I, pp. 71–72. For the growing literature on dal Pozzo, see the bibliography in *Cassiano dal Pozzo's Paper Museum*, I, ed. Ian Jenkins et al. (Olivetti, 1992).

107. Evelyn, *Diary*, II, p. 223.

108. Jan. 10, 1662, Evelyn, *Diary*, III, pp. 309–10.

109. Jan. 18, 1671, ibid., pp. 567–68. An alternative version is that it was Peter Lely who discovered Gibbons working at the Dorset Gardens Theatre who brought him to the attention of the King; see George Vertue, *Note Books*, I (Walpole Society, 18, 1930), p. 125, and J. Douglas Stewart, "New Light on the Early Career of Grinling Gibbons," *Burlington Magazine*, 118 (1976), p. 509; Geoffrey Beard, *The Work of Grinling Gibbons* (London, 1989), pp. 15–16.

110. From a manuscript inventory of 1702, quoted in David Green, *Grinling Gibbons: His Work as Carver and Statuary 1648–1721* (London, 1964), pp. 84–85.

111. June 16, 1683, Evelyn, *Diary*, pp. 316–17. Gibbons also carved Evelyn's portrait in wood, perhaps the one illustrated in Keynes, *Evelyn*, pl. 2.

112. George Vertue, commenting on a marble of Charles II that had broken, in the *Notebooks*, V (Walpole Society, 26, 1937–38), p. 59.

113. Evelyn, *Sylva* (1706), in Green, *Grinling Gibbons*, p. 16.

114. "This Monument requires the more Attention, as it has given Offence to Men of the best Taste": *An Historical Description of Westminster-Abbey* (London, 1764), pp. 130–31. Joseph Addison was one of the first to complain; March 30, 1711, *Spectator*, ed. G. G. Smith, 4 vols (London, 1907), I, pp. 96–99.

115. See also earlier, Evelyn to Pepys, Jan. 30, 1680, in Marburg, *Pepys and Evelyn*, pp. 115–17. Evelyn had made himself an expert on this too, first with another translation from the French, of Gabriel Naudé's *Instructions for the Erecting a Library* (1661). As for his own remarkable library, he made several catalogues which may still be seen among the Evelyn manuscripts, and there is an auction catalogue of his library, published by Sotheby's at its dispersal in 1977.

116. Evelyn to Pepys, Aug. 12, 1689, Evelyn, *Corr.*, III, pp. 439–40. One of Arundel's agents, who was helping him to collect in the East, Thomas Roe, summed up their value perfectly in a letter of 1626.

I have recalled that I saw you marshalling ancient coins and medals, delighting in the records of virtuous times, virtuous men, and virtuous actions. This curiosity of antiquities, though by some severe men censured, hath yet divers uses besides delight, not to be condemned. They are a land of lay humanity, teaching and inciting devotion to moral virtue, as well . . . They propose a living chronology on the one side, and a representation of history, heroic or great actions, on the other. They carry in them a shadow of eternity, and kindle an emulation of glory, by seeing dead men kept long among the living by their famous deeds.

Thomas Roe to the Countess of Bedford, Dec. 9/19, 1626, Roe, *Negotiations*, ed. Richardson, pp. 583–84; Howarth, *Arundel*, p. 234n.

117. Evelyn to Pepys, Aug. 12, 1689, Evelyn, *Corr.*, III, pp. 439–43. Unfortunately, Evelyn grew more garrulous with old age. "One thing leads to another," writes the exasperated Geoffrey Keynes of the *Numismata*, "and it would not be easy to reconstruct the passages by which Evelyn arrived at reminiscences of what Queen Henrietta Maria said to him about her spaniels, and why, in Evelyn's opinion, the creatures have an unsavory breath": Keynes, *Evelyn*, p. 231.

118. Evelyn, *Numismata*, pp. 120, 239. For further details on the contest and the two brothers, Thomas and Abraham Simon, see Vertue, *Notebooks*, V, pp. 46–47; and I, pp. 123–24. Sir George Hill retells the story and comments that "Charles had the bad taste to prefer Rotiere's work": *Medals of the Renaissance*, revised Graham Pollard (London, 1978), p. 159. In 1678, Evelyn visited Roettiers in the Mint, "that incomparable Graver, who emulates the Antients in both metal and Stone;

he was now moulding of an Horse for the King's statue to be cast in silver of a Yard high": July 20, 1678, *Diary*, IV, p. 138. Pepys was equally impressed on an earlier visit, March 26, 1666, *Diary*, VII, pp. 82–83.

119. See Lindsay Stainton and Christopher White, *Drawing in England from Hilliard to Hogarth* (London, 1987), nos 77–78, p. 113.

120. Evelyn to the Countess of Sunderland, Aug. 4, 1690, Evelyn *Corr.*, III, pp. 463–65.

Chapter 2 Evelyn between the Ancients and the Moderns

1. Too bad we have lost Evelyn's "description of a villa" from the *Elysium Britannicum*. See Douglas Chambers who cites a letter to Evelyn, Jan. 9, 1695, " 'Elysium Britannicum not printed neere ready, etc': The 'Elysium Britannicum' in the Correspondence of John Evelyn," *Evelyn's Elysium Britannicum*, ed. Therese O'Malley and J. Wolschke-Bulmahn (Washington, D. C., 1998), p. 118.

2. For what follows I have had to tread in the footsteps of Richard Foster Jones, to whose work, *Ancients and Moderns*, 2nd edn (St Louis, 1961), I am much indebted, although I have criticized it in the past; see Joseph M. Levine, "Ancients and Moderns Reconsidered," *Eighteenth Century Studies*, 15 (1981), pp. 72–89. Very helpful are the many contributions of Michael Hunter, some of them collected in *Establishing the New Science: The Experience of the Royal Society* (Woodbridge, 1989); and also his *Science and Society in Restoration England* (Cambridge, 1981), both with useful bibliographical essays.

3. Evelyn, *Memoires for my Grand-son*, ed. Geoffrey Keynes (Oxford, 1926), p. 40. Michael Hunter tells us that references to Bacon fill Evelyn's massive commonplace book; see "John Evelyn in the 1650s: A Virtuoso in Quest of a Role," in *Science and the Shape of Orthodoxy* (Woodbridge, 1995), p. 74.

4. Their enemies, therefore, had to deny this. According to Henry Stubbe, "The truth is the Lord Bacon is like great piles, when the Sun is not high, they cast an extraordinary shadow over the Earth, which lesseneth as the Sun grows vertical." But he only found fault with Bacon's account of the sweating sickness in his history of Henry VIII; see Stubbe, *Legends no Histories or a Specimen of some Animadversions upon the History of the Royal Society* (London, 1670), pp. 28–29.

5. Evelyn, *Numismata* (London, 1697), p. 340.

6. The work was the *Commentarii Collegii Coimbricensis* (1601–11); see Evelyn to John Evelyn III, Aug. 5, 1699, in W. G. Hiscock, *John Evelyn and his Family Circle* (London,

1955) , p. 211; and Ralph Bohun to Evelyn, n. d., Evelyn Christ Church MS Corr., no. 301. Bohun recognized Aristotle as a great methodizer, and still of some use, but not as an experimentalist, and thus incapable of making new discoveries.

7. For what follows, see my article, "Natural History and the New Philosophy: Bacon, Harvey, and the Two Cultures," in *Humanism and History* (Ithaca, NY, 1987), pp. 123–54.

8. Both the Mechanical Committee and the Committee for Collecting Natural Phenomena specifically invoked the *Parasceve* (1664); see Hunter, *Establishing the New Science*, pp. 92, 104. In 1680, Evelyn reports that he met with the Council of the Royal Society, "and [it] made an order that the next experiments to be examin'd, should be my L Verulam's, and an account to be given of them to the publique from yeare to yeare 'til we had gon through them": *Diary*, June 24, 1680, IV, p. 205.

9. For the social composition of the Royal Society, see Michael Hunter, *The Royal Society and its Fellows 1660–1700* (Chalfont St Giles, 1982). According to a contemporary (1710) source, "Most of their Members were either Men of considerable Fortune and Quality as well as Learning, or such as make their Studies their Business" (p. 27).

10. Evelyn to Mr Maddox (on behalf of Dr Needham), Jan. 10, 1658, Evelyn Corr. Wheatley, III, pp. 224–26. For Maddox, see Evelyn, *Diary*, III, p. 222n. See also Evelyn to Mr Carter, Nov. 27, 1665, advising him on a trip to Italy, Evelyn, Christ Church MS Corr., no. 264; and Evelyn to his grandson, advising him to add natural philosophy and mathematics to his Latin and Greek, *Memoires*, ed. Keynes, p. 37.

11. Another inspiration may have been from the French. In 1661 the Royal Society asked Evelyn to translate a letter from Samuel Sorbières to Thomas Hobbes, describing a proposal for such a society in France; see the transcript dated Feb. 1, 1658, in *The Carl H. Pforzheimer Library: English Literature 1475–1700*, 3 vols (New York, 1940), III, pp. 1206–7. The first article advocates the "advancement of the utilities of life."

12. Evelyn, *Diary*, Nov. 27, 1655, III, pp. 162–63. Recent work in the Hartlib papers at Sheffield University has turned up immense quantities of material, some of which is explored by Charles Webster in *The Great Instauration: Science, Medicine and Reform 1626–1660* (London, 1975) and in his edition of some documents, *Samuel Hartlib and the Advancement of Learning* (Cambridge, 1970). The older work of George H. Turnbull

remains indispensable, *Hartlib, Dury and Comenius* (Liverpool, 1947).

13. Hiscock, *Family Circle*, pp. 51–52. See also Hartlib to Evelyn, Sept. 24, 1659, and other related correspondence in BL Add. MS 15,948, f. 66ff.; and Evelyn to Beale, July 11, 1679, *Evelyn Corr.*, III, pp. 190–92. For Beale see Mayling Stubbs, "John Beale, Philosophical Gardener of Hampshire, I," *Annals of Science*, 38 (1982), p. 469.

14. Evelyn to Boyle, Sept. 3, 1659, *Evelyn Corr.*, III, pp. 261–67.

15. See the illustrations reproduced in Hunter, *Establishing the New Science*, pp. 181–84, pl. 11.

16. See Evelyn, *Diary*, Jan. 2, 1661, III, p. 266 and note.

17. "His Majestie was pleased to discourse with me concerning several particulars relating to our Society and the Planet Saturn, etc., as he sat at Supper in the withdrawing roome to his Bed-Chamber": ibid., May 14, 1661, p. 288.

18. Gabriel Naudé, *Instructions for Erecting of a Library*, trans. John Evelyn, ed. John C. Dana (Cambridge, 1903), dedication pp. ix–lxxvi; Evelyn, *Diary*, III, pp. 303–4, 306. See Keynes, *Evelyn, A Study*, no. 30, pp. 103–8.

19. Evelyn, *Diary*, Jan. 16, 1661, III, p. 268. See E. S. de Beer, "John Evelyn (1620–1706)," *Notes and Records of the Royal Society*, 15 (1960), p. 233; Michael Hunter, "John Evelyn in the 1650s," *Science and the Shape of Orthodoxy*, pp. 75–82.

20. Keynes, *Evelyn, A Study*, no. 33, pp. 116–22. *Sculptura* was presented to the Society in June; see Evelyn, *Diary*, III, p. 325; it was edited with an unpublished second part by C. F. Bell (Oxford, 1906). A manuscript account by Evelyn on the history of mezzotint has disappeared, although extracts appear in the English translation of Bayle's *Dictionary* (1734–41), I, p. 131.

21. Copies were delivered to the Royal Society, Feb. 16, 1664, and to the King, the Lord Treasurer and the Lord Chancellor; see Keynes, *Evelyn, A Study*, no. 40, pp. 130–40; no. 52, pp. 148–51; and no. 57, pp. 154–56. For its collaborative character, see Michael Hunter, "An Experiment in Corporate Enterprise," in *Establishing the New Science*, p. 76.

22. Evelyn, *Diary*, April 29, 1675, IV, pp. 62–63. The work was published the following year as *A Philosophical Discourse of Earth*; see Keynes, *Evelyn, A Study*, pp. 206–11. Other contributions to the Society by Evelyn may be followed in Thomas Birch, *The History of the Royal Society of London*, 4 vols (London, 1756–57), for which an index of proper names has been prepared in the *Notes and Records of the Royal Society*, 28 (1973), pp. 263–329. Evelyn drew on his observations abroad to make contributions to Boyle's *New Experiments and Observations touching the History of Cold* (1665); Hooke's *Micrographia* (1665); and John Houghton's *Collection for the Improvement of Husbandry and Trade* (1681); he also contributed several papers to the *Philosophical Transactions*; see Keynes, *Evelyn, A Study*, pp. 260–62.

23. "This is what abortives the perfection of the most glorious and useful undertakings": *Acetaria: A Discourse of Sallets* (London, 1699). Evelyn was referring to his incomplete manuscript *Elysium Britannicum*; but the comment could have applied equally to the history of trades which he gave up earlier. For a list of these manuscript projects, see the *Index of English Historical Manuscripts*, II, ed. Peter Beal (London, 1987), pp. 468–87.

24. "Be more assiduous in your Prayers," Evelyn wrote characteristically to his son (March 1680), "reading holy things morning and evening and consider your selfe in the presence of God." All his life Evelyn read theology and scrupulously reported the sermons he heard. His aim was to steer between "poperie and phanatisme," as he advised his wife in 1685. In 1654 he began an ambitious *History of Religion* which was printed posthumously by R. M. Evanson, 2 vols (London, 1850).

25. In July 1679, Evelyn complains to Beale about what he has "written and collected for above these 20 yeares upon this fruitfull and inexhaustible subject . . . not yet fully digested to my mind . . . I am almost out of hope that I shall ever have strength to bring it to maturity": Evelyn *Corr.*, III, pp. 190–92. In the preface to the *Acetaria* he is still writing wistfully about this enormous work, much of which has since been lost, but whose table of contents still survives there. It was printed first in a single sheet; see BL Add. MS 19,950, f.143. For details about the manuscript, see the essays by O'Malley and Ingram in *Evelyn's Elysium Britannicum*.

26. Evelyn to the Countess of Sunderland, Aug. 4, 1690, Evelyn Christ Church MS *Corr.*, no. 1560. See also the letter from Joseph Glanvill applauding its success, Jan. 15.

27. Evelyn to Thomas Browne, Jan 28, 1660, *The Works of Thomas Browne*, ed. Geoffrey Keynes, 4 vols (London, 1964), IV, p. 274. (For the date, see E. S. de Beer, "The Correspondence between Sir Thomas Browne and John Evelyn," *The Library*, 4th ser., 19

(1938–39), pp. 103–6.) The chapter was intended as book III, ch. 7 and was, according to Evelyn, "in a manner finished by itselfe." But he only supplied heads for Browne, probably as the broadsheet, "Plan of a Royal Garden," which survives in the British Library, MS 19,950, f.143. In the *Elysium* manuscript, it appears to have occupied book III, ch. 9, pp. 727–886, but it does not seem to have survived.

28. Taylor to Evelyn, April 16, 1656, Evelyn, *Corr.*, III, pp. 211–13. Pepys too admired it extravagantly; see *The Diary of Samuel Pepys*, ed. Robert Latham and William Matthews, 11 vols (Berkeley, 1970–83), VI, pp. 97, 253. Evelyn engraved a plan of the garden in 1653; see *Directions for the Garden at Sayes-Court*, ed. Geoffrey Keynes (London, 1932).

29. See the manuscript passage which seems to have been meant for Browne's *Garden of Cyrus*, in Browne, *Works*, ed. Keynes, I, p. 227. The *Garden of Cyrus* was first printed with the *Hydriotaphia* in 1658.

30. Quoted in Michael Leslie, "The Spiritual Husbandry of John Beale," *Culture and Cultivation in Early Modern England*, ed. Michael Leslie and Timothy Raylor (Leicester, 1992), p. 164. Douglas Chambers points out Beale's combination of classical humanism and Christian purpose; see his "'Wild Pastoral Encounter': John Evelyn, John Beale, and the Regeneration of Pastoral in the Mid-Seventeenth Century," ibid., p. 181. For Beale's modernity with respect to science and technology, see Beale to Hartlib (forwarded to Evelyn), March 16, 1660, BL Add. MS 15,948, ff.92–94.

31. Taylor to Evelyn, Feb. 10, 1660, *Corr.*, III, pp. 275–77. There is a swift general survey of the subject in John Prest, *The Garden of Eden: The Botanic Garden and the Re-creation of Paradise* (New Haven, 1981), with the "Elisium Britannicum" treated at pp. 47–48.

32. Evelyn, *Elysium Britannicum*, p. 155.

33. R. F. Jones describes some of the background, as well as recounting the squabble over the Royal Society, in his *Ancients and Moderns*. Unfortunately, Jones did not see that the proponents of scientific modernity (such as Evelyn) could side with the ancients in other matters.

34. Evelyn, *An Apologie for the Royal Party (1659); and A Panegyric to Charles the Second (1661)*, ed. Geoffrey Keynes (Augustan Reprint Soc., no. 28 1951), p. 14.

35. South gave an oration at Oxford, July 9, 1669, since lost, which apparently "consisted of satyrical invectives against Cromwell,

fanaticks, the Royal Society, and new philosophy." (So John Wallis to Robert Boyle, Boyle, *The Works*, 2nd edn, 6 vols (London, 1772), V, pp. 514–15.) Evelyn thought it all "very foolish and untrue, as well as unreasonable": *Diary*, July, 9, 1669, III, pp. 531–32. South had already condemned the Society in 1667: *Sermons Preached upon Several Occasions*, 7 vols (Oxford, 1823), I, pp. 373–75. See Beale to Oldenburg, June 1, 1667, *The Correspondence of Henry Oldenburg*, ed. A. Rupert Hall and Marie Boas Hall, III (Madison, 1966), pp. 425–30, and note; Marjorie Nicolson, *Pepys Diary and the New Science* (Charlottesville, 1965), p. 159.

36. Meric Casaubon, *A Letter to Peter du Moulin* (Cambridge, 1669), facsimile in Michael Spiller, *Concerning Natural Experimental Philosophie: Meric Casaubon and the Royal Society* (The Hague, 1980), app. I. Spiller also provides some extracts from Casaubon's unpublished *On Learning* (1667) and a long introduction. But see Michael Hunter, "Ancients, Moderns, Philologists, and Scientists," *Annals of Science*, 39 (1982), pp. 187–92. For the attacks on classical learning during the Interregnum, see Webster, *The Great Instauration*, ch. 3, "The Advancement of Learning," pp. 100–245; A. G. Debus (ed.), *Science and Education in the Seventeenth Century: The Webster–Ward Debate* (London, 1970).

37. Even his biographer finds his motives in entering the fray unclear; see James Jacob, *Henry Stubbe: Radical Protestantism and the Early Enlightenment* (Cambridge, 1983), ch. 5. He was certainly a more complicated and puzzling figure, and less consistently "ancient," than appears in Jones. For more on Glanvill, see Jackson I. Cope, *Joseph Glanvill, Anglican Apologist* (St Louis, 1956).

38. See the exchange between Stubbe and Glanvill quoted by Jones, with his comment, *Ancients and Moderns*, p. 338.

39. "Dr. Sprat's talent," Evelyn wrote in admiration of his sermons, "was, a great memorie, never making use of notes, a readinesse of expression, in a most pure and plaine style, for words and full matter, easily delivered," *Diary*, Nov. 23, 1679, IV, p. 188. For Sprat's employment as a polished author rather than as a scientist, see Michael Hunter, "Latitudinarianism and the 'Ideology' of the Royal Society: Thomas Sprat's *History of the Royal Society* (1667) Reconsidered," *Establishing the New Science*, pp. 49–50. Hunter also supplies an up-to-date account of the composition of the work, with some lost marginalia in Evelyn's copy and some

useful references to the Evelyn–Beale correspondence about it.

40. Thomas Sprat, *The History of the Royal Society*, ed. Jackson I. Cope and H. W. Jones (St Louis, 1958), pp. 35–36; and pt. 3, sect. ii, "Experiments will not injure Education," pp. 323–27.

41. See H. Fisch and H. W. Jones, "Bacon's Influence on Sprat's *History of the Royal Society*," *Modern Language Quarterly*, 12 (1951), pp. 399–406; and Paul Wood, "Thomas Sprat's *History of the Royal Society*," *British Journal of the History of Science*, 13 (1980), pp. 1–26.

42. Beale to Evelyn, n.d., Evelyn Christ Church MS Corr.; see Hunter, *Science and Society*, app. pp. 194–97. Cowley's verses, "To the Royal Society," repeat the views of Evelyn and Beale.

43. Perhaps this is the long letter to Electra (Mrs Blagge, later Lady Godolphin), July 1, 1676, in the Christ Church Letterbook, where Evelyn writes of the Royal Society that "our businesse is not to raise a new theorie of Philosophie, but collect plenty of Materials by new and joint Attempts for the Work." Materials must be gathered even "before the foundation is layd or any superstructure dream't of." The exchange with Beale 1668–69 remains unpublished in the Christ Church correspondence in the British Library; the letter to Glanvill, June 24, 1668, is in Evelyn *Corr.*, III, pp. 356–57.

44. Evelyn to Glanvill, June 24, 1668, Evelyn *Corr.*, III, pp. 356–57. Glanvill had praised the *Sylva* and the *Elysium Britannicum*, as well as Evelyn's contributions to sculpture, painting and architecture, "and the like practical useful things with which he hath enrich't it": *Plus Ultra* (London, 1686), pp. 73–74.

45. "The Members of the Royal Society bring in occasional Specimens, not compleat Systemes, but as Materials and particulars which may in time amount to a rich and considerable Magazine," and which will lead, eventually, "to a most august and noble structure": Evelyn to Beale, July 27, 1670, Christ Church Letterbook, no. cccxxix.

46. Evelyn here echoes a letter he had written to Cowley in 1667, urging him to contribute to the cause. "In a word our Registers have outdon Pliny, Porta, and Alexis, and all experimentalists, nay, the great Verulam himself, and have made a noble and more faithful collection of real secrets, usefull and instructive, than has hitherto been shown": Evelyn to Cowley, March 12, 1667, Evelyn *Corr.*, III, pp. 349–51.

47. Gassendi *The Mirrour of True Nobility and*

Gentility, trans. W. Rand (London, 1657), sig. A3v–A4. See Walter E. Houghton, "The English Virtuoso in the Seventeenth Century," *Journal of the History of Ideas*, 3 (1942), pp. 51–73, 190–219. For Evelyn's predecessor, see Georges Cahen-Salvador, *Un Grand Humaniste Peiresc 1580–1637* (Paris, 1951).

48. It is taken, Evelyn says, from an essay on the utility of travel by Samuel Sorbière. Here I quote from the preface to the Bell edition: Evelyn, *Sculptura*, ed. C. F. Bell (Oxford, 1906).

49. Evelyn, *Diary*, Aug. 25, 1678, March 28, 1688, IV, pp. 143, 576. In the *Sylva*, Evelyn remembers "the late elegant and accomplished Sir W. Temple," leaving his heart to be buried in his garden at his death; Arthur Posonby, *John Evelyn* (London, 1933), p. 319.

50. Temple's essay of 1685 was printed in the *Miscellanea, The Second Part* (1690), and is reprinted from the 1692 edition in *Five Miscellaneous Essays*, ed. Samuel Holt Monk (Ann Arbor, 1963), pp. 1–36. I have tried to anatomize the quarrel in "Ancients and Moderns," pp. 72–89, and to tell the whole long story in my *Battle of the Books: History and Literature in the Augustan Age* (Ithaca, N.Y., 1991).

51. July 6, 1679, Evelyn, *Diary*, IV, pp. 172–73.

52. See the exchange of letters, July 7 and Aug. 10, 1694, Samuel Pepys, *Letters and the Second Diary*, ed. R. G. Howarth (London, 1933), pp. 242–43, 247.

53. Wotton devotes a whole chapter to philology in the *Reflections upon Ancient and Modern Learning*, 2nd edn (London, 1697), ch. 27, pp. 310–21.

54. Richard Bentley, "A Dissertation upon the Epistles of Phalaris," appended to Wotton's *Reflections*.

55. See Levine, *Battle of the Books*, chs 2–3.

56. Evelyn to the Earl of Clarendon, Nov. 27, 1666, *Corr.* III, pp. 346–48. Sprat also acknowledges the useful work of the "Criticks and Philologists" who first rescued the ancients from the neglect of the Middle Ages, but cautions against remaining satisfied with the past: *History*, pp. 24–25. Evelyn's unfinished work, "Of Manuscripts," is in the *Miscellaneous Writings*, pp. 433–48.

57. Bentley to Evelyn, April 21, 1698; *Correspondence of Richard Bentley*, ed. Christopher Wordsworth, 2 vols (London, 1842), I, p. 167. Levine, *Battle of the Books*, p. 69.

58. Evelyn, *Numismata*, pp. 2–3, 51, 64, 72; Levine, *Battle of the Books*, pp. 338–42. Evelyn corrects Perrault's *Parallel between the*

Antient and the Modern Learning at one point in favor of Wotton; *Numismata*, p. 179.

59. Evelyn adds a marginal note in the new edition against those "Malevolents" who had tried to divide the Royal Society from Oxford University, and welcomes their present close association: "To the Reader," *Sylva*, n.p.

60. For the "modernity" of antiquarian scholarship, see "The Antiquarian Enterprise, 1500–1800," in Joseph M. Levine, *Humanism and History: Origins of Modern English Historiography* (Ithaca, N.Y., 1987), pp. 73–106; and *Battle of the Books*, pp. 327–73. For Evelyn and the *Britannia*, see ibid., p. 329.

61. Bentley to Evelyn, Apr 21, 1698, *Correspondence of Richard Bentley*, I, p. 152. Evelyn refers to a "club" which included Bentley and Pepys, with some other learned men, in a letter to his grandson, June 12, 1699, in Hiscock, *Family Circle*, pp. 209–11. A few years earlier, he was invited by Pepys to dinner with Newton, and Dr Thomas Gale. With Boyle gone, Pepys wrote, Evelyn would be their Peireskius. Pepys to Evelyn, Jan. 9, 1692, Pepys, *Private Correspondence 1679–1703*, ed. J. R. Tanner, 2 vols (London, 1929), I, pp. 51–52.

62. Among other things, Evelyn sent Wotton a copy of a poem on gardens by René Rapin without mentioning that his son had once translated it into English. The *Hortorum libri IV* (Paris, 1665) was a Virgilian imitation, or rather continuation, much in keeping with Rapin's critical stance in favor of the ancients over the moderns. Wotton especially recommends the dissertation that was appended, entitled *De universa hortensis culturae disciplina*, with its historical chapters, 6–7, in book 4. Wotton used it, and Evelyn included some of the poem in his second edition of *Sylva*. A second translation by James Gardiner appeared in 1706 and has been reprinted with an introduction by Irving T. McDonald (Worcester, Mass., 1932).

63. Evelyn to Wotton, Oct. 28, 1696, *Corr.*, IV, pp. 9–11.

64. Preface to La Quintenaye, *The Compleat Gard'ner* (London, 1693). The translation was attributed to Evelyn, but as he explained to his brother, it was only devised to sell the book, which was really by George London. John to George Evelyn, March 24, 1693, Evelyn Christ Church MS Corr., no. 1586. Evelyn particularly praises Louis XIV's gardener, Le Notre.

65. Evelyn to Wotton, Oct. 1701, Evelyn Christ Church MS Corr., no. 1683.

66. Evelyn to Wotton, June 26, 1697, Evelyn Christ Church MS Corr.

67. Wotton, *Reflections*, ch. 22, p. 293.

68. To be sure, Wotton did believe in the possibility that the moderns might one day come to rival the ancients in the humanities, while Temple did not; and he left open some fields where he thought they might have already done so, like architecture. But neither he nor Bentley had any wish to denigrate the general ancient superiority here, unlike some of their more radical modern counterparts abroad.

69. Charles Hatton to Evelyn, June 3, 1699, Evelyn Christ Church MS Corr., no. 873.

70. Sprat, *History*, p. 19.

Chapter 3 Dryden and the Moderns

1. For a good example of the latter, see Robert D. Hume, *Dryden's Criticism* (Ithaca, N.Y., 1970).

2. According to James Sutherland, "Dryden was so open-minded, and he fluctuated so often in his critical attitude that only a chronological treatment would give an adequate account of his changing critical positions." That is what I have tried to supply here, in close detail. And I have come to something of the same conclusion about Dryden's ambivalence, that "the chronic hesitation between a deep respect for the Ancients and an awareness that the modern world was very different from that of ancient Athens and Rome [and] was shared in various degrees by most of his contemporaries": *English Literature of the Late Seventeenth Century* (Oxford, 1969), p. 396.

3. See Joseph M. Levine, *The Battle of the Books: History and Literature in the Augustan Age* (Ithaca, N.Y., 1991) pp. 54–56; Charles E. Ward, *The Life of John Dryden* (Chapel Hill, 1961), pp. 10–12; James Winn, *John Dryden and his World* (New Haven, 1987), pp. 36–47.

4. Dryden to Busby (1682), *The Letters of John Dryden*, ed. Charles Ward (1942, reprinted New York, 1965), pp. 18–20. Speaking Latin was a requirement in many English public schools, though how thoroughly it was enforced is hard to say.

5. Headnote to the second satire of Persius, Charles E. Ward, *The Life of John Dryden* (Chapel Hill, 1971), p. 11.

6. For the reformers, see Richard L. Greaves, *The Puritan Revolution and Educational Thought* (New Brunswick, 1969); *Samuel Hartlib and the Advancement of Learning*, ed. Charles Webster (Cambridge, 1970), and Webster's monumental *Great Instauration* (New York, 1976). Hoole's subtitle continues

"Written about Twenty three yeares ago, for the benefit of Rotheram School, where it was first used; and after 14 years trial by diligent practise in London in many particulars enlarged, and now at last published for the general profit, especially of young Schoole-Masters." There is a modern version by E.T. Compagnac (London, 1913). My references are to the facsimile by Scolar Press (Menston, 1973).

7. See Joseph M. Levine, *Humanism and History* (Ithaca, N.Y., 1987), pp. 128–38.

8. See the essays by Morris Croll and George Williamson in *Seventeenth-Century Prose*, ed. Stanley Fish (New York, 1971).

9. Thus John Locke, another Busby student at Westminster, made some effort in his educational writing to de-emphasize the classics, even while holding to their practical importance; see my discussion in *Battle of the Books*, pp. 277–78.

10. Hoole, *New Discovery*, p. 144.

11. Ibid., p. 151.

12. May 13, 1661, *The Diary of John Evelyn*, ed. E. S. de Beer, 6 vols (Oxford, 1955) III, pp. 286–87.

13. Ibid., pp. 155, 166.

14. Ibid., p. 168.

15. See Arthur Hoffman, "Dryden's Panegyrics and Lyrics," *John Dryden*, ed. Earl Miner (London, 1972), pp. 120–55. For the association of Charles and Augustus, see in particular the closing lines of Dryden's *Astraea Redux: A Poem on the Happy Restoration and Return of his Majesty Charles the Second* (1660). Dryden also welcomed the Restoration and reproved the Interregnum in some lines that he contributed to a collection of Sir Robert Howard's in that same year. Evelyn's *Panegyric to Charles the II* has been reprinted by Geoffrey Keynes for the Augustan Reprint Society (28, 1951). The best expression of political Augustanism may be the magnificently illustrated folio volume of John Ogilby, *The Entertainment of Charles II through the City of London* (1662). See the facsimile edition by Ronald Knowles (Binghamton, 1988), and Gerrard Reedy, "Mystical Politics: The Imagery of Charles II's Coronation," *Studies in Change and Revolution*, ed. Paul Korshin (Menston, 1972), pp. 22–23. Ogilby had been responsible for the "poetical part" of the Coronation ceremony to which Dryden refers in his own welcoming poem, "To his Sacred Majesty: A Panegyric on the Coronation" (1661). All this was something of a volte-face for Dryden, who had earlier supported the Commonwealth and whose verses commemorating Cromwell (1659) were

reprinted in 1682 to embarrass him. Eventually both Evelyn and Dryden had to temper their first enthusiasm with the realities of Restoration kingship and politics.

16. See Lillian Feder, "John Dryden's Use of Classical Rhetoric," *PMLA*, 69 (1954), pp. 1258–78; Max Nanny, *John Drydens rhetorische Poetik* (Bern, 1959).

17. According to Congreve, "He had something in his Nature that abhorr'd Intrusion into any Society whatever." As a result, "he was Personally less known, and consequently his Character might become liable both to Misapprehensions and Misrepresentations": *The Dramatick Works of John Dryden*, 6 vols (London, 1717), epistle dedicatory; in *William Congreve Letters and Documents*, ed. John C. Hodges (New York, 1964), pp. 124–29. We have finally had a large-scale biography by James A. Winn *John Dryden and his World* (New Haven, 1987), which furnishes much context and criticism, though it does not offer much more, biographically, than Ward's much slimmer older volume.

18. The California edition of *The Works of John Dryden*, 20 vols (Berkeley, 1961–89), (hereafter cited as *Works*), XVII, pp. 73–74.

19. For his "curious inconsistency," see Hugh Macdonald, "The Attacks on John Dryden," *Essays and Studies*, 21 (1955), pp. 41–74, esp. 45, 73.

20. Evelyn, Nov. 26, 1661, *Diary*, III, p. 304.

21. Had we not for the pleasure found new wayes
  You still had rusty arras had, and thredbare playes;
  Nor Scenes nor Women had they had their will,
  But some with grizl'd Beards had acted Women still.

  Second prologue to Shadwell's *Tempest* (1674), *London Stage*, p. xxvii.

22. For all these matters, see the introduction to *The London Stage*, pt. 1: *1660–1700*, ed. William van Lennep (Carbondale, 1965), pp. xxii–xxx.

23. Dryden always disparaged his own comedies, which he thought "inferior" to any other dramatic writing and as a result neglected defending them. See the preface to *An Evening's Love: or the Mock Astrologer* (1671), *Of Dramatic Poesy and Other Critical Essays*, ed. George Waston, 2 vols (London, 1962). Hereafter cited as *Essays*, I, pp. 144–55.

24. See *The Dramatic Works of Roger Boyle, Earl of Orrery*, ed. William C. Clark, 2 vols (Cambridge, Mass., 1937).

25. See Montagu Summers, *The Playhouse of Pepys* (New York, 1935), ch. 1; and for a fresh

reading of the relationship, David B. Haley, *Dryden and the Problem of Freedom* (New Haven, 1997), pp. 140–72.

26. H. J. Oliver argues persuasively (against the usual view) that Howard did indeed deserve the credit that he took for the lion's share of the work, *Sir Robert Howard* (Durham, N.C., 1963), pp. 66–67.

27. Evelyn, *Diary*, Feb. 5, 1664, III, pp. 398–99.

28. Tuke proclaimed the "newness" of his venture in the prologue. Evelyn went to see a rehearsal and performance of *The Adventures of Five Hours* on Dec. 23, Jan. 8 1662–63, and admired it, though he found the "language stiff and formal." Evelyn, *Diary*, III, pp. 348, 350. Pepys thought it one of the best plays he had ever seen, *The Diary of Samuel Pepys*, ed. Robert Latham and William Matthews, 11 vols (Berkeley, 1970–83). Jan. 8, 1663, IV, p. 8. Evelyn's notes are on some loose pages now together with the first scene of *The Originals* in the Christ Church manuscripts in the British Library. *Thersander*, which is also among them, is a nearly finished play, though Evelyn seems to have been dissatisfied with the introductory act which has been rewritten and crossed out. The theme pits the political obligations of the prince against the overwhelming passion of love; its language seems stiff and formal too, but that was undoubtedly one of the faults of the genre.

29. Pepys, *Diary*, VI, p. 289.

30. Orrery's account of how he was induced to write by the King after the new fashion is recounted in a much-quoted letter to the Duke of Ormonde, Jan. 23, 1662; see Mervyn L. Poston, "The Origin of the English Heroic Play," *Modern Language Review*, 16 (1926), pp. 19–20. For Dryden's access to Orrery's unpublished works, see Kathleen M. Lynch, *Roger Boyle, First Earl of Orrery* (Knoxville, 1965), pp. 20–26, 71–109; Haley, *Dryden and the Problem of Freedom*, pp. 152–55.

31. Preface to Dryden, *The Rival Ladies* (1664), *Essays*, ed. Watson, I, pp. 1–9.

32. George Williamson, "The Occasion of *An Essay on Dramatic Poesy*," *Modern Philology*, 44 (1946), pp. 1–9; reprinted in *Essential Articles for the Study of John Dryden*, ed. H. T. Swedenberg (Hamden, Conn., 1966), pp. 65–82. For the text, see Dryden, *Works*, XVII; *Essays of John Dryden*, ed. W.P. Ker, 2 vols (Oxford, 1900) (hereafter cited as *Works*, ed. Ker); *Essays*, ed. Watson.

33. Dryden to Charles Buckhurst, *Works*, XVII, pp. 3–6.

34. James M. Osborn, *John Dryden: Some Biographical Facts and Problems* (Gainesville,

1965), pp. 196–97; text in Dryden, *Works*, II, pp. 43–44.

35. Many years later, Dryden praises Plutarch, who was content to, "only to propound and weigh opinions, leaving the Judgment of his readers free without presuming to describe Dogmatically": preface to Plutarch's *Lives* (1683), *Works*, XVII, p. 249.

36. See Frank L. Huntley, "On the Persons in Dryden's *Essay on Dramatic Poesy*," *Modern Language Notes*, 63 (1948), reprinted in *Essential Articles*, ed. Swedenberg, pp. 88–95. Edmond Malone was the first to try to identify them, *The Critical and Miscellaneous Prose Works*, 3 vols (London, 1800), I, pt. i, pp. 62–67. Recently, David Haley has reconsidered the problem and offered his own view, *Dryden and the Problem of Freedom*, pp. 165–72.

37. Orrery, *The Dramatic Works*, ed. Clark, I, pp. 23–24, 33, 37–38. See also William S. Clark, "Dryden's Relations with Howard and Orrery," *Modern Language Notes*, 42 (1927), pp. 16–20.

38. See Tuke's prologue which credits the King and proclaims the "newness" of the play, *The Adventures of Five Hours*, ed. A. E. H. Swaen (Amsterdam, 1927), p. 51. Allison Gaw showed a long time ago how Dryden responded to Tuke's play in the *The Wild Gallant* and in *The Essay on Dramatic Poesy*, *Sir Samuel Tuke's Adventures of Five Hours in Relation to the Spanish Plot and to Dryden* (Baltimore, 1917), pp. 14–15, 21–22.

39. Campion, "Observations in the Art of English Poesie" (1602); Daniel, "Defence of Rhyme," (1603), in *Elizabethan Critical Essays*, ed. G. Gregory Smith, 2 vols (Oxford, 1904), II, pp. 327–55, 356–80. Rhyme had been attacked earlier by Ascham and Puttenham.

40. Daniel, "Defence," *Elizabethan Critical Essays*, pp. 366–67.

41. Ibid., pp. 371–72.

42. Smith, Intro., ibid., pp. lxiii–iv. But see my *Battle of the Books*, for a more qualified opinion, p. 295; and Author Ferguson, "The Historical Thought of Samuel Daniel: A Study in Renaissance Ambivalence," *Journal of the History of Ideas*, 32 (1971) pp. 185–202.

43. Ben Jonson told Drummond that he had answered Daniel; see too his "A Fit of Rime against Rime," *Underwoods*, *Works*, 11 vols (Oxford, 1947), VIII, pp. 183–84.

44. See John M. Aden, "Dryden, Corneille and the *Essay of Dramatic Poesy*," *Review of English Studies*, n. s. 6 (1955), pp. 147–56; Lawrence E. Padgett, "Dryden's Edition of Corneille," *Modern Language Notes*, 71 (1956), pp. 173–74; Pierre Legouis,

"Corneille and Dryden as Dramatic Critics," *Seventeenth Century Studies: Essays to Herbert Grierson* (1938, reprinted New York, 1967), pp. 269–91; R. V. LeClercq, "Corneille and *An Essay of Dramatic Poesy*," *Comparative Literature*, 22 (1970), pp. 319–27.

45. Sprat, *Observations on Monsieur de Sorbier's Voyage into England* (London, 1668), pp. 214–16.

46. Intro. to *The Rival Ladies*, Dryden, *Works*, VIII, pp. 272–74 (and *Essays*, ed. Watson, pp. 1–9). For a recent discussion and useful bibliography, see Derek Hughes, *Dryden's Heroic Plays* (London, 1980). William B. Piper points out that the new verse still kept a close relation with its classical predecessor, especially the elegiac distichs of Ovid and Martial, "The Inception of the Classical Heroic Couplet," *Modern Philology*, 66 (1968–69), p. 321.

47. It was, incidentally, the "ancient" Francis Atterbury, who was to edit Waller in 1690 and insist on his classical status. *The Second Part of Mr Waller's Poems* (London, 1690).

48. "To the Reader," Dryden, *Four New Plays* (London, 1665). Dryden's "Defence of the Essay on Dramatic Poesy," prefixed to the *Indian Emperour* (2nd edn, 1668), in *Essays*, ed. Watson, I, p. 130. See John Harrington, "The Dryden–Howard Collaborations," *Studies in Philology*, 51 (1954), pp. 54–74; J. H. Oliver, *Sir Robert Howard 1626–98* (Durham, N.C. 1963), ch. 6. For the personal and political motives that also divided the two men, see George McFadden, *Dryden the Public Writer 1660–1685* (Princeton, 1978), pp. 59–87.

49. Oliver, *Sir Robert Howard* opposes the identification, p. 100, relying on George R. Noyes, "Crites in Dryden's *Essay on Dramatic Poesy*," *Modern Language Notes*, 38 (1923), pp. 333–37; see also Huntley in *Essential Articles*, ed. Swedenberg, p. 84.

50. Dryden, *Essay on Dramatic Poesy*, *Works*, XVII, p. 12; *Essays*, ed. Watson, I, p. 23. The Latin is from the *Satyricon*.

51. *Essays*, ed. Watson pp. 12–13.

52. Ibid., p. 37.

53. "To my Honored Friend, Dr. Charleton," *Works*, II, pp. 43–44. Charleton had written in his *Immortality of the Soul* (1657) – for which Dryden may have written the preface – "all Scholars should have reverend esteem of Antiquity, as a good guide for our younger Reason into the waies of Nature; Yet I think it scarce safe for any man to follow it implicitly and without examination . . . The Ancients indeed have left us large and noble Foundations; but few com-

pleat Buildings . . . [the moderns] advance Superstructures of their own": ibid., p. 251. See Osborn, *John Dryden*, pp. 190–91. This may well have been Dryden's view at the time. To be sure, Earl Wasserman thought that the praise of science in the ode was merely a political ploy, *The Subtler Language* (Baltimore, 1959), p. 15.

54. See the discussion by Ella T. Riske, Lewis I. Bredvold and others in *Publications of the Modern Language Society*, 46 (1931), pp. 951–62, and Bredvold "Dryden, Hobbes, and the Royal Society," *Modern Philology*, 25 (1928), pp. 417–38; *Essential Articles*, ed. Swedenberg, pp. 314–40. Earl Miner doubted Dryden's enthusiasm for the new science, "Dryden and the Issue of Human Progress," *Philological Quarterly*, 40 (1961), pp. 120–29. His mature view is set out in his praise of Plutarch many years later (1683), when he argued that moral philosophy was superior to natural philosophy because it admitted less doubt, and because it was "more conducing to the benefit of human life. For after the example of Socrates he had found that the Speculations of Natural Philosophy were more delightful than solid and profitable; that they were abstruse and thorny, and much of Sophism in the Solution of appearances." Even mathematics, "tho' they made him wiser, they made him no more virtuous." As a result, Plutarch, according to Dryden, learned some science, but "made it his Recreation, not his business": *Works*, XVII, pp. 249–50. See also *Don Sebastian*, preface. (1690), ibid., XV, pp. 65–66.

55. Dryden, *Essay of Dramatick Poesie*, *Works*, XVII p. 41.

56. Ibid., p. 43. For Jonson's reputation as the imitator of the ancients, see Robert G. Noyes, *Ben Jonson on the English Stage 1660–1776* (Harvard Studies in English, 17, 1935), p. 17.

57. Dryden, *Works*, XVII, pp. 54–55, 58–63.

58. Ibid., pp. 57, 64. See Arthur Colley Sprague, *Beaumont and Fletcher on the Restoration Stage* (Cambridge, Mass., 1926).

59. Ibid., pp. 71–73.

60. *Essays*, ed. Watson, I, pp. 123–24.

61. So Legouis, "Corneille and Dryden," pp. 280–81.

62. Evelyn dined with Howard, Feb. 16, 1685, "pretending to all manner of Arts and Sciences for which he had been the subject of Comedy, under the name of Sir Positive; not ill-natured, but unsufferably boasting": *Diary*, IV, p. 316. The play was Shadwell's *Sullen Lovers* (1668).

63. Sir Robert Howard, "To the Reader," "The

Great Favorite, or the Duke of Lerma"
(1668), in *Five New Plays* (London, 1672);
Oliver, *Howard*, p. 107.

64. "Defence of an Essay," *Essays*, ed. Watson, I,
p. 122. In the preface to the *Annus Mirabilis*,
Dryden writes of Virgil, "I must own . . .
that he has been the master in this poem.
I have followed him everywhere, I know
not with what success, but I am sure with
diligence enough; my images are many of
them copied from him, and the rest are
imitations of him. My expressions also are
as near as the idioms of the two languages
would admit in translation": *Essays*, ed. Ker,
I, p. 17.

65. "Defence," *Essays*, ed. Watson, I, p. 124.

66. Prologue to *Sacred Love*, Dryden, *Works*, IX,
p. 119; *Essays*, ed. Ker, I, p. 109. In fact the
play is a tragicomedy and decidedly irregular! It was written 1665–66, performed
1667, and published in 1668 (*Essays*, ed.
Watson, p. 104). The preface to the *Annus
Mirabilis* is signed Nov. 10, 1666; see *Essays*,
ed. Ker, I, p. 10.

67. Janet M. Bateley, "Dryden's Revisions in the
Essay of Dramatic Poesy," *Review of English
Studies*, n. s., 15 (1964), pp. 268–82; Irene
Simon, "Dryden's Revision of the *Essay of
Dramatic Poesy*," ibid., 14 (1963), pp. 132–41;
Janet Bateley, "Dryden and Branded Words,"
Notes and Queries, 210 (April 1965),
pp. 134–39.

68. Samuel Johnson, *Lives of the English Poets*, ed.
G. Birkbeck Hill, 3 vols (Oxford, 1905), I,
p. 412.

69. The shift is noticed by Mary Thrale,
"Dryden's Dramatic Criticism: Polestar of
the Ancients," *Comparative Literature*, 18
(1966), pp. 36–54.

70. Howard's preface to *The Woman's Conquest*
(London, 1671) defends the Elizabethans
with a strong argument for modernity, only
to qualify it as usual. "Most men are naturally inclin'd to give to Antiquity its due
respects, and there is some reason for it (if
no more) in that we must be old our selves;
but we were weakly an admirer of times
past, that by our own dotage on them,
would continue himself in a childhood of
knowledge." Nevertheless, English is still not
up to Latin or Greek, Virgil is the prince of
poets, etc.

71. See, for example, *The Usurper*, performed in
1664, and published four years later, along
with the pamphlet by R. F. (perhaps Richard
Flecknoe), *A Letter from a Gentleman to the
Hon. Ed. Howard* (1668); and Howard's *The
Six Days Adventure* (1671). In the preface to
The Woman's Conquest, Howard continued
the attack on rhyme, but declared himself

on the side of modernity, though with the
usual qualifications. "He were weakly an
admirer of times past, that by an over-dotage
on them, would continue himself in the
Childhood of knowledge; since that were to
go backward with ingenuity, as we set too
forward theirs. They have their fame and we
must expect ours; though at present they
challenge so long a prescription, that until
ours doe number more than the three parts
of an age in equal repute with theirs, I make
some doubt whether the best Rhime or
reason that the Stage is now beholding to,
will establish us as great in the judgment of
those who shall succeed us."

72. Pepys, *Diary*, Sept. 19, 1668; see Thomas
Shadwell, *The Complete Works*, ed. Montagu
Summers, 5 vols (London, 1927), I, p. lxix.

73. Shadwell, *Sullen Lovers*, *Works*, I, pp. 9–11.

74. Ibid. p. 187. See R. Jack Smith, "Shadwell's
Impact on John Dryden," *Review of English
Studies* 20 (1944), pp. 29–44. For Pepys on
the *Sullen Lovers*, see *Diary*, May 2, 4, 8, 14.

75. Dec. 14, 1671, Evelyn, *Diary*, III, p. 529.

76. Buckingham, *The Rehearsal*, ed. Edward
Arber (Westminster, 1902), pp. 33, 136. There
is a more recent version by D. E. L. Crane
(Durham, N.C., 1976), who notes that the
third edition (1675) adds more references to
Dryden. See John Harrington Smith,
"Dryden and Buckingham: The Beginnings
of a Feud," *Modern Language Notes*, 69
(1954), pp. 242–45. There were nearly 300
performances between 1671 and 1777. For
Rochester's "attitude of veneration towards
classical antiquity," see David M. Veith, *Attribution in Restoration Poetry: A Study of
Rochester's Poems of 1680* (New Haven, 1963),
p. 221.

77. John Reichart, "A Note on Buckingham
and Dryden," *Notes and Queries* (June 1962),
pp. 220–21.

78. Earl of Rochester, *Complete Poems*, ed. David
M. Veith (New Haven, 1963), p. 221; see
Howard Weinbrot, "An Allusion to Horace:
Rochester's Invective Mode," *Studies in
Philology*, 69 (1972), pp. 348–68; Frank L.
Huntley, "Dryden, Rochester, and the
Eighth Satire of Juvenal," *Philological Quar-
terly*, 18 (1939), pp. 269–84; *Essential Articles*,
ed. Swedenberg, pp. 91–111.

79. Preface to the *Mock-Astrologer* (1671), *Essays*,
ed. Watson, I, pp. 148, 154.

80. Mary Evelyn to Ralph Bohun [1671],
Evelyn, *Diary and Correspondence*, ed. H. B.
Wheatley, 4 vols (London, 1906), IV, pp.
56–57. John Evelyn's comment is in Feb. 9,
1671, Evelyn, *Diary*, III, pp. 569–70. In 1668,
he had found Dryden's *Evening's Love*
foolish and very profane, "the stage degen-

erated and poluted by the licentious times":
Diary, III, pp. 510–11. In 1676, he wrote
about plays to a lady friend: "Not onely the
Fathers have universally decry'd them as
impious and abominable, but the whole
current of Divines and Religious men . . .
[do] utterly condemn them." He was especially offended by the women actors who
exposed themselves on the stage, "repugnant
to the Vows and natural Modestie of the
Sex." At that time, he had been to the
theater only once in four or five years;
Evelyn to Electra [Mrs Blagge], July 1, 1676;
Evelyn Christ Church MS Corr. Later, he
advised his son Jack to be careful about
where he went in London, the playhouses
being especially dangerous, April 18, 1690,
ibid.

81. Dryden, "Of Heroic Plays," *Essays*, ed.
    Watson, I, p. 156.

82. *Gondibert*, ed. David F. Gladish (Oxford,
    1971); Cornell M. Dowlin, *Sir William
    Davenant's Gondibert* (Philadelphia, 1934).

83. Dryden, "A Defence of the Epilogue, or An
    Essay on the Dramatic Poetry of the Last
    Age" (1672); *Essays*, ed. Watson, I, p. 169.

84. In an exchange of pamphlets in 1673,
    Dryden was attacked and defended for his
    "superbosity in prostrating the fame of
    defunct, and breathing Authors." The four
    pamphlets, for and against, are printed in
    Dryden: The Critical Heritage, ed. James and
    Helen Kinsley (London, 1971). See H. R.
    Steeves, "The Athenian Virtuosi and the
    Athenian Society," *Modern Language Review*,
    7 (1912), pp. 358–71. The quotation is from
    the anonymous *The Athenian Virtuosi
    Answered*, p. 105.

85. Dryden, "Defence of the Epilogue," *Essays*,
    Watson, I, p. 169.

86. Ibid., p. 170.

87. See Robert D. Hume, *The Development of
    English Drama in the Late Seventeenth Century*
    (Oxford, 1976), pp. 281–82.

88. The texts are provided by Maximilian
    Novak, *The Empress of Morocco and its Critics*
    (Augustan Reprint Soc., special publication,
    1968). According to the hostile Langbaine,
    Settle's attack "shewed Mr. Dryden was not
    Infallible, but notwithstanding his Brava-
    does, he himself was as faulty as others":
    Dryden, *Works*, XVIII, p. 387. See also Anne
    Doyle, "Dryden's Authorship of *Notes and
    Observations* (1674)," *Studies in English Liter-
    ature*, 6 (1966), pp. 421–45.

89. McFadden, *Dryden the Public Writer*, pp.
    57–58.

90. Dedication to *The Conquest of Granada*, in
    Works (Saintsbury), IV, pp. 11–17. See Walter
    Scott's remarks on the improbable character

of Almanzor and its indebtedness to
romance, ibid., pp. 1–10.

91. The pejorative terms are all borrowed from
    D. W. Jefferson, "The Significance of
    Dryden's Heroic Plays," in *Restoration
    Drama: Modern Essays in Criticism*, ed. John
    Loftis (New York, 1966), p. 177. See also
    Bruce King, *Dryden's Major Plays* (Edin-
    burgh, 1966). The Augustan verdict is much
    the same; see George Granville, Lord Lan
    downe, "An Essay upon Unnatural Flights
    in Poetry," *A New Miscellany* (London,
    1701), pp. 311–22. Jefferson makes a valiant
    attempt to rescue Dryden from this criti-
    cism by suggesting that the sometimes
    comical effect of the plays was intentional
    rather than inadvertent. John Heath-Stubbs
    also notices the "element of ironic comedy
    in Dryden's heroic tragedies": "Dryden and
    the the Heroic Ideal," *Dryden's Mind and Art*,
    ed. Bruce King (Edinburgh, 1969). Robert
    Hume is not convinced about this view of
    Dryden's intentions, I think rightly, but he
    accepts the anomalies of Dryden's form and
    style, and leaves the critical problem unre-
    solved: *Development of English Drama*, pp.
    187–91.

92. Hume, *Development of English Drama*, pp.
    318–19.

93. Dryden, "Notes and Observations on the
    Empress of Morocco" (1674), *Works*, XVII,
    pp. 180–84. See Doyle, "Dryden's Author-
    ship of *Notes and Observations*," pp. 421–45.

Chapter 4 Dryden and the Ancients

1. René Rapin, *The Whole Critical Works*, ed.
   B. Kennett 2 vols (London, 1706), I, sig.
   A2v. Thomas Pope Blount collects some
   contemporary tributes in his *De Re
   Poetica: Or Remarks upon Poetry with
   Characters and Censures* (London, 1694), pp.
   186–88.

2. Rapin, *Works*, I, p. 321.

3. Ibid., p. 485.

4. Ibid., II, p. 447.

5. Ibid., pp. 384–85.

6. "Design of the Work," ibid., I, sig. b.

7. René Rapin, *Reflections on Aristotle's Treatise
   of Poesie with Reflections on the Whole of the
   Ancient and Modern Poets and the Faults Noted*
   (London, 1974) [sig. b3]. The original has
   been edited by E. T. Dubois, *Les Réflexions
   sur la poétique* (Geneva, 1970).

8. Rapin, *Reflections on Aristotle*, pp. 16–17.

9. Ibid., pp. 52–53.

10. Ibid., p. 55.

11. For Rymer's life, see Thomas Duffus Hardy,
    Syllabus of Rymer's Foedera, 3 vols (London,
    1969), I, intro., pp. xv–xxvi.

12. For Rymer's verse, see James M. Osborn, "Thomas Rymer on Rhyme," *Philological Quarterly*, 54 (1975), pp. 152–77. *Edgar* was probably written between 1672 and 1677 and published in 1678; it was damned by Dryden, who read it before publication, in his preface to *Love Triumphant*. See Rymer, *The Critical Works*, ed. Curt Zimansky (New Haven, 1956), pp. 216–23.

13. Macaulay proclaimed him "the worst critic who ever lived!" Hardy, *Syllabus*, p. xxi. For recent (but uncharacteristic) praise, see T. S. Eliot, *John Dryden, the Poet, the Dramatist, the Critic* (New York, 1932), p. 55. Earl Miner offers a more qualified judgment in "Mr Dryden and Mr Rymer," *Philological Quarterly*, 54 (1975), pp. 137–51.

14. See George P. Dutton, "The French Aristotelian Formalists and Thomas Rymer," *PMLA*, 29 (1914), pp. 1528–88; and Rymer, *Critical Works*, ed. Zimansky, p. xxix.

15. *The Tragedies of the Last Age*, Rymer, *Critical Works*, ed. Zimansky, p. 2 (cf. p. 18).

16. Ibid., pp. 2–3.

17. Ibid., pp. 4, 122.

18. Ibid., p. 18.

19. This is the argument of Saint-Evremond, for example; see ch. 7 below.

20. *The Tragedies of the Last Age*, Rymer, *Critical Works*, ed. Zimansky, p. 19 (cf. p. 57).

21. Ibid., p. 19.

22. Ibid., p. 21.

23. Ibid., p. 74.

24. Ibid., p. 75.

25. "I protest to you, as I am an Author . . . I can hardly keep my self from quoting Aristotle and Horace, and talking to you of the Rules of Writing (like the French Authors) to shew you and my Readers I understand 'em": William Wycherley, *The Plain Dealer* (1677), *The Plays*, ed. Arthur Friedman (Oxford, 1979), p. 369.

26. Dryden to the Earl of Dorset [1677], *The Letters of John Dryden*, ed. Charles Ward (1942, reprinted New York, 1965), pp. 13–14.

27. Wycherley to the Earl of Mulgrave, Aug. 20, 1677 (*Times Literary Supplement*, April 18, 1935), p. 257); Samuel Butler, *Prose Observations*, ed. Hugh de Quehen (Oxford, 1979), pp. 131, 143, 184–86, 203–4, 257–58); "Upon Critics who Judge of Modern Plays Precisely by the Rules of the Ancients," *Genuine Remains* (1759), reprinted in *Critical Essays of the Seventeenth Century*, ed. Joel Spingarn, 3 vols (Oxford, 1957), II, pp. 278–81; Rymer, *Critical Works*, ed. Zimansky pp. 193–94.

28. *The Letters of John Dryden*, ed. Charles E. Ward (Durham, N.C. 1942), pp. 13–14.

29. See Robert D. Hume, "Dryden's *Heads of an Answer to Rymer*: Notes toward a Hypothetical Revolution," *Review of English Studies*, 19 (1968), pp. 373–86; George Watson, "Dryden's First Answer to Rymer," ibid., n.s., 14 (1963), pp. 17–23; Fred G. Walcott, "John Dryden's Answer to Thomas Rymer's *The Tragedies of the Last Age*," *Philological Quarterly*, 15 (1936), pp. 194–214. The text is given in Dryden, *Essays* Watson, I, pp. 210–20.

30. Dryden, *Essays*, ed. Watson, I, pp. 212, 218.

31. Ibid., p. 214.

32. Ibid.

33. Ibid., pp. 215–17. See the different views on this point by Watson, "Dryden's First Answer to Rymer," and Robert D. Hume, *Dryden's Criticism* (Ithaca, N.Y., 1970), pp. 118–20.

34. Dryden, *Essays*, ed. Watson, I, pp. 218–19.

35. See Jules Brody, *Boileau and Longinus* (Geneva, 1958); and for Dryden and Boileau, A. F. B. Clark, *Boileau and the French Classical Critics in England* (1925, reprinted New York, 1965); Frank L. Huntley, "Dryden's Discovery of Boileau," *Modern Philology*, 45 (1947), pp. 112–17; John M. Aden, "Dryden and Boileau: The Question of Critical Influence," *Studies in Philology*, 50 (1953), pp. 491–509.

36. It was translated in 1695, as a *Treatise of the Epick Poem*, by W. J. In the preface, the translator applauds Rapin and alludes to the quarrel between Temple and Wotton.

38. Dedication to Mulgrave, Dryden, *Aureng-Zebe* (1676) in *Essays*, ed. Watson, I, pp. 190–91.

39. Prologue, *Aureng-Zebe*, I, p. 192.

40. Epilogue, ibid., I, pp. 192–93. For Dryden's debt to the French playwrights, see Harold F. Brooks, "Dryden's *Aureng-Zebe*: Debts to Corneille and Racine," *Revue de la littérature comparée*, 46 (1972), pp. 5–35.

41. See Clark, *Boileau*, who, however, overestimates it.

42. See Sister Marie Philip Haley, *Racine and the Art Poétique of Boileau* (Johns Hopkins Studies in Romance Languages and Literature, extra ser., 12, reprinted New York, 1976), pp. 95, 98–100.

43. Dryden, *Works*, II, pp. 124–56 and commentary, pp. 368–73; Clark, *Boileau*, pp. 275–76, 388; Julian E. White, *Nicholas Boileau* (New York, 1969), pp. 20–21.

44. The Davenant–Hobbes exchange can be read in Davenant's *Gondibert*, ed. David F. Gladish (Oxford, 1971); see C. M. Dowlin, *Sir William Davenant's Gondibert, its Preface, and Hobbes's Answer: A Study in English Neo-Classicism* (Philadelphia, 1934). See H. T. Swedenberg, Jr, *The Theory of the Epic in England 1650–1800* (1944, reprinted New York, 1972), ch. xi, pp. 266–305.

45. Different estimates of influence are offered by Huntley, "Dryden's Discovery," pp. 112–17, and John M. Aden, "Dryden and Boileau."

46. Martin Clifford, *Notes upon Mr Dryden's Poems in Four Letters* (1687), p. 8, Dryden, *Works*, XVII, p. 336. La Mesnardière's *Poétique* was published in 1639; Hédelin, the abbé d'Aubignac, published his *Pratique du théâtre* in 1657 (see below, ch. 7). For their relation to Dryden's thought, see Cecil V. Deane, *Dramatic Theory and the Rhymed Heroic Play* (London, 1931).

47. *The Complete Plays of William Congreve*, ed. Herbert Davis (Chicago, 1969), pp. 141–42, with Dryden's verses to Congreve, pp. 123–24. See also the Earl of Mulgrave, *An Essay on Poetry* (London, 1682), pp. 20–21. Dryden calls Bossu "the best of modern critics," *Grounds of Criticism*, *Essays*, ed. Watson, I, p. 246. For his use by Dryden in the *Grounds*, see D. W. Hopkins, "Dryden, Le Bossu and Ovid's Speeches of Ajax and Ulysses," *Notes and Queries*, 223 (1978), pp. 30–31. And for more characteristic praise of Bossu (coupling him with Rapin), see Samuel Wesley, "Essay on Heroic Poetry," prefixed to his *Life of the Saviour* (1697), *Essays on Poetry*, ed. Edward N. Hooker (Augustan Reprint Soc., 1947), p. 1; and Basil Kennett, *The Lives and Characters of the Ancient Grecian Poets* (London, 1697), pp. 15–24.

48. John Toland says Howard was a "great admirer" of Milton to his dying day: *Life of John Milton with Amyntor* (London, 1761), p. 129.

49. Morris Freedman, "Dryden's Reported Reaction to *Paradise Lost*," *Notes and Queries*, 203 (Jan. 1958), pp. 14–16; William Riley Parker, *Milton: A Biography*, 2 vols (Oxford, 1968), II, pp. 1115–16.

50. David Masson, *Life of John Milton*, 7 vols (London, 1859–94), VI, p. 634; Parker, *Milton*, pp. 603–4.

51. Preface, "On Verse," *Paradise Lost*, *The Works of John Milton*, 18 vols (New York, 1931), II, pt 1, p. 6.

52. Though Earl Miner doubts it, "Dryden's Admired Acquaintance, Mr Milton," *Milton Studies*, 11 (1978), p. 7.

53. *Samson* was composed between 1667 and 1670, and licensed July 2, 1670; see William Riley Parker, "The Date of *Samson Agonistes*," *Philological Quarterly*, 28 (1949), p. 145; Parker, *Milton*, pp. 903–17; Mary Ann Radzinovicz, *Toward Samson Agonistes* (Princeton, 1978), app. E, pp. 387–407.

54. See Annette C. Flower, "The Critical Context of the Preface to *Samson Agonistes*," *Studies in English Literature*, 10 (1970), pp. 409–23.

55. "Of that sort of Dramatic Poem which is call'd Tragedy," preface to *Samson Agonistes*, Milton, *Works*, I, pt 2, p. 331.

56. Ibid., p. 332.

57. Ibid. See Gretchen L. Finney, "Chorus in *Samson Agonistes*," *Publications of the Modern Language Association*, 58 (1943), pp. 649–64.

58. Milton, *Works*, I, pt 2, p. 333.

59. See John M. Steadman, "Passions Well Imitated: Rhetoric and Poetics in *Samson Agonistes*," *Calm of Mind*, ed. J. A. Wistreich (Cleveland, 1971), p. 182.

60. See for example F. Michael Krouse, *Milton's Samson and the Christian Tradition* (Princeton, 1949), p. 9; idem, "Two Athenian Models for *Samson Agonistes*," *Publications of the Modern Language Association*, 42 (1927), pp. 910–20. Anthony Low, *The Blaze of Noon: A Reading of Samson Agonistes* (New York, 1974), ch. 2; and the essays in *Twentieth-Century Interpretations of Samson Agonistes*, ed. Galbraith M. Crump (Englewood Cliffs, N.J., 1968).

61. Toland, *Life of Milton*, p. 128.

62. For Coleridge, see the lectures on Shakespeare, quoted by Krouse, *Milton's Samson*, p. 9. See too Goethe; quoted by William Riley Parker, *Milton's Debt to Greek Tragedy in Samson Agonistes* (1937, reprinted New York, 1969), p. 195.

63. Harris Fletcher, *The Intellectual Development of John Milton*, 2 vols (Urbana, 1961), I, pp. 273–88; II, pp. 361, 402; J. C. Maxwell, "Milton's Knowledge of Aeschylus: The Argument from Parallel Passages," *Review of English Studies*. n. s. 3 (1952), pp. 366–71.

64. See Parker, *Milton's Debt*, pp. 246–47. Parker finds eighteen unmistakable references to Euripides, eight to Sophocles, and one to Aeschylus.

65. See Brooks, "Dryden's *Aureng-Zebe*," pp. 5–35; Edward S. Le Conte, "*Samson Agonistes* and *Aureng-Zebe*," *Études anglaises*, 11 (1958), pp. 18–22. Earl Miner reverses the terms of their neoclassicism in *Milton Studies* (n. 52 above), pp. 22–23.

66. See Morris Freedman, "Dryden's Miniature Epics," *Journal of English and Germanic Philology*, 57 (1958), pp. 211–19; Mark Van Doren, *The Poetry of Dryden* (New York, 1920), pp. 103–5; Charles E. Ward, *The Life of John Dryden* (Chapel Hill, 1961), pp. 70–75; and especially Ann Davidson Ferry, *Milton and the Miltonic Dryden* (Cambridge, Mass., 1968).

67. See Morris Freedman, "Dryden's Memorable Visit to Milton," *Huntington Library Quarterly*, 18 (1955), pp. 99–108; Dryden's Reported Reaction," pp. 14–16. Dryden refers obliquely to a conversation with

Milton about Spenser in his preface to *Fables Ancient and Modern* (1700), *Essays*, ed. Watson, II, p. 271.

68. John Aubrey, *Brief Lives*, ed. A. Clark, 2 vols (Oxford, 1898) II, p. 72.

69. From the *Monitor* (1713); see G. Thorn-Drury, "Some Notes on Dryden: Dryden and Milton," *Review of English Studies*, 1 (1925), pp. 80–81.

70. "On Mr Milton's *Paradise Lost*," *The Poems and Letters of Andrew Marvell*, ed. H. M. Margoliouth, 2nd edn, 2 vols (Oxford, 1952), I, pp. 131–32, and note, pp. 260–61; see also William Riley Parker, *Milton's Contemporary Reputation* (1940, reprinted New York, 1940), pp. 113–15.

71. Ward, *Life of Dryden*, pp. 104–5, 348–50. For more on opera, see ch. 7 below.

72. "The Author's Apology for Heroic Poetry," Dryden, *Essays*, ed. Watson, p. 196.

73. Lee, "To Mr Dryden on his Poem of Paradise" (1677), quoted in Roswell G. Ham, *Otway and Lee: Biography from a Baroque Age* (New Haven, 1931), pp. 156–57; Dryden responded by writing several prefaces to Lee's plays.

74. For Bentley, see my essay in the *The Battle of the Books: History and Literature in the Augustan Age* (Ithaca, N.Y., 1991), pp. 245–63, reprinted from the *Journal of the History of Ideas*, 50 (1989), pp. 549–68; for Atterbury, see his letter to Pope, June 15, 1722, in the *Correspondence of Alexander Pope*, ed. George Sherburn, 5 vols (Oxford, 1956), II, pp. 124–25. Atterbury writes that the poem was written "in the very spirit of the Ancients," and could be "improv'd with little trouble into a perfect Model and Standard of Tragic Poetry."

75. Dryden, "A Discourse concerning Satire" (1693), *Essays*, ed. Watson, II, pp. 149–52. Later still, Dryden remembered that Milton had told him that Spenser was his original; preface to *Fables Ancient and Modern* (1700), ibid., p. 271.

76. Walter Scott's life of Dryden in *Dramatic Works*, ed. Walter Scott, revised George Saintsbury, 18 vols (Edinburgh, 1882–92), I, pp. 144–49; and his introductory remarks ibid., V, pp. 996–99.

77. "Yet Mr Dryden at that time knew not half the Extent of his Excellence, as he confess'd to me, and as is pretty plain from the writing of the *State of Innocence*," from *Original Letters* (1721), in John Dennis, *The Critical Works*, ed. Edward N. Hooker, 2 vols (Baltimore, 1943), II, p. 169. For a modern (and unusual) appreciation of the work, see James Winn, *John Dryden and his World* (New Haven, 1987), pp. 265–69.

78. Dryden, "Apology," *Essays*, ed. Watson, I, p. 196.

79. Ibid., pp. 198–99.

80. Ibid., p. 200.

81. Ibid., pp. 200–1.

82. Milton in the *Reason of Church Government* (1641), questions "Whether the rules of Aristotle herein are strictly to be kept or nature to be followed, which in them that know art and use judgment is no transgression, but an enriching of art" [book 2, preface], quoted by Allan H. Gilbert, "Is *Samson Agonistes* Unfinished?" *Philological Quarterly*, 28 (1949), p. 101.

83. On Oct. 23, 1667, James Langham wrote to Evelyn asking his opinion about Phillips as a tutor for the Countess of Huntington's son. BL Add. MS 15,857, f.52.

84. Edward Phillips, *History of the Literature of England and Scotland*, trans. David C. Calder and Charles R. Folkes (Salzburg Studies in English Literature, 21, 1973). See R. G. Howarth, "Edward Phillips' *Compendium Enumeratio Poetarum*," *Modern Language Review*, 54 (1959), pp. 321–28.

85. See Sanford Golding, "The Sources of the *Theatrum Poetarum*," *Publications of the Modern Language Association*, 76 (1961), pp. 48–53; and for the opposite view, Harris Fletcher, "Milton's Index Poeticus the *Theatrum Poetarum* by Edward Phillips," *Journal of English and Germanic Philology*, 55 (1961), pp. 35–40.

86. Edward Phillips, *Theatrum Poetarum*, sig. ★★★3.

87. Ibid., sig. ★★4v.

88. Ibid., sig. ★★4v–5.

89. Ibid., p. 113.

90. George McFadden, "Dryden's 'Most Barren Period' and Milton," *Huntington Library Quarterly*, 24 (1961), pp. 283–96.

91. See *All for Love: A Collection of Critical Essays*, ed. Bruce King (Englewood Cliffs, N.J., 1968).

92. *Antony and Cleopatra* (1677) in Charles Sedley, *The Poetical and Dramatic Works*, ed. V. de Sola Pinto, 2 vols (London, 1928). See H. Neville Davis, "Dryden's *All for Love* and Sedley's *Antony and Cleopatra*," *Notes and Queries*, 212 (June 1967), pp. 221–27.

93. Preface to *All for Love*, *Essays*, ed. Watson, I, pp. 221–22. The text has been newly edited by David M. Veith (Lincoln, 1972).

94. Scott's introduction to *All for Love*, Dryden, *Dramatic Works*, ed. Scott-Saintsbury, V, p. 308.

95. Gerard Langbaine, *An Account of the English Dramatic Poets* (Oxford, 1691), p. 142.

96. Preface to *All for Love*, in Dryden, *Essays*, ed. Watson, I, p. 225.

97. Ibid., p. 230.
98. There is a useful survey in Veith's edition. See also Howard Weinbrot, "Alexas in *All for Love*," *Studies in Philology*, 64 (1967), pp. 625–39.
99. Preface, in Dryden, *Works*, ed. Scott-Saintsbury, VI, p. 131.
100. Roswell G. Ham, "The Collaboration of Lee and Dryden," *Otway and Lee*, pp. 156–63.
101. Dryden, *Works*, VII, p. 131.
102. Ibid., p. 133.
103. Ham, "The Collaboration," p. 163. Ferry, *Milton*, p. 13.
104. In the *Essay of Dramatick Poesie* (1668), Dryden notices that the Greek tragedies and Seneca were "to be had"; in the 1684 revision, he says that they "are in our hands" (*Essays*, ed. Watson, I, p. 31n.). Whether he could read Greek remains problematical; see William Frost, "More about Dryden as Classicist," *Notes and Queries*, 217 (1972), pp. 23–26. His Latin, on the other hand, was fluent; see J. M. Bottkol, "Dryden's Latin Scholarship," *Modern Philology*, 40 (1942–43), pp. 241–54.
105. *Oedipus*, Dryden, *Dramatic Works*, ed. Scott-Saintsbury, I, prologue, p. 135.
106. Preface, ibid., VI, p. 133.
107. Dryden, *Essays*, ed. Watson, I, p. 240.
108. See, however, Hazelton Spencer, *Shakespeare Improved* (Cambridge, Mass., 1927), pp. 231–32, 236–37. Noyes thinks that *Troilus* marks Dryden's "conversion to the classic point of view": *Select Dramas of John Dryden* (Chicago, 1910), p. 1.
109. Dryden, *Essays*, ed. Watson, I, p. 242.
110. Ibid., p. 239.
111. Ibid., p. 246.
112. Ibid., pp. 246–47.
113. Ibid., p. 257.
114. Ibid., p. 260.
115. Ibid., pp. 274–79. The preface is dated 1680.
116. Dryden complains again about the low state of the stage in the prologue and epilogue to John Banks' *Unhappy Favorite* (1693), Ward, *Life of Dryden*, pp. 164–65.
117. Preface to a *Parallel between Poetry and Painting* (1695), *Essays*, ed. Watson, II, p. 207.
118. Preface to *The Spanish Friar*, ibid., I, pp. 276, 277. "A true Poet often misses of applause because he cannot debase himself to write so ill as to please his Audience": preface to *An Evening's Love: or the Mock Astrologer* (1671), ibid., pp. 145–55.
119. See Edward L. Saslow, "Dryden in 1684," *Modern Philology*, 72 (1975), p. 255; Louis I. Bredvold, "Notes on Dryden's Pension," *Modern Philology*, 30 (1933), pp. 267–74. In the preface to *All for Love*, Dryden had written, "Thus the case is hard with writers;

if they succeed not, they must starve; and if they do, some malicious satire is prepared to level them for daring to please without their leave": *Essays*, ed. Watson, I, p. 227.
120. For a full and precise description of Dryden's turn to Tory politics, see Philip Harth, *Pen for a Party: Dryden's Tory Propaganda in its Contexts* (Princeton, 1993).
121. Roswell Ham, "Dryden as Historiographer-Royal," *Essential Articles for the Study of John Dryden*, ed. H. T. Swedenberg (Hamden, Conn., 1966), pp. 135–53; Edward L. Saslow, "Dryden as Historiographer Royal and the Authorship of *His Majesties Declaration Defended*," *Modern Philology*, 75 (1977–78), pp. 261–72.
122. See Dryden's introduction to his translation of Louis Maimbourg's *History of the League* (1684), Dryden, *Works*, XVIII, and more especially his preface to the translations of Plutarch and Polybius, for more about which see below, ch. 3, n. 18. Of some use is Wallace Maurer, "Dryden's Knowledge of Historians, Ancient and Modern," *Notes and Queries*, 204, n. s. 6 (1959), pp. 264–66; Aschsah Guibborg, "Dryden's Views of History," *Philological Quarterly* 52 (1973), pp. 187–204; and my own *Battle of the Books*, pp. 273–77.
123. Preface to Ovid's *Epistles*, Dryden, *Essays*, ed. Watson, I, pp. 268–72. Dryden returned to the subject in the preface to *Sylvae* (1685), ibid., II, pp. 18–33. See in general, William Frost, *Dryden and the Art of Translation* (New Haven, 1959).
124. Dryden, *Essays*, ed. Watson, I, p. 271.
125. Nevertheless, he was criticized for taking liberties by his old enemy Shadwell, preface to *The Tenth Satyr of Juvenal* (1687), Dryden, *Works*, V, p. 293.
126. See the *Short Account of Some Passages in the Life and Death of Wentworth late Earle of Roscommon* by Kneightly Chetwood, Baker MS, Cambridge University Library, MS 1. 47, pp. 31–32; O. F. Emerson, "John Dryden and a British Academy," *Proceedings of the British Academy*, 10 (1921–23), pp. 45–58, reprinted in *Essential Articles*, pp. 363–80; Carl Niemeyer, "The Earl of Roscommon's Academy," *Modern Language Notes*, 49 (1934), pp. 32–37.
127. Elijah Fenton (1730), quoted by Niemeyer, "Earl of Roscommon," p. 432. Chetwood, in *Short Account*, says that Roscommon thought Dryden a "naturall rather than a correct poet": p. 39.
128. Chetwood, *Short Account*, pp. 39–40.
129. Emerson, "John Dryden and a British Academy," pp. 45–58; *Essential Articles*, pp. 263–80. For Evelyn, see p. 216, n. 65

above; for Swift, see Levine, *Battle of the Books*, pp. 377–81.

130. Dryden, *Works*, II, pp. 172–74. Dryden now turns against rhyme and repeats some other commonplaces of the party of the ancients.

131. See John Harold Wilson, *The Court Wits of the Restoration* (1948, reprinted London, 1967).

132. Mulgrave, *An Essay upon Poetry* (London, 1682), p. 4; Hume, *Dryden's Criticism*, p. 144.

133. Robert Wolseley, preface to Rochester's *Valentinian* (1685), quoted in Wilson, *Court Wits*, p. 191, along with the praises of Addison, Pope, et al., p. 193.

134. Dryden to Tonson, *Letters*, pp. 22–23.

135. *The Percy Anecdotes*, ed. John Timbs (Chandos Classics, London, n.d.), 4, p. 81. For some other contemporary tributes to Dorset as poet and patron, and his patronage of Dryden, see Brice Harris, *Charles Sackville Sixth Earl of Dorset: Patron and Poet of the Restoration* (Urbana, 1940). Pope praised him to Joseph Spence, in Spence, *Observations, Anecdotes, and Characters*, ed. James M. Osborn, 2 vols (Oxford, 1966), I, pp. 200–1.

136. See Arthur Sherbo, "The Dryden-Cambridge Translation of Plutarch's *Lives*," *Études anglaises*, 32 (1979), pp. 177–84.

137. Hugh Macdonald, *John Dryden: A Bibliography of Early Editions* (Oxford, 1939), pp. 168–69. Thomas Rymer was one of the contributors!

138. Dryden, *Works*, XVII, intro., p. 429ff.

139. "Life of Plutarch," ibid., p. 287.

140. Preface to the Duke of Ormonde, ibid., pp. 227–28.

141. Ibid., pp. 227–29.

Chapter 5 Dryden and the Battle of the Books

1. Sir William Temple, "Of Poetry," *Five Miscellaneous Essays*, ed. Samuel Holt Monk (Ann Arbor, 1963), p. 182.

2. Ibid., pp. 180–81.

3. Ibid., p. 181.

4. Ibid., p. 188.

5. Ibid., p. 194.

6. Ibid., p. 195.

7. Ibid., p. 202.

8. Ibid., p. 199.

9. Ibid., p. 201.

10. Preface to *Don Sebastian* (1690), Dryden, *Of Dramatic Poesy and Other Critical Essays*, ed. George Watson, 2 vols (London, 1962), II, p. 45. For some light on Dryden's financial problems, see Louis I. Bredvold, "Notes on Dryden's Pension," *Modern Philology*, 30 (1933), pp. 267–74; Charles E. Ward, "A Biographical Note on John

Dryden," *Modern Language Review*, 27 (1932), pp. 206–10.

11. For the politics in these late plays, see David Bywaters, *Dryden in Revolutionary England* (Berkeley, 1991).

12. Preface to *Don Sebastian*, Dryden, *Essays*, ed. Watson, II, pp. 48–49. In 1679, in the "Grounds of Criticism," he quoted Longinus to that effect: ibid., I, p. 242. As early as 1671, he was defending himself from the charge with classical precedents; see the preface to *An Evening's Love*, ibid., pp. 153–55. For the politics of the play itself, see Stephen Zwicker, *Lines of Authority: Politics and English Culture 1649–1689* (Ithaca, N.Y., 1993), pp. 190–97.

13. Dryden, *Essays*, ed. Watson, II, p. 49.

14. The setting is Sparta, the source Plutarch; the situation, a failed rebellion and exile, naturally raised suspicions about Dryden's view of the contemporary political situation, which nearly led to the banning of the play and delayed its performance and publication. See "Biographical Note," Charles E. Ward, *The Life of John Dryden* (Chapel Hill, 1971), pp. 254–55; James Winn, *John Dryden and his World* (New Haven, 1987), pp. 451–53.

15. Preface to *Cleomenes*, Dryden, *The Dramatic Works*, ed. Walter Scott, revised George Saintsbury, 18 vols (Edinburgh, 1882–92), VIII, pp. 220–21.

16. I use the version in *Essays*, ed. Watson, II, pp. 71–155. It is dated Aug. 18, 1692; The *Satires of Juvenal and Persius* appeared in folio later that autumn. For Dryden and Dorset, see Brice Harris, *Charles Sackville, Sixth Earl of Dorset* (Urbana, 1940).

17. Dryden, *Essays*, ed. Watson, II, pp. 73–74.

18. Ibid., pp. 80–81.

19. "But suppose that Homer and Virgil were the only of their species, and that nature was so much worn out in producing them that she was never able to bear the like again; yet the example only holds in heroic poetry" – not in tragedy and satire, where we have Shakespeare and Dorset! Ibid., p. 81.

20. Ibid., pp. 83–84.

21. Ibid, p. 96.

22. Ibid., p. 88.

23. Ibid., pp. 90, 96.

24. Ibid., p. 144.

25. Thomas Rymer, *Critical Works*, ed. C. A. Zimansky, 2 vols (New Haven, 1956), pp. 82–83. The reference is to the *Aeneid*, II, l. 274. Rymer remembers the controversy over Corneille's *Cid*, ibid., p. 88.

26. So Rymer, *Critical Works*, p. xvi.

27. T. S. Eliot, *Selected Essays* (New York, 1932), pp. 97n., 121n.

28. For André Dacier's uncompromising *ancien-*

neté, see "An Essay upon Satyr," translated in Père Bossu's *Treatise on the Epick Poem* (London, 1695), pp. 275–76; and Joseph M. Levine, *The Battle of the Books: History and Literature in the Augustan Age* (Ithaca, N.Y., 1991), pp. 127–28.

29. Was Rymer really "a learned and strict critic," asked Spence of Pope? "Aye, that's exactly his character," replied Pope. "He is generally right, though rather too severe in his opinions of the particular plays he speaks of, and is on the whole one of the best critics we ever had": Joseph Spence, *Observations, Anecdotes, and Characters of Books and Men*, ed. James M. Osborn, 2 vols (Oxford, 1966), I, p. 205.

30. Rymer, *Critical Works*, p. 170.

31. Dryden, *Essays*, ed. Watson, II, pp. 156–68.

32. Ibid., p. 158.

33. Ibid., p. 160.

34. Ibid., p. 161.

35. Ibid., p. 164.

36. Ibid., p. 161.

37. "To My Dear Friend Mr Congreve, on his Comedy Called the *Double-Dealer*" (1694), ibid., pp. 169–72," ll. 41–46.

38. Dedication to *Love Triumphant* (1694), Dryden, *Dramatic Works* (Scott-Saintsbury), VIII, p. 374.

39. Ibid., p. 376.

40. Dryden to Walsh [May 9 or 10, 1693], *The Letters of John Dryden*, ed. Charles E. Ward (Durham, N.C., 1942), p. 54.

41. Ibid. [Dec. 12, 1693], pp. 61–62.

42. Dryden to Dennis [c. Mar. 1693], ibid., pp. 70–74. H. G. Paul, *John Dennis: His Life and Criticism* (New York, 1911); Fred S. Tupper, "Notes on the Life of John Dennis," *English Literary History*, 5 (1938), pp. 211–17.

43. The text (1693) appears in John Dennis, *The Critical Works*, ed. Edward N. Hooker, 2 vols (Baltimore, 1939), I, pp. 11–41; and in *Critical Essays of the Seventeenth Century*, ed. J. E. Spingarn, 3 vols (Oxford, 1957), III, pp. 148–97.

44. Dennis, *Critical Works*, I, p. 11.

45. Ibid., p. 13.

46. Ibid., p. 22.

47. "Certain it is, that Nature is the same, and Man is the same, he loves, grieves, hates, envies, has the same affections and passions in both places, and the same springs that give them motion. What mov'd pity there, will here also produce the same effect": *Tragedies of the Last Age*, in Rymer, *Critical Works*, p. 19.

48. "Shakespeare and Fletcher have written to the genius of the age and nation in which they lived; for though nature, as he [Rymer] objects, is the same in all places, and reason

too the same, yet the climate, the age, the disposition of the people, to whom a poet writes, may be so different, that what pleased the Greeks will not satisfy an English audience": "Heads of an Answer," Dryden, *Dramatic Works*, ed. Scott-Saintsbury, XV, p. 385.

49. Dennis, *Critical Works*, I, p. 39. See also Dennis to Walter Moyle, in John Dennis, *Letters upon Several Occasions* (London, 1696), p. 125.

50. Terence, *Comedies* (London, 1694, 2nd edn 1698). Eachard admired Dryden's *All for Love*, and believed that modern English playwrights could yet outdo the ancients. He repeats the commonplace that the rules should be observed, because they were "pure Nature only Methodiz'd": preface, pp. xiii, xvi.

51. Dennis, *Critical Works*, I, p. 41.

52. Dryden, *Letters*, pp. 70–74. The letter was printed in *Letters upon Several Occasions*, p. 53ff.

53. *Remarks on a Poem Entituled Prince Arthur* (1696), in Dennis, *Critical Works*, I, pp. 46–144 (pp. 46, 84–89). Dennis's work is praised by H. T. Swedenberg as an exemplary piece of neoclassical criticism, for its "combination of established theory, good sense, and critical perspicacity": *The Theory of the Epic in England 1650–1800* (1944, reprinted New York, 1972), pp. 52–54.

54. For Blackmore's criticism, see Spingarn, *Critical Essays*, III, pp. 229–34. Paul, *John Dennis* (p. 29) thinks this was the provocation, but Hooker is dubious (see his note in Dennis, *Critical Works*, I, pp. 447–48). Dryden complains in his preface to the *Fables Ancient and Modern* (1700) (*Essays*, ed. Watson, II, pp. 291–93) that Blackmore stole his idea about Christian machinery, as he certainly did his subject of King Arthur. In fact, Dennis and Blackmore, as so often then, agreed about much and later made up their quarrel. *Arthur* was still being praised as just below Homer and Virgil by the translator of Bossu, W. J., who generally prefers Wotton to Temple: *Treatise of the Epick Poem*, 2 vols (London, 1719), I, sig. a3v.

55. John Dennis, *The Advancement and Reformation of Modern Poetry* (1701), *Critical Works*, I, pp. 200–1.

56. Ibid., p. 203.

57. Ibid., p. 209, and the next two chapters which explore the advantages that the ancients were alleged to have, and which Dennis denies, p. 14.

58. Ibid., p. 271.

59. He remembers to quote Bacon that it is the moderns who are the true ancients, with three thousand years of additional experi-

ence; and he still proposes Milton as often equaling and sometimes surpassing, both the Greeks and Romans. Dennis, *Reflections Critical and Satyrical upon a Late Rhapsody, Call'd An Essay on Criticism* (1711), *Critical Works*, I, pp. 407–8. Earlier, he supports Boileau over Perrault in the *querelle*, pointing out that he did not support the ancients out of mere reverence for their antiquity, and only chose the best, ibid., pp. 399–400. He also casts suspicion on the sincerity of Pope's praise of Dryden, now that he was dead, ibid., p. 416 and note, p. 530.

60. André Dacier, "Essay upon Satyr," *Miscellany Poems upon Several Occasions*, ed. Charles Gildon (London, 1692), n. p., from Dacier's translation of Horace (book 6).

61. Charles Gildon, *Miscellaneous Letters and Essays on Several Subjects* (London, 1694), preface.

62. Ibid., pp. 10, 39–40.

63. Ibid., pp. 64–118, esp. pp. 87–88.

64. Ibid., p. 87.

65. Ibid., p. 221.

66. Ibid., pp. 67–68.

67. Ibid., p. 86.

68. Ibid., p. 92.

69. Ibid., p. 145.

70. Ibid., p. 152.

71. Gildon, *The Complete Art of Poetry*, 2 vols (London, 1718), I, pp. 129, 206, 225. See Frances E. Litz, "The Sources of Charles Gildon's *Complete Art of Poetry*," *English Literary History*, 9 (1942), pp. 118–35. The second dialogue, "Of the Use and Necessity of Rules in Poetry," is printed in *Critical Essays of the Eighteenth Century 1700–25*, ed. Willard H. Durham (New Haven, 1915), pp. 18–75.

Chapter 6 Dryden's Virgil and the Triumph of Antiquity

1. For what follows, see Joseph M. Levine, *The Battle of the Books: History and Literature in the Augustan Age* (Ithaca, N.Y., 1991), pp. 34–46.

2. Wotton, *Reflections upon Ancient and Modern Learning* (London, 1694), p. 28.

3. "Of Ancient and Modern Eloquence and Poesie," ibid., ch. 3, pp. 20–45.

4. Ibid., ch. 4, "Reflections upon Monsieur's Hypothesis, That Modern Orators and Poets are more excellent than Ancient," pp. 45–55.

5. Ibid, p. 39.

6. Ibid., p. 50.

7. Wotton, *Reflections*, pp. 52–53.

8. Ibid., pp. 45–46.

9. Polybius and Tacitus, Dryden believed, were "without dispute, the best Historians in their several kinds." The first was more

useful to those who lived in a republic, the second those in a monarchy. See Dryden's "Character of Polybius," prefixed to the *History of Polybius*, trans. Sir Henry Shere (1693), in Dryden, *Works*, ed. Walter Scott, revised George Saintsbury, 18 vols (Edinburgh, 1882–92), XVII, pp. 34–35. For the immediate circumstances, and Dryden's debt to Casaubon and Julien Pichon, see ibid., pp. 317–26, 336–37. Dryden later contributed to a collaborative translation of Tacitus: *The Annals and History* (1698), *The Works of John Dryden*, 20 vols (Berkeley, 1961–89), XX, pp. 231–93; 386–97.

10. *The Diary of John Evelyn*, ed. E. S. de Beer, 6 vols (Oxford, 1955), V, p. 164.

11. Dryden to Walsh, Dec. 12, 1693, *The Letters of John Dryden*, ed. Charles E. Ward (Durham, N.C., 1942), p. 64. See C. E. Ward, "The Publication and Profits of Dryden's *Virgil*," *Publications of the Modern Language Association*, 8 (1938), pp. 807–12; John Bernard, "Dryden, Tonson, and Subscriptions for the 1697 Virgil," *Papers of the Bibliographical Society of America*, 57 (1963), pp. 129–51.

12. With joy I learn'd, Dryden designs to crown
    All the things he has already done:
    No loss, no change of vigour can he feel,
    Who dares attempt the sacred Mantuan
        still.

    Charles Hopkins to Antony Hammond, quoted in Dryden, *Works*, VI, p. 877.

13. Dryden, *Letters*, pp. 70–71; The article in the *Gentleman's Journal* was by Peter Motteux; see Dryden, *Works*, VI, pp. 877–88.

14. "A Discourse concerning Satire," Dryden, *Essays*, ed. Watson, II, p. 80.

15. For Dryden's many allusions to Virgil, see William Frost, "Translating Virgil, Douglas to Dryden," *Poetic Traditions of the English Renaissance*, ed. Maynard Mack and George deForest Lord (New Haven, 1982), pp. 278–79. Dryden had expressly taken Virgil as his model for the *Annus Mirabilis* (1667); see the "Account of the Ensuing Poem," addressed to Sir Robert Howard, *Annus Mirabilis* (1667), *The Poetical Works of John Dryden*, ed. George R. Noyes (Cambridge, 1950), pp. 23–26.

16. Dedication to the *Aeneis*, Dryden, *Works*, V, p. 267. For other expressions of this commonplace, see ibid., VI, p. 941n. Dryden notices that he must confute Aristotle here and his modern exponent, André Dacier, p. 274. In the end, he allows, however, that "they are both the Master-Pieces of Humane Wit," p. 275.

17. Ibid., p. 273. See the apology before *The State of Innocence* (1677), Dryden, *Essays*, ed. Watson, I, pp. 189–90; and the *Discourse of*

Satire (Works, V, p. 26). For the Apologie, see Works, XVII, p. 75.

18. Dryden, Works, V, pp. 275–76. Milton might have made it, had "the Devil not been his Heroe instead of Adam": p. 276.

19. Examen poeticum: Being the Third Part of Miscellan Poems (1693), preface in Essays, ed. Watson, p. 167. Dryden contributed about a quarter of the volume, including translations of Ovid and Homer.

20. Essays, ed. Watson, p. 167.

21. For Milton's effort to surpass the ancients, see Louis Martz, Poet of Exile, 2nd edn (New Haven, 1986), chs 9, 12; for "Dryden's Unwritten Epic," see Mary Thrale, Papers in Language and Literature, 5 (1969), pp. 423–33. For the uproar over Blackmore's pretentious efforts, see Richard C. Boys, Sir Richard Blackmore and the Wits (Ann Arbor, 1949). Blackmore attacked Dryden in the preface to Prince Arthur (1695) for his religion and politics and was satirized by Dryden in turn (Dryden, Works, VI, p. 1114, Boys, Sir Richard Blackmore, pp. 12–18).

22. "A Discourse Concerning Satire" (1693), Essays, ed. Watson, II, pp. 89–90.

23. Yet Edward Howard, who remained uncompromisingly modern, looked forward now to Dryden's outdoing Virgil, to making him speak, as he put it, better than his original had thought. See his An Essay upon Pastoral as also an Elegy dedicated to Mary the Second (London, 1695), proem. He later contributed some commendatory verses to the folio volume.

24. Ibid., p. 305. Dryden substitutes Versailles for the Louvre in Segrais's argument.

25. Anon. preface (by Robert Wolseley) to the Earl of Rochester's Valentinian, in Critical Essays of the Seventeenth Century, ed. Joel Spingarn (Oxford, 1909), III, p. 16. The commonplaces are drawn from Simonides of Ceos, as reported in Plutarch's Moralia 346f.; and from Horace, Ars poetica, I, 361. For Dryden, see the ode, "To the Memory of the Accomplish'd Young Lady, Mrs Anne Killigrew, Excellent in the Two Sister-Arts of Poesie and Painting," Dryden, Works, III, pp. 109–15. In general, see Jean H. Hagstrum, The Sister Arts (Chicago, 1958); Rensselaer W. Lee, Ut Pictura Poesis: The Humanistic Theory of Painting (New York, 1967); William G. Howell, "Ut Pictura Poesis," PMLA, 24 (1909), pp. 40–123; Dean T. Mace, "Ut Pictura Poesis: Dryden, Poussin and the Parallel of Poetry and Painting in the Seventeenth Century," Encounters: Essays on Literature and the Visual Arts, ed. John Dixon Hunt (New York, 1971), pp. 58–81.

26. Vertue saw the portrait for which Dryden "made that fine Poem," at Lord Malton's, with its inscription, "presentit to Mr Dryden by G. Kneller." George Vertue, Note books, IV (Walpole Soc., 24, 1935–36), p. 186.

27. For what a song, or senseless opera
    Is to the living labor of a play;
    Or what a play to Virgil's work would be,
    Such is a single piece to history. (ll.
    146–54)
    "To Sir Godfrey Kneller" (1694), Dryden, Works, IV, pp. 461–64.

28. Ibid., p. 46, ll. 166–68.

29. D. C. Stewart, "William III and Sir Godfrey Kneller," Journal of the Warburg and Courtauld Institutes, 33 (1970), pp. 330–36; and in general, idem, Sir Godfrey Kneller and the English Baroque Portrait (Oxford, 1983).

30. Vertue bid for a large historical painting of the Duke of Marlborough which sold for a paltry seven and a half guineas at his death: Note Books, V, p. 88. See also J. Douglas Stewart, "Sir Godfrey Kneller as Painter of Histories and Portraits Histories," Art and Patronage in the Caroline Courts (Cambridge, 1993), pp. 243–63.

31. Vertue, Notebooks, II, p. 121; John Harris, "Kneller Hall, Middlesex," The Country Seat: Studies in the History of the Brtitish Country House presented to Sir John Summerson, ed. Howard Colvin and John Harris (London, 1970), pp. 81–84.

32. Thomas Tickell, To Sir Godfrey Kneller at his Country Seat (London, 1722).

33. Marshall Smith, The Art of Painting (1692), p. 23. See also the life by B. Buckridge in Roger de Piles, Art of Painting (London, 1750), pp. 393–98, esp. p. 394.

34. Stewart, Kneller, pp. 7, 63–64, 84–85.

35. Cf. Cicero, Orator, ii. 7–iii. 10 and Seneca, Ad Lucilium lxv. 4–8; lviii. 16ff. with Plato in the Republic and elsewhere; see Richard McKeon, "Literary Criticism and the Concept of Imitation in Antiquity," Critics and Criticism, ed. R. S. Crane (Chicago, 1952), pp. 147–75; Hagstrum, Sister Arts, pp. 13–14; Erwin Panofsky, Idea: A Concept in Art Theory, trans. Joseph J. S. Peake (Columbia, SC, 1968), pp. 105–9; Lee, Ut Pictura Poesis, pp. 13–16. Dennis Mahon puts the origins of these ideas earlier: see his "Agucchi and the Idea della Belleza: A Stage in the History of a Theory," Studies in Seicento Art and Theory (London, 1947), pp. 141–43, 153–54. Charles Alphonse du Fresnoy (1611–65) wrote his work in Rome sometime between 1633 and 1653 and published it as De arte graphica (1668); Dryden used the prose French translation by Roger de Piles

(1668). For Bellori, see Kenneth Donahue, "The Ingenious Bellori," *Marsyas*, 3 (1946), pp. 108–38. And for further background, see André Fontaine, *Les Doctrines d'art en France de Poussin à Diderot* (Paris, 1909), p. 17ff.; Leon Mirot, *Roger de Piles* (Paris, 1924); Jacques Thuillier, "Les Observations sur la peinture de Charles-Alphonse du Fresnoy," *Walter Friedlaender zum 90 Gebertstag* (Berlin, 1965) pp. 193–210.

36. The passage from Bellori is omitted from Watson; I quote it from Dryden's "Parallel" in the *Works*, XX, p. 41. The original is from Bellori's *L'Idea del pittore, dello scultore, e dell'arcitetto* (1664), which was also prefixed to his *Le vite de pittore* (1672). Bellori (followed by Dryden) adds more from Cicero's *Orator*, and from various Renaissance sources, including Alberti, and Dryden adds a long paragraph from Philostratus's *Imagines* (p. 46).

37. Text and commentary in Dryden, *Works*, XX, pp. 37–206, 337–70. Watson gives an abridged version, leaving out some long extracts from Bellori, in *Essays*, II, pp. 181–208. Dryden used the French translation by Roger de Piles of the Latin original (1668). It was revised in 1716 and reprinted several times, and there were several other translations of the poem in the eighteenth century.

38. Dryden, *Works*, XX, pp. 59–60. Dryden thanks Moyle also for furnishing him all the relevant passages in Aristotle and Horace to explain the art of poetry by painting, which he hoped to include in any later edition of the essay. The notion that beauty and harmony must be preferred to likeness is illustrated in a story told by John Elsum. "Apelles having drawn the Picture of Alexander the Great, the Emperor reprimanded him for making his Legs crooked; the Painter, to justify what he had done, answer'd that Nature had made them so: To Whom the King reply'd, Tell not me of Nature, had I paid Nature as I have paid you, I'd have as good Legs as any Prince in the Universe": *The Art of Painting after the Italian Manner* (London, 1703), pp. 47–48.

39. "Thus at least I have shewn, that in the most perfect Poem, which is that of Virgil, a perfect Idea was requir'd and follow'd, and consequently, that all succeeding Poets ought rather to imitate him, than even Homer": Dryden, *Works*, XX, pp. 50–51.

40. Ibid., p. 57.
41. Ibid.
42. Ibid., p. 58.
43. Watson points out that the three parts of painting and poetry, invention, disposition and coloring, resemble the three "happi-

nesses" of the poet, invention, fancy and elocution, in the preface to *Annus Mirabilis* (1667). Dryden, *Essays*, II, p. 194n.

44. Ibid., p. 62.
45. "The Gothique manner, and the barbarous Ornaments, which are to be avoided in a Picture, are just the same with those in an ill-order'd Play. For example, our English Tragicomedy must be confess'd to be wholly Gothique." Dryden includes his own *Spanish Fryar* as presenting "an unnatural mingle": ibid., pp. 70–71.

46. Preface to the *Fables Ancient and Modern* (1700), ibid., p. 272.
47. Dedication to the *Aeneis*, *Works*, V, p. 337.
48. Dryden corrected the preface himself for the second edition; see Dryden to Chetwood [Dec. 1697], *Letters*, pp. 98–100.
49. Dryden, *Works*, V, p. 153. Dryden had earlier preferred the *Georgics* as the "divinest part of all his writings": see the "Account of the Ensuing Poem," *Annus Mirabilis* (1667), *Poetical Works*, Noyes, p. 25. On the other hand, Dryden believed the *Pastorals* of Virgil to be inferior to Theocritus: Dryden to Elizabeth Thomas, Nov. 1699, *Letters*, pp. 127–28.
50. "Had I been born early enough, I must have known and loved him," Pope to William Wycherley, Dec. 26, 1704, Pope, *Correspondence*, ed. George Sherburn, 5 vols (Oxford, 1956), I, p. 2. Pope remembered seeing Dryden when he was about twelve years old: "I looked upon him with the greatest veneration even then": Joseph Spence, *Observations, Anecdotes, and Characters of Books and Men*, ed. James M. Osborn, 2 vols (Oxford, 1966), I, p. 25. As Maynard Mack points out, almost all his early friends had been friends of Dryden's: *Alexander Pope: A Life* (New Haven, 1985), p. 837. For Pope's *ancienneté*, see Levine, *Battle of the Books*, pp. 181–217.
51. The work appeared in the summer with a postscript and some notes and observations; Dryden corrected it later that year for a second edition in 1698. See Dryden, *Letters*, pp. 97, 179; Dryden, *Works*, VI, p. 846.
52. Dryden, *Works*, V, p. 75.
53. Ibid., p. 280.
54. Ibid., p. 278. See Steven N. Zwicker, *Politics and Language in Dryden's Poetry* (Princeton, 1984), ch. 6, pp. 177–205; Murray G. H. Pittock, "The *Aeneid* in the Age of Burlington: A Jacobite Text?" *Lord Burlington: Architecture, Art and Life*, ed. Toby Bernard and Jane Clark (London, 1995), pp. 234–36.
55. Luke Milbourne, *Notes on Dryden's Virgil* (London, 1698), p. 8. It has been suggested that Dryden's collaboration in a translation of Tacitus in 1698 may have appealed to him

as a republican critique of arbitrary power against William III; see Stephen Zwicker and David Bywaters, "Politics and Translation: The English Tacitus of 1698," *Huntington Library Quarterly*, 59 (1989), pp. 319–45. Dryden was necessarily too circumspect to leave much direct evidence about his political opinions in these years. The safest thing to say was that he died pretty much disillusioned by all sides; see Jay Arnold Levine, "John Dryden's *Epistle to John Driden*," *Dryden's Mind and Art*, ed. Bruce King (Edinburgh, 1969), pp. 114–42.

56. "If he had not well studied his Patron's Temper, it might have Ruin'd him with another Prince": Dryden, *Works*, V, p. 280, and Dryden's note, ibid., VI, pp. 822–23.

57. Ibid., V, p. 281.

58. Ibid. "The court rather speaks kindly of me, than does anything for me, though they promise largely . . . If they will consider me as a Man, who have done my best to improve the Language, and especially the Poetry, and will be content with my acquiescence under the present Government, and forbearing satire on it, that I can promise, because I can perform it: but I can neither take the Oaths, nor foresake my Religion": Dryden to Elizabeth Steward, Nov. 7, 1699, *Letters*, pp. 122–224. Bywaters (Berkeley, 1991) argues that the political aim of *Cleomenes* was already to show how admiration for James II could be reconciled with patriotic obedience to William, *Dryden in Revolutionary England*, pp. 94–103. And William C. Cameron shows convincingly how the same position informs Dryden's reading of the *Aeneid* and his choice of Mulgrave as his patron: "John Dryden's Jacobitism," *Restoration Literature: Critical Approaches*, ed. Harold Love (London, 1972), pp. 277–308. For more on the political implications of the *Aeneis*, see Zwicker, *Politics and Language*, pp. 181–88, and Bywaters, *Dryden*, pp. 146–60.

59. See the *Aestraea Redux* (1660), which was reprinted in 1688, and Dryden's dedication to *All for Love* (1678), where he sets out his view of monarchy and revolution. For the political message of the translation, see L. Proudfoot, *Dryden's Aeneid and its Seventeenth Century Predecessors* (Manchester, 1977), pp. 197–207, 258–64.

60. It is not clear that Dryden approved. He says of Tonson, "But however he has missd of his design in the Dedication: though He had prepard the Book for it: for in every figure of Eneas, he has caused him to be drawn like K. William, with a hookd Nose": Dryden to his sons, Sept. 3, 1697, *Letters*, p. 93. Zwicker quotes a contemporary verse making fun of Tonson's "hook-nosed head" and its parallel, p. 234n., and discusses the political implications of the plates, most of which had been used for Ogilby's previous translation, see Zwicker, *Politics and Language*, pp. 190–96.

61. Dryden, *Works*, V, p. 281.

62. He quotes Segrais approvingly: "Virgil had consider'd that the greatest Virtues of Augustus consisted in the Art of Governing his People; which caus'd him to Reign for more than Forty years in great felicity. He consider'd that his Emperour was Valiant, Civil, Popular, Eloquent, Politick, and Religious. He has given all those Qualities to Aeneas. But knowing that Piety alone comprehends the whole Duty of man towards the Gods, towards his Country, and towards his relations, he judg'd, that this ought to be his first Character": ibid., p. 288. There follows a long section borrowed from Segrais defending Aeneas for showing fear (and shedding tears) and for abusing Dido's love. It was the modern, Perrault, who had accused Aeneas of shedding tears on every occasion. "Cette manière de trembler en sortes d'occasions ne me semble point héroïque, ny convenir au fondateur de l'Empire et au Père de tous les Cesars," Perrault, *Parallèle des anciens et des modernes* (1692), p. 135.

63. Virgil was no proponent of absolutism: "Oblig'd he was to his Master for his Bounty, and he repays him with good Counsel, how to behave himself in his new Monarchy, so as to gain the Affections of his Subjects, and deserve to be call'd the Father of his Country": Dryden, *Works*, V, p. 283.

64. "Life of Lucian," written in 1696 but published only in 1711 as a preface to the *Works of Lucian translated by Several Eminent Hands*, Dryden, *Essays*, ed. Watson, II, p. 215.

65. Dryden was defending the notion of translation that he had set out in his version of Ovid, and more recently in his Juvenal and Persius in the "Discourse on Satire," *Works*, V, p. 330; *Essays*, ed. Watson, I, pp. 268–72; II, p. 152. The *locus classicus* is Horace, *Ars poetica*, ll. 133–34.

66. Once at least Dryden admits this; for line 979, he placed Dido's guest at her side "in the modern fashion" sitting at table, since "the Ancient custom of lying on Beds, had not been understood by the Unlearn'd Reader": *Works*, VI, p. 817. For some political examples, involving "violence" to the original, see T. W. Harrison, "Dryden's

Aeneid," *Dryden's Mind and Art*, ed. Bruce King (Edinburgh, 1969), pp. 130–67.

67. *A Full and True Account of the Battel between the Antient and the Modern Books*, in Swift, *A Tale of a Tub and the Battel of the Books*, ed. A. C. Guthkeltch and D. Nichol Smith (Oxford, 1958), pp. 246–47. Dryden is further mocked in *A Tale* for writing four score and eleven pamphlets in three reigns, "for the Service of six and thirty Factions," and for using his prefaces to promote his (otherwise dubious) poetical reputation: ibid., pp. 69–71, 131.

68. According to Dr Johnson, *Lives of the English Poets*, ed. George Birkbeck Hill, 3 vols (Oxford, 1905), III, pp. 7–8 and note. Some other disparaging references by Swift to Dryden are collected in *Dryden: The Critical Heritage*, ed. James and Helen Kinsley (London, 1971), pp. 245–48.

69. Dryden resumes the stock contrast between Homer and Virgil in the preface to *Fables Ancient and Modern* (1700), in *Essays*, ed. Watson, II, pp. 274–77. "My thoughts at present," Dryden wrote just before his death, "are fix'd on Homer: And by my translation of the first Iliad: I find him a Poet more according to my Genius than Virgil: and consequently hope I may do him more justice, in his fiery way of writing; which, as it is liable to more faults, so it is capable of more beauties, than the exactness, and sobriety of Virgil": Dryden to Charles Montague [*c.* Oct. 1699], *Letters*, pp. 120–21. John Sherwood suggests that nearly all the critical judgments of the preface are consistent with the classical rules, which remind him of Temple's "Of Poesy." "Dryden and the Rules: The Preface to the *Fables*," *Journal of English and Germanic Philology*, 52 (1953), pp. 13–26.

70. Dryden, *Works*, V, p. 328; *Aeneid*, II, 724 (Loeb).

Chapter 7 Saint-Evremond and the Moderns

1. There is a brief treatment in John M. Aden, "Dryden and Saint-Evremond," *Comparative Literature*, 6 (1954), pp. 232–39. For Saint-Evremond's importance in England, see (among others), A. F. B. Clark, *Boileau and the French Classical Critics in England* (1925, reprinted New York, 1965), pp. 288–93.

2. "The Life of Monsieur de Saint-Evremond," in *The Works of Monsieur de Saint-Evremond*, ed. Pierre des Maizeaux, 2nd edn, 3 vols (London, 1728), I, p. vi. The papers of Des Maizeaux are in the British Library, MS Add. 4281–89, from which it seems he made an honest attempt to restore

the original texts of Saint-Evremond (as he explains in his preface), but sometimes modified, deleted and added new passages; see D. C. Potts, "Desmaizeux and Saint-Evremond's Text," *French Studies*, 19 (1965), pp. 239–52. See also René Ternois, "En écoutant Saint-Evremond," *Revue d'histoire littéraire de la France*, 60 (1960), pp. 165–76. Des Maizeaux used the French edition of Saint-Evremond's works published in London in 1705, which he and Pierre Silvestre edited from the manuscripts, as the foundation of this enlarged and corrected version. He identifies and excludes many spurious works that had been fostered on his very popular author – and he leaves out the poetry. The best modern edition of the works is by Ternois, *Oeuvres en prose*, 4 vols (Paris, 1962–69), with a fine discussion of the early editions and bibliographical problems. On Des Maizeaux, see Leon Petit, *La Fontaine et Saint-Evremond* (Toulouse, 1953), app. 1, pp. 381–87.

3. Saint-Evremond, *Works*, I, pp. vii–ix; III, p. xxxv; "To the Mareschal de Créqui," ibid., II, p. 71. For more on the distinction between "a polite and a learned Person," see "Of Study and Conversation," ibid., pp. 267–73.

4. See for example the poem, "Sur les Vaines Occupations des savans et des controversistes," on the "stérilité de leur Génie pour les commerce des honnête gens." In *Oeuvres*, ed. Pierre Des Maizeaux, 4 vols (Amsterdam, 1726), IV, pp. 356–60.

5. See Paul Chaponnière, "Les Premières Années d'exil de Saint-Evremond," *Revue d'histoire littéraire de la France*, 29 (1922), pp. 385–408; Gustave Cohen, *Le Séjour de Saint-Evremond en Hollande* (Paris, 1926).

6. René Ternois, "Saint-Evremond et la politique Angloise 1665–1674," *XVIIe siècle*, 57 (1962), pp. 3–23; Walter Melville Daniels, *Saint-Evremond en Angleterre* (Versailles, 1907), pp. 104–9; Earl of Arlington to Temple, April 29, 1670, *Letters to Sir William Temple*, 2 vols (London, 1701), I, pp. 432–33; Saint-Evremond to Arlington, in Cohen, *Le Séjour* app., pp. 89–93. Silvestre tells also how he managed to convert his French assets into a generous pension and annuity; Saint-Evremond, *Works*, III, p. xxxviii.

7. Saint-Evremond, *Works*, II, pp. 51–52; idem, *Lettres*, ed. René Ternois, 2 vols (Paris 1967), I, pp. 156–58; *The Letters of Saint-Evremond*, trans. John Hayward (London, 1930), pp. 104–5.

8. See Cyril Hartmann, *The Vagabond Duchess* (London, 1927), pp. 220–21; Georges Mongrédien, *Une Aventurière au grand siècle: La Duchesse de Mazarin* (Paris, 1952), ch. 6,

pp. 153–66. Des Maizeaux included the Duchess's memoirs (which he attributed to the abbé St Real), in the *Works*, III, pp. 105–77.

9. Saint-Evremond, *Works*, III, p. xxx. He declined a new invitation to France as late as 1686; see Quentin M. Hope, "Huet and Saint-Evremond," *Modern Language Notes*, 72 (1957), pp. 575–77. There is a nice appreciation by Le Clerc, reviewing his works in the *Bibliothèque choisie*, 9 (1706), pp. 319–36.

10. Paul Bonnefon, "Une Lettre inédite sur la mort de Saint-Evremond," *Revue d'histoire littéraire de la France*, 13 (1906), pp. 322–25. For Anthony Hamilton, Count de Grammont, who knew him well, "he was a Philosopher equally remote from Superstition and Impiety, a Voluptuary, who has no less aversion for Debauchery, than inclination for Pleasure," from the *Memoirs of Count Grammont*, quoted in Des Maizeaux's "Life," in Saint-Evremond, *Works*, I, p. clvii. For Saint-Evremond as an epicure, see René Ternois, "Saint-Evremond et Gassendi," *Modern Language Notes*, 72 (1957), pp. 575–77, and for his generally tolerant, but thoroughly Erastian religion, see his letter to Henri Justel (1681), in *Works*, II, pp. 271–80; *Letters,* trans. Hayward, pp. 231–40; and his "Reflections upon Religion," ibid., pp. 333–36, Ternois, *Oeuvres*, III, pp. 360–66; and H. T. Barnwell, *Les Idées morales et critiques de Saint-Evremond* (Paris, 1957), ch. 5, pp. 91–115.

11. I have restricted myself to those works authenticated by Ternois, though it is likely that some of the many others attributed to Saint-Evremond (some included by Des Maizeaux, who made strenuous efforts to distinguish them) may be genuine.

12. Saint-Evremond, *Works*, I, p. cxlii.

13. *La Comédie des académistes*, ed. G. L. Van Roosbroeck (New York, 1931). See Henry Carrington Lancaster, *A History of French Dramatic Literature in the Seventeenth Century*, pt 2, 2 vols (Baltimore, 1932), I, pp. 295–98.

14. In 1653, Saint-Evremond was committed briefly to the Bastille for making fun of Mazarin; he was more seriously compromised by a long criticism he made of Mazarin in a letter to a friend, the Marquis de Créqui, and by his association with the suddenly displaced Fouquet, and was compelled to leave France for exile. See Saint-Evremond, *Works*, I, pp. xxii–xxxvi. He had earlier lost his captaincy of the guard for making fun of the Prince de Condé. On the other hand, it should be said that Saint-Evremond resisted the entreaties of the *frondeurs* and remained loyal to the crown, for which he received some reward.

15. Pierre Corneille, *Le Cid*, ed. Peter H. Nurse (Baton Rouge, 1978); J. B. Segall, *Corneille and the Spanish Drama* (New York, 1902), pp. 30–93.

16. Pierre Corneille, *Writings on the Theatre*, ed. H. T. Barnwell (Oxford, 1965), app. A, pp. 174–75; E. B. O. Borgerhoff, *The Freedom of French Classicism* (Princeton, 1950 reprinted New York, 1968), pp. 67–68.

17. *Les Sentiments de l'Académie Française sur le Cid*, ed. Colbert Searles (University of Minnesota Studies in Language and Literature, 3, 1916); Armand Gaste, *La Querelle du Cid: pièces et pamphlets* (Paris, 1898); Paul Reynier, *Le Cid de Corneille: étude et analyse* (Paris, n. d.). See also Louis Rivaille, *Les Débuts de P. Corneille* (Paris, n. d.), and Lancaster, *A History*, I, pp. 118–44.

18. The "ancients" were impressed but not persuaded; see Chapelain to Balzac, Feb. 19, 1640, in Chapelain, *Opuscules critiques*, ed. Alfred C. Hunter (Paris, 1936), p. 418.

19. Other candidates are *Medée* and *Horace*; see the introduction to *Medée* by André de Leyssac (Textes littéraires de France, 258, 1978), and for *Horace*, Peter H. Nurse, *Classical Voices* (Totowa, N.J., 1971), pp. 13–66.

20. See the text in Corneille's *Writings on the Theatre*, pp. 91–94.

21. Whether the unities of time, place and action are indeed Aristotelian, and how they migrated from Italy to France is still a tangled subject; but see Geoffrey Brereton, who dates their arrival in France to the 1630s, *French Tragic Drama in the Sixteenth and Seventeenth Centuries* (London, 1973), pp. 133–37.

22. See John M. Aden, "Dryden, Corneille, and the *Essay of Dramatic Poesy*," *Review of English Studies*, n.s., 6 (1955), pp. 147–56; R. V. Le Clercq, "Corneille and the *Essay of Dramatic Poesy*," *Comparative Literature*, 22 (1970), pp. 319–27; Pierre Legouis, "Corneille and Racine as Dramatic Critics," *Seventeenth Century Studies: Essays to Herbert Grierson* (1938, reprinted New York, 1967), pp. 269–91. Amanda Ellis found that of nineteen passages taken by Dryden from Horace fourteen probably derived from Corneille: "Horace's Influence on Dryden," *Philological Quarterly*, 4 (1925), p. 48.

23. The three discourses of 1660 may now be read in translation: "On the Uses and Elements of Dramatic Poetry," in *European Theories of the Drama*, ed. Barrett H. Clark (New York, 1936), pp. 139–47; idem, "Discourse on Tragedy, and of the Methods of Treating it, According to Probability [*vraisemblance*] and Necessity," in *Dramatic Essays of the Neoclassic Age*, ed. H. H. Adams and Baxter Hathaway

(New York, 1950), pp. 2–34; idem, "Of the Three Unities of Action, Time, and Place," in *The Continental Model: Selected French Critical Essays of the Seventeenth Century* ed. Scott Elledge and Donald Schier (Ithaca, N.Y., 1970), pp. 101–15. The originals may be conveniently consulted in Corneille's *Writings on the Theatre*.

24. Georges May assembles many examples in "Corneille and the Classics," *Yale French Studies*, 38 (1967), pp. 143–44.

25. Saint-Evremond, *Works*, I, p. xl.

26. *Sir Politick Would-Be*, ed. Robert Finch and Eugène Joliet (Geneva, 1978).

27. See the letter purportedly by Saint-Evremond to Mme Mazarin, first printed in the *Works of the Earls of Rochester, Roscommon and Dorset*, 2 vols (London, 1731), I, p. xxvi. Rochester, writes Saint-Evremond, had it in for Dryden after his great successes, possibly because "he was sensible that he deserved not that applause for his Tragedies which the mad, unthinking audience gave them – which corruption of taste [Saint-Evremond adds] was afterward corrected by the Duke of Buckingham's *Rehearsal*." He goes on to recall how when Crowne's *Destruction of Jerusalem* came to rival Dryden's *Conquest of Granada* ("with as wild and unaccountable Success"), Rochester again took umbrage and withdrew his favor.

28. See René Bray, *La Tragédie cornélienne devant la critique classique d'après la querelle de Sophonisbe (1663)* (Paris, 1927).

29. Ternois prints the two letters, *Oeuvres*, II, pp. 76–83. For the circumstances, see Saint-Evremond to the comte de Lionne (1668), *Works*, I, pp. 246–48; *Letters*, ed. Ternois, pp. 69–72. The quarrel over *Sophonisbe* is discussed in René Bray, *La Tragédie cornélienne*; and Georges Couton, *La Vieillesse de Corneille* (Paris, 1949), pp. 46–57.

30. See for example, Robert J. Nelson, *Corneille and Racine: Parallels and Contrasts* (Englewood Cliffs, N.J., 1966), with selections from Longuepierre (1686), La Bruyère (1688), Fontenelle (1693), etc.; Georges May, *Tragédie cornélienne, tragédie racinienne* (Urbana, 1948), Gordon Pocock, *Corneille and Racine* (Cambridge, 1973).

31. "A Dissertation on Racine's Tragedy called *The Grand Alexander*," Saint-Evremond, *Works*, I, p. 232; Ternois, *Oeuvres*, II, p. 84.

32. Saint-Evremond, *Works*, I, p. 235.

33. Ibid.

34. Ibid. pp. 236–38.

35. "Saint-Evremond n'avait pas tort, qui disait que les moeurs d'*Alexandre* étaient celles des chevaliers errants . . . Il est en verité remarquable que le jeune helléniste ait si com-

plètement réussi à oublier la Grèce: sa tragédie évoque, non Plutarque ou Quinte-Curce, mais le *Roman d'Alexandre* ou d'*Eneas*," Philip Butler, *Classicisme et baroque dans l'oeuvre de Racine* (Paris, 1959), p. 118. Racine had several medieval romances in his library beside the classics, ibid., p. 137 n.

36. Saint-Evremond to the comte de Lionne, *Works*, I, pp. 220–21; *Lettres*, ed. Ternois, I, pp. 132–34; *Letters*, trans. Hayward, pp. 62–63.

37. Corneille was "never aware that he was not creating a modern counterpart of Greek tragedy," Borgerhoff, *Freedom of French Classicism*, pp. 71–72.

38. R. C. Knight, "The Evolution of Racine's Poétique," *Modern Language Review*, 35 (1940), pp. 19–39.

39. "Pouvez-vous ne pas convenir que ce sont Sophocle et Euripide qui ont formé M. Racine?" Boileau to Perrault; seconded by Fénelon, "M. Racine . . . avait fort etudié les grandes modèles de l'antiquité," both quoted by Knight, *Racine et la Grèce* 2nd edn (Paris, 1974), p. 7.

40. *La Pratique du théâtre*, ed. Hans-Jorg Neuschafer (Geneva, 1971). The English translation rearranges the chapters in books 3 and 4. There is a helpful biography in Charles Arnaud, *Les Théories dramatiques au xviie siècle: étude sur la vie et les oeuvres de l'abbé d'Aubignac* (Paris, 1888), pp. 9–56.

41. D'Aubignac, *The Whole Art of the Stage* (1684, reprinted New York, 1968), I, pt. 1, p. 12.

42. Ibid., pp. 123, 19.

43. "Of Probability and Decency," ibid., II, pt. 2, pp. 74–122. See René Bray, *La Formation de la doctrine classique en France* (Paris, 1927), pp. 191–214, 215–30.

44. D'Aubignac, *Whole Art*, III, ch. 1, p. 13.

45. Ibid., II, p. 125.

46. Ibid., p. 127.

47. See *Rodogune* (1647), ed. and trans. William C. Chubb (London, 1974); Pocock, *Corneille and Racine*, p. 99. Martin Turnell calls *Polyeucte* "certainly his greatest play": *The Classical Moment* (London, 1947), p. 37.

48. D'Aubignac, *Whole Art*, III, p. 13. See Bray, *Doctrine*, p. 17.

49. D'Aubignac, *Whole Art*, III, pp. 13–14.

50. Ibid., p. 44.

51. Ibid., p. 45.

52. Ibid., IV, p. 101.

53. For the conflict between *vrai* and *vraisemblance* in Corneille and contemporary theory, see Jacques Scherer, *La Dramaturgie classique en France* (Paris, 1950), pp. 369–71; Bray, *Doctrine*, pp. 202–5, 211–12. Scherer finds that Corneille preferred the one, Racine the other.

54. So too Chapelain and La Mesnardière who both preferred *vraisemblance* to *la verité historique*; see Helen Reese, *La Mesnardière's Poetique* (Baltimore, 1937), p. 73.

55. Besides Bray, *Doctrine* (pp. 225–26), see Gustave Lanson, *Corneille* (Paris, 1898), pp. 68–72; P. J. Yarrow, *Corneille* (London, 1963), pp. 265–67; H. T. Barnwell, "Reflections on Corneille's Theory of Vraisemblance," *Forum for Modern Language Studies*, 1, pp. 295–310.

56. See Prosser Hall Frye, *Romance and Tragedy* (1908, reprinted Lincoln, 1961), p. 163.

57. Corneille to Saint-Evremond [1668], *Works*, II, pp. 26–27; *Lettres*, ed. Ternois, I, pp. 166–67; *Letters*, trans. Hayward, pp. 72–73.

58. Saint-Evremond to Corneille [1668], *Works*, II, pp. 28–29; *Lettres*, ed. Ternois, I, pp. 168–70; *Letters*, trans. Hayward, pp. 75–76.

59. From an anecdote by Racine's son, Louis; see Eugène Vinaver, *Racine and Poetic Tragedy*, trans. P. M. Jones (Manchester, 1957), p. 66.

60. Preface to Racine, *Alexander the Great*, in the *Complete Plays*, trans. Samuel Solomon, 2 vols (New York, 1967), I, p. 73.

61. To be sure, George Saintsbury thought that *Agesilaus* was almost worthless! See his edition of *Horace* (Oxford, 1882), p. xx.

62. "Never did one shadow of mistrust cloud this bond": Karl Vossler, *Jean Racine* (New York, n.d.), p. 10.

63. H. T. Barnwell finds the same tendency in some other contemporary dramatists; see "From *La Thebaid* to *Andromaque*," *French Studies*, 5 (1951), pp. 30–35.

64. Bray distinguishes Corneille thus: "Ce qui fait l'originalité de son système tragique, ce qui le différencie du système de Racine et en général du système proprement classique, ce n'est donc pas l'attachement à l'histoire, à l'égard de laquelle il marque dans son oeuvre autant de désinvolture q'un d'Aubignac, mais bien la recherche du fait extraordinaire, du sujet générateur de merveille, qui, dépassant la vraisemblance ordinaire, à laquel s'attachent après Chapelain tous nos classiques, a besoin de se parer, pour se faire accepter du public, de l'authenticité historique. Le respect de Corneille pour l'histoire n'est donc qu'une facade. Elle ne doit pas nous masquer . . . la realité de ses infidélités historiques": *Doctrine*, pp. 225–26. According to May, "Racine modifie l'histoire pour se rapprocher autant que possible des connaissances traditionelles du public. Corneille les modifie pour s'eloigner autant qu'il le peut de ces connaissances. En consequence, l'un retranche surtout, tandis que l'autre ajoute." May, *Tragédie cornélienne*, p. 223.

65. Menestrier, it is true, asks for period costumes in ballets, as far as possible. C. F. Menestrier, *De Ballets anciens et des modernes* (Paris, 1682), pp. 250–57. But the actual designs of Jean Berain combine Roman and contemporary motifs for the supposedly Greek protagonists; see James Laver, *Drama: Its Costume and Decor* (London, 1951), pp. 150–56; and John C. Lapp, *Aspects of Racinian Tragedy* (Toronto, 1955), p. 191. So too Giovanni Battista Doni advised producers to costume their players in the dress of the times and places of their portrayal, but apparently to as little effect. Simon T. Worsthorne, *Venetian Opera in the Seventeenth Century* (Oxford, 1954), p. 2. This was true in England too, despite Pepys's praise for the (spurious) Roman garments he saw in *Heraclius*; see Montage Summers, *The Restoration Theatre*, (London, 1934), p. 279.

66. For an exhaustive study of Racine's knowledge and debt to ancient Greece, see Knight, *Racine et la Grèce*; idem, "Racine and Greek Tragedy," *Racine: Modern Judgments* (London, 1969), pp. 161–73; Lapp, *Aspects*, pp. 15–63.

67. The annotations on D'Aubignac appear in the Pléiade edition of *Oeuvres complètes*, ed. Raymond Picard, Racine, 2 vols, (Paris, 1960), II, pp. 991–92; on the *Poetics* and the Greek tragedians, ibid., pp. 843–80, 931–32. See also Sister Marie Philip Haley, *Racine and the Art Poetique of Boileau* (Johns Hopkins Studies in Romance Literatures and Languages, extra vol., XII, reprinted New York, 1976), p. 113.

68. Racine, *Oeuvres complètes* (Pléiade edn), I, pp. 259–62. For the originality of *Andromaque*, see Paul Benichou, *Man and Ethics: Studies in French Classicism*, trans. Elizabeth Hughes (New York, 1971), pp. 142–52, 157. Its comparative simplicity and love story may be compared with Corneille's *Agesilaus* of that same year, Barnwell, "From *La Thebaide* to *Andromache*," pp. 30–35.

69. See the note in the Pléiade edition of Racine *Oeuvres complètes*, p. 1102; and Lancaster, *A History*, p. 59.

70. Racine, *Oeuvres complètes* (Pléiade), I, pp. 403–7.

71. But see Philip Butler's skeptical remarks in his edition of *Britannicus* (Cambridge, 1967), p. 18.

72. See H. C. Lancaster, "A Passage in the First Preface of *Britannica*," *Modern Language Notes*, 51 (1936) pp. 8–10.

73. After Terence in the prologue to *Andria*.

74. Racine, *Complete Plays*, I, pp. 376–79.

75. C. L. Walton in his edition of *Bérénice* (Oxford, 1965), p. 37.

76. "Berenice has nothing to do with Palestine; and it is impossible to care whether she is a queen or not. She does not inhabit that mortal realm in which racial tradition, geography, social status, and the historical context have their fatal importance": Francis Ferguson, *The Idea of a Theater* (Princeton, 1948, reprinted New York, 1954), p. 68. See Maurice Bowra, "The Simplicity of Racine," (1956) reprinted in *Racine: Modern Judgments*, ed. R. C. Knight (London, 1969), pp. 24–48, and H. T. Barnwell, "The Simplicity of Racine –Yet Again," *French Studies*, 31 (1977), pp. 304–406.

77. Mme de Sévigné to Mme de Grignan, March 16, 1672, Mme de Sévigné, *Lettres* (Pléiade edn), I, ed. Gerard-Gailly (Paris, 1956), pp. 496–500.

78. Saint-Evremond to the comte de Lionne (1668), *Works*, I, pp. 218–20; *Letters*, trans. Hayward, pp. 59–62.

79. Saint-Evremond to the comte de Lionne (1667–68), *Lettres*, ed. Ternois, I, pp. 144–47; *Letters*, trans. Hayward, pp. 50–52. See Quentin M. Hope, "Molière and Saint-Evremond," *Publications of the Modern Langurage Association*, 76 (1961), pp. 200–4.

80. Saint-Evremond to the comte de Lionne (1668), *Works*, I, pp. 221–24; *Lettres*, ed. Ternois, I, pp. 134–38; *Letters*, trans. Hayward, pp. 64–66.

81. Saint-Evremond, *Works*, I, p. 244–46; *Lettres*, ed. Ternois, I, pp. 138–41; *Letters*, trans. Hayward, pp. 67–69, and Hayward note, p. 65.

82. *Letters*, trans. Hayward, pp. 77–78. Hayward points out that these words only appeared in the *Nouvelles Oeuvres de Saint-Evremond* in 1700 and are not in Des Maizeaux.

83. Saint-Evremond to the comte de Lionne (1669–70), *Works*, II, pp. 124–25; *Lettres*, ed. Ternois, I, pp. 152–54; *Letters*, trans. Hayward, pp. 81–84.

84. Saint-Evremond, *Works*, II, pp. 154–58; *Oeuvres*, ed. Ternois, III, pp. 21–31.

85. Saint-Evremond, *Works*, II, p. 154.

86. Ibid., p. 155.

87. Ibid., p. 156.

88. Ibid., p. 157.

89. For the expression and its use in the period, see Scherer, *La Dramaturgie classique*, pp. 383–421. As with *vraisemblance*, Scherer points out that it was a means of adapting the piece to public taste.

90. See above, p. 114ff. For D'Aubigny, see Ternois, "Un ami de Saint-Evremond: l'abbé d'Aubigny," *Studi francesi*, 7 (1963), pp. 26–39.

91. Saint-Evremond, *Works*, II, p. 158.

92. Saint-Evremond, *Works*, II, pp. 159–72; *Oeuvres*, ed. Ternois, III, pp. 32–60.

93. Saint-Evremond, *Works*, II, p. 159.

94. Ibid, p. 162.

95. Ibid., p. 170.

96. Ibid., p. 171.

97. For Molière against the rules, see Dorante in *School for Wives* (1663), scene vii.

98. Saint-Evremond, *Works*, II, pp. 112–20; *Ouevres*, ed. Ternois, III, pp. 324–37. Ternois agrees with Des Maizeaux in placing it about 1672.

99. Saint-Evremond, *Works*, II, p. 117.

Chapter 8 Saint-Evremond, Dryden and the Opera

1. James R. Anthony, *French Baroque Music from Beaujoyeulx to Rameau* (New York, 1974), p. 5. I have not seen the revised and improved version of this useful work, *La Musique en France à l'époque baroque*, trans. Beatrice Vierne (Paris, 1981).

2. For Doni, see the full summary in John Hawkins, *A General History of the Science and Practice of Music*, ed. Charles Cudworth, 2 vols (New York, 1963), II, pp. 628–35, and Charles Burney who gives an extract from Doni's work, in which Doni (whom he calls "extremely warped in his judgment by a predilection for antiquity") recalls the origins of Florentine opera. Burney also describes Galilei's work "upon the abuse of modern Music": *A General History of Music*, 2nd edn (1776–89), ed. Frank Mercer, 2 vols (New York, 1957), II, pp. 511–14. See too Burney's comments on Pietro della Valle in favor of the moderns (1640), pointing out sympathetically that Plato was already complaining that music had declined two thousand years ago, and doubting that there ever was a golden age (pp. 524–26, 534). An extract from Galilei's *Dialogo della musica antica e della moderna* (1581) may be found in *Source Readings in Musical History*, ed. Oliver Strunk (New York, 1950), pp. 302–22.

3. Giulio Caccini (the composer of *Euridice*) recalls the learned discussions in the Florentine "camerata," and welcomes the new in *Le nuove musiche* (1602, and again in 1614), a work which found an English translation in an abridged form in John Playford's *Introduction to the Skill of Musick* (1655), and went through fourteen editions by 1700. A corrected translation is provided by Strunk, *Source Readings*, pp. 377–92; see the edition by H. Wiley Hitchcock (Madison, 1970), and Hitchcock's article, "Caccini's 'Other' *Nuove musiche*," *American Musicological*

Society, 27 (1974), pp. 438–60. The Rinuccini and Peri dedications are translated in Strunk, *Source Readings*, pp. 367–69; 373–76. For general discussion, see Robert Donnington, *The Rise of Opera* (London, 1981); Claude V. Palisca, *Humanism in Italian Renaissance Thought* (New Haven, 1985), ch. 14, pp. 408–34; M. Bukofzer, *Music in the Baroque Era* (New York, 1947), pp. 25–26, 56–57. See also Charles Palisca, "Marco Scacchi's Defence of Modern Music," *Words and Music . . . in Honor of A. Tillman Merritt*, ed. Laurence Berman (Cambridge, Mass., 1972), pp. 189–235.

4. Thomas Blount, *Glossographia* (1656), quoted by H. L. Reyher, *Les Masques anglais* (1909, reprinted New York, 1964), p. 470n.

5. Saint-Evremond, *Works*, I, p. clvi; III, p. xxxvi. On one occasion (1678), Saint-Evremond set a pastoral to music and had it sung in the salon, "before a great many persons of distinction": ibid., I, p. xcix. The text of the *Idylle en musique* is given in the French edition of the works; see Saint-Evremond, *Oeuvres*, ed. Des Maizeaux, 4 vols (Amsterdam, 1739), III, pp. 430–43.

6. See Romain Rolland, "The First Opera Played in Paris," *Some Musicians of Former Days*, trans. Mary Blaiklock (1915, reprinted Freeport, N.Y., 1968), pp. 70–128; for some other early efforts, see Henri Prunières, *L'Opéra italien en France avant Lulli* (Paris, 1913), and more recently, Neal Zaslaw, "The First Opera in Paris: A Study in the Politics of Art," *Jean Baptiste Lully and the Music of the French Baroque*, ed. John Hajdu Heyer (Cambridge, 1989), pp. 7–23. Rossi's airs were well known in London in such collections as the one dedicated to Henry Howard, *Scelta di canzonette italiane di diversi autori* (London, 1679).

7. Dryden attacks its incredibility in the *Essay of Dramatick Poesie*, in *The Works of John Dryden*, 20 vols (Berkeley, 1961–89), XVII, p. 50. Corneille himself suspected that his work, *Andromède* (1650), with its great use of machines, did not measure up to *Cinna* or *Rodogune*, though he had made a genuine effort to reform his Italian models; see Ternois's useful introduction to Saint-Evremond's essay, *Oeuvres*, III, pp. 134–35, and Prunières, *L'Opéra italien*, pp. 324–28. Corneille's *examen*, in which he emphasizes the subsidiary role of the music, is included in H. T. Barnwell, *Pierre Corneille: Writings on the Theatre* (Oxford, 1965), pp. 140–49.

8. John Orrell, "A New Witness to the Restoration Stage, 1670–1680)," *Theater Research International*, 1 (1976), p. 91; Pierre Danchin, "The Foundation of the Royal Academy of Music in 1674 and Pierre Perrin's *Ariane*," *Theater Survey*, 25 (1984), p. 61; John Buttrey, "New Light on Robert Cambert in London, and his *Ballet en Musique*," *Early Music*, 23 (1995), pp. 198–219. See also Ternois, who quotes from the accounts of the French ambassador that Charles II especially admired the beauties of the chorus and musicians, and who believes that Saint-Evremond took part. *Oeuvres*, ed. Ternois, III, pp. 141–42. Evelyn reported seeing an "Italian Opera in musique, the first that had ben in England of this kind": Jan. 5, 1674, *The Diary of John Evelyn*, ed. E. S. de Beer, 6 vols (Oxford, 1955), IV, p. 30, which Alfred Loewenberg thinks might have been a rehearsal of *Ariane*, but De Beer suggests is more likely to have been an Italian performance of something staged for Mary of Modena, the new Duchess of York; see Alfred Loewenberg, *Annals of Opera 1597–1940*, 2 vols (Geneva, 1955), I, pp. 54–55; Evelyn, *Diary*, p. 30n. Cambert's "opera" (so entitled) was sung in French, but the libretto was translated into English. Upon his arrival in London in 1673 Cambert founded a short-lived "Royall Academy of Musick" in Covent Garden, and died early in 1677. Norman Demuth calls *Pomone* (1671), "the first genuine French opera": *French Opera: Its Development to the Revolution* (Sussex, 1963), pp. 97–118, 275–78, 288.

9. *Ariadne; or the Marriage of Bacchus. An Opera or a Vocal Representation, first composed by Monsieur P.P. Now put into Music by Monsieur Grabu* (London, 1674). The frontispiece is reproduced in *Theatre in Europe: A Documentary History: Restoration and Georgian England 1660–1788*, ed. David Thomas (Cambridge, 1989), p. 102.

10. See Donald J. Grout, "Some Forerunners of the Lully Opera," *Music and Letters*, 22 (1941), pp. 1–25.

11. Perrault's life appears among *Les Hommes illustrés qui ont paru en France pendant ce siècle*, 2 vols (Paris, 1697–1700). See too Voltaire's verdict on Quinault's operas, "Si l'on trouvait dans antiquité un poème comme *Armide* ou comme *Attys*, avec quelle idolatrie il serait reçu! Mais Quinault était moderne": *Le Siècle de Louis XIV*, ch. 32. For an appreciation of Quinault as librettist, see Yves Giraud, "Quinault et Lully ou l'accord de deux styles," *Marseille*, 3rd ser., 95 (1973), pp. 195–212; Patrick J. Smith, *The Tenth Muse* (New York, 1970), pp. 47–62; and in general the monumental work of Etienne Gros, *Philippe Quinault: sa vie et son oeuvre* (Paris, 1926).

12. Charles Perrault, *Memoirs of My Life*, trans. Jeanne Morgan Zarucchi (Columbia, Miss., 1989), pp. 108–10.

13. *Le Banquet des dieux pour la naissance de Monseigneur le Duc de Burgogne* (1682); the *New Grove Dictionary* ("Perrault") also mentions an earlier operatic collaboration between Perrault and Oudot (1677).

14. For Charles Perrault defending Quinault–Lully, see the *Parallèle des anciens et des modernes*, III (Paris, 1692), pp. 239–42. There is a facsimile edition by Hans Robert Jauss and Max Imdahl (Munich, 1964). The *Siècle de Louis le Grand* with its praise of modern opera (p. 20) appeared first in 1687, and was reprinted in the first volume of the *Parallèles*, 4 vols (Paris, 1688–97).

15. *La Critique de l'opéra ou examen de la tragédie intitulée Alceste ou le Triomphe d'Alcide* appeared in 1674. Paul Bonnefon attributes it to Charles, in "Charles Perrault, essai sur sa vie et ses ouvrages," *Revue d'histoire littéraire française*, 11 (1905), p. 410; followed by André Hallays, *Les Perraults* (Paris, 1926), p. 144n. Racine's quotation is from Quintilian, *Institutio Oratoria*, X, i, 26; his *Iphigénie* was first printed with its preface in 1675.

16. See Gros, *Quinault*, p. 730ff.; R. C. Knight, *Racine et la Grèce*, pp. 328–30. Knight relies on the prefaces, but he is aware already (p. 333) of Lucien Goldmann's warning that they must not be taken too literally to describe the plays. See p. 251 n. 16 below.

17. "Lettre à M. Chapelain sur la préface de l'Iphigénie de M. Racine," ed. Paul Bonnefon, *Revue d'histoire littéraire* (July–Sept. 1904); *Parallèles*, IV, pp. 337–42.

18. The tract was published in Perrault's *Essais de physique*, II (Paris, 1680); see Hubert Gillot, *La Querelle des anciens et des modernes en France* (Nancy, 1914), pp. 576–91. He had already declared himself on the matter in the notes to his translation of Vitruvius (1673). For Perrault and Quinault, see Hallays, *Les Perraults*, app. VIII, pp. 271–74.

19. Colbert's sons asked Racine and Lully to write a cantata celebrating the King which was performed as an *Idyll sur la paix* in 1685. According to Boileau, Racine would never admit that there could be a good opera; Quinault got his commission only because the King intervened. See Boileau's account in his preface to a *Fragment d'un prologue d'opéra*, in *Oeuvres poétiques* (Paris, 1853), p. 409. As for his own attack on opera, provoked in 1686 by the Lully–Quinault collaboration, *Armide*, see Boileau's tenth satire, ibid., ll. 131–49. Quinault himself gave up writing operas because of moral scruples late in life.

20. See besides Gillot, Maurice Barthélemy, "L'Opéra français et la querelle entre les anciens et des modernes," *Lettres romanes*, 10 (1956), pp. 379–91.

21. "An Essay upon the Ancient and Modern Learning" (1690), William Temple, *Five Miscellaneous Essays*, ed. Samuel Holt Monk (Ann Arbor, 1963), p. 57.

22. Hawkins quotes Temple's passage at the outset of his work, as by an author, "whose zeal for a favorite hypothesis, had led him to write on a subject he did not understand": *A General History of the Science and Practice of Music*, 2 vols (New York, 1963), I, pp. 1–2. Burney reviews the whole quarrel in his "Dissertation on the Music of the Ancients," in the *General History of Music*, I, esp. pp. 105–2. The first volumes of Burney and John Hawkins both appeared in 1776. The full story of music in the English quarrel between the ancients and moderns remains to be told; for some suggestions, see Warren Dwight Allen, *Philosophies of Music History* (1939, reprinted New York, 1962), and William Weber, *The Rise of Musical Classics in Eighteenth-Century England* (Oxford, 1992).

23. *Roger North on Music*, ed. John Wilson (London, 1959), p. 350; and Danchin (relying on the reports of the French ambassador, Courtin), "Foundation," pp. 64–65. For Charles's love of Lully, see Buttrey, "New Light," pp. 205–9. Lully's first *tragédie en musique, Cadmus et Hermione* (1673) was performed in London by a French troupe in 1686; see Anthony, *French Baroque Music*, p. 106. For more on Lully's influence in England, see Demuth, *French Opera*, app. 42, pp. 293–301.

24. Romain Rolland, "Notes on Lully," *Some Musicians*, pp. 129–250, esp. sect. 3, "Lully's Recitative and Racine's Declamation," pp. 176–209. See also Lois Rostow, "French Baroque Recitative as an Expression of Tragic Declamation," *Early Music*, 11 (1983), pp. 468–79, and Manfred Bukofzer who writes that "the French conceived the recitative in rhetorical rather than musical terms," *Music in the Baroque Era*, p. 156. As for the English, the preface to the *Fairy Queen* (1692) points out that "he must be a very ignorant Player, who knows not there is a Musical Cadence in speaking, and that a Man may as well speak out of Tune, as sing out of Tune." The similarity between tragic declamation and classical oratory is also discussed at length by Thomas Betterton, the great actor who produced most of the English opera in the period; see Charles Gildon, *The Life of Mr Thomas Betterton* (London, 1710).

25. Saint-Evremond to d'Harvart [Barthélemy Herwarth], Feb. 4, [1676], *Lettres,* I, pp. 217–19; *Letters,* pp. 160–62. Many of the English Restoration versions of Corneille added music; see Richard Luckett, "Exotick but Rational Entertainments: The English Dramatic Operas," *English Drama: Forms and Development,* ed. Marie Axton and Raymond Williams (Cambridge, 1977), pp. 134–35.

26. Saint-Evremond, *Works,* II, pp. 173–74. He is probably referring to the preface to *Andromède.*

27. "All that belongs to Conversation, all that relates to Intrigues and Affairs, all that belongs to Council and Action, is proper for Actors to rehearse, but ridiculous in the Mouths of Musicians to sing": ibid., p. 177.

28. Saint-Evremond actually wrote some complimentary lines to Lully for his opera *Armide* which was given in Paris 1686; see the *Oeuvres mêlées,* ed. Charles Giraud, 3 vols (Paris, 1865), II, pp. 549–51.

29. Among the many "ancients" who opposed opera, there were besides Boileau and Racine, La Fontaine and La Bruyère; see Gros, "Les Adversaires de l'opéra," *Quinault,* ch. 6, pp. 715–41.

30. Saint-Evremond, *Works,* I, p. cv–cvi. See Donald J. Grout, "Seventeenth-Century Parodies of French Opera," *Musical Quarterly,* 27 (1941), p. 213, and Ternois who supplies a summary and the key scene, Act II, scene iv, Saint-Evremond, *Oeuvres,* II, pp. 143–47.

31. See Rémond de Saint-Mard, *Réflexions sur l'opéra* (The Hague, 1741); Max Graf, *Composer and Critic* (New York, 1946), p. 96.

32. There were several projects to perform Italian operas between 1660 and 1667, but nothing seems to have come of them; see J. A. Westrup, *Purcell,* 3rd edn (New York, 1962), p. 127.

33. For a contemporary account, see Richard Flecknoe, *A Short Discourse of the English Stage* (London, 1664). See also Reyher, *Les Masques anglais,* pp. 469–75. However, Ann-Mari Hedback has found some evidence of Venetian operatic influence; see the introduction to her edition of *The Siege of Rhodes* (Uppsala, 1973), pp. lxxi–lxxii. The *Siege* was entered in the Stationer's Register (Aug. 27, 1656) as a "masque" but Davenant referred to it elsewhere as a "costly opera": Edmond, pp. 127–28. Needless to say, the term and the genre were (and remain) flexible to suit the hybrid character of the form; see the remarks of Richard Luckett, "Exotick but Rational Entertainments", pp. 130–32.

34. See D. J. Gordon, "Poet and Architect: The Intellectual Setting of the Quarrel between Ben Jonson and Inigo Jones," *The Renaissance Imagination,* ed. Stephen Orgel (Berkeley, 1975), pp. 77–101.

35. See Lily B. Campbell, *Scenes and Machines of the English Stage during the Renaissance: A Classical Revival* (Cambridge, 1923), p. 178; John Peacock, "The Stuart Court Masque and the Theater of the Greeks," *Journal of the Warburg and Courtauld Institutes,* 56 (1993), pp. 183–208; and idem, *The Stage Designs of Inigo Jones: The European Context* (Cambridge, 1995).

36. This passage has been questioned, for example by Dennis Arundell, *The Critic at the Opera* (London, 1957), pp. 51, 57, but John Aubrey and Anthony Wood seem to confirm it. "Being freed from imprisonment," Aubrey remembered, "because playes, scil. Tragedies and Comoedies, were in those Presbyterian times scandalous, he [Davenant] contrives to set up an Opera *stylo recitativo*": *Brief Lives,* ed. Andrew Clark, 2 vols (Oxford, 1898), I, p. 208. Cf. Anthony Wood, *Athenae Oxoniensis,* ed. Philip Bliss, 5 vols (London, 1813–20), III, pp. 805–6. For the immediate circumstances, Hyder E. Rollins, "Contribution to the History of the English Commonwealth Drama," *Studies in Philology,* 18 (1921), uses some contemporary documents to show that the government distinguished plays and operas, prohibiting only the former, pp. 329–30. And Leslie Hotson, *The Commonwealth and Restoration Stage* (1928, reprinted New York, 1961), pp. 141–60, illustrates the danger with a letter of Dec. 14, 1658, which predicts that, "the Opera will speedily go down; the godly party are so much discontented with it," and an ominous order a week later by the Council of State.

37. "The First Dayes Entertainment at Rutland-House," Davenant, *Works,* 2 vols (London, 1673), I, pp. 341–59; see Hotson, *Commonwealth and Restoration,* pp. 149–51 (with an interesting contemporary description), and Mary Edmond, *Rare Sir William Davenant* (New York, 1987), pp. 123–36.

38. A contemporary remarks that some plays were put on by stealth, "under pretence of Rope-dancing," Rollins, "Contribution to the History," p. 307; and for more on the subject, ibid., pp. 311, 313–15. See also the ballad "Peru," satirizing Davenant and printed by Rollins, ibid., pp. 326–28; and Arundell, *Critic at the Opera,* pp. 60–72. It was printed in Dryden's third and last *Examen poeticum, being the third part of the Miscellany Poems* (London, 1716), pp. 323–25.

39. See "The Designs for the First Moveable

Scenery on the English Public Stage,"
Burlington Magazine, 25 (1914), pp. 29, 85.

40. May 5, 1659, Evelyn, *Diary*, III, p. 229. Evelyn
is usually thought to refer to Davenant's
Siege, but Edmond thinks it more likely to
have been *The History of Sir Francis Drake*. A
masque by James Shirley, *Cupid and Death*,
had been performed and published
in 1653, and these "private entertainments,"
with music, dance, scenery and costumes,
apparently survived even the worst days
of the Interregnum. Much later, Evelyn
attended John Crowne's extravagant masque,
Callisto, in December 1674 with "a great
presse of people": *Diary*, IV, pp. 50–51 and
described it in his *Life of Mrs Godolphin*,
ed. Harriet Sampson (London, 1939), pp.
52–55, app. C, pp. 231–36. For the details of
this wonderfully documented occasion, see
Eleanor Boswell, *The Restoration Court Stage
(1660–1702) with a particular account of Callisto*
(Cambridge, 1932), pp. 175–227, app. F,
pp. 303–43; Andrew Walkling, "Masque and
Politics at the Restoration Court: John
Crowne's *Callisto*," *Early Music*, 24 (1996),
pp. 27–61. *Callisto* was divided into five acts
with singing and dancing in the long prologue, and the *intermedii* between the acts and
at the end, without much connection to the
plot. Even John Blow's fully fledged opera,
Venus and Adonis (*c.* 1682), still calls itself a
masque.

41. Edward Howard, preface to the *Woman's
Conquest*, quoted in *The Dramatic Works of
William D'Avenant*, 5 vols (Edinburgh,
1874), V, pp. 399–400. Dryden, "Of Heroic
Plays: An Essay," prefixed to the *Siege of
Granada* (1672), Dryden, *Essays*, ed. Watson,
I, pp. 156–58. Burney agreed with Dryden,
disputing with Alexander Pope, who had
credited the *Siege* in *Imitations of Horace* as
being the first English opera on the erro-
neous ground that it was sung by eunuchs!
General History, II, pp. 640–41.

42. Shadwell's participation is a vexed problem
that has created a large controversy; see,
for example, Charles E. Ward, "*The Tempest*:
A Restoration Opera Problem," *English
Literary History*, 13 (1946), pp. 119–30;
Maximilian Novak, "Elkannah Settle's
Attacks on Thomas Shadwell and the
Authorship of the Operatic Tempest," *Notes
and Queries*, 213 (1968), pp. 263–65. Price
describes it as "One of the very few works
to occupy the rocky ground between true
opera and play . . . [it] had behind it the
great Elizabethan and Jacobean traditions of
the masque and lyrical spoken drama." It
combined spoken dialogue with interludes
sung by other actors. Curtis Alexander

Price, *Henry Purcell and the London Stage*
(Cambridge, 1984), pp. 203–4.

43. The first stage direction reads as follows:
"While the Overture is playing, the Curtain
rises, and discovers a new Frontispiece,
joined to the Pilasters, on each side of the
Stage. This Frontispiece is a noble Arch,
supported by large wreathed Columns
of the Corinthean Order. On the Cornice,
just over the Capitals, sits on either side a
Figure, with a trumpet in hand, and a Palm
in the other, representing Fame. A little
further on the same Cornice . . . lie a lion
and a Unicorn, the Supporters of the Royal
Arms of England . . . Beyond this is the
Scene, which represents a thick Cloudy Sky,
a very rocky Coast, and a Tempestuous
sea in perpetual Agitation. This tempest
(suppos'd to be rais'd by Magick) has
many dreadful objects in it, as several
Spirits in horrid shapes . . . When the ship
is sinking, the whole House is darken'd,
and a shower of Fire falls upon 'em. This
is accompanied by Lightening, and several
Claps of Thunder." Edward J. Dent,
Foundations of English Opera (Cambridge,
1928), pp. 139–44; William Barclay Squire,
"The Music of Shadwell's *Tempest*," *Musical
Quarterly*, 7 (1921), p. 567. According to
Moore, "the play is a fascinating illustration
of the baroque passion for piling
into a single work so wide a diversity of
appeals as to land it straight in the lap of
the grotesque," yet, "its very absurdity made
it delightful": Robert Eldridge Moore,
Henry Purcell and the Restoration Theater
(1961, reprinted Westport, Conn., 1974), pp.
183, 188. It was swiftly parodied by Thomas
Duffet in the *Mock-Tempest*, and is already
scoffed at in the *Rehearsal*.

44. Arundell, *Critic at the Opera*, pp. 114–28. See
also James Vernon to Joseph Williamson,
Aug. 22, 1673, writing in anticipation of
the "great machines" and "dancers out of
France": Charles E. Ward, *The Life of John
Dryden* (Chapel Hill, 1961), pp. 103–4.

45. John Downes, *Roscius Anglicanus* (1708),
p. 35. It too was soon burlesqued by Thomas
Duffet, as *Psyche Debauched*. In general,
for scene-painting in drama and opera, see
Montagu Summers, *The Restoration Theatre*
(London, 1934), pp. 212–49.

46. The Davenant–Dryden collaboration is
reprinted in *Shakespearian Adaptations*
(London, 1922), ed. Montague Summers;
the Shadwell opera in Thomas Shadwell,
Complete Works, ed. Montague Summers, 5
vols (London, 1927), II, with a discussion of
the variants, pp. 349–54. See Dent, *Foundations*, pp. 105, 138; Albert Borgman, *Thomas*

Shadwell (1928, reprinted New York, 1969), pp. 28–29.

47. The series (1673–92) which begins with *The Tempest* and includes Dryden's *Albion* and *King Arthur*, were all produced by the actor-manager, Thomas Betterton, for the new Dorset Garden theater designed by Christopher Wren, and were characterized by their extravagant machinery and cost; see Judith Milhous, "The Multimedia Spectacular on the Restoration Stage," *British Theatre and the Other Arts 1660–1800*, ed. Shirley Strum Kenny (Washington, 1984), pp. 41–66. It was probably some of the earlier Davenant productions that Saint-Evremond means when he says, "I have seen Plays in England, wherein there is a great deal of musick": *Works*, II, p. 178.

48. Dryden's prologue was published in *Miscellany Poems* (1684), *The Prologues and Epilogues of John Dryden*, ed. William B. Gardner (New York, 1951), pp. 60–61. See Ward, *Life of Dryden*, pp. 104–7; Winn, *Dryden*, pp. 262–64.

49. Preface to *Albion and Albanius: An Opera* in Dryden, *Essays*, ed. Watson, II, p. 41. For the circumstances, see Ward, *Life of Dryden*, app. E, pp. 330–32; Dryden, *Works*, XV, pp. 323–55; Phillip Harth, *Pen for a Party* (Princeton, 1993), pp. 254–68.

50. Evelyn, *Diary*, II, pp. 449–50. He was still recalling the event fondly half a century later, Evelyn to Henshaw, March 1, 1698, *Diary and Correspondence*, ed. Henry Wheatley, 4 vols ((London, 1896), IV, p. 22. Evelyn also saw operas in Rome and Milan, 1644–45, ibid., II, pp. 261, 388–89, 503. For other enthusiastic appreciations, see Michael Tilmouth, "Music on the Travels of an English Merchant: Robert Bargrave (1628–61)," *Music and Letters*, 53 (1972), pp. 143–59; and Eric Walter White, *A History of English Opera* (London, 1983), pp. 49–55.

51. Irving Lowens suggests that Saint-Evremond's essay may have been published in the *Mixt Essays* as a response to *Albion and Albanius*, "Saint-Evremond, Dryden, and the Theory of Opera," *Criticism*, 1 (1959), p. 242.

52. Preface to *Albion and Albanius*, Dryden, *Works*, XV, p. 3.

53. It was alleged by at least one critic (in Thomas Durfey's *Pills to Purge Melancholy*, 1721) that he was tone deaf, a charge that Arundell finds (too easily) plausible, *Critic at the Opera*, pp. 140–41.

54. Dryden, *Works*, XV, p. 4.

55. Ibid., pp. 4, 10. For Dryden's intentions and his indebtedness to Isaac Vossius, see D. T. Mace, "Musical Humanism, the Doctrine of Rhythmus, and the St Cecilia Odes of Dryden," *Journal of the Warburg and Courtauld Institutes*, 27 (1964), pp. 251–92.

56. Postscript, Mace, "Musical Humanism," p. 12. The reference is to Isaac Vossius, *De poematum cantu et viribus rhythmi* (Oxford, 1673). His work is summarized contemptuously ("an unintelligible rhapsody . . . futile and unsatisfactory") in Hawkins, *History*, pp. 659–61. For the friendship between Vossius and Saint-Evremond, see Saint-Evremond, *Works*, I, pp. cxi–cxiii.

57. Dent is very hard, perhaps too hard, on Dryden's opera: *Foundations*, pp. 163–65. Compare the apologetical comments in Dryden, *Works*, XV, p. 355.

58. *Gentleman's Journal*, Jan. 1692, pp. 7–8, quoted in Lucyle Hook, "Motteux and the Classical Masque," *British Theater and the Other Arts*, pp. 106–7; see too Franklin B. Zimmerman, *Henry Purcell 1656–95: His Life and Times*, 2nd edn (Philadelphia, 1983), p. 197.

59. See "The Introduction of Semi-Operas," *Roger North on Music*, ed. John Wilson (London, 1959), pp. 306–7.

60. For Dryden's part, see Roswell G. Ham, "Dryden's Dedication for *The Music of the Prophetesse*, 1691," *Publications of the Modern Language Association*, 50 (1935), pp. 1065–75. For analysis of text and music, see Price, *Henry Purcell*, pp. 270–88.

61. For a reading with recent bibliography, see James Anderson Winn, *"When Beauty Fires the Blood": Love and the Arts in the Age of Dryden* (Michigan, 1992), pp. 273–302.

62. "Epistle Dedicatory for the Vocal and Instrumental Musick of the Prophetess," Dryden, *Works*, XVII, pp. 324–26. The manuscript draft with variants is given by Ham, "Dryden's Dedication," pp. 1070–71, where it is used to confirm Dryden's authorship.

63. "There was nothing that ever had appeared in England like the representations he made of all kinds, whether for pomp or ceremony, in his grand chorus, etc., or that exquisite piece called the freezing piece of musick; in representing a mad couple, or country swains making love, or indeed any kind of musick whatever": Thomas Tudway, quoted from his manuscript collection 1714–20, in White, *History of English Opera*, p. 128.

64. Dryden's original was more sharply turned against his predecessors and may have been toned down by Purcell for publication; the next words, "and leave the hedge notes of our homely Ancestors," were excised from the printed version. See Ham, "Dryden's Dedication," p. 1071; Price, *Henry Purcell*, pp. 264–65. So was a long passage on the

parallel of painting with the other two arts, which anticipates what Dryden has to say later in his lines to Kneller and his translation of Fresnoy's *Parallel*.

65. Westrup describes the semi-opera as "an apposition, not a combination, of drama and music." Typically, the principal actors did not sing: *Purcell*, pp. 145–47. See too Burney, *General History*, II, p. 648. The author of *A Comparison between the Two Stages* (1702) [Charles Gildon?] complains with reference to the *Prophetesse* (as in operas generally) that its songs and dances were not always related to the story and therefore absurd and ridiculous (ed. Staring B. Wells, Princeton, 1942, p. 30). Downes, on the other hand, appreciated the "Costly Scenes, Machines and Cloaths" that "got the Author great Reputation" (*Roscius Anglicanus*, p. 42) and are fully described in the stage directions; and Moore (who tries manfully to restore the baroque sensibility of his subject) appreciates it for its music, despite its bad verse and lack of either realistic or classical virtues: *Henry Purcell and the Restoration Theater*, pp. 130–49.

66. The original was supposed to have been "a Tragedy mix'd with Opera," see Price, *Henry Purcell*, pp. 289–319, who suggests Shadwell's *Psyche* as the model, pp. 296–97. I use the text in Dryden, *Works*, ed. Walter Scott, revised George Saintsbury, 18 vols (Edinburgh, 1882–92), VIII, pp. 123–201. The score is printed in *The Works of Henry Purcell*, ed. Dennis Arundell (London, 1928), XXVI.

67. Prologue, in Dryden, *Works*, ed. Scott–Saintsbury, VIII, p. 12.

68. Dedication to the Marquis of Halifax, ibid., p. 135.

69. Music and drama are "principalls, and we know not which to apply our attention to most. In such case nothing is so sure, as that everyone will be better pleased with one or the other, the consequence is this, that the delight of one, kills the other and makes it hatefull. And that must be a fault." Betterton answered, "I was for dining on one dish rather than two . . .": "Some Memorandums concerning Musick," quoted in North's *Musical Grammarian*, ed. Mary Chan and Jamie C. Kassler (Cambridge, 1990), p. 216n.

70. Downes, *Roscius Anglicanus*, p. 42. Robert Moore has analysed its problems for our sensibilities, its "serene disregard of artistic rules in favor of muddling through," and its "taste for grandiose heroics combined with irrelevant grandiose spectacle, a taste eminently baroque," and properly warns against judging it anachronistically against the future course of opera: *Henry Purcell and the Restoration Theater*, pp. 96–97.

71. So Zimmermann, *Purcell*, pp. 252–53. The original *Indian Queen*, writes Charles Gildon, was "formerly Acted with great Applause . . . but now turn'd into an Opera, and many times represented at the same Theater with like success": in Gerard Langbaine, *The Lives and Characters of the English Dramatic Poets* (London, 1699), p. 75. For a modern appreciation, see Moore, *Purcell and the Restoration Theater*, pp. 155–77.

72. Rymer, *Short View of Tragedy* (1693), *Critical Essays of the Seventeenth Century*, ed. Joel E. Spingarn, 3 vols (Oxford, 1957), II, p. 214.

73. John Dennis, *Essays on the Opera's after the Italian Manner* (1706), *The Critical Works*, ed. Edward Niles Hooker, 2 vols (Baltimore, 1939), I, pp. 382, 391–92. The prevailing view seems to have been that only the choruses were sung in ancient tragedy; but Luckett quotes an anonymous English annotator of François Raguenet's work, to the contrary: "Exotick but Rational," pp. 138–40. Raguenet's *Parallèle des Italiens et des Français* (1702), was translated into English, perhaps by J. E. Galliard (1709), and is reprinted in the *Musical Quarterly*, 32 (1946), pp. 411–36. It was answered by Le Cerf de la Vieville in 1705, who also rebutted the Perraults and Fontenelle in what is clearly a further instalment of the *querelle*.

74. *The Spectator*, March 6 and 15, 1711; *Tatler*, 4, April 18, 1709. Hooker provides a useful summary of opinion in a note to Dennis, *Critical Works*, I, p. 523. See Siegmund A. E. Betz, "The Operatic Criticism of the *Tatler* and *Spectator*," *Musical Quarterly*, 31 (1945), pp. 318–30.

75. Gildon, *Life of Betterton*, p. 158. Though Gildon preferred Purcell to Handel, the English to the Italians, he seems to accept ancient Athens, as he imagines it, with its "happy mixture of Reason and Musick," as his ultimate model: p. 172.

76. "Ancient and Modern Tragedy," Voltaire, *Works*, reprinted from the Smollett edition, 22 vols (New York, 1901), XIX, pp. 122–23. See also Voltaire's preface to *Semiramis* (1748), where he expressly defends Lully's operas as successfully reiterating the idea of Greek drama, in *The Essence of Opera*, ed. Ulrich Weisstein (Glencoe, 1964), pp. 74–78.

77. Burney (the modern) was satisfied that the declamation of the Greeks and Romans was like modern recitative, *General History*, I, pp. 145, 534. Hawkins (the ancient) is still quoting Saint-Evremond respectfully and at length: *History*, I, p. xxxix.

Chapter 9 Saint-Evremond in England

1. Saint-Evremond to D'Hervart, Dec. 1 [1674], Saint-Evremond, *Lettres*, ed. René Ternois, 2 vols (Paris, 1967), I, pp. 214–17; *The Letters of Saint-Evremond*, trans. John Hayward (London, 1930), pp. 157–60.

2. *The Works of Monsieur de Saint-Evremond*, ed. Pierre des Maizeaux, 2nd edn, 3 vols (London, 1728), II, pp. 101–11; Saint-Evremond, *Oeuvres en Prose*, ed. René Ternois, 4 vols (Paris, 1962–69), IV, pp. 166–84. Ternois puts it in 1674 or a little later and sees it as a response to the strict *ancienneté* of Boileau in the *Art poétique* published just then, admiring the ancients, though not accepting the strait-jacket of the rules.

3. Saint-Evremond, *Works*, II, pp. 101–2.

4. Ibid., p. 102. For Gassendi as a source of Saint-Evremond's Epicureanism, see René Ternois, "Saint-Evremond et Gassendi," *Revue d'histoire littéraire de la France*, 69 (1969), pp. 576–82.

5. Saint-Evremond, *Works*, II, pp. 352–58; idem, *Oeuvres*, IV, pp. 185–95. Ternois (correcting Des Maizeaux) believes it was written about 1675. Both pieces were first published in 1692.

6. "Of Antient and Modern Tragedy," Saint-Evremond, *Works*, II, pp. 103–4. For Boileau, Saint-Evremond, and the contemporary reception of the play, see J. Calvet, *Polyeucte, de Corneille* (Paris, n. d.), pp. 291–302.

7. Saint-Evremond, *Works*, II, pp. 109–10.

8. William Wotton, *Reflections on Ancient and Modern Learning* (London, 1694), p. 110.

9. Saint-Evremond, *Works*, p. 111.

10. The preface is translated in *European Theories of the Drama*, ed. Barrett H. Clark (1918, revised edn, 1947), pp. 117–23. The reply by Chapelain, "Lettre sur la règle des vingt-quatre heures" (1630), is in his *Opuscules critiques*, edn. Alfred Hunter (Paris, 1936), pp. 113–26. The episode is described in Geoffrey Brereton, *French Drama in the Sixteenth and Seventeenth Centuries* (London, 1973), pp. 112–14.

11. Saint-Evremond to D'Hervart, Dec. 1, 1674, *Lettres* ed. Ternois, I, pp. 214–17; *Letters* trans. Hayward, pp. 157–60.

12. "Discours prononcé à l'Académie Française a la réception de MM. de [Pierre] Corneille et de Bergeret" (1685), Racine, *Oeuvres complètes*, ed. Raymond Picard, 2 vols (Pléiade edn, Paris, 1951–60), II, pp. 345–46.

13. "Sophocle, Euripide, Térence, Homère et Virgile nous sont encore en vénération, comme ils l'ont été dans Athènes et dans Rome": preface for an edition of two letters to the author of *Lettres sur l'hérésie imaginaire* (1666), ibid., II, p. 20; Sister Marie P. Haley, *Racine and the Art Poétique of Boileau* (Baltimore, 1976), p. 109.

14. Both were members of the Lamoignan circle; see Racine to Bouhours, in Racine, *Oeuvres complètes*, II, pp. 462, 466; and to Rapin, ibid., p. 477–78. The President de Lamoignan was, according to Boileau, "un homme d'un savoir étonnant, et passione admirateur de tous les bons livres de l'antiquité": see Haley, *Racine*, pp. 95–96.

15. So Corneille in *Segraisiana*, quoted by Paul Mesnard, *Oeuvres de J. Racine*, 6 vols (Paris, 1865), VI, pp. 452–53.

16. Lucien Goldmann emphasizes the disjunction between what Racine says in his prefaces and what he does in his plays. He quotes Racine himself that "Poets are like hypocrites in this, that they always defend what they do, but are never left in peace by their own conscience." Separating "conceptual thought and literary creation" has the advantage for us that we may see Racine (and for that matter Dryden) as both ancient and modern, or caught somewhere between the two. See Lucien Goldmann, *The Hidden God*, trans. Philip Thody (London, 1964), pp. 318–19. For Lancaster, typically, Racine was a dramatist who continued the work of his predecessors, including Corneille, "but to distinguish himself from them, he appealed to the Greeks . . . He became, not a neo-Greek dramatist, but the most Hellenic of the French dramatists": Henry C. Lancaster, *A History of French Dramatic Literature in the Seventeenth Century*, pt. 3, 2 vols (Baltimore, 1936), II, p. 584.

17. According to Gustave Lanson, "The seventeenth century would make the ancients in their own image, more yet than they would make themselves in the image of the ancients, and – in the absence of a historical sense coming to the aid of their rationalism – they would undermine antiquity." Quoted in Haley, *Racine*, pp. 196–97. For some instances of Greek teaching and learning, and its limits, see E. Egger, *L'Hellenisme en France*, 2 vols (Paris, 1869), II, pp. 44–148.

18. "A Defence of Some Dramatic Pieces of M. Corneille," "Saint-Evremond to M. de Barillon" (1677), Saint-Evremond, *Works*, II, pp. 227–29; idem, *Oeuvres*, IV, pp. 422–25.

19. Saint-Evremond to the Duchess Mazarin, *Works*, II, pp. 231–32.

20. "A Judgment upon some French Authors": Saint-Evremond to the Duchess Mazarin (1692), Saint-Evremond, *Works*, II, pp. 417–19; idem, *Oeuvres*, IV, pp. 342–45; *Letters*, trans. Hayward, pp. 298–300.

21. See Howard Jordan, who attributes the borrowing to Théophile de Viau (1623), "Théophile de Viau's Fragments d'une *Histoire Comique* and a Letter of Saint-Evremond's," *Modern Language Notes,* 53 (1938), pp. 586–87.

22. "Some Observations upon the Taste and Judgment of the French," Saint-Evremond, *Works,* II, pp. 307–8; idem *Oeuvres,* III, pp. 127–28. Des Maizeaux placed the work in 1684–85, but it may have been written much earlier; see Ternois's introduction, Saint-Evremond, *Oeuvres,* III, pp. 118–20.

23. Saint-Evremond, *Works,* III, pp. 45–46; *Letters,* trans. Hayward, pp. 319–20. About this time (1692), according to Des Maizeaux, he also wrote some verses defending modern philosophy, wit and gallantry against the ancients: *Works,* I, p. cxxxiv; and *Lettres,* ed. Ternois, II, p. 177.

24. "In his old days," his friend Silvestre remembered, "he affected to praise and commend every thing . . . This was rather an effect of Fear and Distrust, the ordinary Companions of old Age, than a change of his Temper and Inclination": Saint-Evremond, *Works,* III, p. xxxvii.

25. Des Maizeaux puts the request in 1692: ibid., I, p. cxxiv.

26. "A Judgment upon some French Authors": ibid., II, pp. 417–19; Saint-Evremond, *Oeuvres,* IV, pp. 343–45; *Letters,* trans. Hayward, pp. 298–300.

27. See "On the Morals of Epicurus," Saint-Evremond, *Works,* II, pp. 364–70; and "To the Maréschal de Créqui," ibid., p. 281. In late old age he vigorously defended Bayle's *Dictionary,* ibid., III, p. cxxxvii.

28. Ibid., II pp. 308–10; *Letters,* trans. Hayward, pp. 264–66.

29. Saint-Evremond, *Works,* I, p. xlv. See "A Judgment on the Sciences to which a Gentleman may apply himself," ibid., pp. 49–54; and "On the Morals of Epicurus," ibid., II, pp. 363–70.

30. "A Discourse upon the French Historians," ibid., pp. 126–43; Saint-Evremond, *Oeuvres,* III, pp. 61–95. Des Maizeaux placed it in 1674, but as with most of his work, Saint-Evremond kept rewriting and correcting his earlier pieces; it was first published in a collection by Barbin in 1684, but Des Maizeaux used a more complete copy corrected by Saint-Evremond himself, and Ternois as always goes back to the manuscripts.

31. "Observations on Sallust and Tacitus," in an address to Isaac Vossius, Saint-Evremond, *Works,* I, pp. 224–32; idem, *Oeuvres,* II, pp. 54–69.

32. "Observations on the different Genius of the Roman People, at the different times of the Republick," Saint-Evremond, *Works,* I, pp. 55–134; idem, *Oeuvres,* II, pp. 199–365. The piece was probably begun in England in 1663–64, but was only published complete in 1684.

33. Saint-Evremond, *Works,* I, p. 63.

34. Ibid., pp. 65–66.

35. "Of the Poems of the Antients," ibid., II, pp. 344–51; Saint-Evremond, *Oeuvres,* III, pp. 344–59. The piece may have been provoked by La Valterie's translation of Homer (1681), or (as Ternois suspects) by the first volume of Perrault's *Parallèles* and Fontenelle's *Digression sur les anciens et des modernes* (1688). It is quoted to good effect by one of the first Itaian moderns of the new century, Count Francesco Montani of Pesaro; see D. W. Thompson, "Montani, Saint-Evremond, and Longinus," *Modern Language Notes,* 51 (1936), pp. 10–17.

36. Saint-Evremond, *Works,* II, pp. 347–48.

37. Ibid., pp. 349–50.

38. Ibid.

39. Ibid., p. 351.

40. Ibid.

41. "For our Novelties have often a cast of extravagance; and the good Sense which is often found in our Writings, is generally borrow'd from Antiquity, rather than of our own growth." Nevertheless, though the ancients (who were themselves once novel) may still teach us how to think, Saint-Evremond counsels against too literal a borrowing. Saint-Evremond to the Duchess Mazarin [1677 or 1678], *Works,* II, pp. 254–58; *Lettres,* ed. Ternois, I, pp. 343–49.

42. "To the Maréschal de Créqui, Who ask'd the temper of my Mind, and my thoughts of all things, in my old Age," Saint-Evremond, *Works,* II, pp. 53–91 (esp. p. 58); *Letters,* trans. Hayward, pp. 111–46; Saint-Evremond, *Oeuvres,* IV, pp. 103–39. Ternois assigns its composition to 1669–71; its first publication to 1692.

43. For D'Ablancourt and the *belles infidèles,* see R. W. Ladborough, "Translation from the Ancients in Seventeenth-Century France," *Journal of the Warburg Institute,* 2 (1938), pp. 85–104; Roger Zuber, *Les Belles Infidèles et la formation du goût classique* (Paris, 1968). Ladborough suggests that D'Ablancourt was an advocate of the ancients, even while he modernized them, a position that was only reversed later in the century during the *querelle* when it was the moderns who became the advocates of free translation and the ancients who demanded accuracy. In 1676, John Evelyn wrote to his father

from Paris that D'Ablancourt's translations were cheap and very much esteemed and promised to send them all at the very first opportunity, Feb. 1, 1676, Evelyn Christ Church MS Corr.

44. "Reflections upon the French Translators," Saint-Evremond, *Works*, II, pp. 144–53 (esp. p. 144); idem, *Oeuvres*, III, pp. 96–117. Ternois supposes that the work was provoked both by Segrais's translation of the *Aeneid* (1668) and Rapin's *Comparaison des poèmes d'Homère et de Virgil* (1667) – to which it replies – and prefers to place it in 1669, as opposed to Des Maizeaux's 1674.

45. Saint-Evremond, *Works*, II, p. 146.

46. Ibid., p. 153.

47. "Some Observations upon the Taste and Judgment of the French," ibid., pp. 303–8 (esp. pp. 307–8); Saint-Evremond, *Oeuvres*, III, pp. 118–28. Des Maizeaux suggested 1684–85, but Ternois thinks it might have been much earlier, perhaps 1668.

48. Saint-Evremond to the Duchess Mazarin, *Works*, II, pp. 254–58; *Lettres*, ed. Ternois, II, pp. 35–40; *Letters*, trans. Hayward, pp. 163–67.

49. Silvestre notices the objections that had been made to Saint-Evremond's style, that it was not always clear and sometimes affected, with "a too exact and labour'd measure, and too frequent Antitheses." He does not deny some negligence; Saint-Evremond, "could not bear those who write in a manner always exact, but too uniform; and one of the advices he gave to write well, was to vary as much as possible the construction and turn of the Phrase." If Silvestre had known the term, he might have called the style "baroque": Saint-Evremond, *Works*, III, pp. xvii–xviii.

50. The play was actually performed in London (Dec. 1, 1662) and printed almost simultaneously with the French. Pepys saw it twenty-six years later, but found its blank verse very dull. It was translated again by William Popple in 1691. See Dorothea F. Canfield, *Corneille and Racine in England* (New York, 1904), pp. 3–14, 104–7.

51. Gerard Langbaine, *An Account of the English Dramatic Poets* (1691), quoted approvingly by George Ballard, *Memoirs of British Ladies* (London, 1755), pp. 287–96. Evelyn coupled her with Lady Newcastle and Aphra Behn (*his* Sappho) in the *Numismata*; Dryden used her as a model for Anne Killigrew in his ode. See Philip W. Souers, *The Matchless Orinda* (Cambridge, 1931); and Orinda's *Collected Works* (Stump Cross, 1990), I, edited with a useful introduction by Patricia Thomas. For Mrs Phillips, see Souers, *The*

Matchless Orinda, pp. 169–71, 185–204, 228–31.

52. Published with an apologetical preface in 1670, but not apparently performed. There is some interesting correspondence about the rival versions in *Letters from Orinda to Polearchus* (London, 1705). Corneille's *Heraclius* was also translated by Ludowick Carlell in 1664 and *Nicomède* by John Dancer in 1670. Sir William Lower translated *Polyeucte* (1655) and *Horatius* (1656), and there were one or two others.

53. Abel Boyer, *Achilles, or Iphigenia in Aulis* (London, 1700), advertisement; see Katherine E. Wheatley, *Racine and English Classicism* (Austin, 1956), pp. 82–92. Boyer's adaptation makes room for much music and spectacle, including a song by Purcell, but otherwise follows the original closely. Unfortunately it appeared in the same week as another version by John Dennis, and the two *Iphigenias*, "clashd together, like two rotten ships, which cou'd not endure the shock, and sunk to rights": Dryden to Mrs Steward, Dec. 14, 1699, *The Letters of John Dryden*, ed. Charles E. Ward (Chapel Hill, 1961), pp. 130–31.

54. "Had it been acted in the good well meaning times, when the Cid Heraclius and other French Playes met such applause, this could have passed very well; but since our Audiences have tasted so plentifully the fine English Wit, then their Regalio's will not down": Epistle to the Reader, *Andromache: A Tragedy* (London, 1675). Crowne seems to have revised someone else's translation.

55. *The Dramatic Works of John Crowne*, ed. James Maidment and W. H. Logan, 4 vols (London, 1873), II, p. 238; Wheatley, *Racine*, pp. 3–25.

56. See Pocock, p. 190; and Canfield, *Corneille and Racine*, pp. 140–66. Wheatley, *Racine*, deplores the changes, pp. 118–38. The *Spectator* greeted it warmly, Feb. 1, and March 25, 1712; and an anonymous author attacked it bitterly, *A Modest Survey of that Celebrated Tragedy, the Distrest Mother* (1712). But it held the stage for a century.

57. Preface to *All for Love* (1678), Dryden *Essays*, ed. Watson, I, pp. 224–25. Racine's *Phèdre* appeared the year before as *Phèdre et Hippolyte* and Euripides's work was Rymer's principal example in *The Tragedies of the Last Age* (1678).

58. Saint-Evremond, *Mixt Essays* (London, 1685), preface, n. p.

59. Saint-Evremond, *Miscellanea, or Various Discourses upon Tragedy, Comedy, the Italian, the English Comedy and Operas*, trans. Ferrand Spence (London, 1686), sig. A3.

60. Ibid., sig. A4–[A5].

61. Ibid., sig. d *et seq*. See Lowens, p. 243.

62. See Spence's defense of his deliberate modernization of Lucian in Lucian's *Works*, 5 vols (London, 1684), I, sig. A4. It was Giles Ménage, apparently, who coined the sobriquet, *belles infidèles* (*Menagiana*, Paris 1693, 385); see R. C. Knight, *Racine et la Gréce*, p. 47.

63. Temple makes a reference at one point to Almanzor in his essay, "Of Heroic Virtue," that sounds as if he may be thinking of Dryden's defense of that hero in his "Of Heroic Plays," prefixed to *The Conquest of Granada* (1672) (in *Essays*, ed. Watson, I, pp. 163–66). See William Temple, *Five Miscellaneous Essays*, ed. Samuel Holt Monk (Ann Arbor, 1963), p. 156.

64. Joseph M. Levine, *The Battle of the Books: History and Literature in the Augustan Age* (Ithaca, N.Y. 1991), pp. 29–30.

65. See the fourth of the *Essays upon Several Subjects* (London, 1691), pp. 63–76. Blount was a country gentleman who gained a considerable reputation for a critical anthology he published in 1690, *Censura Celebriorum Authorum*, and another in 1694, *De Re Poetica, or Remarks upon Poetry*, which showed very wide learning. The *Essays* received a third edition with additions in 1697. See Blount's biography in Andrew Kippis, *Biographia Britannica*, 5 vols (London, 1790), II, pp. 378–80.

66. Blount, *Essays*, p. 77.

67. Ibid., pp. 79, 82–83.

68. Ibid., pp. 78–79. See also the fifth essay, "Whether the Men of this present Age are any way inferior to those of former Ages, either in respect of Vertue, Learning or long life," in which he concludes, "there is no one thing hath stunted the growth of Learning, than a stiff adhering to the dictates of the Ancients": p. 87. Temple is cited approvingly for his theory of climate at p. 167.

69. Blount, *Essays upon Several Subjects*, 3rd edn (London, 1697), pp. 131–32.

70. *Miscellaneous Essays by Monsieur St-Evremond* (London, 1692). It translates most of the essays in the edition of Barbin (1689) and in the same order. Saint-Evremond, *Oeuvres*, III, p. 218.

71. John M. Aden also notices (and perhaps exaggerates) the differences between the two, "Dryden and Saint Evremond," *Comparative Literature*, 6 (1959), p. 233.

72. "A Judgment upon Seneca, Plutarch and Petronius" (1664, corrected 1689), Saint-Evremond, *Works*, I, pp. 153–71; idem, *Oeuvres*, I, pp. 145–86.

73. Saint-Evremond, *Works*, I, p. 153.

74. See Paul Benichou, *Man and Ethics: Studies*

in French Classicism, trans. Elizabeth Hughes (New York, 1971), pp. 63–74.

75. Saint-Evremond, *Works*, I, pp. 203–7; idem, *Oeuvres*, II, pp. 24–33; *Letters*, trans. Hayward, pp. 41–49.

76. Saint-Evremond, *Works*, II, pp. 51–52; *Lettres*, ed. Ternois, I, pp. 156–58; *Letters*, trans. Hayward, pp. 104–5.

77. "Upon Friendship" (1678), Saint-Evremond, *Works*, II, p. 202–11; *Letters*, trans. Hayward, pp. 195–205. Saint-Evremond goes on to remember the disgrace of his old friend, Fouquet.

78. See Paul Hammond, "Dryden's Employment by Cromwell's Government," *Transactions of the Cambridge Bibliographical Society*, 8, pt 1 (1981), pp. 130–36.

79. Dryden objects to Saint-Evremond's criticism in his "Life of Plutarch," prefixed to *Plutarch's Lives*, I (1683), in *The Works of John Dryden*, 20 vols (Berkeley, 1961–89), XVII, pp. 281–87.

80. Ibid., p. 282.

81. For Dryden's conversational prose style, modeled on Cicero's letters to Atticus, see Irene Simon, "Dryden's Prose Style," in *Seventeenth-Century Prose*, ed. Stanley E. Fish (New York, 1971), p. 556.

82. "A Dissertation upon the Word Vast [1678–81]," Saint-Evremond, *Works*, II, p. 183; Ternois, *Oeuvres*, III, pp. 375–76. Cf. "To the Marischal de Créqui," *Works*, II, p. 58–59, and for the mixed benefaction of the Emperor Augustus, "Reflections on the different Genius of the Roman People at the different times of the Republick," ibid., ch. 16, pp. 113–27. The "Character" by Dr N. in the *Works*, 2 vols (London, 1702), praises Saint-Evremond extravagantly as an Augustan. "When he speaks of the Ancient Romans, you would believe you are reading one of the same Age and Nation" (A3v).

83. *Miscellaneous Essays . . . with a Character by a Person of Honour here in England. Continued by Mr Dryden* (London, 1692). There is a modernized text in Dryden, *Works*, ed. Walter Scott, revised George Saintsbury, 18 vols (Edinburgh, 1882–92), XVIII, pp. 13–17.

84. The California editors distinguish the enthusiastic Chetwood from the more ambiguous Dryden: *Works*, XX, pp. 309–10.

85. Saint-Evremond, *Works*, II, pp. 144–53; idem, *Oeuvres*, III, pp. 96–117. Saint-Evremond had known Segrais, whose *Eneide* appeared in 1668.

86. "A Character of Saint-Evremond," in Dryden, *Works*, XX, p. 7; *Miscellaneous*

Essays, sig. A2–A3. There is a line that interrupts the text at sig. A4 that seems to mark the place where Chetwood stopped and Dryden began his continuation.

87. Ibid., sig. A4–[A6]; Dryden, *Works*, XX, pp. 7, 9.

88. Dryden, *Works*, XX, p. 10; René Bossu, *Traité du poème épique* (Paris, 1675), pp. 66–71.

89. Dryden, *Works*, XX, p. 11.

Chapter 10 Restoration Architecture and the Young Christopher Wren

1. The claim goes back to Vitruvius, but Inigo Jones had to reassert it (on the authority of the Renaissance Italians) against a skeptical Ben Jonson, and the idea only slowly caught hold in England. See D. J. Gordon, "Poet and Architect: The Intellectual Setting of the Quarrel between Ben Jonson and Inigo Jones," *Journal of the Warburg and Courtauld Institutes*, 11 (1948), pp. 152–78.

2. "To my Dear Friend, Mr Congreve on his Comedy, call'd The Double Dealer," John Dryden, *The Poems*, ed. James Kinsley, 4 vols (Oxford, 1958), II, pp. 852–54.

3. William Temple, "An Essay upon the Ancient and Modern Learning," *Five Miscellaneous Essays*, ed. Samuel Holt Monk (Ann Arbor, 1963), p. 58.

4. Though for style, Addison preferred the Pantheon; see *Spectator*, 415, June 26, 1712.

5. J. B. Fischer von Erlach, *Entwurf einer historischen Architectur* (Leipzig, 1725), trans. Thomas Lediard as *A Plan of Civil and Historical Architecture* (n. p., 1730), Book 1. The topos goes back at least to Philo of Byzantium and forward at least to Karl Friedrich Schinkel (1812).

6. Ch. 6: "Of Ancient and Modern Architecture, Statuary, and Painting," Willian Wotton, *Reflections upon Ancient and Modern Learning* (London, 1694), pp. 61–77.

7. Charles Perrault, *Parallèle des anciens et des modernes*, 2 vols (Paris, 1690), I, p. 138.

8. Wotton, *Reflections*, pp. 67–68.

9. Wotton made no changes in the chapter for the 1697 and 1705 editions. In October 1703, Wotton wrote to Evelyn rejoicing at the prospects of a new edition of Evelyn's work: Evelyn, *Diary and Correspondence*, ed. Henry B. Wheatley, 4 vols (London, 1906), III, pp. 398–99.

10. See the dedication (Aug. 20, 1664) to Charles II in Evelyn's translation of Fréart's *Architecture* (see Note 16 below).

11. *The Diary of John Evelyn*, ed. E. S. de Beer, 6 vols (Oxford, 1955), Nov. 4, 1644, II, pp. 214, 223, 247. The sketches in the *Catalogue of the*

Drawings of the Royal Institute of British Architects, 3 (1972), figs 84–85, include a façade of S. Andrea in the Via Flaminia, Rome, with measurements.

12. Evelyn, *Diary*, II, pp. 255–61, 313, 371–72.

13. Ibid., I, p. 63.

14. "The Character of England" (1659), in Evelyn, *Miscellaneous Writings*, (London, 1825), p. 151. See the *Survey of London*, XXXVI *Parish of St. Paul Covent Garden* (London, 1970), ch. 3, pp. 63–76.

15. R. T. Gunther, *The Architecture of Sir Roger Pratt* (Oxford, 1928), p. 23. Pratt had lived with Evelyn in Rome in 1644. He later practiced architecture in England; Evelyn praised the great house in Piccadilly that he designed for the Earl of Clarendon, as "the best contriv'd, the most usefull, gracefull, and magnificent house in England": Evelyn to Viscount Cornbery, Jan. 20, 1666, *Diary and Correspondence*, ed. Wheatley, III, pp. 340–41.

16. Fréart's *Parallèle de l'architecture antique avec la moderne* was published in 1650; Evelyn began his translation about 1652 and resumed it ten years later at the insistence of his friend, the architect Hugh May, who helped him with the plates. See Geoffrey Keynes, *Evelyn: A Study in Bibliophily and a Bibliography* (Oxford, 1968), pp. 166–72. I use the facsimile published by Gregg (Farnborough, 1965), *A Parallel of the Antient Architecture with the Modern* (London, 1664). It seems that Evelyn helped May design the chapel at Cornbury House, Oxford: Howard M. Colvin, *A Biographical Dictionary of English Architects, 1600–1840*, 2nd edn (London, 1978), p. 303.

17. Evelyn's preface to Fréart's *Parallel* p. 2.

18. Ibid., preface, p. 8.

19. John Evelyn, "Account," pp. 118–19.

20. See Evelyn to Joseph Glanvill, June 24, 1668, praising the *plus ultra* of the Royal Society, *Corr.*, ed. Wheatley, III, p. 204. Glanvill, defending the Royal Society that year, popularized the expression for that purpose; see his *Plus Ultra, or, the Progress and Advancement of Knowledge since the Days of Aristotle* (London, 1668), described by Jackson I. Cope in *Joseph Glanvill* (St Louis, 1956), pp. 42–72. Glanvill commends Evelyn's *Sylva* there (pp. 73–74), for which he received Evelyn's gratitude, *Corr.* pp. 356–57. The expression was associated with an inscription on Hercules's columns and is post-classical; see Earl Rosenthal, "*Plus Ultra, Non Plus Ultra*, and the Columnar Device of Charles V," *Journal of the Warburg and Courtauld Institutes*, 34 (1971), pp. 204–28.

21. See André Hallays, *Les Perraults* (Paris, 1926); Joseph M. Levine, *The Battle of the Books:*

History and Literature in Augustan England (Ithaca, N.Y., 1991).

22. The office is described by Louis Hautecourt, *Histoire de l'architecture classique en France: le règne de Louis XIV*, 2 vols (Paris, 1948), II, p. 442.

23. See Ragnar Josephson, "Quelques Dessins de Claude Perrault pour le Louvre," *Gazette des beaux-arts*, 69 (1927), pp. 171–92; Christopher Tadgell, "Charles Perrault, François Le Vau and the Louvre Colonnade," *Burlington Magazine*, 122 (May, 1980), pp. 326–36.

24. The English translation of Perrault's *Abrégé des dix livres d'architecture* (Paris, 1674) begins with an encomium for Vitruvius's two great patrons, Julius Caesar and Augustus in "an Age when all things were come to the highest degree of Perfection": *An Abridgment of the Architecture of Vitruvius by Mons. Perrault* (London, 1692), p. 2; *Abrégé*, pp. 2–3.

25. An abridged version of the preface appears with a useful introduction in *La Théorie architecturale à l'âge classique*, ed. Françoise Fichet (Brussels, 1979), pp. 205–50.

26. For what follows, see especially, Wolfgang Herrmann, *The Theory of Claude Perrault* (London, 1973).

27. "To make a just Comparison, then, between Musick and Architecture, we must consider Consonances barely in themselves, which are all naturally such as cannot be chang'd, but the Manner of making use of them, which is different by different Musicians, and in divers Nations, like as the Proportions of Architecture are in different Authors and Buildings": preface, Perrault, *A Treatise of the Five Orders of Columns in Architecture*, trans. Thomas James (London, 1708), p. iv.

28. Ibid., pp. xiv–xv.

29. Ibid., p. xvi.

30. Ibid., pp. xviii, xx.

31. See Levine, *Battle of the Books*, pp. 254–55.

32. "I do not hold the conviction," Blondel wrote in the *Cours d'architecture* (Paris, 1675), "of those who do not allow anything in architecture that does not have an example in the works of the ancients. On the contrary, I know that there are many things in the buildings of the ancients whose usage I would not advise." See the extract in Fichet, *Théorie*, p. 140. As a result, Blondel was quite willing to applaud the invention of the modern composite order: *Cours*, I, p. 250. Blondel's work was printed in 1675, 1683, 1685, and in a second edition in 1688. Nevertheless, Louis Hautecouer aptly describes the *Cours* as the *art poétique* of architecture, and compares Perrault to Saint-Evremond. *Histoire de l'architecture clas-*

sique, II, pp. 485, 490. See also Alberto Perez-Gomez, *Architecture and the Crisis of Modern Science* (Cambridge, 1983), pp. 17–47.

33. Dorothea Nyberg, "La Sainte Antiquité," *Essays in the History of Architecture presented to Rudolf Wittkower*, ed. Douglas Fraser et al. (London, 1967), p. 169, fig. 4.

34. See Wolfgang Herrmann, "Unknown Designs for the 'Temple of Jerusalem' by Charles Perrault," ibid., pp. 143–58.

35. *In Ezechielem explanationes et apparatus urbis ac Templi Hierosolymitani, commentarius et imaginibus illustatus* (Rome, 1596–1605), II, ii. Villalpando insisted that the Temple of Ezechiel was identical with the Temple of Solomon.

36. Fréart, *Architecture*, pp. 72–73. An early model by Jacob Judah Leon (1641) seems to have been brought to England and come to the attention of Christopher Wren; see Huyghens to Wren, Helen Rosenau, *Vision of the Temple: The Image of the Temple in Judaism and Christianity* (London, 1979), p. 141n. Another by J. J. Erasmus (1694) was later exhibited in London; see J. Rykwert, *On Adam's House in Paradise* (New York, 1972), p. 132. Another early attempt to visualize the Temple appears in Samuel Lee, *Orbis Miraculum, or the Temple of Solomon* (London, 1659).

37. See the correspondence between Locke and Nicolas Toinard in 1680: *The Correspondence of John Locke*, ed. E. S. de Beer, 8 vols (Oxford, 1976–89), II, pp. 273, 276–79, 282–85, etc.

38. *Ordonnance des cinq espèces de colonnes* (Paris, 1683), p. xviii. Perrault had already complained about this in his *Vitruvius* (1673); see Herrmann, *Theory*, p. 143.

39. *Memoirs of Sir Isaac Newton's Life by William Stukeley* (1752), ed. A. Hastings White (London, 1936), pp. 17–18. See also Stukeley to Roger Gale, March 17, 1729, *Family Memoirs* (Surtees Soc. 76, 1883), pp. 261–63; Isaac Newton, *The Chronology of Ancient Kingdoms Amended* (London, 1728), p. 333.

40. Perrault explains in his Vitruvius that he has invented a sixth order by joining the columns in pairs, *Les Dix Livres d'architecture de Vitruve* (Paris, 1673), p. 76n.

41. See Jean Marie Pérouse de Montclos, "Le Sixième Ordre d'architecture, ou la pratique des ordres suivant les nations," *Journal of the Society of Architects*, 38 (1977), p. 238.

42. Blondel denounced the double columns in the *Cours*. See Reginald Blomfield, *A History of French Architecture 1661–1774* (London, 1921), p. 80; Paul Léon, *La Vie des monuments français* (Paris, 1951), pp. 43–45.

43. Evelyn to the bookseller, Place, Aug. 17, 1696, *Corr.*, ed. Wheatley, III, pp. 360–63. The *Parallel* had been reissued in 1669; retitled in 1680 as *The Whole Body of Antient and Modern Architecture*; rededicated to Wren in 1697; and was finally republished in 1707.

44. Evelyn to Bentley, Dec. 22, 1697, *Corr.*, ed. Wheatley, III, pp. 365–66. (Christ Church MS, Letterbook (1699), p. 231).

45. I use the text in Evelyn's *Miscellaneous Writings*, pp. 365–70.

46. Ibid., pp. 365–67.

47. Cf. Evelyn to Pepys, Aug. 12, 1689, *Diary and Correspondence of John Evelyn*, ed. William Bray, 4 vols (London, 1863), II, pp. 294–311.

48. Though Evelyn could find occasional praise for a Gothic building, as at York or Salisbury (*Diary*, III, pp. 113, 129, 134), it was not sufficient to override his basically neoclassical sensibility; see Kerry Downes, "John Evelyn and Architecture: A First Inquiry," *Concerning Architecture, Essays to Nicholaus Pevsner*, ed. John Summerson (London, 1968), p. 35.

49. Evelyn in *Miscellaneous Writings*, pp. 410–11.

50. Ibid., pp. 413–14.

51. Jean de la Bruyère, *The Characters or the Manners of the Age* (London, 1699), p. 22.

52. *Parentalia, or, Memoirs of the Family of the Wrens* (London, 1750), p. 354.

53. Jones's copy of Palladio's *Quattro libri* (1601) remains at Worcester College, Oxford; see John Orrell, *The Theatres of Inigo Jones and John Webb* (Cambridge, 1985), p. 8; John Harris and A. A. Tait, *Catalogue of the Drawings by Inigo Jones, John Webb and Isaac de Caus at Worcester College* (Oxford, 1979).

54. Fréart, *Parallel*, 2nd edn (London, 1707), p. 8.

55. *Les Édifices antiques de Rome: dessines et mesures très exactement* (Paris, 1682) with 22 plates. For what follows, see Wolfgang Herrmann, "Antoine Desgodets and the Académie Royale d'Architecture," *Art Bulletin*, 40 (1958), pp. 23–53. There is a facsimile of Desgodets's work in the *Printed Sources of Western Art*, ed. Theodore Bestermann, I (Portland, Oregon, 1972). The English translation is by G. Marshall, *Edifices, The Ancient Buildings of Rome* (London, 1771).

56. The *Procès-verbaux de l'académie royale d'architecture* has been edited by H. Lemonnier, 10 vols (Paris, 1911–30). For the cool reception by the Academy, see Herrmann, "Desgodets," pp. 25–29.

57. François Blondel, *Cours d'architecture*, (Paris, 1683), p. 748, quoted by Herrmann, *Cours*, p. 28.

58. Fréart, *Parallel*, 2nd edn, p. 10.

59. Perrault took most of his measurements of Roman buildings, admitting his debt to Desgodets in the *Ordonnance*, p. xxvii; see Herrmann, *Desgodets*, p. 31n.

60. Evelyn, *Diary*, III, p. 106.

61. July 13, 1654, ibid., pp. 110–11.

62. *Parentalia*; *Wren Society*, ed. A. T. Bolton and H. D. Hendry, 20 vols (London, 1923–43). The title page of the *Parentalia* attributes the work to Christopher Wren, Jr, the publication to the grandson, Stephen. I use the interleaved copy which has been reproduced by Gregg, for which see Lawrence Weaver, "The Interleaved Copy of Wren's *Parentalia* with Manuscript Insertions," *Journal of the Royal Institute of British Architects [RIBA]*, 3rd ser., 18 (1911), pp. 569–85.

63. It is John Summerson who notices the parallel in a brilliant essay on "The Mind of Wren," in *Heavenly Mansions and Other Essays on Architecture* (New York, 1963), p. 67.

64. See James Winn, *John Dryden and his World* (New Haven, 1987), pp. 261–65. The playhouse opened with a revival of Fletcher's *The Beggar's Bush*, with a prologue by Dryden that tells the story of the "plain built house": *The Prologues and Epilogues of John Dryden*, ed. William B. Gardner (New York, 1951), pp. 60–61. Dryden got a share in the company and continued for a while to write for it. The theater seems to have been designed to allow the audience a perspective view of the setting, an innovation in design that helped to make the transition from the Elizabethan open stage to the modern picture-frame stage. Richard Leacock attempts a reconstruction from a Wren drawing in "Wren's Drury Lane," *Architectural Review*, 110 (1951), pp. 43–46, figs 1–3. But see also Edward A. Langham, "Wren's Restoration Playhouse," *Theatre Notebook*, 18 (1964), pp. 91–100; David Mullin and Bruce King, "Christopher Wren's Theatre Royal," ibid., 21 (1967), pp. 180–87. For a suggestive account of the long story of the transition from the Italian Renaissance stage to Restoration England by way of Serlio and Palladio, see Licisco Magnagnato, "The Genesis of the Teatro Olimpico," *Journal of the Warburg and Courtauld Institutes*, 14 (1951), pp. 209–20.

65. *Survey of London: The Theatre Royal Drury Lane*, XXXV (London, 1970), p. 40. According to the authors of the *Survey*, the frontispiece to Perrin's *Ariadne* (1674) probably shows the original proscenium in the theater: p. 44.

66. The account by John Ward still remains useful, *The Lives of the Professors of Gresham*

College (London, 1740), pp. 95–110. Christopher Wren Jr assisted him with it; see their correspondence in the British Library, BL Add. MS 6209. See also H. W. Jones, "Sir Christopher Wren and Natural Philosophy: with a Checklist of his Scientific Activities," Notes and Records of the Royal Society, 13 (1958), pp. 19–37; Michael Hunter, "The Making of Christopher Wren," Science and the Shape of Orthodoxy (Woodbridge, 1995), pp. 45–65.

67. See too Newton to Halley, May 27, 1686, and Halley to Newton, June 29, 1686; The Correspondence of Isaac Newton, ed. H. W. Turnbull et al., 7 vols (Cambridge, 1959–77), II, pp. 433–35, 441–43.

68. Thomas Sprat, History of the Royal Society (1667), ed. Jackson I. Cope and Harold W. Jones (St Louis, 1959), pp. 311–18.

69. "Catalogue of New Theories, Inventions, Experiments, and Mechanick Improvements," Parentalia, pp. 198–99.

70. J. A. Bennett insists on the close connection between Wren's mathematical and scientific and architectural activities throughout his life, The Mathematical Science of Christopher Wren (Cambridge, n.d.).

71. "He attained very early by his own Genius and modesty alone, a Masterly Pensil in the Art of Designing and Drawing, was expert also in the Arts of Graving, Etching, and Turning: all his Schemes, Instruments, and Machines, in every Part of the Mathematicks, and in Anatomy, were executed by his own hand": "Of the Life of My Father," BL Add. MS 25,071, f. 38.

72. His description of an instrument for drawing the outlines of any object in perspective appeared in the Royal Society's Philosophical Transactions, 45 (March 1669), p. 898. "He [also] exhibited a great Variety of sciographical, scenographical, dioptical and catoptical Experiments": Parentalia, pp. 213, 221–24, 243.

73. Inaugural lecture in Parentalia, pp. 200–6. Wren's father had anticipated many of his interests in natural philosophy but resolutely opposed Copernicus; see Rosalie Colie, "Dean Wren's Marginalia and Early Science at Oxford," Bodleian Library Record, 6 (1960), pp. 541–51.

74. Wren to the Royal Society, Parentalia, pp. 221–24.

75. Since the time of Archimedes, Hooke wrote, there was never so perfect a mechanical hand joined to so philosophical a mind: Robert Hooke, Micrographia (London, 1665), sig. g2. See J. A. Bennett, "Hooke and Wren and the System of the World: Some Points towards an Historical Account,"

British Journal for the History of Science, 8 (1975), pp. 32–61.

76. Robert Hooke, The Diary 1672–80, ed. Henry W. Robinson and William Adams (London, 1935), pp. 307, 334, 344, 349–50, and many other entries.

77. Ibid., pp. 317, 320–21. For Hooke's interest in architecture, see M. I. Batten, "The Architecture of Robert Hooke" (Walpole Soc. 25, 1937), pp. 83–113. In 1689 he may be found "querying" Perrault: R. T. Gunther, Life and Work of Robert Boyle (Early Science at Oxford, 10, 1935), p. 134.

78. See R. A. Beddard, "Wren's Mausoleum for Charles I and the Cult of the Royal Martyr," Architectural History, 27 (1984), pp. 36–48. On January 29, 1678, the House of Commons voted £70,000 for the monument, which Wren designed after the example of Bramanti's Tempietto; see Parentalia, pp. 331–32; Howard Colvin, The History of the King's Works, 6 vols (London, 1963–76), V, p. 324. Wren also attempted reconstructions of the Temple of Diana at Ephesus and the Mausoleum at Halicarnassus: Parentalia, pp. 360, 367; Wren Society, XIX pp. 134, 138.

79. For the introduction of such terms as symmetry, pilaster, perspective, portico, etc., see B. Sprague Allen, Tides in English Taste, 2nd edn, 2 vols (Cambridge, Mass., 1937), I, pp. 2–5.

80. In 1665, Evelyn asked Wren for help in finding a tutor for his son. "The qualities I require are that he be a perfect Grecian, and . . . more than vulgarly mathematical": April 4, 1665, Corr., ed. Wheatley, III, p. 305.

81. Sprat to Wren on his translation of Horace's "Epistle to Lollius," Parentalia, pp. 255–56. Wren (1663) replied with a rhetorical exercise on "wit": ibid., pp. 256–60. He was rewarded when Sprat addressed the Observations on Monsieur de Sorbier's Voyage into England to him (1665).

82. Sprat, Observations, p. 283. For Sprat's rhetorical talents, see Evelyn, Nov. 23, 1679, Diary, IV, p. 188.

83. Hunter points out that Wren is not easily placed as a Whig or a Tory, but that he seems to have endorsed Sprat's desire to see a Restoration regime, "justly compos'd of a sufficient liberty, and restraint." See Sprat's Observations, pp. 283–89, in Hunter's Science and the Shape of Orthodoxy, pp. 51–52.

84. See Wren's essay, "Architecture has its Political Use," Parentalia, p. 351; and "Wren's Mausoleum for Charles I and the Cult of the Royal Martyr," Architectural History, 27 (1984), pp. 36–47.

85. See Evelyn, A Character of England (1659),

and *Fumefugium: or The Inconveniencie of the Aer and Smoak of London Dissipated* (London, 1661), "To the Reader," p. 21. Both are reprinted in the *Miscellaneous Writings*, pp. 141–67; 205–42. Evelyn was answered by the anonymous author of *Gallus Cistratus*; see Allen, *Tides*, I, p. 36.

86. There are several letters of advice from Evelyn to young people going to Italy; see Evelyn to Fr. Carter, Nov. 27, 1665, Christ Church Letterbook no. cclxiv; to his nephew, George, Aug. 24, 1661, no. clxxxii,; March 30, 1664, no. ccxii. He particularly hoped his nephew would see the latest buildings in Rome, especially those by Bernini. See Evelyn to Dr Pope, March 30, 1664, ibid., no. ccxiii.

87. Nicholas Hawksmoor, *Remarks on the Royal Hospital at Greenwich* (1728), in *Wren Society*, VI, p. 18.

88. James Ralph, *Critical Review* (1734), quoted in *Parentalia*, pp. 269–70. Evelyn thought his plan not unlike Wren's; see his *Londinium redivum*, edited with an introduction by E. S. de Beer, as *London Revived* (Oxford, 1938). The King and Council were momentarily interested, but nothing came of it. See Oldenburg to Boyle, Sept. 16, 1666, and Evelyn to Oldenburg, Dec. 22, 1666, in, *The Correspondence of Henry Oldenburg*, ed. A. Rupert Hall and Marie Boas Hall, 11 vols (Madison, 1965–77), III, pp. 229–31; 299–300; and pp. 237–39, 244–46. For a comparison of both plans with Palladio, and Wren's Royal Exchange with the Roman Forum, see Allen, *Tides*, I, pp. 165–68.

89. Wren had been offered the reversion of Sir John Denham's post as Surveyor-General of the Royal Works in 1661 but declined; in March 1669 he accepted.

90. See Evelyn *Diary*, III, p. 387.

91. *Parentalia*, pp. 335–39. Eduard Sekler prefers to credit Barbaro's edition of Vitruvius and the Du Perac representation of the Theater of Marcellus to Serlio: *Wren and his Place in European Architecture* (New York, 1956), pp. 39–40.

92. Wren showed a model to the Royal Society in April 1663; Thomas Birch, *The History of the Royal Society*, 4 vols (London, 1756), I, p. 230.

93. Robert Plot, *The Natural History of Oxfordshire*, 2nd edn (Oxford, 1705), p. 278 (with plate).

94. Sir John Summerson, *Christopher Wren* (London, 1953), p. 48. See also Summerson, "The Mind of Wren," in *Heavenly Mansions*, which continues and develops the Latin analogy, pp. 51–86.

95. Edward Croft-Murray, *Decorative Painting in*

England, 2 vols (London, 1962), I, pp. 44–45. According to his biographer, Richard Graham in his supplement to Roger de Piles's *Abrégé*, translated as *The Art of Painting* (London, 1706), pp. 464–66, Streater had a good collection of Italian books, drawings and prints. "To do him but Justice, he was the greatest, and most Universal Painter that ever England had, which we owe, in some meanes, to his Reading, he being reported a very good Historian": Tancred Borenius, "Robert Streater," *Burlington Magazine*, 84 (1944), pp. 3–12.

96. William Sanderson, *Graphice. The Use of Pen and Pensel, or the Most Excellent Art of Painting* (1658), pp. 19–20.

97. William Soper of Wadham College as amended by Robert Plot in his *Natural History of Oxfordshire* (Oxford, 1677), p. 276.

98. That future ages must confess they owe To Streeter more than Michael Angelo.

Robert Whitehead, *Urania or a Description of the Painting of the Top of the Theater at Oxford* (London, 1669); *The Diary of Samuel Pepys*, ed. Robert Latham and William Matthews, 11 vols (Berkeley, 1970–83), Feb. 1, 1669, IX, p. 44.

99. Richard Graham, in his addition to Roger de Piles, *Abrégé*, pp. 464–66; quoted in "Robert Streater," p. 3. Graham especially applauds Streater's history, architecture and perspective, the truth of his outlines and his skill at foreshortening, as well as his abilities in landscape and still life.

100. Margaret Whinney and Oliver Millar, *English Art 1625–1714* (Oxford, 1957), p. 292. Among other things, they are not satisfied with the foreshortening of the tumbling figures. Nikolaus Pevsner quotes James II and finds the painting unreservedly "poor," *Oxfordshire* (Buildings of England, Harmondsworth, 1974), pp. 41–42, 256.

101. Oct. 25, 1664, and July 9, 1669, Evelyn, *Diary*, III, pp. 384–85, 530–31.

102. "Very glorious scenes and perspectives, the work of Mr. Streeter who well understands it." Feb. 10, 1671, ibid., p. 570. Evelyn later assisted "that excellent Painter of Perspective, etc. and Landscip," through an attack of stone: Jan. 20, 1675, ibid., IV, pp. 51–52. See also ibid., III, pp. 374, 570, 625–26; IV, p. 288.

103. For South and the ceremony, see besides Evelyn, John Wallis to Boyle, July 17, 1669, *The Works of Robert Boyle*, ed. Thomas Birch, 6 vols (London, 1772), VI, pp. 458–60; and Wallis and Glanvill to Oldenburg, July 16 and 19, 1669, *Oldenburg, Correspondence* ed. Hall and Hall, VI, pp. 129–31, 137–39.

104. Pevsner, *Oxfordshire*, p. 255.

Chapter 11   *Restoration Architecture between the Ancients and the Moderns*

1. *Parentalia, or, Memoirs of the Family of the Wrens* (London, 1750), pp. 261–62; Evelyn to Wren, April 4, 1665, *Diary and Correspondence*, ed. Henry B. Wheatley, 4 vols (London, 1906), III, pp. 304–6. See in general, Margaret Whinney, "Wren's Visit to Paris," *Gazette des beaux arts*, 51 (1958), pp. 229–42.

2. Wren to Bathurst, June 22, 1665, *Wren Society*, ed. A. T. Bolton and H. D. Hendry, 20 vols (London, 1923–43), V, p. 14. For the report that follows, see the letter in *Parentalia*, pp. 261–62; *Wren Society*, XIII, pp. 40–42.

3. See Cecil Gould, *Bernini in France: An Episode in Seventeenth-Century History* (London, 1981).

4. Evelyn to Pepys [Aug. 21, 1669], Clara Marburg, *Mr Pepys and Mr Evelyn* (Philadelphia, 1935), app., pp. 101–8. Evelyn was once again full of advice and letters of recommendation for Pepys's trip; see his additional note on the same day, in Pepys, *Letters and Second Diary of Sanuel Pepys*, ed. R. G. Howarth (London, 1932), pp. 35–36.

5. Edward Browne to Sir Thomas Browne, Sept. 30, 1665, in Whinney, "Wren's Visit," pp. 232–34. Wren's guide seems to have been Henri Justel; see Justel to Oldenburg, in *The Correspondence of Henry Oldenburg*, ed. A. Rupert Hall and Marie Boas Hall, 11 vols (Madison, 1965–77), III, p. 12. For a description of the quays under Colbert, see Louis Hautecout, *Histoire de l'architecture classique en France*, 2 vols (Paris, 1948), II, i, pp. 429–31. For the failure to build a Thames quay after the fire of London, and Wren's involvement, see Wren to Sancroft, Sept. 16, 1671, *Wren Society*, XIII, p. 50; T. F. Reddaway, *The Rebuilding of London after the Great Fire* (London, 1940), pp. 221–43.

6. Wren to his son, doubting the expense of a trip, March 7, 1698, *Wren Society*, XIX, p. 119. Of course, Wren had access to Rome through engravings and Italian books on architecture; for the influence of the Pantheon, see Viktor Furst, *The Architecture of Sir Christopher Wren* (London, 1956), p. 138ff.

7. For the general reliability of the documents reproduced by Christopher Wren, Jr in the *Parentalia*, see J. A. Bennett, "Christopher Wren: The Natural Causes of Beauty," *Architectural History*, 15 (1972), pp. 5–22; and idem, "A Study of *Parentalia*, with Two Unpublished Letters of Sir Christopher Wren," *Annals of Science*, 30 (1973), pp.

129–47. Bennett uses three manuscript copies to show that the work was composed long before publication, when Wren Sr was still alive, and he supplies a letter to Petty (*c.* 1656) from the British Library manuscript (BL 25,074, ff.92–93), that vividly describes Wren's scientific activities (pp. 146–47).

8. Most of the surviving drawings for the cathedral are reproduced in *Wren Society* II, III and VIII; and more completely by Kerry Downes, *Sir Christopher Wren: The Designs of St Paul's Cathedral* (London, 1982).

9. See Joseph Rykwert, *The First Moderns: The Architecture of the Eighteenth Century* (Cambridge, Mass., 1980), p. 144.

10. Wren to Sancroft, May 7, 1666, *Wren Society*, XIII, p. 44.

11. See Wren's report to the commissioners, May 1, 1666, *Parentalia*, pp. 274–77; *Wren Society*, XIII, pp. 15–17. The designs now at All Souls are reproduced by Kerry Downes, *The Architecture of Christopher Wren* (New York, 1982), pls 20–21. Wren seems to have been guided by Pratt's advice, Wren to Sancroft, Aug. 5, 1766, *Wren Society*, XIII, pp. 44–45.

12. *Parentalia*, p. 275.

13. *Wren Society*, XIII, p. 18, and for Pratt's later objections to Wren's model, pp. 25–26; R. T. Gunther, *The Architecture of Roger Platt* (1928, reprinted New York, 1972), pp. 196, 213–14.

14. Aug. 27, 1666, *The Diary of John Evelyn*, ed. E. S. de Beer, 6 vols (Oxford, 1955), IV, p. 449.

15. For the great column, see M. I. Batten, "The Architecture of Robert Hooke," (Walpole Soc., 25, 1937), pp. 84–85.

16. [James Ralph] *A Critical Review of the Publick Buildings, Statues and Ornaments in and about London and Westminster* (London, 1734), p. 12. For St Stephen's, see *Wren Society*, X, pp. 77–88, 112–23; for St Mary-le-Bow, ibid., pp. 57–76. The latest discussion is in Paul Jeffrey, *The City Churches of Christopher Wren* (London, 1996).

17. *Wren Society*, V, pp. 32–34; reproduced in the appendix to *The Making of the Wren Library: Trinity College Cambridge*, ed. David McKitterick (Cambridge, 1985), pp. 142–45. See especially the essay there by Howard Colvin, pp. 28–46.

18. Nikolaus Pevsner, *Cambridgeshire*, 2nd edn (Buildings of England, Harmondsworth, 1970), p. 173. Kerry Downes sees in the building some affinity to the late baroque architecture of Guarini and Fontana, *Architecture of Wren*, p. 76.

19. Sir John Summerson, *Heavenly Mansions and Other Essays on Architecture* (New York,

1963), p. 85; and Kerry Downes's note in *Sir Christopher Wren*, p. 55. For Pevsner, it was "one of Wren's most mature and perfect works": *Cambridgeshire*, p. 31. See also Howard Colvin in *The Making of the Wren Library*, pp. 28–49.

20. *Parentalia*, p. 282.

21. "The Surveyor in private Conversation, always seem'd to set a higher Value on this Design, than any he had made before or since; as what was made with more Study and Success," *Parentalia*, p. 282. A plan known as the Greek Cross preceded it but contains most of its basic features; see John Summerson, *Architecture in Britain 1530–80*, 4th edn (Baltimore, 1963), p. 130. The Great Model, according to Downes, is "Wren's most classical design in the sense of the word that denotes the balance, restraint, rationality, linguistic orthodoxy and ordered inevitability of the High Renaissance." *Architecture of Wren*, p. 69.

22. *Parentalia*, p. 282.

23. Several resident canons and several bishops on the commission objected to the Greek Cross of the Great Model; see ibid., p. 282; Jane Lang, *Rebuilding of St Paul's* (London, 1956), p. 69.

24. *Parentalia*, p. 182.

25. Summerson, *Architecture in Britain*, pp. 106–7. Elsewhere, he agrees that the "absurd classic-gothic steeple" was undoubtedly "bizarre." It was, of course, eventually replaced by an elegantly designed dome. Summerson, ibid., p. 131.

26. "The Cupolo, were it finished," wrote Wren to the commissioners in 1697, "would be so remarkable an ornament to this mighty City, which is yet inferior in Publick Buildings to many Cities of lesse note and wealth, that all Persons natives or forreigners will be extremely satisfied": *Wren Society*, XVI, pp. 85–86. The transition from the Warrant design to the actual building has been traced by John Summerson through an intermediate design; see "The Penultimate Design for St Paul's Cathedral," *Burlington Magazine*, 103 (1961), pp. 83–89.

27. Oct. 5, 1694, Evelyn, *Diary*, V, p. 192.

28. *An Account* (dated Feb. 21, 1697) in Fréart, *Parallel* (1707), *Miscellaneous Works*, pp. 351–52.

29. "The manner now in general Use, first introduced by that great Lover and Patron of the good Arts, the Illustrious Thomas late Earl of Arundel and Surrey . . . incited others to build with Stone and brick after the present Gusto, and which Inigo Jones since pursued in that Stately Pile at White-hall now mentioned, the Church and Piazza

in Covent Garden . . . but that which is at this day exalted (namely Architecture) to a much greater (if I may say, even to the highest Pitch of Perfection) by our most worthy Friend Sir Christopher Wren": Evelyn, *Numismata* (London, 1697), p. 50.

30. Evelyn to Place, Aug. 17, 1696, *Corr.*, ed. Wheatley, IV, pp. 8–11.

31. Wren's protest (Oct. 28, 1717) is in *Wren Society*, XVI, pp. 130–31. For a list of many other setbacks and rejections in Wren's long career, see ibid., 19, p. xi.

32. Typical is Sekler's observation that the great main portal can be seen "in strictly antique Roman terms but the two windows in the niches at the base of the towers come from the Rome of the baroque, perhaps from the Palazzo Barberini": Eduard Sekler, *Wren and his Place in European Architecture* (New York, 1956), pp. 143–44. For Nikolaus Pevsner the domes one inside the other provide "an ingenious solution of the engineering problem in hand, a scientist's solution rather than a born architect's who might have taken exception to the ugliness of the cone, regardless of the fact that it is not visible": *London: The Buildings of England* (Harmondsworth, 1952), p. 121.

33. See p. 266, n. 113 below. For Nikolaus Pevsner, Wren's church style was classical, "but it was a baroque version of classicism": *An Outline of European Architecture* (London, 1968), p. 326; for John Summerson, Wren's architecture is characterized by an "element of compromise, of disunity of conception . . . of inconsistency." Though he was temperamentally not in accord with the baroque spirit, he handled classic forms "in a loose, unconventional fashion which, allowing for a strong individual trend, can be called by no other name": *Heavenly Mansions*, pp. 79, 84. See too V. Fuerst, *The Architecture of Christopher Wren* (London, 1956), p. 178.

34. A catalogue of Wren's library may be found in *Wren Society*, XX, pp. 74–77.

35. *Parentalia*, p. 289.

36. Ibid. This might be compared with Evelyn's view of modeling English on the Latin and Greek writers, and even some of the moderns, "so a laudable and unaffected imitation of the best and choicest recommended." Evelyn to Pepys, Oct. 4, 1689, Pepys, *Letters and the Second Diary*, ed. Howarth, p. 209. Evelyn had served on the Royal Society committee to improve the English language; see Evelyn to Peter Wyche, June 20, 1665, *Diary and Correspondence*, ed. Wheatley, III, pp. 309–12.

37. James Elmes, *Memoirs of the Life and Works of*

Sir Christopher Wren (London, 1823), p. 320. Elmes was himself an architect as well as a critic; see Howard Colvin, *A Biographical Dictionary of British Architects 1600–1840* (New York, 1978), pp. 291–92. According to Eduard Sekler, Wren was "a follower of a classicist ideal forced by the artistic climate of his time to achieve Baroque creations": Sekler, *Wren*, p. 94.

38. Memorial of Wren, Oct. 28, 1717, *Wren Society*, XVI, pp. 131–33, taken from Elmes, *Memoirs of Wren*, p. 508. Wren was already protesting about this in 1711; see his letter to the Archbishop, Jan. 25, 1711, ibid., pp. 154–55, and the commissioners' reply, pp. 157–58. Wren seems to have withdrawn from the work about that time.

39. Lawrence A. Turner, "The Crafts at St Paul's," *Sir Christopher Wren 1632–1723: Bicentenary Memorial Volume* (London, 1923), p. 81. Nevertheless, it appears that the overall scheme for the decoration at Trinity College was by Henry Aldrich; see Hiscock, on Jonathan Maine in *Country Life*, Dec. 1948.

40. "It seems to be the case that Gibbons filled in the decorative work [at Hampton Court] on inch-scale drawings of Wren's work as drawn in outline and supplied to him": *Wren Society*, IV, p. 17, pls 27–46. Among the many others who worked there under him was Robert Streater, who did much of the preliminary preparations for painting: ibid., pp. 58–59. As the editors point out, Wren's activity extended to the smallest things and was prodigious.

41. *Parentalia*, p. 88; David B. Green, *Grinling Gibbons: His Work as Carver and Statuary* (London, 1964), pp. 87–94.

42. "For this Purpose he had projected to have procured from Italy four of the most eminent Artists in that Profession; but as this Art was a great Novelty in England, and not generally apprehended, did not receive the Encouragement it deserved; it was imagined also the Expence would prove too great, and the Time very long in Duration; but tho' these and all Objections were fully answered, yet this excellent Design was no further pursued": *Parentalia*, p. 292. As an apostolic church, the Anglicans traced their origins back to the very beginning of Christendom, perhaps to a mission by St Paul himself. Wren supposed that the first churches were destroyed in the early persecutions, but rebuilt under Constantine, "after the pattern of the Roman Basilica of St Peter and St Paul in the Vatican," and he tried to place the new St Paul's exactly on the original Roman site: ibid., p. 271.

43. Feb. 28, 1711, *Wren Society*, XVI, p. 174.

44. Wren to a gentleman, May 14 [1687?], *Wren Society*, XII, p. 23; Howard Colvin, *History of the King's Works*, 6 vols (1963–76), V, p. 20. See Carol Gibson-Wood, "The Political Background to Thornhill's Paintings in St Paul's Cathedral," *Journal of the Warburg and Courtauld Institutes*, 56 (1993), pp. 229–37.

45. See Edward Croft-Murray, *Decorative Art in England 1537–1837*, 2 vols (London, 1962), I, pp. 50–60.

46. It was here that Wren had been employed for the great tomb for Charles I which was designed but never funded. And it was here too that Kneller added an impressive painting of William III to the original celebration of his predecessors.

47. June 16, 1683, Evelyn, *Diary*, IV, pp. 316–17; Sept. 6, 1685, ibid., p. 465. Evelyn repeats the compliments in his own copy of Fréart's *Idea of the Perfection of Painting*. Almost all of Verrio's work was replaced a century later under George III and George IV.

48. Oct. 10, 1683, Evelyn, *Diary*, IV, p. 344. If Evelyn's enthusiasm seems excessive, Croft-Murray reminds us that "the full-blooded experience of the baroque had never been let loose on such a scale in this country," *Decorative Art*, I, p. 55. Evelyn also admired the gardens that Verrio laid out at St James (after Le Notre's Versailles) as "a very delirious paradise." *Diary*, IV, p. 57.

49. Dec. 1686, Evelyn, *Diary*, IV, pp. 543–45; Colvin, *King's Works*, V, pp. 290–93.

50. Verrio did much work at Burghley House and Chatsworth, before returning to Windsor (1699) and Hampton Court. See Edgar Wind, "Julian the Apostate at Hampton Court," *Journal of the Warburg Institute*, 3 (1939–40), pp. 127–37, reprinted in *Hume and the Heroic Portrait*, ed. Jaynie Anderson (Oxford, 1986), pp. 53–62. Verrio died in 1707.

51. According to Vertue, it was "a truly curious work alluding to Painting, finely thought, correctly deliniated, and well color'd ... one of his masterpieces": George Vertue, *Note Books*, IV (Walpole Soc., 24, 1935–36), p. 125. At Hampton Court, Laguerre was put to work by William III to repair Mantegna's *Triumphs of Caesar*, one of the ultimate sources for all subsequent historical painting. See also Whinney and Millar, pp. 302–6; Croft-Murray, *Decorative Art*, I, pp. 61–68.

52. The term "decorative painting" seems to me a misnomer; the period preferred to think of these ceilings and wall paintings as histories. William Aglionby explains that this meant "assembling many Figures in one Piece, to Represent any Action of Life, whether True

or Fabulous, accompanied with all its Ornaments of Landskip and Perspective": *Painting
Illustrated in Three Dialogues* (London, 1686),
n. p. Later Thomas Page elaborates: "History
is a Picture consisting of divers Figures,
representing the Manner and Form of
some Adventure, that has been perform'd by
the noted Actions of Men." The choice of
subject must be "according to the Taste and
Manner of the Ancients, without which all
our Workes would be Gothick and monstrous, for they are the Rule of Beauty and
Gracefulness. Wherefore we must be curious
in the Imitation of their Statues and Paintings
. . .": *The Art of Painting: in its Rudiments,
Progress, and Perfection* (Norwich, 1720), pp.
106–7.

53. The music, it was feared, being recitative,
might not be immediately acceptable; see
the preface in Burney's *History of Music*, 2
vols (New York, 1957), II, p. 655. The opera
which opened at the Drury Lane, London
on June 16, 1705 was in fact a great success.
Meanwhile, the rival theater at Lincoln's Inn
Fields, was putting on Dryden's *Amphytrion*,
"with the proper Entertainments of Singing
and Dancing in between the Acts." See
Judith Milhous, "New Light on Vanbrugh's
Haymarket Theatre Project," *Theatre Survey*,
17 (1976), pp. 151, 156.

54. Vertue, *Note Books*, IV, p. 125. Vertue had
studied with Laguerre and admired him as
a person and an artist.

55. March 3, 1709 (with Wren counted present),
Wren Society, XVI, p. 107.

56. Feb. 11, 1710, ibid., p. 109. The decision was
made finally on June 25, 1715, when Thornhill was instructed to proceed with his design
for a basso-relievo; ibid., p. 116. *Gentleman's
Magazine*, Nov. 1790, and George Vertue,
Note Books, II (Walpole Soc., 20, 1932), p. 125.
See William R. Osmun, "A Study of the
Work of Sir James Thornhill" (unpublished
dissertation, London University, 1950), to
which I owe much of what follows.

57. Vertue says that Ricci was thought "by the
best judges" to be the best historical painter
in England and that his appearance in
England was the cause of Pellegrini's depar-
ture, as Thornhill's victory was to be the
cause of his: *Note Books*, I (Walpole Soc., 18,
1930), pp. 39, 45, 74. Henry Talmon wrote
from Italy in November 1711, protesting
against his appointment; see Carol Gibson-
Wood, "The Political Background",
p. 235. George Knox sees the Pellegrini–
Ricci rivalry as a reenactment of the
Venetian–Roman, color–design argument:
Antonio Pellegrini (Oxford, 1995), p. 85. To
be sure, the painters had actually worked

together in London in 1709 on the sets
for operas by Scarlatti and Bononcini. See
also, Jeffrey Daniels, *Sebastiano Ricci* (Hove,
1976).

58. Wren to the commissioners, Jan. 25, 1711,
Wren Society, XVI, pp. 154–57; Osmun, "A
Study," pp. 395–97. In April, William Trumbull reported that, with the appointment of
a deputy, John James, Wren felt "quite dis-
carded": *Wren Society*, XVI, p. 178. Just a year
or two before, the *Tatler* had extolled Wren's
modesty and patience before his enemies
under the guise of "Nestor," *Tatler*, 52
(1709).

59. Thornhill succeeded Kneller as director in
1716, but was later undone by a new faction.
The story of the rivalry is too complicated
to tell here, but it is related (with other
useful material about Thornhill) by Ronald
Paulson in the first volume of his magisterial life of Hogarth (Cambridge, 1991),
p. 101ff.

60. *The Diary of Dudley Ryder 1715–1716*, ed.
William Matthews (London, 1939),
pp. 307–8.

61. In 1661 Evelyn gave the poet, Sir John
Denham, then the King's Surveyor, some
advice about siting the palace that was
to be rebuilt at Greenwich, but Denham
objected, "so I came away knowing Sir John
to be a better Poet than Architect, though
he had Mr Webb (Inigo Jones' man) to assist
him": *Diary*, III, pp. 300–1.

62. "Preferring in this, as in every other Passage
of his Life, the Public Service to any private
Advantage of his own, by the Acquist of
Wealth, of which he had a great contempt":
Parentalia, quoted in Philip Newell, *Green-
wich Hospital* (Greenwich, 1984), p. 56.

63. The story is recalled by Hawksmoor in his
*Remarks on the Founding and Carrying out of
the Buildings of the Royal Hospital at Greenwich* (1728), abridged in the *Wren Society*,
VI, pp. 17–27.

64. Evelyn, *Diary*, V, pp. 209–12, 243, 249, 399,
etc. *Wren Society*, VI, p. 41. In 1702, Evelyn
brought a report to Parliament, "to their
great satisfaction." He had by then paid out
nearly £100,000: *Diary*, V, pp. 447, 492, 495.

65. In 1705, when the hospital began to admit
seamen, Evelyn took his whole family
to visit and found the building "very
magnificent": *Diary*, V, p. 600.

66. See Lawrence Whistler, *Sir John Vanbrugh,
Architect and Dramatist 1664–1726* (London,
1938), pp. 71–75; Kerry Downes, *Hawksmoor*, 2nd edn (London, 1979), pp. 83–98.
On the answer depends whether Wren
should be seen as moving toward the
baroque himself, or at least approving of it

in his friends, but the documentation to settle the point is lacking.

67. At the outset, the board ordered some changes in Thornhill's design; Vanbrugh was present at the meeting on July 17, 1707, but Wren was not. *Wren Society*, VI, p. 57. Much later, Thornhill insisted on closing up some of the windows for his painting and (with Wren long since retired) this was approved by Vanbrugh and the board: ibid., p. 79.

68. Pevsner, *London*, p. 149. "The epitome of baroque illusionism": Edgar de N. Mayhew, *Sketches by Thornhill at the Victoria and Albert Museum* (London, 1967), p. 6.

69. The *Lover*, 33, May 11 (London, 1715), pp. 223–24. *An Explanation of the Painting in the Royal Hospital at Greenwich* (n. d.).

70. There is an encomium to Thornhill, and his triumph over foreign competition, in Elkanah Settle's funeral poem to Wren, *Threnodia Apollinaris* (London, 1723), pp. 6–7.

71. Edgar Wind, "The Revolution in History Painting," *Journal of the Warburg Institute*, 3 (1938–39), pp. 116–27, esp. 122–24; reprinted in *Hume and the Heroic Portrait* ed. Anderson, pp. 88–99. Paulson traverses much of the same ground in *Hogarth*, I, pp. 123–24.

72. Thus typically according to Thomas Page, one should follow the ancient models, "By the advantage of which, forming to our selves a Model of the superior Beauties, and reflecting on them, [we may] endeavor to correct and amend their common Nature, and to represent it as it ought to be," not too literally. On the other hand the painting should be true to the circumstances of the text: time and place and customs, though leaving out all "trivial" circumstances: *The Art of Painting*, pp. 106–7.

73. I use the transcription in Lindsay Stainton and Christopher White, *Drawing in England from Hilliard to Hogarth* (London, 1987), p. 234; and Osmun, "A Study," pp. 264–65.

74. Paulson, *Hogarth*, pp. 95–100, 119.

75. Marshall Smith, *The Art of Painting according to the Theory and Practise of the Best Italian, French and German Masters*, 2nd edn (London, 1693), pp. 86–87.

76. *Spectator*, 129, July 28, 1712.

77. Martin Lister, *A Journey to Paris in the Year 1698*, ed. Raymond P. Stearns (Urbana, 1967), pp. 28–30.

78. For the background, see Dianna de Marly, "The Establishment of Roman Dress in Seventeenth-Century Portraiture," *Burlington Magazine*, 117 (1975), pp. 443–51. For the discussion later in the eighteenth century, see Edgar Wind, "The Revolution

of History Painting," *Hume and the Heroic Portrait*, ed. Anderson, pp. 88–99.

79. *Wren Society*, VI, pp. 77–79.

80. Colin Campbell, *Vitruvius Britannicus*, 3 vols (London, 1715–25, reprinted New York, 1967), I p. 6. Aglionby, *Painting Illustrated*, preface. There is a story that may reflect the peculiar position of history painting, though it may be apocryphal. It seems that Godfrey Kneller asked Thornhill to paint his staircase at Whitton, but when he heard that Thornhill was also painting portraits in his spare time, he fired him, saying that "no portrait painter would ever decorate his house": Michael Morris Killanin, *Sir Godfrey Kneller and his Times* (London, 1948), p. 26 (with no citation). Vertue laments the fact that no artist was then allowed to venture out of his professional domain, and suggests that Thornhill in particular suffered from his pretensions to architecture: *Notebooks*, III, p. 55.

81. Bentley to Evelyn, Oct. 21, 1697, Bentley, *Correspondence*, ed. C. Wordsworth, 2 vols (London, 1842), I, p. 152.

82. Four of them are given in *Parentalia*, pp. 351–60; a fifth in Lucy Phillimore, *Sir Christopher Wren: His Family and his Times* (London, 1881), app. III, pp. 340–50; all are reproduced from the above in *Wren Society*, XIX, pp. 121–45. Christopher Wren Jr pointed out to Ward that they were "only the first rough Drafts, not perfected, nor intended by him for the Press": BL Add. MS 6209, f.215.

83. *Wren Society*, XIII, p. 41.

84. Ibid., p. 126.

85. Ibid., p. 127.

86. For the first, see Bennett, "Christopher Wren."

87. Howard Colvin, "Roger North and Sir Christopher Wren," *Architectural Review*, 110 (1951), pp. 257–60. For North's reading in Renaissance theory (including Evelyn's translation of Fréart), see his autobiography in *Lives of the Norths*, ed. Augustus Jessopp, 3 vols (London, 1890), III, p. 61. In a manuscript of 1698, North writes, "It bears much of arrogance to pretend outdoing antiquity; and we have not many Michael Angelos to pretend to that": Roger North, *Writings on Architecture*, ed. Howard Colvin and John Newman (Oxford, 1981), p. 20.

88. See Colvin, "Roger North," pp. 259–60.

89. Tract III, *Wren Society*, XIX, p. 133.

90. Tract II, ibid., p. 128.

91. "Observations on the Temple of Peace built by the Emperor Vespasian," *Parentalia*, pp. 362–63.

92. Tract II, *Wren Society*, XIX, p. 129.

93. Tract V, ibid., p. 142 (Tract IV, *Parentalia*, pp. 359–60). It is possible that Wren's attention was first called to the subject in 1670 by Christian Huyghens who had written a popular tract on the Temple and now planned to exhibit a large wooden model in London based on Villalpando. (Perrault was a friend of Huyghens and could also have known it.) See Huyghens to Oldenburg, Sept. 27, 1674, Oldenburg, *Correspondence*, XI, p. 93; Helen Rosenau, *Vision of the Temple* (London, 1979), p. 141n. Leon's work, *Ritrato de Templo de Solomono* (1642) with engravings was soon turned into Dutch, French, German and Latin; see Herrmann, "Unknown Designs," pp. 148–49.

94. Tract V, *Wren Society*, XIX, pp. 140–45.

95. *Parentalia*, pp. 264–67. See Joseph M. Levine, *Dr. Woodward's Shield: History, Science and Satire in Augustan England* (Berkley, 1987), pp. 134–35.

96. Tract V, *Wren Society*, XIX, pp. 143–44 (*Parentalia*, pp. 360–61, 362–63). In the little tempietto above the entrance to Queen's College Oxford there was a copy of the shrine of the statue of Diana at Ephesus, contributed by Wren: *Parentalia*, p. 134.

97. *Parentalia*, p. 307.

98. See Wren's report ibid., pp. 295–302; *Wren Society*, XIII, pp. 303–6.

99. Wren found much to admire in Salisbury Cathedral, compared to the late Gothic that followed, but pointed out numerous "errors" in the design, and concluded that this was why "this Forme of Churches hath been rejected by moderne Architects abroad, who use the better and Roman Forme of Architecture": Wren to Seth Ward, Aug. 31, 1668, *Parentalia*, pp. 304–6.

100. See Atterbury's preface to *The Second Part of Mr Waller's Poems* (London, 1690); Joseph M. Levine, *The Battle of the Books: History and Literature in Augustan England* (Ithaca, N.Y., 1991), pp. 59–61.

101. Levine, *Battle of the Books*, p. 302.

102. Wren to Fell, Dec. 3, 1681, in W. Douglas Caroe, *Tom Tower: Some Letters of Sir Christopher Wren to John Fell* (Oxford, 1923), pp. 31–32. For Wren's designs see *Wren Society*, XI, pp. 35–45, pls 15–18.

103. Hawksmoor protested his loyalty and obligations to Wren in an eloquent statement late in life, while Vanbrugh steadfastly refused to take Wren's place, when offered the opportunity; see Sir John Vanbrugh, *The Complete Works IV: The Letters*, ed. Geoffrey Webb (London, 1928), p. x.

104. Anthony Blunt, *Baroque and Rococo: Architecture and Decoration* (London, 1978), p. 14.

105. See Margaret Lyttleton, *Baroque Architecture in Classical Antiquity* (Ithaca, N.Y., 1974).

106. There are five views and plans signed by Hawksmoor. See Summerson, *Architecture in Britain*, pp. 191–93; Kerry Downes, *Hawksmoor* (London, 1969), p. 197; Timothy F. Rub, "A *Most Solemn and Awful Appearance*: Nicholas Hawksmoor's East London Churches," *Marsyas*, 21 (1981–82), p. 26n.

107. Jan. 7, 1724, Downes, *Hawksmoor*, 2nd edn (London, 1979), app. A, pp. 243–44. See also the letters of Hawksmoor, invoking classical authority for his great mausoleum there: Geoffrey Webb, "The Letters and Drawings of Nicholas Hawksmoor relating to the Building at Castle Howard 1726–42" (Walpole Soc., 19, 1931), pp. 117–19, 133–37, 148–49. See also Charles S. S. Smith, *The Building of Castle Howard* (London, 1990). According to Vertue, who wrote Hawksmoor's obituary, "He was perfectly skilld in the history of Architecture and could give an exact account of all the famous buildings, both antient and modern in every part of the World": *Note Books*, I, pp. 77–78. This is given credence by the sale catalogue of his library (1740); see Kerry Downes, "Hawksmoor's Sale Catalogue," *Burlington Magazine*, 95 (Oct. 1953), pp. 331–35.

108. See the long and important letter from Hawksmoor to the Dean of Westminster, in Downes, *Hawksmoor* (1969), pp. 255–58.

109. As he wrote on one drawing, "I think Lord Carlisle cannot have a Nobler Building, entirely after the Antique." See also the letters of Hawksmoor to Carlisle, Oct. 1732, quoted by Smith, in *Building of Castle Howard*, pp. 172–80, who suggests that there were economic motives too.

110. See Philip Olleson, "Vanbrugh and Opera at the Queen's Theatre, Haymarket," *Theater Notebook*, 26 (1971–72), pp. 94–101; Judith Milhous, "New Light on Vanbrugh's Haymarket Theatre Project," *Theatre Survey*, 17 (1976), pp. 143–61. For Vanbrugh as architect, see Whistler, *Sir John Vanbrugh*; Geoffrey Beard, *The Work of John Vanbrugh* (London, 1986); Kerry Downes, *Sir John Vanbrugh, A Biography* (London, 1987). The conjunction of careers has never been satisfactorily explained, but it was the cause of great fun to Jonathan Swift, who satirized and paralleled the two in his poem, "Van's House," for which see Whistler, *Sir John Vanbrugh*, pp. 304–7.

111. Geoffrey Webb in Vanbrugh, *Complete Works*, IV, p. xxiii. See especially the brilliant article by S. Lang, "Vanbrugh's Theory and Hawksmoor's Buildings," *Journal of the*

Society of Architectural Historians, 24 (1965), pp. 127–45. The best expression of Vanbrugh's ideas is the "Proposals for Building the New Churches" (1711), printed in Lawrence Whistler, *The Imagination of Vanbrugh and his Fellow Artists* (London, 1954), app. 2, pp. 257–58. For Vanbrugh's debt to Palladio, see besides Lang, "Vanbrugh's Theory," pp. 138–39, Kerry Downes, *Vanbrugh*, 2nd edn (London, 1977), pp. 111–26.

112. Kerry Downes, *English Baroque Architecture* (London, 1966), p. 26. For the anxiety about fancy in the period, see David Cast, "Seeing Vanbrugh and Hawksmoor," *Journal of the Society of Architectural Historians*, 43 (1984), pp. 315–17.

113. Some critics associate a late Wren style with Hawksmoor and Vanbrugh; so Rykwert describes it as "High Tory Gothic baroque": *First Moderns*, p. 154. Webb too places the late Wren and his students in an "international baroque style": Geoffrey Webb, "Baroque Art," *Proceedings of the British Academy*, 33 (1947) pp. 145–46.

114. See his letter of March 6, 1712, the Earl of Shaftesbury, *Characteristicks*, 5th edn (London, 1732), III, p. 400. At the same time, Wren began to lose control of the financial administration of the office of the King's Works: see Howard Colvin, "The End of Wren's Regime," in *King's Works*, pp. 47–56.

115. The *World*, 50, Dec. 13, 1753. Was Burlington recalling Dryden's lines to Congreve? See Arthur W. Hoffman, "Dryden's *To Mr Congreve*," *Modern Language Notes*, 75 (1960), pp. 553–56.

116. Pope to Jervas, July 9, 1716, Pope, *Correspondence*, ed. George Sherburn, 5 vols (Oxford, 1956), I, pp. 346–47; see also III, pp. 187–88, 356, 313–15.

117. See John Gay, "Epistle to Paul Methuen" (1720), ll. 59–62, 67–70; and *Trivia* (1716), ll. 493–500; in *Poetical Works*, ed. G. C. Faber (London, 1926, reprinted New York, 1969), pp. 76, 161; Jonathan Swift, in the *Poems*, ed. Harold Williams (Oxford, 1958), III, p. 893; Carole Fabricant, *Swift's Landscape* (Baltimore, 1982), pp. 109–13. For more on Burlington, see Fiske Kimball, "Burlington Architectus, Parts One and Two," *RIBA Journal*, 34 (1927), pp. 675–93; 35 (Nov. 1927), pp. 14–16; James Lees-Milne, *Earls of Creation* (London, 1962), pp. 103–69; Rudolf Wittkower, *Palladio and Palladianism* (New York and London, 1974), pp. 114–32. It was Horace Walpole who called Burlington "the Apollo of the Arts," Walpole, *Anecdotes of Painting*, ed. Ralph N. Wornum, 3 vols (London, 1888), III, pp. 53–56.

118. The Italian visitor, Scipione Maffei, gave Burlington a copy of Alessandro Pompei's *Cinque ordine* inscribed to him as "il Palladio e il Jones de' nostri tempi": John Wilton-Ely, "Lord Burlington and the Virtuoso Portrait," *Architectural History*, 27 (1984), p. 378n.

119. "An Epistle to the Right Honorable Richard Earl of Burlington. Occasion'd by his Publishing Designs of the Baths, Arches, Theatres, etc. of Ancient Rome," a sixteen-page folio, in Pope, *Epistles to Several Persons*, ed. F. W. Bateson (Twickenham edn), *Poems of Alexander Pope* (London, 1961), III, ii, p. 128–56. See William Gibson, "Three Principles of Renaissance Architectural History: Theory in Pope's *Epistle to Burlington*," in *Pope: Recent Essays by Several Hands*, ed. Maynard Mack and James A. Winn (Hamden, Conn. 1980), pp. 352–71; Howard Erskine-Hill, "Heirs of Vitruvius: Pope and the Idea of Architecture," *The Art of Alexander Pope*, ed. Erskine-Hill and Anne Smith (New York, 1979), pp. 144–56; and Erskine-Hill, "'Avowed Friend and Patron': The Third Earl of Burlington and Alexander Pope," in *Lord Burlington, Architecture, Art and Life*, ed. Toby Bernard and Jane Clark (London, 1955), pp. 217–29.

120. "The Portico of Covent-garden Church had been just then [1727] restored and beautify'd at the expence of Richard Earl of Burlington, who at the same time, by his publication of the designs of that great Master and Palladio, as well as many noble buildings of his own, revived the true Taste of Architecture in this Kingdom": Alexander Pope, *Dunciad*, ed. James Sutherland, Twickenham edn, *Poems of Alexander Pope*, (London, 1963), V p. 189n. These judgments are also reflected in James Ralph's *Critical Review*, pp. 17–22 (on St Paul's Cathedral), p. 29 (on St Paul's, Covent Garden), etc.

121. In his advice to the traveler, Edward Brown typically recommends Vicenza, "by reason that Palladius hath here shown great skill in Architecture in his Rotunda, in imitation of the Pantheon in Rome in his theatre exactly proportioned . . . and other fair houses in town": *A Brief Account of Some Travels in Divers Parts of Europe* (London, 1685). In a note on Palladio (1636), Inigo Jones had written, "in my opinion, Palladio Immitates the best . . . but allwaes the libberty of composing with reason is not taken awaye, but who followes the best of the ancients cannot much erre": *On Palladio*, 2 vols (Newcastle, 1970), I, p. 62. Palladio himself claimed to use as his guides the ancient Romans, "who vastly excelled all those who have been

since their time," i. e. Vitruvius and the ancient buildings themselves, exactly observed. See *The Four Books of Andrea Palladio's Architecture*, trans. Isaac Ware, and dedicated to Burlington (London, 1738), n. p.

122. Thus Evelyn found the Teatro Olympico in 1646, "the most perfect [theater] now standing in all the world . . . in exact imitation of the Antient Roman," Evelyn, *Diary*, II, p. 482. Arundel had already made the point in his instructions to Evelyn, *Remembrances of Things worth seeing in Italy*, ed. John Martin Robinson (London, 1987), p. 23. See too Evelyn in his translation of Fréart's *Parallel*, p. 22.

123. Palladio's *Quattro libri* (1550), Scamozzi's *Idea dell'arcitectura universale* (1615), and Daniele Barbaro's version of Vitruvius (1556), all in Jones's library. According to Esther Eisenthal, Webb worked independently of Jones and sought a reconstruction that was "comprehensive, complete, and as authentic as the illustrated sources would allow." See "John Webb's Reconstruction of the Ancient House," *Architectural History*, 28 (1985), pp. 7–18; and also John Orrell, *The Theatres of Inigo Jones and John Webb* (Cambridge, 1985).

124. The Burlington House façade, designed by Colin Campbell in 1725, displayed "two Niches in Flank, fronting each other, where the noble Patron has prepared the statues of Palladio and Jones."

125. For this central episode in the Battle of the Books, and Aldrich's complicity, see my *Battle of the Books*, pp. 47–84.

126. See W. G. Hiscock, *Henry Aldrich of Christ Church (1648–1710)* (Oxford, 1960). Evelyn several times advised his grandson at Oxford to get drawing lessons with Aldrich.

127. For the importance of the Christ Church wits in the quarrel, see Levine, *Battle of the Books*, pp. 47–84.

128. Henry Aldrich, *The Elements of Architecture according to Vitruvius and other Ancients and . . . Palladio*, ed. and trans. Philip Smyth (Oxford, 1789). Typically Aldrich emphasizes the authority of the rules (p. 29), but allows some freedom for variation, "For Architecture, as well as the sister Arts, Painting and Poetry, claims some indulgences, and may be permitted to use them, when compatible with taste and elegance" (p. 24).

129. *The Architecture of A. Palladio, Revis'd, Design'd, and Publish'd by Giacomo Leoni*, 5 pts (London, 1715–20), text in English, French and Italian; 2nd edn (in English only), 1721. Leoni followed it with a translation of

Alberti in 1726. See Colvin, *Dictionary*, pp. 511–14, and Rudolf Wittkower, "Giacomo Leoni's Edition of Palladio's *Quattro libri dell'architettura*," *Arte Veneta*, III (1954), pp. 310–16; idem, "English Neoclassicism and the Vicissitudes of Palladio's *Quattro Libri*," *Palladio*, pp. 73–92.

130. Campbell, *Vitruvius Britannicus*, sig. B. See T. P. Connor, "The Making of *Vitruvius Britannicus*," *Architectural History*, 21 (1978), pp. 14–30; and idem, "Colin Campbell as Architect to the Prince of Wales," *Architectural History*, 22 (1979), pp. 64–71. For more on Campbell, see Howard E. Stutchbury, *The Architecture of Colin Campbell* (Manchester, 1967).

131. He praises St Paul's Covent Garden, as "the only Piece the Moderns have yet produced, that can admit of a just Comparison with the Works of Antiquity, where a Majestick Simplicity commands the Approbation of the Judicious": Campbell, *Vitruvius Britannicus*, II, p. 1. See Downes, "Anti-Baroque," *English Baroque Architecture*, pp. 9–11.

132. For Campbell's influence on Burlington, see *The Survey of London: The Park of St James Westminster* (London, 1963), 32 pp. 401–2. Their dispute may have been only over a carpenter's bill, but by 1720 Burlington had replaced Campbell with William Kent; see Walter Ison, "The Architecture of Burlington House," *Apollo*, 89 (1969), p. 6. Campbell seems to have learned his Palladianism from the Scot, James Smith, who had been to Italy *c.* 1670–75; see Howard Colvin, "A Scottish Origin for English Palladianism," *Architectural History*, 17 (1974); John Harris, *The Palladians* (London, 1981), p. 16.

133. Campbell, *Vitruvius Britannicus*, I, p. 4. The first architect was probably Hugh May; Gibbs took over about 1717, and was supplanted by Campbell in 1719–20. In 1720, Kent described the house to a friend as having a "true Palladian front." *Survey of London*, pt 2, pp. 390–423, esp. pp. 400–2.

134. Graham's dedication to Burlington in his "Short Account" appended to C. A. De Fresnoy, *De arte graphica*, trans. John Dryden (London, 1716). See George Knox, "Sebastiano Ricci at Burlington House: A Venetian Decoration *alla romana*," *Burlington Magazine*, 127 (1985), pp. 601–7.

135. *Wren Society*, XI, pp. 35–45; Harris, *The Palladians*, fig. 53, p. 72. Colvin, *King's Works*, pp. 47–66.

136. John Molesworth to Galilei, in Ilaria Toesca, "Alessandro Galilei in Inghilterra," *English*

Miscellany, 3 (1952), p. 220. Apparently, Burlington did disapprove of Michelangelo; see Joseph Spence, *Observations, Anecdotes and Characters of Books and Men*, ed. James M. Osborn, 2 vols (Oxford, 1966), II, p. 558.

137. Vertue, *Note Books*, VI (Walpole Soc., 29, 1940–42), pp. 139–41; Rudolf Wittkower, "Lord Burlington and William Kent," *Palladio*, pp. 115–32. Kent was much freer than Burlington in his reliance on the ancients, so that their collaboration has puzzled many, but it was based on their common Italian experience and built on mutual esteem. See Cinzia Maria Sicca, "On William Kent's Roman Sources," *Architectural History*, 29 (1986), pp. 134–47.

138. See the various criticisms quoted by Osmun, "A Study," pp. 187–89. Toward the end, Thornhill got tired of his work at Greenwich and farmed off some of it to assistants; Paulson charts the abrupt decline in commissions from twenty-one between 1715 and 1725, to only one between 1725 and 1734, *Hogarth*, pp. 197–98.

139. See Arlene Meyer, *Sir James Thornhill and the Legacy of Raphael's Tapestry Cartoons* (New York, 1996). The catalogue of Thornhill's collections prepared for auction after his death describes these works as "finished with the utmost Care and Judgment, to preserve to future Ages a just Idea of these Divine Originals": Tancred Borenius, "Sir James Thornhill's Collections," *Burlington Magazine*, 82 (1943), pp. 133–36. Vertue describes a visit to Thornhill while he was working at Hampton Court and trying to copy the cartoons exactly in full-size, half-size and quarter-size versions. He was impressed but dissatisfied with some of the sketches: Vertue, *Note Books*, III (Walpole Soc., 22, 1934), pp. 38–39. The cartoons had been engraved in their new setting by Simon Gribelin. The story of their transmission and appreciation from their acquisition by Charles I is sketched by John Shearman, *Raphael's Cartoons in the Collection of her Majesty the Queen* (London, 1972), pp. 139–51. See also F. J. B. Watson, "On the Early History of Collecting in England," *Burlington Magazine*, 85 (1944), pp. 226–27; and Paulson, *Hogarth*, p. 359. It is clear from Vertue, who mentions still other copies, that there was a sudden intense interest in these neglected works.

140. See Rykwert, *First Moderns*, p. 186ff.; Colvin, *Dictionary*, pp. 558–59. Morris's preface (p. xvii) advocates "the strictest Adherence to the Practice of those unerring Rules, those perfect Standards of the Law of Reason and Nature, founded upon Beauty and Necessity." If the rules were observed, he says later (p. 85), we might have an architecture "that might even stand above Competition with the Ancients."

141. Morris, *Essay*, title page. Stephen Switzer believed that Pope's precepts could also be applied to gardening; see *The Noblemen, Gentlemen and Gardener's Recreation* (London, 1715).

142. Morris, *Essay*, pp. xii, 23, 25–27, 40, 66; Morris, *Lectures on Architecture Consisting of Rules* (London, 1734–36), pp. 59–61. Nevertheless, Morris typically denies being "such a bigot to Antiquity as some may imagine": ibid. p. 65. For Morris, see Colvin, *Dictionary*, p. 559ff.; and especially, David Leatherbarrow, "Architecture and Situation: A Study of the Architectural Writings of Robert Morris," *Journal of the Society of Architectural History*, 44 (1985), pp. 48–59. Morris published several other literary and architectural works, one of them anonymously, *The Art of Architecture, A Poem in Imitation of Horace's Art of Poetry* (1742), which has been reprinted (without attribution) by William Gibson (Augustan Reprint Soc., 144, 1970).

143. In his brief introduction, Burlington describes his search for Palladio's work on ancient Roman buildings and his fortunate discovery of the unpublished drawings; he regrets his inability to find Palladio's commentary. He promises a second volume and concludes, "Finally, I cannot avoid asserting that the studies of so great a Man have to be more greatly valued as they are particularly Pertinent to our Era, which perhaps no other has demonstrated so great a proclivity toward costly Buildings, nor produced more ignorant Pretenders who lead others astray from the true trace of fine Art": *Fabriche antiche disegnate da Andrea Palladio* (London, 1730), "All'Intendente Lettore."

144. For more on Pope and Palladianism, see besides Erskine-Hill and Gibson (above, n. 119), James Sambrook, "Pope and the Visual Arts," *Writers and their Background: Alexander Pope*, ed. A. P. and Peter Dixon (London, 1972), pp. 143–71; Morris R. Brownell, *Alexander Pope and the Arts of Georgian England* (Oxford, 1978), pp 276–94; Peter Martin, *Pursuing Innocent Pleasures: The Gardening World of Alexander Pope* (Hamden, Conn., 1984).

145. Pope, *Correspondence*, I, p. 45. Brownell, *Pope and the Arts of Georgian England*, pp. 283–86.

146. The old view that all of this was inspired by a Whig political purpose has been challenged recently by Jane Clark, who argues

that Burlington was a closet Jacobite, in "'Lord Burlington is Here,'" *Lord Burlington, Architecture, Art and Life*, ed. Toby Bernard and Jane Clark (London, 1995), pp. 251–310. Howard Colvin finds the case unproved, in the introduction to the volume, but suggests, I think rightly, that partisan politics will not do as an explanation for the triumph of the Palladian style: ibid., pp. xxiii–xxix. I hope to deal with this issue more directly in *Why Neoclassicism? Politics and Culture in Eighteenth-Century England*. For more on Burlington's overt Whig career, see Eveline Cruickshanks, "The Political Career of the Third Earl of Burlington," in the same volume pp. 201–16.

147. Kimball, "Burlington Architectus," p. 693; Harris, *The Palladians*, p. 72. According to Wittkower, "Burlington undoubtedly wanted to go beyond even Palladio's classics and to recreate for modern use the ancient villa suburbana," Fritz Saxl and Rudolf Wittkower, *British Art and the Mediterranean* (Oxford, 1948), p. 54.

148. Robert Castell, *The Villas of the Ancients Illustrated* (London, 1727). See Marianne Fischer, *Die frühen Rekonstuktionen der Landhäuser Plinius' des Jungeren* (Berlin, 1962), pp. 91–121; Lees-Milne, *Earls of Creation*, p. 145. According to Richard Hewlings, Burlington was more interested in reproducing antiquity than Palladio at Chiswick, though he used Palladio as a guide: "Chiswick House and Gardens: Appearance and Meaning," *Lord Burlington*, ed. Bernard and Clark, pp. 1–150.

149. "The Goths were those barbarous nations from the north of Europe, who overspread Italy and ruin'd the Roman Empire . . . They introduced a bad manner not only in Architecture but in all other arts and sciences. We have been upwards of 200 years endeavoring to recover ourselves from this Gothicism. Yet there are still too many amongst us whose bad taste neither example nor precept will ever rectify, and therefore are to be left to themselves. For Goths will always have a Gothic taste": John Clerk of Penicuik, note to his manuscript poem "The Country Seat" (1727), in Stuart Piggott, "Sir John Clerk and *The Country Seat*," and "Aubrey's *Chronologia Architectonic*," *Concerning Architecture*, ed. John Summerson (London, 1968), pp. 1–2.

150. Chesterfield was pleased that his son would learn something about classical architecture – a frequent subject of conversation. It was important to have good taste. He would do well to "read about one-third of Palladio's Book of Architecture with some skilful person . . . and examine the best buildings by those rules." But he must not overdo it, as had Burlington. Chesterfield to his son, Oct. 17, 1749, *The Letters of Chesterfield*, 6 vols, ed. Bonamy Dobrée (London, 1932), IV, pp. 1418–22.

151. Avril Henry and Peter Dixon, "Pope and the Architects: A Note on the Epistle to Burlington," *English Studies*, 51 (1970), pp. 437–41. For Pope's attack on Timon's villa (which was usually taken to be Lord Chandos's Cannons or Walpole's Houghton) and the scandal it caused, see George Sherburn, "Timon's Villa and Cannons," *Huntington Library Record*, 8 (1935), pp. 131–50; Kathleen Mahaffey, "Timon's Villa: Walpole's Houghton," *Texas Studies in Language and Literature*, 9 (1967), pp. 193–222. See also Charles Beaumont, "Pope and the Palladians," ibid., 17 (1975), pp. 461–79; and Maynard Mack, *The Garden and the City* (Oxford, 1969), pp. 122–26.

152. Saxl and Wittkower, *British Art and the Mediterranean*, p. 59; Wittkower, *Palladio*, p. 141. According to Horace Walpole, "Lord Hervey said of the new house at Chiswick, that it was too small to live in, and too big to hang a Watch": *Horace Walpole's Journals of Visits to Country Seats*, ed. Paget Toynbee (Walpole Soc., 16, 1927–28), p. 23. For a modern rebuttal which suggests that Chiswick was meant to be lived in, see T. S. Rosoman, "The Decoration and Use of the Principal Apartments of Chiswick House 1727–70," *Burlington Magazine*, 127 (1985), pp. 663–67. The Duchess of Marlborough complained of York, that the columns were like nine-pins: "Nobody with a hoop petty coat can pass through them." Wittkower, *Palladio* p. 142. Nevertheless, the contemporary historian of York, Francis Drake, claimed (in *Eboracum, or the History and Antiquities of York*, 1736) that the Assembly Rooms were "in a truer and nobler taste in architecture than, in all probability, Roman Eboracum could ever boast of," and Fiske Kimball agrees: "Burlington Architectus," p. 690.

153. James Bramston, *The Man of Taste, Occasion'd by an Epistle of Mr Pope's on that Subject* (London, 1733), p. 10.

154. "The Views and Prospects of the Most Noted County Seats," B. Sprague Allen, *Tides of Taste*, 2 vols (New York, 1937), I, p. 109.

155. The print, called "The Taste of the Town," is unsigned but was generally believed to be by Hogarth, though doubts have arisen; see Ronald Paulson, *Hogarth's Graphic Works*,

2nd edn, 2 vols (New Haven, 1970), I, pp. 299–300 (pl. 321). It was first printed as the frontispiece to the attack on Pope by Concannen and Welsted in *A Miscellany of Taste* (1732). Nevertheless, it has been possible to find elements of *ancienneté* even in Hogarth; see J. T. A. Burke, "A Classical Aspect of Hogarth's Theory of Art," *Journal of the Warburg and Courtauld Institutes*, 6 (1943), pp. 151–53.

156. "Miscellaneous Reflections", in the Earl of Shaftesbury, *Characteristicks*, 2nd edn, 3 vols (London, 1714), III, pp. 138–41. See Ernst Cassirer, "Shaftesbury und die deutsche Geistesgeschichte," *Vorträge der Bibliothek Warburg* (1932), p. 154. Shaftesbury severely criticized Wren's St Paul's as "a false and counterfeit Piece of magnificence", in a "Letter Concerning Design," which was printed in the fifth edition of the *Character-*

isticks (1732). For more on the precocious taste for Greece in England, see Sir Thomas Hewett to Alessandro Galilei, Feb. 21, 1720, in Toesca, "Alessandro Galilei." Even before the Burlingtonian revival, Hewlett, Galilei and Sir George Markham formed a "new Junta for Architecture" to introduce a more classical style into English architecture. This was one of several "false starts and private initiatives" that anticipated, and perhaps paved the way for, Burlington's Palladianism; see Colvin, "A Scottish Origin", pp. 5–6.

157. For this, and much else on the triumph of neoclassicism, see my forthcoming volume, *Why Neoclassicism?*

158. See Joseph M. Levine, "Giambattista Vico and the Quarrel between the Ancients and the Moderns," *Journal of the History of Ideas*, 52 (1991), pp. 55–79.

Index